Within and Above Ourselves:
Essays of Political Analysis

Within and Above Ourselves

Essays of Political Analysis

by

Gerhart Niemeyer

Intercollegiate Studies Institute
Wilmington, Delaware

Library of Congress Catalog Card Number
95-081660

ISBN 1-882926-11-0

Published in the United States by:

Intercollegiate Studies Institute
3901 Centerville Road
P.O. Box 4431
Wilmington, DE 19807-0431

Manufactured in the United States of America

Contents

Beliefs and Structures

Social Forces and Concepts of Order

Acknowledgements

The author and the publisher gratefully acknowledge the publications in which the articles in this volume first appeared.

"History and Civilization" first appeared in the *Review of Politics* 19 (July 1957): 403-409.

"Are There 'Intelligible Parts of History'"? was first published in German in *The Philosophy of Order Essays on History, Conciousness and Politics:* 302-315, to honor Eric Voegelin on his 80th birthday.

"This Terrible Century" was first published in *The Intercollegiate Review* 29 (Fall 1993): 3-10.

"The Reality of the Good" first appeared as a review of *The Imperative of Responsibility: In Search of an Ethics for the Technological Age* by Hans Jonas, in *Modern Age* 30 (Spring 1986): 157-161.

"The Recovery of 'The Sacred'"? was published in *The Intercollegiate Review* 24 (Spring 1989): 3-12.

"Redeeming the Time" was published in *The Hillsdale Review* 3 (Spring/Summer 1986): 3-13.

"Reconstituting Political Theory" was published as a review of Eric Voegelin's *Science, Politics, and Gnosticism*, in the journal *Religion and Society* 2 (April 1969): 42-46.

"Faith and Reason in Eric Voegelin"has never been published.

"Christian Faith, and Religion, in Eric Voegelin's Work" was published in *The Review of Politics:* 91-104.

"God and Man, World and Society: The Last Work of Eric Voegelin" was first published in *The Review of Politics* (Winter 1989): 107-123.

"Beyond Institutions and Patterns of Power"was originally published in Germany, in Südosteuropa-Studie #50: *Von der Ost-West-Konfrontation zur Europäischen Friedensordnurg,* Ed. Günther Wagenlehner. München, 1992: 301-303.

"After Lenin—Who Helps Whom?" has never been published.

"Forces That Shape the Twentieth Century" was delivered at an ISI conference held at Piety Hill, Mecosta, Michigan.

"A Christian Sheen on a Secular World" was first published in *Modern Age* 31 (Summer/Fall 1987): 355-361.

"Christianity, in a Time-Bound Perspective" first appeared in *Modern Age* 33 (Summer 1990): 184-192.

"The New Need for the Catholic University" was first published in *The Review of Politics* 37 (October 1975): 479-489.

"In Praise of Tradition" was published in *Modern Age* 36 (Spring 1994): 233-236.

"After Communism—What"? was first published in *Pacific Community: An Asian Quarterly Review* (January 1971): 307-317.

"A Reappraisal of the Doctrine of Free Speech" first appeared in *Thought* 25 (June 1950): 251-274.

"Myth and Order in Our Time"was delivered as a speech at the 4th annual meeting of the Open Court Editorial Advisory Board and later published by the Open Court Publishing Company in La Salle, Ill. in 1973: 83-97.

"The Nation, Myths, and Mores" was first published in *Triumph* 3 (December 1968): 16-18, 37.

"The Social Whole and the Solitary Thinker" was first published in *Saints, Sovereigns, and Scholars: Essays in Honor of Frederick D. Wilhelmsen* (Peter Lang: New York, 1994).

"A Query about Assumptions On International Organization" was published first in *World Politics* 7 (January 1995): 337-347.

"Enlightenment to Ideology" first appeared in two parts: *Modern Age* 35 (Fall 1992, Winter 1993).

"On Authority and Alienation" first was published in *The Review of Politics* (Summer 1991): 530-546.

"We possess this unity within ourselves and yet above ourselves, for both grounds and preserves our being and life."

—John Ruusbroec

Introduction

BY

MARION MONTGOMERY

What a formidable task, mine—to presume an introduction to these essays by an old friend. It is not the friendship that makes me feel presumptuous, but that he is so formidable a presence, to me and to many others, those who have learned so much from him over the years. An invited guest, I am in an awkward position, having arrived early at the feast here before us. Here at the portal, feeling somewhat an intruder, though generously invited, I speak over my shoulder as the door is being opened, perhaps saying the wrong thing in an intent to honor our host for his generosity of spirit. There is nothing for it but to conduct myself with the best manners possible, hoping that the moment's awkwardness will dissolve as we arrive before the healthful and so wisely seasoned fare our host has first husbanded and now lays before us out of his generous care.

Gerhart Niemeyer's *Within and Above Ourselves* is a restoring offering, out of his full experience as husbandman to intellect. As an awkward guest, I am awed by his firm learning. But I am put somewhat at ease by his generosity of spirit, so that it remains in my thanksgiving to remark my (our) obligation as we make ourselves welcomed: an obligation to intellectual integrity, the only appetite proper in these circumstances. We are obliged, in honoring our host, to an openness of reason toward truth in these intellectual matters before us. Perhaps my sense of awkwardness is in part a response to this unusual expectation, considering the current intellectual community, especially its failures of intellectual manners which we may observe all about us, but especially in the current academy. Anciently, our mothers used to remind us, as we set out on social calls, to mind our manners, out of respect not only for whatever host or hostess, but in respect for our own family as an orderly part of a community established through manners. The obligation of mannerly openness through reason to truth in the intellectual community, as our host knows well, underlies and supports and sustains community in that complexity we call civility, a civility foregone so radically in our day as to endanger families to isolation and thereby threaten the fabric of social order. As we may discover in these essays, the destruction is precisely because intellectual manners in respect for truth itself is so considerably decayed.

Intellectual integrity seems such an uncommon expectation of guests in what passes for intellectual community at this moment that to remember is to make us aware with some discomfort that intellectual manners make us singularly obliged to integrity, each within his own gifts. That we have so generally failed the obligation is made daily more evident, to the point that social manners are now legislated as a substitute for intellectual manners, as we become more and more coerced by the "politically correct" to exercise manners divorced from intellectual integrity, under penalty of the law. The letter of the law as a substitute for social or intellectual manners, as we begin to discover grudgingly, denies the spirit. Law as letter freed of spirit yields only a new jungle, the jungle made of shadows of "universalism" bequeathed us both by Descartes and by Kant, and especially by Kant, who has proved so successful in divorcing universalisms from nature, leaving intellect in its own high vacuum as the only authority of all actions in nature. That is the condition to intellectual spirit from which our host would recall us here.

What is expected of us as guests here is not the high learning of our host but an old-fashioned honesty of intent to the truth of things, remembered as a tradition to intellectual community reaching at least as far back as Plato's Academy. We are not required the same or a larger formidable learning than our host possesses, or else he might well be calling on us rather than we on him. We are required to maintain common sense toward the prospect of wisdom, whatever the limits of our formal learning. If, along with this initial sense of awkwardness, there is also a recognition of how much has been lost to intellectual communion in the academy this past hundred or so years, we might be tempted to an anger out of our deprivation. In the presence of our host, however, that anger may for a moment turn to sadness. We may regret that our own present good fortune as guests to this wise presence speaks almost elegiacally of our general loss of intellectual heritage. We might even, at such a poignant moment, suspect that our host must feel himself lingering among us with a sense of absence, like that which Ezra Pound felt when told of the death of his old companion T.S. Eliot: "Who is there now for me to share a joke with?" Who is there now for Gerhart Niemeyer to share his great learning with, since among others his old friend Eric Voegelin is no longer here.

But that is to misunderstand altogether. Gerhart Niemeyer, unlike Pound, looks forward—bringing the viable past with him to us; handing it to us. For him Eric Voegelin is always present, as are Plato and Aristotle, St. Augustine and St. Thomas Aquinas, and on and on. We could name a goodly presence of company, of intellectual community now vitally present, evidenced in these essays. So let us remember here at least Eric Voegelin's uncovering of that long, spiritual wandering in the desert, presented in his *Israel and Revelation*, the Hebrew "leap in being" beyond Egyptian captivity in that old closed view of existence. To remember is at once to recognize our host's witness to the necessity of our own leap into being, out of the dominant intellectual pride of Modernism in its power over non-being, a pride becoming pervasive of the Western intellectual community since the Renaissance. What we are recalled to, in Professor Niemeyer's prophetic phrase, is the "royal majesty of truth," beyond the pride of autonomous intellect as the "lord of being", whose Dantesean characterization might be our present awakening from Modernism to discover ourselves as the lords, not of everything as autonomous intellect dreams of becoming, but "lords of nothingness", since by pride of intellect we have rejected being itself.

With his invitation, then, we enter into his present intellectual witness of these essays to a recovery of *somethingness*. And we remember that the nature of the prophet is to recall us to known but forgotten things. It would be an error to understand our host as if he were merely a "conservative" spokesman, an uncertain term, standing against Modernist "liberalism," though given the erosive effects of Modernism upon our spiritual and intellectual inheritance a secularized liberalism of the past two centuries is steadily called into question here. Our host is neither "conservative" nor "liberal" as those terms have becomes limited to political questions. Let us say rather that he is a *traditionalist*, in a special sense of the term beyond how it is now used in popular jargon. That is, he is a philosopher and theologian as prophet: he is concerned with the abiding truth of things. He recalls us to that which we discover we have actually known by living, but forgotten or rejected: man's particular nature as intellectual soul incarnate. For man is that most peculiar of all creatures in the orders of being, a *person*. In his final essay, "After Communism—What?", our host releases us to our own witness to truth, reminding us that "Religion and philosophy...and ideology are antithetical" in any age, though it is an exacerbated antipathy with which we must deal in our own.

In dealing with this antipathy, insofar as we are drawn to consider the truth of things, we need all the help we can get, so that we can ill afford to be anything less than such a traditionalist as Gerhart Niemeyer. With his help, we see that ideology is intellect's reductionism of reality to the convenience of intellect's own present interest, particularly its interest in a present power over existence itself. Science, divorced of philosophy and theology, will establish ideology as a version of both, in doctrines inimical to human community. For it is tempting to intellect to suppose that knowledge—science—by reductionism elevates knowledge as supreme arbiter of truth, rather than truth of knowledge. Indeed, *science* in popular expectations is considered such an instrument, though its ends, to the popular imagination, is primarily the satisfaction of a variety of appetites. That distortion has led some concerned philosophers to distinguish *scientism* from *science*, in a defense of valid and honorable science. Not successfully, since the popular mind has been supported deceptively by allies whose calling is to science but whose uses of science has been a scientism. The geneticist R. C. Lewontin, of Harvard, calls our particular attention to this reductionism in his *Biology as Ideology: The Doctrine of DNA*, quoting a fellow geneticist, Richard Dawkins, who confidently pronounces that humans are "lumbering robots." We are "created...body and mind" by our genes. What Professor Dawkins does not tell us, of course, is from what detached and transcendent sphere in the orders of being he is enabled to his pronouncement.

Now one of the callings of our host is as "political scientist," though the more apt title (as these essays show) would be "political philosopher." Of course, as a formal discipline (though with growing exceptions, praise the Lord) political science as an academic discipline ought to be listed in curricula catalogues as "political scientism." It practices reductionism through historicism as an ideological address to tradition, dependent in its authority (underneath its considerable "data bases") on opinion. This is a theme of concern evident in Gerhart Niemeyer's essays. Thus in "History and Civilization" he reminds us that the unity of history is not to be extrapolated from the succession of mundane events, the data bases without which journal papers and formal academic conferences would become entirely (rather than largely, as now evident from published contents pages and programs) exercises in political correctness. Events may be focused about a time center by the historian of course, as in the works of Herodotus, Thucidides, Polybius, Ssu-ma Ch' ien, Vico, Gibbon, Spengler, and their like.

But the center is not event but the consciousness of the particular person engaged by event or by the memory of event—by the participant or his historian. True unity and order are not determined by event, as the various species of determinists under the Modernist aegis insist, but reside *within* the specific intellect's consent to an openness to the truth of existence. What is at issue for consciousness, most fundamentally, is not order in the world as directed by science—by gnosis—on the principle of a determinism of human *being* by event. Nevertheless, order within event itself is a responsibility of man as steward of being, as opposed to his conduct as dictator of being as in the Modernist intent. The order of the discrete soul is at issue—the order of the *within*. It is an order to be recovered through the good, the beautiful—the true as realities *above* intellect's temptations to reductionism, yet inclusive of the intellectual soul as it participates in "history." In this recovery of person to an order *within* lies the valid prospect of any recovery of a community of persons. That is why political science without philosophy can only reach the level of political scientism. Furthermore, that is why we must recognize and listen to such a political philosopher as Gerhart Niemeyer.

We suggested that, as an obligation of manners in our presence to our good host, we are required the conduct of common sense as a proper ordering of each intellectual *within*. That is the precondition to that more inclusive formal conduct of intellect called philosophy, whatever the category of philosophical concern. By common sense, we respond to the self-evident which is granted intellect—to that which as intellectual creature we know through the actual experience of living. The self-evident is the initial—the initiating—truth to intellect. Thus intellect discovers itself possessed of knowledge before its subsequent necessity to a rational articulation in sharing what it knows. For articulation—the proper using of signs of one intellect to another—is the fundamental necessity to our existence as community, our existence as viable body *above* each person's within whether as intellectual, or political, or social, or religious community requires a degree of common understanding through a consent to signs accepted in a communal piety.

Professor Niemeyer's formal concern, very often in these essays, is with our having lost community through violations of our common signs through ideological intent. Knowing that the beginnings of community lie in each person's common sense engagement of reality through his own experience, he would remind us that we share in the common consent of intellects, a concert of intellectual community, to the truth of things known in common. Thus *con-sentire*, a *feeling with* as intuitive to our nature, becomes properly a *knowing-with*. By such consent, supported by rational understanding of common sense, it becomes possible to draw together as a body of persons, as a community—whatever parameters exist to particular communities—academic, political, or religious. The erosive effect in signs falsely taken, with ideological intent, is the malady to communal body from which we suffer so conspicuously. Such an essay as "A Reappraisal of Free Speech" therefore cuts to the heart of ideological distortions of common sense (*feeling with*) responses to truth itself—an essay one wishes required reading for media ideologists in particular.

Community is justified, not by the actuality of our knowing the self-evident by experience, but by the truth of that which we know. With this distinction, we are enabled to avoid the intolerable isolation within community effected by the ideological uses of sign, the intellectual malaise of alienation in response to which ours has been an age of philosophical obsession with epistemology. What we have forgotten, and what our philosophical prophet here recalls us to, is the actuality of truth, independent of our act of knowing (*pace* Descartes), and that truth (known through the grace of our natures) binds us to reality, more firmly binds us that ideology's authority in loosing us from reality to float "free" into alienation. That is why our host in these essays reminds us often that our task is to recover "metaphysical reality, moral and spiritual order," first within the self so that as persons we may flourish in community beyond the self, *above* the self as now so largely alienated *beneath* itself by ideology. The truth of things, then, known by the experience of our actually living as intellectual creature, is the measure of knowing's validity and not knowing the measure of truth. A true community of persons is built on that principle as guide, requiring a recovery of virtue, most notably prudence and humility. The abstract, universalized principle of intellectual autonom of willed intellectual act divorced from truth as its measure, has led to our general collapse as community, a course inevitable when intellect willfully separates itself from the nature of things in order to exercise power over the being of things. The father of all ideologies, autonomous intellect, can only leave the specific person or the subscribing community to ideological separation from reality, alienated from reality with most painful social, political, and religious consequences.

That is why, to the necessity of communal order, we require the loving offices of the philosopher, who assures us of our inclination to order against disorder as proper to our nature as person. For which reason, what is necessary to us is not *science*, especially in the popular appropriation of that term since Francis Bacon, but *love*. Not *knowing*, however much it may appear sufficient to the *within* through an ordering of the *above* by ideological control of existence itself, but *love*. It is a love *toward*, an opening *toward*, the truth of things as proper to the fulfillment of our nature as intellectual creatures. Thus, by this "openness to being" we are turned "above" our "self" through a desire for the beautiful, the true, the good. It would be a mistake, therefore, to read these essays, in the light of their subtitle, as concerned merely with the *process* of political, social, religious, scientific thought, as if the concern at issue were at the level of the *within*, not only the *within* of consciousness as reduced by Modernism to biological limits, but to the *within* of history.

But it would also be a mistake not to see what authority our host, Mr. Niemeyer, deals with our political and social history as that history is used in deliberate reductionism through an authority presumed justified by autonomous intellect. He has been around for a long time, through many wars and many flawed reconciliations advanced as "peace" out of our increasingly desperate hope. Desperate hope, because our century in particular has so insistently commanded us to attend to the within and to deny the above, insofar as the above suggests any transcendent as the proper tendency of our desire through the beautiful, the true, and the good. We cannot neglect recognizing that our host, then, is not only a political philosopher, but theologian—indeed a priest—as well.

As priest, he has a special concern for our given nature as intellectual soul, but especially because we seem easily seduced by Modernism from transcendent concerns proper to that nature. Through ideological reductionism, intellect is encouraged to suppose itself capable of the illusion that the imminent is the limit of being, a closed arena within which autonomous intellect may exercise its authority as the only transcendent. Modernist ideology has as its *within* the egocentric confidence of self-autonomy as the only cause of the beautiful, the true, and the good. And the arena for the practice of that autonomy is the existential world, considered variously as mechanistic, materialistic, even illusional reality. Common to ideological reductionisms is the presumption of limited existence, upon which to practice ideological reconstitutions. It is of this which Voegelin cautions us, when he says that modern gnosticism intends "power over being." That power becomes operative, first of all, by a denial of being itself as significant of any truth transcendent. It is by this Modernism, then, that we find ourselves returned to a closed world, that from which the Hebrew children in the desert made a leap in being—a leap into being and so their recovering of the relation of the *within* and the *above*.

Professor Niemeyer is attuned as philosopher and theologian, as a member of that continuing body of traditionalists concerned with the human soul, to the strategic subtlety of Modernist philosophy, which has its own "theology," as it has its own metaphysicians of material and biological existence. That ideology has seized and used the *within* which is self-evidently real and true—the "person" made collective persons ("individuals"), concentrating argument upon the limit to reality as that *within*, emphasizing a limited response to the *above* (the closed arena of "nature") as the only possibility to the person: that limited response is will's necessity in its attempt to reconstitute being itself. It is a strategy requiring a manipulation of the signs through which community is bonded. First, the reality of *being* must be denied. The world of things, known self-evidently by the experience of consciousness to *be*, must be reconstituted by an inverse Platonism, whereby existence is to be conferred by intellect itself, as will also be conferred truth and good and beauty. The existential world, through sign manipulated, is made a "shadow" of the light of intellect itself, and that light is justified in making whatever patterns of order, its own shadows, it desires to make. Thus the beautiful, the true, the good have origin and end in autonomous intellect itself—in the subjective as absolute.

Actual, existing things—know by common sense—are addressed as a shadowy prime matter by the new "religion" of Modernism, to be in service to gnostic intent. These essays are rich and incisive in exposing this shell-game as employed against any genuine community of persons in the world. We see here that ideological con game which makes both community and the world a circus, to be enjoyed by the self—by egocentric man—in pursuit of his ultimate desire as appetite for the *within* at a temporal and spatial limit, beyond which there can be no admission of truth, or of the good. The *within* of the self is thus to be served by the *within* of nature as ordered to the self. Some of these perpetrators Professor Niemeyer names and exposes, not only here but in the body of his work. Here, they are Descartes, Voltaire, Comte, and others, but we remember as well his considerable expose of Modernist ideology in his *From Nothingness to Paradise* and in his *Aftersight and Foresight*, making the body of his work a whole.

Ideological con games have "victimized" community since the Renaissance, then, with some of these artists of the sign themselves self-deceived. One might cite Kant in particular, who by his purity of intent in pursuit of pure reason bequeaths us the most corrosive "virtue" out of ideology, namely *sincerity*, to take the place of *humility* which once governed the intellectual community's devotion to beauty, truth, and goodness. Sincerity becomes a sufficient self-justification, whereby we are, although all victims of our own errors, incapable of willful sin. As victims, though we may differ in levels of angry protest,—the decibels of physics which we increasingly substitute for reasoned argument in the social, political, and theological arenas of our concerns— we insist upon our victim-status as justifying our *rights* through the *sincerity* of the *noise* we make. It is in the name of our recovery as persons to community existence through the true, the beautiful, the good that Father Niemeyer invites us in those offerings. And most especially he invites our reasoned exploration or what we know by common sense to be a necessary recovery of the "majesty of truth." That his offerings have immediate *relevance* (that much abused term) to our recovery of the virtue of prudence through humility and is not a reserved offering as if separate from the immediacy of our living: this we may discover, each for himself. All that is required is our common sense recognition of the truth of our own immediate experiences of living, as here so persuasively celebrated in these words toward a recovery of viable community.

Crawford, Georgia

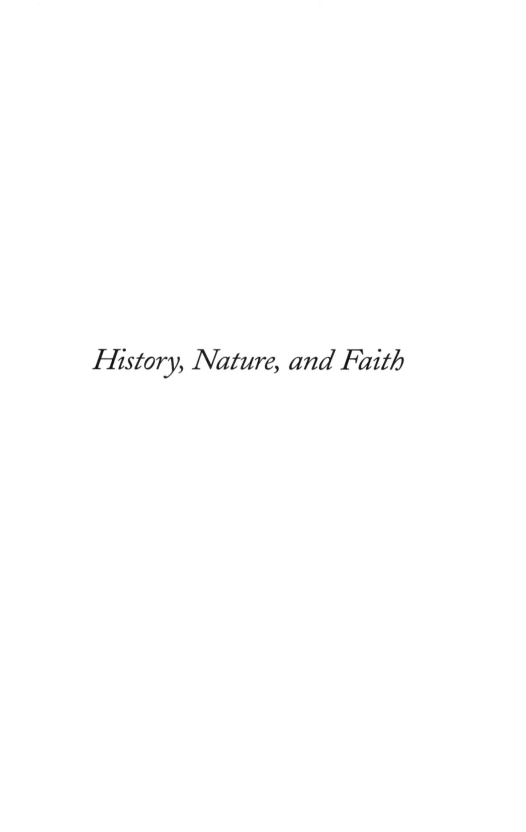

History, Nature, and Faith

History and Civilization

History, like being, nature, and cosmos, is a concept of unity. The peculiar difficulty with this concept is not the element of time. Time is also involved in the processes of growth and the metamorphoses of nature where it has never stood in the way of unifying concepts. The difficulty in the case of history comes from the freedom of man which makes possible acts, achievements, and events that are singular rather than typical. Singular deeds and works, contingent upon the singularity of human characters and souls, are phenomenal; but men need to conceive their ensemble also as essential. Chronicles of the *res gestae* of rulers and peoples gather the phenomena but do not penetrate to any kind of unity. Outstanding historiographers in the past sought to go further. Herodotus, Thucydides, Polybius in the West, and Ssu-ma Ch'ien in China attempted to group events, peoples, cultures, and even mythical memories around a contemporary time center: in Herodotus the Persian wars of Greece, in Thucydides the Peloponnesian war, in Polybius the Punic wars, and in Ssu-ma Ch'ien the wars attending the downfall of the harsh Ch'in dynasty, and the establishment of the Confucianist Han Dynasty. The time center in each case figured not merely as a contest of unusual dimension and scope, but also as a struggle carrying a universal significance. Yet none of these "histories" called forth, in the language of contemporary philosophy, something one could call "historiology" (on the analogy of cosmology, anthropology, or theology). Neither Plato, nor Aristotle, nor the Stoics, nor Cicero, nor Augustine, nor Chu Hsi built anything like philosophical or existential unity on the kind of time center emphasized by the historiographers. A center consisting of certain mundane events has a way of passing into insignificance after a few centuries. Herodotus and Polybius are more than chroniclers, but they did not attain anything like a universal unity concerning singular human deeds and works.

That concept was achieved alone by Augustine, from whose thought our civilization has received it as the core of its cultural form, so that there can be no Western civilization without a notion of history. We either have a sound notion of history or else a perverted one, for if we destroy within us a valid view of the unity of singularities found in the notion of history we immediately rush to fill the void with some counterfeit. Our present age is full of counterfeit notions, each of which erect some kind of idol of history, attributing to it substance, will, intention, or purpose; attaching to it a preordained schedule of mundane movement ("moving into the Twentieth century," "the next step in history," "historically necessary") toward the present (self-centered evolutionism) or the future (evolutionary or revolutionary progressivism). It is these counterfeit "substances" of history that have lent to civilization and civilizational works a salvific character, resulting necessarily in elevating to divine rank some particular civilization, enterprise, or political organization of which redeeming power or mission is predicated. Since our dependence on the concept of history goes back to Augustine, it behooves us to look closely again at what Augustine meant.

The following theses about Augustine's historiology seem defensible:

    a) Augustine never deliberately formulated what we today would call a concept of history. Above all, he did not extrapolate unity from a succession of mundane events in time, nor group a multitude of events around a time center (not even around the Incarnation), but rather combined his own anthropology with an Aristotelian ontology to discover the historiological dimension of being.

b) Augustine's ontology was both fuller and more systematic than that of Aristotle, above all full in the addition of an elaborated theology completing Aristotle's brief metaphysical hints.

c) Augustine's anthropology resembled that of modern Existentialism and to this extent differed from that of both Plato and Aristotle. Augustine, again, has an anthropology more complete and systematic than the Existentialists in that it is linked to a fully elaborate ontology and thus need not do without the concept of natures.

d) It is the interplay of his anthropology and his ontology, complete with theology, that allows Augustine to discover that purposeful movement in human existence from which we derive our sense of history, even though Augustine himself never used the word in this sense but rather constructs all being as historiological, setting out with the movement of mutables and culminating in eschatological completion of all movements begun and sustained.

Augustine's psychology is proverbial, his theology almost a commonplace, but both are saturated with his ontology. Rudolf Schneider, in his *Seele and Sein* (1957) has demonstrated the basic similarity of Augustine's ontology to Aristotle's. Augustine's teaching of subjective experience roots in his teaching of objective being. Nor can one separate Augustine's theology from his ontology. His teaching about God, his Christology, his doctrines about sin and grace are all woven through with concepts of being. Ontology is the basic element in all of Augustine's disciplines. All the same, Augustine's ontology is not our main concern here, so that one may sketch it very summarily. *Deus creator omnium*, the hymn which he intones in the sixth book of *de musica*, is the cornerstone of the structure. God alone is being pure and simple, without accidents. In the sense of the scriptural *I am that I am* God is existence, the underlying ground of all particular beings. God has created all things out of nothing. He did not create things out of preexisting matter, but he also created matter as something capable of being formed and constituting "some kind of life." Mutable things created out of nothing both are and are not. They are needy, since God alone is the fullness of being, so that mutable created things "have" being threatened by nothingness and must adhere to God to save it. With regard to intelligent creatures, for instance, Augustine distinguishes between *esse* and *vivere*, and again between *vivere* and *sapienter vivere*.[1] The formulation of both spiritual and corporeal matter always involves a turning to God who truly and always is.[2] Thus movement attends things created out of nothing, not merely the movement of growth according to their nature, but also movement stemming from their neediness. "For the body is borne by its gravity, as the spirit by love, whithersoever it is borne."[3] In the structure of being, God alone is the unchangeable good. The good of creatures consists in *habere*, having. They have their natures which are created good, so that to each creature belongs its *ordo* and *pax*, the terms order and peace being almost synonyms in Augustine. Like nourishment, they are needed for life, for life depends on having what is needed. The existence of created things is thus characterized by the possibilities of gain or loss, *habere* and *deficere*. But the good of mutables has its ground in the immutable good of God. In all of this, Augustine surpasses Aristotle, who, while seeing God alone as unmoved though causing all movement, and alone as *actus purus*, did not push this insight to the obvious conclusion that God is the good that is needed by all mutable creatures.

Of all created things, man is that thing created in God's image, having the gift of intellect and the freedom of will that goes with it. Thus man is the only created thing capable of altering his own nature by his will. This is the point where Augustine's anthropology links up with his ontology. Augustine's ontology differs from that of Aristotle mainly in the fuller elaboration of the theological dimension: "Augustine has established the dominance of theology in ontological manner. In other words: He has universally validated his ontology with the help of theology."[4] Augustine's anthropology, however, is vastly different from Aristotle's. Aristotle, as Heidegger once remarked, looked upon man in the same way in which he looked on things and animals: each has its attributes, its built-in goal, its good. His anthropology therefore is merely a piece of his perception of all kinds of natures. Augustine's anthropology, however, centers in the notion that among all things and creatures man exists in an utterly different and unique way, so that the problem of human existence cannot be grasped fully through concepts of nature and natures. This is the insight which Augustine has in common with today's Existentialists, and it is no accident that Heidegger studied Augustine before writing his *Sein und Zeit*. The difference of Augustine from the Existentialists is, however, precisely his insistence on ontology. While exploring man and his possibilities through the depth of the soul and the experiences, the mind and memory, he never forgot that man's peace is something belonging to his nature.

Even man's basic experience of *dolor*, the sorrow of existence, comes from his understanding of the human situation, its frailty, precariousness, and a velleity for nothingness. This experience is a straight ontological inference. But then there also was Augustine's own stormy career of experiences, beginning with doubt, restlessness, anxiety, despair. There was the decisive turn of this turbulence toward peace through his conversion. Moreover, his conversion came not as a subjectively isolated happening, but was embedded, as it were, in his observation of a similar event befalling Victorinus, the report of the conversion of two state officials as reported by Ponticianus, the example of St.

Anthony, and further on the horizon the conversion of St. Paul and Plato's *periagoge*. Man's possibility of missing his existence or attaining it came to Augustine as a series of experiences of which each was singular, although the aggregate appeared typical.

A number of concepts may serve for a brief outline of Augustine's anthropology. "Internalization" is frequently mentioned as the salient characteristic of modern man, particularly since Rousseau. Augustine, still in unbroken contact with his ontology, developed a complex and profound insight into the crucial reality of the "inner man." A central concern of this inner man is the equivalence of *unum* and *esse*, and, above all, Augustine's teaching of the affect as the access to the transcendental One. This teaching one finds already in his early work *de ordine*, where he shows that the mind moves within a unifying horizon, and, coming to itself, comprehends the world as *unus*. Just like a circle centers in one point from which everything is measured, so the mind's understanding consists in seeing in the natural multiplicity the central unity. This is the inner horizon which constitutes the mind's world. There is a similar unity of time, which comes through memory. In the *Confessions* Augustine stands in awe before the mystery of the mind: "Great is the power of memory; its deep and boundless multiplicity is something fearful, O my God! And this is the mind, and I am this myself. What, then, am I, O my God? What is my nature? A life of many aspects and many ways, strikingly immeasurable."[5] "These are not the only things which the vast capacity of my memory bears. Here, also are all these things which have been grasped from the liberal disciplines and which have not yet been forgotten—put aside, as it were, in an inner place which is not a place. Nor do I carry the images of these, but the things themselves."[6] The unity of time is perceived in the following way: "But how is the future, which does not yet exist, decreased or eaten up, or how does the past, which is no longer existing, increase, unless because of the fact that three functions occur in the mind which is doing this? It looks ahead, it attends, and it remembers—in such a way that what it looks forward to passes through what it is attending to into what it is remembering.... So, the long future is not a long time, but a long expectation of the future; nor is past time long, for it is nonexistent, but a long past is a long memory of that which is past."[7] This means that the human life occurs in something like a temporal space, which also forms a horizon.

Man's reason, comprising the unifying horizon, numbers, memory, constitutes a "life of its own" in a sense in which the body is not life.[8] The mode of this life is in speaking. Memory consists in speaking, knowledge manifests itself in speaking, no action occurs without speaking. "For the thought that is formed by the thing which we know, is the word which we speak in the heart; which word is neither Greek, nor Latin, nor of any other tongue."[9] Speaking, however, always presupposes a partner. Hence the life of reason is *esse cum*, being with the other. And here the affect enters into the picture, primarily love. "For instance, he who knows righteousness perfectly, and loves it perfectly is already righteous."[10] "Whenever, then, the mind knows and loves itself, its word is joined to it by love. And since it loves knowledge and knows love, both the word is in love and love is in the word, and both are in him who loves and speaks."[11] Thus the rightly attained existence is the beloved word speaking true knowledge. The inner man, then, consists of memory, understanding, and love. This is the setting for the rational creature's life. In this trinitarian combination consists *esse posse*, man's ability fully to be.

Augustine's main question—what is attainment of existence—was already formulated in his early works, *contra academicos* and, above all, in *de beata vita*, the title of which implies his answer.[12] In these two, and another of his early writings, *de musica*, Augustine lists three designs of human existence which he characterizes by the terms *sentire—scire—amare*. *Sentire* is represented by the view of Zeno who saw the soul as mortal and felt that in the world there was nothing immortal, since the gods themselves consisted of fire. Such a view gives rise to a design of life in which man feels that he can fulfill himself in knowing, controlling, and enjoying the things in the empirical world.[13] Plato stands for the pattern of *scire*, believing, as he did, that there are two worlds, one intelligible, in which truth itself dwells, and the other sensible which is accessible to our seeing and touching. Human existence can be fulfilled only through deep contemplation on the timeless truth behind the sense-appearance of things.[14] *Amare* is the life discovered through Augustine's own experiences and first contrasted to the other two designs in *de musica*, VI, "so that adolescents, or men of any age God has endowed with a good natural capacity, might with reason guiding by torn away...from the fleshly senses and letters...and adhere with the love of unchangeable truth to one God and Master of all things...."[15] "Let us, then, order ourselves between those [things] below us and those above us...."[16] "...this affection or motion of the soul by which it understands eternal things and counts temporal things below them even within itself...."[17]

Augustine describes all three designs as logically self-sufficient and rational in that each, in its own way, "makes sense." All the same, he sees the three as differing from each other in rank. The life-design of having, controlling, and enjoying things of this word he characterizes by the formula *in ipso extra ipsum*. He finds that the multiple things of this world do not provide a unifying center. Also the desire for possession and enjoyment (*frui*) of these things involves "the appetite of the soul to have under it other souls; not of beasts as conceded by divine law but rational ones, that is your neighbors, fellows, and companions...the proud soul desires to operate on them...."[18] This life-design, then, entails the lust for power, the *libido dominandi*. It also sees life's fulfillment in the desire to enjoy the possession of things, which Augustine calls *concupiscere*. The design to complete human life through the philosophical knowledge of essences must still be seen as a desire to have power (mental power), and also, to enjoy things of this world (in this case, one's own thoughts). "They recognize God, but they do not praise and thank him as God, rather lose themselves in their own thoughts."[18] With this criticism of the *have* Augustine introduces the distinction between *scientia* and *sapientia*, by which he means here knowledge and wisdom, though at another place practical and theoretical knowledge. At any rate, the life-design of *scire* he calls *in ipso*, in which intellectual self-centeredness man lives without a partner (*esse sine*) while by contrast "*sapientia non in esse sine*"—wisdom is not a life without fellowship.

While "making sense" in their own terms, these two designs cannot produce the unity which is equivalent of a true human existence. "And so many of these things seem to us disordered and perturbed, because we have been sewn into their order according to our merits, not knowing what beautiful thing Divine Providence purposes for us. For, if someone should be put as a statue in a corner of the most spacious and beautiful building he could not perceive the beauty of the building he himself is part of.... So God has ordered the man who sins as vicious, but not viciously. For he has been made vicious by will, thus losing the whole he who obeyed God's precepts possessed, and has been ordered in part so who did not fulfill the law has been fulfilled by the law...has been ordered in part so he as far as he is man is something good."[20] The life of *amare* is the response of the soul to God in thanks and praise. It is the love of the word that answers God, and the will to enjoy nothing that is lower than God (which means that all things of this world are to be used—*uti*—but not enjoyed—*frui*). This life design is *in te supra me*, the calling and answering relation of the soul to God. It should be noted that in this context Augustine means by *amare* solely the love of God, while in another context, particularly in book 19 of the *City of God*, he speaks of a variety of conceivable loves. Thus man's *esse posse* (ability to be) depends on *esse velle* (will to being). Man's fulfillment of his destiny is in attaining the possibility, provided for him by God, of partnership with God, in which existence his situation is that in between the divinity above him and the things natural below him. For a man to remain below that highest possibility means to be deficient in being (*deficere, deesse, degere*) and to miss his existence. That deficiency is sinful, insofar as the will not to adhere to God is deliberate and fully conscious. Augustine's anthropology, like his ontology, culminates in theology, but one may also speak of his theology as ontological and anthropological theology.

Augustine's formula *amor meus pondus meum* (my love is my center of gravity) governs both his definition of a people and his distinction between the earthly city and the City of God, the two crucial groupings among men. It is Augustine's array of three life-designs which has proved to him that man, capable of a multitude of loves, can arrange his world, both personal and political, in a number of different ways. This insight causes him to reject Cicero's definition of a people as that association which is centered in right notions of justice. In other words, loves other, and lower, than the love of God do not appear necessarily nonsensical to men, even though they are in error. Hence, empirically speaking, peoples can be formed by a variety of loves, because there are many things which appear good in this world, even though they are not the highest and not the true good. That is why Augustine, having previously spoken only of the highest ranking life-design as *amare*, can speak of love as the bond that forms a people and thereby mean any of a variety of loves, including inferior loves. When explaining three different designs of life, *sentire, scire,* and *amare*, he showed that the first, characterized by concupiscence and lust for power, centers in a love for self, and that the desire to enjoy possession and power is one that each man has for himself alone, and that the second design, intellectually turned in on itself, did not get away from this confinement. Only the third life-design, in that it loves the world that gives thanks and praise to God and thus answers God's call for partnership, turns love away from self and in the direction of a good that is common to all men, rather than privy to each individual. It is this distinction that leads Augustine to his concept of two cities, the City of God and the earthly city (not satanic city, as Tyconius had it).

Augustine's vocabulary, in discussing the two cities, strikes us as somewhat less than adequate. Still, he uses *civitas* rather than *respublica*, which was the current Latin translation of the Greek *politeia*, and therefore we also might use a translation that departs from the ordinary, for instance, "citizenry of God," rather than "City of God." For both *civitates* must not be seen as institutions or organizations. Rather, they are groupings of men in terms of those two diametrically opposed loves, that of self and that of God, which are decisive to human existence and its salvation. The "earthly city" is not the state, and the "City of God" is not the Church. All the same, the groupings are real, one might say in a sociological sense, and as real groupings are apt to produce some kind of organizations other than political, some kind of arrangement for purposes of the common pursuit of the respective love. These would be arrangements or organizations not by nature or in response to natural attributes, as is the state, but rather by the two basic orientations constituting the two citizenries, fault and faith, both singular historical manifestations of will. Since Augustine sees neither of the two citizenries as natural, it is all the more remarkable that he describes them as perennial in time. The two coexist basically in the same way through a succession of various kingdoms and empires that have followed each other in time. Histories have reported the rise and fall of political entities and of civilizations, but histories do not report anything like the rise and fall of Augustine's two cities. Where, then, is Augustine's "history"? How did we come to derive from his works that conception which has come to form the center of our culture?

Augustine's *primum cognitum*, Gilson has remarked, is not the cosmos, not even God, but "man within the universe."[21] "Taking man altogether, he observes him, and while he formulates him in ideas, he models his ideas on the empirical content that he has observed." What emerges is a historiology of being. It takes its place in opposition to philosophers who, focusing their eyes on the regularities of observed nature, see things primarily in terms of causes and cyclical processes. Augustine's anthropology, centering in his ontological *Deus creator omnium*, is the observation, in human life, of either the loss or the gain of existence, and, if gain, then the fulfillment of life in blessedness (the *beata vita*) and the secure enjoyment of God. This observation cannot fit into a philosophy of cyclical processes, for the souls who have entered into bliss will never again return to their former misery, so that in that respect there are things which are new and were not before.[22] The same observation does away with causality in human life, for the notion that the revolution of ages should be the cause of what happens in time is plainly false. Thus there are no such cycles at all.[23] The movement of human life toward its destiny obviously is also wholly unlike the motion that Aristotle saw as characteristic of an *entelechy*. Those who do not cleave to God differ from those who do, not by nature but by fault. Their natures are the same, and their natures are created good. It is their will, or love, which contains the motion toward God or away from God, in the latter case injuring the good nature. That will itself has no efficient cause, neither in circumstances of nature nor in those of culture. Augustine thus eliminates causality as an explanation of the affairs of men, on two grounds: first, in rejecting the succession of "ages" or cycles as a cause for what happens in time, and second, in rejecting an efficient cause for either the will that has brought about man's misery or the other which is the turning toward the road of blessedness.

Man, a creature of intellect, expressing his being in language and therefore essentially existing in partnership of the word, lives as he speaks, i.e., discursively. There is a meaningful movement of the understanding, of memory, but, above all, of love. Man's existence cannot be adequately described as the unfolding of genetic forces, but only as the movement of love. Created in the image of God, man can by his loves be carried to one of two ends: either fullness of partnership with God who is *actus purus*, existence *per se*, and the unchangeable good; or else the utter deprivation of that absolute good in a hopelessly solitary self-will. The movement of man's existence, then, cannot be seen as pertaining to or even in analogy with, nature. It must be grasped as history. History belongs to the mutability of the rational creature made in God's image who is *capax dei* and *capax infiniti*, but also capable of willfully botching this high destiny.

One frequently reads a statement to the effect that books 15-19 of the *City of God* contain the "history" of the heavenly city, and this "history" is then seen as the core of Augustine's construction of world history. If we understand by history something like progressive development, then the causal connection of successive events, the famous "six ages" are indeed mentioned but play no role in the shaping of Augustine's historiology which is rather found in books 11 and 12. In books 15-18 we find no more than a listing of the families and individuals who, on the authority of Scripture, have at various times cleaved to God. No causal connections are adduced; sometimes gaps of centuries occur in the narrative. Nor is any progressive development implied. The citizenry of God now is not better or higher than in Abraham's time. Nor is there report of quantitative growth, or any prospect of future dominion over the earth, or of an ultimate improvement of the mind in this mortal life. The men and women of God are simply set side by side with the secular events and kingdoms contemporary with them. In those kingdoms and events, causal connections could be observed, but not with the persons and actions pertaining to the City of God. Christ was born in the time of Caesar Augustus, so in the same way others lived and died at times marked by the records of kings' *res gestae*. That is all. The citizenry of God as such cannot be said to have a history in the sense of evolution or progress. It is engaged in a pilgrimage, but that does not lead from one saint to another; rather it leads all saints in trans-temporal communion and personally, through the vicissitudes of mortal and corruptible life, to God. Progress in Christianity is not linear and horizontal, it is vertical. It aims at eternity, not the spinning out of time.[24] As for the secular events, Augustine must have found that many causalities do not a unity make. How about developments that can be observed in civilization, the arts, and so on? Curiously enough, Augustine, who has delivered himself of the most scathing criticism of this life that has ever been written, calling even the virtues, if they remain aloof from God, nothing but "splendid vices," has also composed a pangyric on the progress of the arts, sciences, industries, and other skills that he observed in the Rome of his time.[25] He numbers them among "the blessings of this life" which men are indeed happy to use, but should not enjoy. For they do not fulfill man's destiny which lies in the movement of his love, and even in their highest development there is not *salus*, no possibility of the *beata vita*.

The result of Augustine's observation of man is his perception of being as a movement toward a goal. Mutable rational creatures have from the beginning set up a drama centering in a conflict between good and evil, so that the entire creation moves toward a corresponding end: "By the end of good, we at present mean, not that by which good is destroyed, so that it no longer exists, but by which it is finished, so that it becomes complete; and by the end of evil we mean, not that which abolishes it, but that which completes its development. These two ends, therefore, are the supreme good and the supreme evil."[26] The completion, then, is historical. Augustine here returns to the ontological concept of order with which he began and in which he reflected on the place of evil in a good creation: "Although the whole life of fools is ordered by themselves hardly logically and almost not at all, it still is included by Divine Providence in the necessary order of things and by an unspoken and eternal law confined, as it were, to a fixed sphere beyond which it is not permitted."[27] Judgment, eternal bliss, and eternal punishment are Augustine's theological terms for the historiology of being induced by the presence of evil loves in good natures. "And when a vitiated nature is punished, besides the good it has in being a nature, it has this also, that it is not unpunished."[28] Being must also be seen historiologically, because its movement transcends man and his race in every direction. The movement comprises the fallen angels, and ultimately transcends time itself, since it comes to its full completion only on the eighth day, beyond the cessation of time.

Augustine's history, then, is not what Voegelin has called historiogenesis, the attempt to trace one's own society back to primeval beginnings in divinities or eponymic heroes. Augustine presents nothing like a continuous succession, nor any constitutive or meliorative power attributed to events, persons, cultures, or ages. Much less is it history as the comprehensive unity of mundane events, in the sense of Hegel and Marx. It is a unified view, the unity comprising movement, but the movement that of the order of being, affected, as it is, by the loves of mutable rational creatures made in the image of god who, because of their speech, have their being in fellowship. In this movement there is some that goes in the direction of nothingness, and some into the direction of blessedness, but it is historical as the movement of love uncaused, unpredicted, uncontrolled, a movement toward a goal and thus meaningful, a destiny first refused and then regained in human will responding to divine grace.

The fact that Western civilization centers on a concept of history is due to Augustine's work. It has been said before that our civilization cannot do without a concept of history and, if refusing to entertain a valid view, will of necessity resort to a counterfeit one. The contemporary age has seen a plethora of counterfeit constructions of history emerge, most of them between 1750 and 1850; false notions of history have crystallized into those millenarian idea systems which are called modern ideologies. Modern notions of history also can be traced to the thought of one man, in this case Voltaire, who in the 1750s coined the new term "philosophy of history," or, as he put it, the study of history "*en philosophe.*"

Voltaire, like Augustine, fashioned a concept of history starting from scratch. This is not quite accurate, for precisely owing to Augustine's legacy, the concept of history as such was available and imposed itself on everyday language. In Voltaire's time, the Augustinian view had been handed down by Bossuet's *Histoire universelle* in a diluted and at times almost caricatured version, and Voltaire set out by despising and rejecting Bossuet's work. If Voltaire was original, then, it was because he, like Descartes, began to reflect in a self-inflicted vacuum. To his credit it should be noted that he did not take the availability of the term "history" as a self-evident assurance that successive events are naturally or teleologically so linked to each other that their flux would add up to a self-evident "meaning." Quite the contrary, the chain of events appeared to Voltaire as a "chaos."[29] The multitude of known facts being nothing but "confusing," their totality constitutes but a "vast warehouse" where one selects only that which one finds "useful" and "worthy to be known by oneself." The title of Voltaire's work already indicates that his preference is for the history of culture, over the history of facts. Even there, however, he finds that "in their manners and laws men always contradict each other."[30] Thus history is something at which Voltaire can arrive only by a process or picking and choosing, of inclusion and exclusion. Here, his distance from Augustine could not be greater. Augustine sees all being in terms of a movement, according to God's order, with the driving forces being the loves of rational creatures and the saving grace of God. In the light of that view, all of the past, all of the future is important. In every action, every event, and every person there occurs the eternally relevant movement toward either the all-embracing absolute good, or else toward the pinpoint of self. In all of memory we discover the mystery of the soul and the destiny of man. In God's providential government, nothing is lost, not even human sinfulness, which is assigned its place in the movement of the whole. Voltaire, by contrast, divides men and events of the past into those that are important, and those which "have decided nothing." "Decided nothing" is a term of causality, meaning that certain happenings have left no great influence on subsequent ones. These he utterly refused to notice. His eyes rest only on the "grand" events, and on the relatively enduring manners and customs of peoples. But even here he selects. What, then, is to be left out? Voltaire is disarmingly candid about his own prejudices: "Let us leave respectfully the divine to those who are its keepers, and attach ourselves solely to history."[31] Between "history" and the divine, then, a great gulf is fixed. Quite consistently, Voltaire designates his subject as "the march of the human mind left to itself."[32] One perceives its itinerary by "seeing things on the grand scale" so that one can "place the centuries before one's eyes without confusion."[33] The "grand scale" is further affected by the requirement of "probability" which Voltaire, in a somewhat cavalier fashion, imposes on the record. This "probability" of events must fit into the framework of "nature" which is "always and everywhere the same."[34] Behind this concept is hidden Voltaire's anthropology, for he observes that in "the enormous variety of manners, customs, laws, revolutions" there lies "the same principle," the "interests." What are these "interests"? "Man, in general, has always been what he is...he has always had the same instinct which induces him to love his own self, in the attendance (*compagne*) of his pleasures."[35] A kind of afterthought introduces a qualification, in that "there is also a love of order"

which "animates the human race secretly"(!) and "has prevented
its total ruin."[36]

What Voltaire sees, to the exclusion of anything else, is the
man of Augustine's earthly city, the self-willed, self-loving, self-
centered creature who has turned away from God. In this pattern
of motives and orientation, man must "necessarily adopt the
same verities and the same errors," so that the consistency of
human thoughts and works "forms the *tableau* of the universe."[37]
Sameness in the midst of change, which characterizes nature,
does not, however, amount to history. Voltaire, having dismissed
God from history, and having excluded the unity provided by an
eschatological end of history, now proceeds to construct his
concept of history with the help of three assumptions: a single
source of history, a subject of history, and a direction. The
subject, as has already been mentioned, is "the human mind left
to itself,"--a vague notion which makes one wonder whether it
refers to any given reality. Whatever is meant by "the human
mind", however, it is "marching on." The march proceeds by way
of imitation, first of the most talented individual men, then of the
more advanced peoples by the more backward ones. The chain
of imitations and lessons may be likened to Aristotle's chain of
motions, and, as all motions must go back to a prime mover, so
Voltaire's successive learnings must be traced to a prime teacher.
That leads Voltaire into an extensive discussion of the antiquity
of peoples and cultures. His prime endeavor is to dethrone the
Jews from their preeminence as the people to whom God has
revealed himself. Page after page he devotes to a persistent effort
to discredit the biblical history of the Jews, from denying them
the authorship of the Book of Job, to identifying Moses with the
Greek god Dionysos. As the history of the Jews is linked with
that of the Egyptians, a secondary thrust demolishes the antiquity of Egyptian culture. Mesopotamia and India are conceded
to be older cultural achievements, but Voltaire eventually asserts
that the oldest annals in the world are those of China. China as

the oldest country must be called a "useful" selection of Voltaire's. For the Chinese "wrote their history with pen and astrolabe in their hands." "What this people wrote, they wrote reasonably...their history does not mention a body of priests...they do not go back to the origin of things; their history covers only historical times...they have perfected morality, which is the first of the sciences...."[38] Voltaire advises Mme. du Chatelet, to whom he dedicated his work: "As you inform yourself about this world *en philosophe*, direct your glance first toward the Orient, the cradle of all the arts."[39] The arts! Men's own works, the product of their mind "left to itself," the making of things that satisfy "the interests" and provide for the "company of the pleasures." The arts are to Voltaire the key to endurance; a nation that possesses them and is not subject to foreign rule can "easily emerge from its ruins and always recover."[40] At this point Voltaire's history is but a step removed from that of Marx who attributed historical continuity to the process of production, while Voltaire saw it in the ensemble of the products. The arts had their beginning in China "which has given the West everything...[they] have every-thing by nature; while we of the northern West owe everything to time, trade, and a belated industry."[41] Here, then, is the single source of history. Here begins the "march of the human mind." In what direction is it headed? Voltaire sees indubitable progress. Western Europe is to him "more populated, more civilized, more wealthy, more enlightened now than before, and is even much superior to the Roman Empire."[42] Of the century of Louis XIV Voltaire says that it is "the most enlightened century that ever was," the best in a group of happy ages comprising Greece from Philip of Macedonia to Alexander, Rome from Caesar to Augustus, and Italy following the conquest of Constantinople by the Turks.[43]

Voltaire looks on the history of civilization without any concern with the problem of saving man's existence, which preoccupied not only Augustine, but also Socrates, Plato, and

Aristotle. By replacing Bossuet's Hebrew center of history with a multitude of different civilizations, some of which he brought first to the attention of educated Europeans, and all of which he placed above the Jews in achievement, education, character, and importance, he emphasized as strongly as he could the utterly secular character of civilization and of history as a whole. In selecting China as the teacher of mankind, he shifted history from man's spirituality to man's artifacts. He construed the general movement of civilization as one from "superstition" and "the miraculous" to reason and nature, but soberly remarked that in spite of that movement men "are what they always have been." Civilization, even while apparently progressing, is thus seen as a kind of veneer, bare of any ontic significance. It follows that "the march of the human mind, left to itself" may have direction but leads to no end, in the sense of a fundamental change in human life, an end that Augustine clearly perceived through the experience of fundamental change in his own life. Voltaire is not interested in ontology and does not see being in historiological terms. Nor does he construe history as a movement of objective character. For him history comes into existence only as he chooses "what is worthy to be known" and "what is of use," and by thus choosing makes "of this chaos a general and well-articulated *tableau*."[44] That makes the *tableau* itself a human artifact, an aspect of civilization, useful to satisfy certain interests of certain men. The unity of Voltaire's history exists only in a subjective sense, like a travelogue, passing a multitude of fascinating impressions before the delighted eye as it dwells on manners and arts rather than on hard facts. In all of this Voltaire does not see any objective mechanism of change, or a necessary succession of phases of history. In fact, history is that which constantly surprises: "Every event leads to another which one did not anticipate."[45] Grand events may be either beneficial or injurious.

What is the function of Voltaire's *tableau*? There is no denying that it seeks to reduce the mystery of history to something like certain knowledge, thereby also putting it effectively under some kind of human control, a control which Voltaire himself demonstrated by constituting history's unity through his deliberate choice of "useful" facts from the "chaos" of events. As the object of rational knowledge, history is vindicated to the autonomous human mind—the autonomy emphasized by the horizon of everyday's "interests" within which everything occurs. One may say that Voltaire has aptly conceived the history of Augustine's earthly citizenry, i.e., of human life turned in on itself, centering on pleasure and power, producing cumulative advances which cannot affect the basic orientation of men's souls. In a certain pride of cyclical honestly, Voltaire does not pretend that that life can attain a perfection of which he can see no evidence. All the same, to his claim of rational knowledge there is also attached a certain hope for rational political management. With a kind of Fabian emphasis, Voltaire singles out two past rulers for highest praise: Peter the Great and Julian the Apostate ("the glory of the Roman Empire"). Peter used autocratic power like meat cleaver to remould his people from "superstition" and "barbarism" to civilization, while Julian made a similarly strenuous effort to return the Romans from Christianity to paganism. The fact that one, in modern lingo, sought to "turn back the clock of history" while the other violently yanked its hands forward underscores what Voltaire found equally admirable in both of them: both executed the movement which Marx later called "ascending from earth to heaven," i.e., placing first man and his "interests," or civilization, and excluding soul, God, salvation, and blessedness.

Voltaire's reductionism, his deliberate disregard of knowledge about man that had been gained in many centuries of great and serious effort, was the flaw in his honestly. Prior to setting his pen to paper, he made up his mind not to see one half of reality. Given that defective "position," however, one cannot but admire his consistency and unfliching clear eye. He wrote the history of the earthly citizenry without blinkers, finding in it no more or less than on the basis of his premise he could observe. Within its unflinching confinement, Voltaire's *Essai sur les moeurs et l'esprit des nations* must be termed a rational and valid construction of a partial history. In this capacity it is the sole conceivable alternative to Augustine. If Augustine's is an onto-theological history, Voltaire's is an anthropo-demiurgic history, centering on man the craftsman of his own world of things. It is this concept that has become the basic pattern of every subsequent "philosophy of history." Hegel, Comte, Marx, and Spengler, wrote their philosophies of history in terms of "the human mind, left to itself," centering on civilization minus spirituality as the core meaning of life. In one important respect they differed from Voltaire, though. We have found that Voltaire put into his *Essai sur les moeurs* all that a history of man-centered civilization contained. The later writers took from Voltaire their clue that such a history was possible. With his pattern as a foundation, however, they added certain mystifying concepts which had nothing to do with civilization and the works of man.

Hegel and Marx, for instance, supplied a mechanism of historical change, Hegel, the "cunning of reason," and Marx, the "laws of history." Hegel and Marx also gave the direction of history an upward tilt so that in their system whatever came later also had to be "higher," calling it "the dialectic." Finally, they had the human mind, or civilization, not only march in a certain direction but also finally arrive at an end figuring as "the riddle or history, solved"; in Hegel's case, "absolute knowledge," in Marx's, "the realm of freedom." Unlike Voltaire, they resorted to pseudotheological notions quite alien to the intramundane civilizational reality to which they pretended to have confined themselves, in the "spirit of science." It is these extraneous and mystifying additions by later beneficiaries of Voltaire's initial effort which account for the salvific pretensions attached to civilizational activities in our time. These are bootlegged notions belonging to Augustine's onto-theological—or, better, to the Gnostic's speculative—rather than to Voltaire's anthropo-demiurgic construction. In any history that claims to remain wholly on the ground of this earth, they are illegitimate intruders, dissimulating impostors that tend to confer on civilization titles and pretensions which cannot possibly be sustained in the court of reason. Moreover, there is no possibility of combining pseudotheological concepts with concepts of civilizational development in an unambiguous way. Any combination of such disparate elements is apt to slant left as well as right and appear in extremist as well as in moderate form, its needle apt to gyrate wildly either within one person or one group. In order to resist such exaggerated claims for civilization, one would do well to return to Voltaire as the originator of a basically modest history confined to civilization, and, for ultimate correction, recall Augustine, the giant who could visualize the great history, encompassing man and God in the movement of being as a whole.

NOTES

1. Augustine, *De genesi ad litt.* 1.c.9 n. 17; also 1.c.5 n. 10.

2. C.J. O'Toole, *The Philosophy of Creation in the Writings of St. Augustine* (Washington, D.C.: Catholic University of America Press, 1944), p. 22.

3. Augustine, *De civ. dei* 11.28.

4. Rudolf Schneider, *Seele und Sein, Ontologic bei Augustine und Aristoteles* (Stuttgart: Kohlhammer, 1957), p. 52.

5. Augustine, *Confessions* 10.17. This and subsequent quotations from *The Fathers of the Church*, trans. R.J. Deferrari (Washington, D.C.: Catholic University of America Press, 1963).

6. Augustine, *Confessions* 10.16.

7. Augustine, *Confessions* 11.37.

8. Augustine, *De trin.* 9.4.

9. Augustine, *De trin.* 15.19.

10. Augustine, *De trin.* 9.14.

11. Augustine, *De trin.* 9.15.

12. In the following remarks I acknowledge my indebtedness to Wilhelm Hoffmann, *Augustinus, Das Problem seiner Daseinsauslegung* (Münster: Aschendorf, 1963).

13. Augustine, *Contra acad.* 3.38

14. Augustine, *Contra acad.* 3.37.

15. Augustine, *De musica* 6.1.

16. Augustine, *De musica* 6.11.

17. Augustine, *De musica* 6.13.

18. Augustine, *De musica* 6.41.

19. Augustine, *Confessions* 7.9.

20. Augustine, *De musica* 6.30.

21. *St. Augustine*, Essays by M.C. D'Arcy et al. (New York: Meridian Books, 1957), pp. 306, 302.

22. Augustine, *De civ. dei* 11.4.

23. Augustine, *De civ. dei* 12.19.

24. A.D. Sertillanges, *Pensées inedites, De la vie, De l'histoire.* Quoted in H.I. Marrou, *Time and Timeliness*, trans. Violet Nevile (New York: Sheed Ward, 1969).

25. Augustine, *De civ. dei* 22.24.

26. Augustine, *De civ. dei* 19.1.

27. Augustine, *De ordine* 3.8.

28. Augustine, *De civ. dei* 12.3.

29. Voltaire, *Essai sur les moeurs et l'esprit des nations*, in *Oeuvres complètes*, ed. E. de la Bedolliere and Georges Avenal, vol. 2 (Paris: Bureau du Siecle, 1867), p. 4.

30. Voltaire, *Essai*, p. 10.

31. Voltaire, *Essai*, p. 65.

32. Voltaire, *Essai*, p. 9.

33. Voltaire, *Essai*, p. 5.

34. Voltaire, *Essai*, p. 8.

35. Voltaire, *Essai*, p. 11.

36. Voltaire, *Essai*, p. 360-361.

37. Voltaire, *Essai*, p. 356.

38. Voltaire, *Essai*, p. 21.

39. Voltaire, *Essai*, p. 49.

40. Voltaire, *Essai*, p. 362.

41. Voltaire, *Essai*, p. 49.

42. Voltaire, *Essai*, p. 361.

43. Voltaire, *Essai*, p. 367.

44. Voltaire, *Essai*, pp. 4, 48.

45. Voltaire, *Essai*, p. 46.

Are There "Intelligible Parts" of History?

If one says that history is the symbolic form of our consciousness one may elicit spontaneous assent, but the statement is far from being clear. Does "history" here mean merely the past, or a whole that includes the future? Does the "symbolic form" include something like a knowable plan, as, for instance, a movement of necessary progress? Can we really "see," even symbolically, History as a unit? Arnold Toynbee opened his *Study of History* by introducing the concept "intelligible field of historical study," imputing intelligibility to "the lives of societies, not states," and calling these societies "the social atoms" with which "students of history have to deal" (V. I, 2nd ed., 44 ff.). The whole here is accessible only because one has empirical access to a part, which as an "intelligible unit" plays a role similar to that of a fossil skull from which one can reconstruct an image of the entire paleontological body. Toynbee, then, sees the "intelligible field" as the analyzable fragment of a whole which is his real object. He quotes Lord Acton in this context: "by Universal History I understand that which is distinct from the combined history of all countries...a continuous development (which) is not a burden on the memory, but an illumination of the soul" (p. 47). Focusing his research on the "intelligible fields," Toynbee both conceals and begs the question of whether there is such a thing as universal History, rather than a multitude of histories.[1]

If, as Toynbee maintains, the historian has access only to "intelligible units" which may be seen as "parts," whence came the intuition of a whole? Our wonderment about this question begins with the first historiographers who were aware that they undertook something different in kind from what the chroniclers did. They intended something they called history. This constituted no mere logical development. Even today there are great civilizations where "the symbolic form of consciousness" is not history but rather the myth; where human life is illumined by a background of stories about gods and goddesses in which the past plays nor more of a role than the future, as illustrated by the following paragraph from E.M. Forster's *A Passage to India*: "Some hundreds of miles westward of the Marabar Hills...Professor Narayan Godbole stands in the presence of God. God is not born yet—that will occur at midnight—but He has also been born centuries ago, not can He ever be born, because He is the Lord of the Universe, who transcends human processes. He is, was not, is not, was" (ch. XXXIII). This kind of consciousness is not ordered by history, so that even the national past remains of but little interest. Time, to use the language of Mircea Eliade, appears "reversible"; past can be both present and future, and vice versa. Myth was the symbolic form of order everywhere, "before philosophy." Philosophy, "the discovery of the mind," introduced intelligibility of things in terms of their own "nature," explaining by means of conceptual syllogisms rather than intuiting through stories about the gods,—which is not the same thing as saying that philosophy sought to understand reality "apart from God."

It looks as if this achievement of philosophy may have induced the writing of history rather than chronicles, as historians took courage about the possibility of explaining past events in terms of intelligible causes and effects. All the same, while historiography in Greece (and in China) followed the event of philosophy, it did not directly grow out of philosophy. This separation is clearly noted by Aristotle (*Poetics* 1451 b): "The distinction between historian and poet is not in the one writing prose and the other verse—you might put the work of Herodotus into verse, and it would still be a species of history; it consists really in this, that the one describes the thing that has been, and the other a kind of thing that might be. Hence poetry is something more philosophic and of graver import than history, since its statements are of the nature rather of universals, whereas those of history are singulars. By a universal statement I mean one as to what such or such a kind of man will probably or necessarily say or do—which is the aim of poetry, though it affixes proper names to the characters; by a singular statement, one as to what, say, Alcibiades did or had done to him."

Apart from the general impulse to look for elements of immanent intelligibility history and philosophy owe nothing to each other. Plato and Aristotle did not philosophize about the results of Herodotus and Thucydides. Greek and Roman historians prided themselves on the truthfulness of their reporting but used concepts of universal necessity or intimated the existence of universal patterns. The language of universals and the intention of nature or natures remained the domain of philosophy; the portraying of singular action, persons, and events, that of history. In the words of Troeltsch, the latter is ideographic, the former nomothetic. It appears, the, that the order of the myth was displaced not only by consciousness symbolically illumined by philosophy, but also by a new reliance on accurate knowledge of the past.

Unlike the philosopher, the historian faced the problem of finding an object of knowledge. He looked out on an unceasing stream of multitudinous "happenings" with no self-evident meaning or structure. He could not help imposing his own frame on such materials. Historiography stood in need of some "thing" to explain. Where to begin, where to end, what to include, and what to omit? What was the principle on which he should conceive his frame? One sees historiographers struggling with this problem as they agreed, successively, to write history on the model of tragedy, or rhetoric. The same need suggested the selection of great wars as the scope of inquiry, since in war a multitude of events hang together in contributing to the outcome. Here, then, is a kind of "whole" and "parts." All the same, this kind of whole is not the whole of history. The problem remained unsolved.

Herodotus focused on two "wholes" rather than one: "I hope to do two things: to preserve the memory of the past by putting on record the astonishing achievements both of our own and of the Asiatic peoples; secondly, and more particularly, to show how the two races came into conflict" (opening paragraph of *The Histories*). This creates a quandary of where to begin. Herodotus takes in not merely the prehistory of the wars but delves deeply into the background of myth. And where to end? His last scenes describe the Athenians recovering the chains with which the Persians built a bridge across the Hellespont, but then he adds some more stories about the fate of certain Persian officers, and there is no evident reason why he should stop there. The "why?" is answered not by explaining various human motives or some higher design but rather the war's significance as it appeared to Herodotus: the preservation of Greek freedom against the threat of Persian tyranny. Thucydides selects his war because it seems to him to be the largest yet: "Indeed, this was the greatest movement yet known in history, not only in Greece, but over a large part of the non-Greek world—I almost said of mankind." What Thucydides "almost" said, Polybius seized and maintained: "Fortune has caused nearly all events in the known world to point in one direction, and she has compelled everything to incline toward one and the same goal. It is therefore my duty to concentrate for the reader through my history, in one overall survey, the working of Fortune through which she has fulfilled her general design. Indeed, it was this that most of all invited and stimulated me to attempt a history. A secondary motive was the fact that no one in my time has essayed a systematic world-history.... For (Fortune) has put on many a showpiece and is constantly taking an active part in the lives of men, but I may safely say that she has never fashioned any work nor accomplished any feat like the one in our times. And this work of hers cannot be seen as a whole by studying writers of historical monographs.... Therefore we must agree that historical monographs contribute very little indeed toward a confident mastery of the whole of world history" (I, 4).

Here a historian for the first time perceives a "whole," the ecumene, as having emerged from the work of Fortune, which now deserves to be mastered by the mind through the telling of its history. Polybius' history comes close to claiming the super-session of philosophy. A similar intention inspired the work of Ssu-ma Ch'ien, who described the war between Hsiang Yu and Liu Chi as the coming-to-be of the cosmic order of the Han-Dynasty, making his point more emphatic by including China's cosmic foundation myths as well as the tradition of rituals, ceremonies, and hymns. Liu chi was friendly to Confucian philosophy, as both the preceding Ch'in-Dynasty and Hsiang Yu were not, so that the victory of the Han-Dynasty secured not only the imperial order but also the order of the sage against amoral power.

Even though the most ambitious of these historiographers talk confidently in terms of "the whole," they do know that they had nothing like "universal history" in their grasp. Polybius' description of Scipio weeping on the ruins of Carthage as he anticipates a similar fate for Rome points to a future in which "the world" of his story will have crumbled. Herodotus again and again insists on the "wheel" of historical changes by which "most of those who were great once are small today; and those which in my own lifetime have grown to greatness, were small enough in the old days. It makes no odds whether the cities I shall write of are big or little—for in this world nobody remains prosperous for long" (I). In ancient historiography, then, Acton's "Universal History" is no object of the mind. Even though they speak of "the whole world," they do not intend an ontological unit, nor an enduring oneness. However big their scope may be, they describe no more than what Thucydides has called "a movement in history."

Still, as compared with the chronicles, these various histories do explain. If the whole of their scope is not intelligible as a part of universal history, what are their "intelligible units"? Livy in the Preface to his *History of Rome* is fairly explicit: "...to perpetuate the achievements of a people, the Lords of the World...what their life and what their manners were; through what men and by what measures, both in peace and in war, their empire was acquired and extended...let [the reader] follow in his thoughts their morals...how they have sunk more and more, then began to fall headlong.... What is particularly salutary and profitable in the study of history is that you behold instances of every variety of conduct displayed on a conspicuous monument; that from thence you may select...that which you may imitate; thence note what is shameful...which you may avoid." Tacitus defines his intention as follows: "And yet this melancholy period, barren as it was of public virtue, produced some examples of truth and honor. Mothers went into voluntary exile with their sons; wives followed the fortune of their husbands; relations stood forth in the cause of their unhappy kindred; sons appeared in defense of their fathers; slaves on the rack gave proof of their fidelity; eminent citizens, under the hard hand of oppression, were reduced to want and misery, and, even in that distress, retained an unconquered spirit" (*The History* I, 3). And in *The Annals*: "The transactions hitherto related, and those which are to follow, may, I am well aware, be thought of little importance, and beneath the dignity of history (and not) comparable with the old republic.... The work in which I am engaged, lies in a narrow compass.... A long and settled calm...a gloomy scene at home...these are the scanty materials that lie before me. And yet materials like these are not to be undervalued; though slight in appearance, they still merit attention, since they are often the secret spring of the most important events" (IV, 32).

It seems, then, that the "intelligible unit" of ancient historiography is not "the world," nor a war, not a people, but the noble deed, or maybe the conspicuous deed, be it noble or vile. It is in terms of particular decisions and personal deeds that larger concatenations of events are explained. The deeds themselves call for an understanding of the actor's character. Thus virtues and vices, rationality and irrationality, deliberations false and correct, are preserved in memory, to the end that later generations may "imitate or avoid" what they read about. The framework or scope may be large and painted in bold strokes. The actual scenery, however, consists of particular human actions and characters, the judgment of which constitutes the coloring. No theory of time functions in these explanations. In fact, as the title of *The Annals* shows, the temporal unit of the narrative is the year, a unit without any meaning other than the weather. One potential temporal unit is conspicuous by its absence: the "age," in the sense of Hesiod's three ages. Historiography, which together with philosophy has replaced the myth, has also left the myth of "ages" behind. Even though Tacitus characterizes his "time," he is not speaking of an "age" that superimposes itself on the lives of all men with the irresistible power of a ruling destiny. Nor does historiography make use of the concept of a "great age" that is found in some philosophers. If neither in philosophy nor in history a concept of "Universal History" is to be found, where and when could our Western consciousness have acquired this concept as its symbolic structure?

Philosophy asked questions about being and natures; historiography about the character of particular human actions. Neither could engender a concept of universal history until questions were asked about an ultimate meaning beyond the stream of "happenings." In the words of Karl Loewith: "History...is meaningful only by indicating some transcendent purpose beyond the actual facts. But, since history is a movement in time, the purpose is a goal."[2] The concept that touched off systematic thinking of an ultimate goal, was eschatology. This notion was alien to Greek thinking and had no place in Greek or Roman historiography. It had arisen in the self-understanding of a people in whose past a miraculous deliverance by God's act had moved them to center their religious creed on this historical fact, and on God's lordship of history. Hebrew thinking was history-centered instead of cosmos-centered. Or rather, the Hebrews saw the world, both events and things, in the perspective of God's invisible though active presence, as temporal-movement-in-God. Eschatological concepts, an unavoidable conclusion, are found in Amos' "Day of the Lord," Isaiah's "remnant," Ezekiel's revived "dry bones," Malachi's eschatological community, Daniels' identification of "the people of the saints of the most High" with "the Son of Man," to list just the outstanding instances. From there eschatology made its way into the Greco-Roman world not so much by theoretical writings as through the liturgy. In the second half of the fourth century, along with the full establishment of Christianity, a great liturgical reform took place, in which the formerly private services became public services. The liturgy of the mass thus brought eschatological concepts to general attention, even though the Greco-Roman mind still had its difficulties with it.

The first function of the mass was recollection, *anamnesis*, but a recollection of a past the reality of which dominated both present and future. In the words of St. John Chrysostom: "What then? Do we not offer daily? Certainly we offer thus, making an *anamnesis* of his death. How is it one and not many? Because it was offered once, like that which was carried (in the O.T., on the Day of Atonement) into the holy of holies...for we ever offer the same Person, not today one sheep and next time a different one, but ever the same offering. Therefore the sacrifice is one. By this argument then, since the offering is made in many places, does it follow that there are many Christs? Not at all, for Christ is everywhere one, complete here and complete there, a single body. Thus, as when offered in many places He is one Body and not many bodies, so also there is one sacrifice. One High-priest is He Who offered the sacrifice which cleanses us. We offer even now that which was then offered, which cannot be exhausted. This is done for an *anamnesis* of what was then done, for 'Do this' said He 'for the *anamnesis* of Me'. We do not offer a different sacrifice like the high priest of old. Or rather we offer the *anamnesis* of the sacrifice."[3] The "inexhaustible past" is also the ever-changing present. Dix sees the second function of the mass as action, essentially the action of an eschatological "becoming what you are." "The Body of Christ, the church, offers itself to *become* the sacrificed Body of Christ, the sacrament, in order that thereby the church itself may become within time what in eternal reality it is before God—the 'fullness' or 'fulfillment' of Christ; and each of the redeemed may 'become' what he has been made by baptism and confirmation, a living member of Christ's body" (p. 247). This is the "realized eschaton," the actuality of fulfillment in historical movement of what Christ is eternally.

Dix, likening eschatology to the mathematical process of sum, in which the answer is both part of the calculation and also contained in it from the beginning, continues: "The 'Day of the Lord', the *eschaton*...is the answer to the agonizing problem of history, with its apparent chaos of good and evil. This completion of history, 'the End' which manifests the 'kingdom'...of God throughout history in all its parts, does not interrupt history or destroy it; it fulfills it. All the divine values implicit and fragmentary in history are gathered up and revealed in the *eschaton*, which is 'the End' to which history moves. In this sense, the 'Day of the Lord' involves a 'judgment' of history as a whole, and of all that goes to make up history. 'The End' is at once within history and beyond time, the 'Age to come'" (p. 258). Turning to the Christian life "in the spirit," Dix remarks: "'The Spirit' is that power of presence of the Ascended Christ...in the 'Body of Christ', the church on earth...thus the church, though 'in Christ' and one with Him in his eternal glory and kingdom, remained within time. 'The End' had come and yet history continued!" Recognizing the difficulty this notion presented to "Greeks" then and now, Dix continues: "...the eschaton had a double significance: (1) it manifested the purpose of history, and (2) it also concluded it. but even in Jewish thought these two aspects were not regarded as necessarily coincident in time....The same eternal fact can touch the process of history at more than one point, and if there is an apparent difference in the effects of such contacts, that difference is entirely on the side of the temporal process" (p. 260 ff.).

This set of symbols made possible Augustine's *City of God* to which we rightly trace our concept of history. It could not have come from Greco-Roman historiography, in spite of Polybius' vision of *telos*, since those historians described movements *in* history, none of which could be conceived as the end of history. Nor could their emphasis of the judgment of human action point to an end, either in or beyond history, of attained goodness. Historiography thus produced evidence of past happenings, something one may call "history" in the lower case, but it could not bring into view "History," the "order of time," since this latter is "not a human institution" but something "whose creator and administrator is God."[4] Nor could a concept of History have come from philosophy, even though, as Eric Voegelin has shown, Plato as well as Aristotle became aware of a new epoch, of a significant distinction between 'before' and 'after.' Plato saw the Nous as "the divinity" of a "new age," beyond that of Zeus.[5] This divine Nous, however, marked a new age of philosophical contemplation rather than of the manifold of historical actions. One may see the full fruition of this philosophical theology in the utterly unhistorical Plotinus. Similarly, Aristotle's God, the 'prime mover' and 'agent of purpose' has no relevance for history, because among other things, he is sketched only with the barest of theological lines.

What are the conceptual elements of Augustine's "History"? First, let us note what we find in him:

a) a concept of time created, having both beginning and end;

b) the vision of an eschatological ultimate perfection in God, beyond time, from which stems;

c) meaning in the temporal succession of particularities: an assured outcome, not to be eventually undone or reversed;

d) a set of events in history experienced and perpetually recalled as "God's mighty acts";

e) a continuity of human beings who, at various time and places, responded adequately to God's active presence, this continuity called the *City of God*;

f) a notion of Providence: the God active in History is the redeemer-god (which does not mean that he is the executor of a bureaucratic master-plan).

Secondly, we do *not* find in Augustine:

a) an attempt to draw inductively some ultimate or partial meaning from the succession of historical particularities;

b) an attempt to construct an *eidos* of history in terms of "ages" as powerful, active patterns of overall temporal order.

This last statement requires an explanation, since Augustine repeatedly mentioned "six ages," both in terms of a single human life and in terms of history (e.g., *City of God*, XXII, 30). Augustine's "ages," however, bear no comparison either with the three ages of Hesiod, or with those of Joachim of Flora, and even less with the later ones of Comte and Marx. Those are mere subdivisions of time. Of most of them no more is said than that they lasted from one date to another. Of some of them, Augustine mentions casually that in them some important event occurred, e.g.: "the law was given." It is not the age, however, which accounts for the event; the age is merely its temporal location. Similarly, he mentions in no more than one sentence the birth of Jesus Christ, in another "age." In no ways did Augustine tie these or other events to a particular age seen as a compelling structural necessity. Of the sixth and last age he remarks that its duration cannot be foretold. Again, however, this is no "last age" in the sense of Joachim, Comte, or Marx: a fulfillment of human destiny within history. Rather, it is compared to man's old age in which accumulated experience enables him to enjoy wisdom: similarly, the realized manifestation of God's Kingdom in Jesus Christ completes God's revelation in time and thus enables mankind to live for the remainder in the relative fullness of this light.

One other thing one cannot find in Augustine: a self-conscious mentioning of the concept of History he achieved, which may indicate that it was more of a by-product than a prime intention. The resulting change, however, cannot be overestimated. Before Augustine, there certainly had developed what could call itself "history," but it was no more than a description of how particular action were linked to each other in the scope of "movements" limited in time and space. Augustine accepted this work as "useful." What he left us, however, was the "seeing," beyond a random succession of passing "movements," of the one great movement arching from the beginning of created time to the eternal Beyond. What is remarkable is his agreement with the historiographers on concrete human action as the intelligible element—the stuff of history—which Aristotle called "the ultimate particular" (*Nicomachean Ethics* VI, 8). The great arching movement is that of creation and redemption. To use the words of Romano Guardini, however, "Salvation does not take place on the natural level, or on the idealistic level, or on that of some exalted individual, but on the level of history and historical development. And what is history but decisions of the hour made by individuals and valid for all men for all time."[6]

It is in this sense that Augustine speaks of the great development: "For the end of our good is that for the sake of which other things are to be desired, while it is to be desired for its own sake; and the end of evil is that on account of which other things are to be shunned, while it is avoided on its own account. Thus by the *end of good*, we at present mean, not that by which good is destroyed, so that it no longer exists, but that by which it is finished, so that it becomes complete; and by the *end of evil* we mean, not that which abolishes it, but that which completes its development." (*City of God* XIX, 1). Characteristically, Augustine notes the envisioned attainment of goodness first in the context of personal life (XII, 13), before he comes to the three great books in which he deals with Judgment, Heaven, and Hell, the imagery of the eschatological end of History, "end" in the sense of both completion and finality (XX-XXII). The ultimate good is the vision of God, assured in eternal life, but also a historical reality. The ultimate evil is an irreversible self-debarment from that vision. Since no mere temporal good, however attractive it may seem, can compare with that eternal one, no political order deserves to be looked on as "the good state" or "the best state," particularly since every state consists of a people in which the City of God and the earthly city are mixed. Thus one is not to count on the millennium of *Rev.* 20:3 as a future state of temporal perfection; rather, the concept is to be read as referring to the present church, the "proleptic eschaton."

Much has been made of Augustine's concept of Providence, as if that by itself created a concept of History. Replacing *tyche* and *fortuna*, Providence removed from history the element of irrational capriciousness. On the other hand it neither eliminates the mystery of History nor can it function as that perfect human hindsight which was beloved by Orosius but utterly rejected by Augustine (XVIII, 52). Nor does the mere Oneness of God suffice to engender the unity of History: In Plotinus, the all-dominant unity of The One has no historical dimension whatever. Rather, History's unity is a tension between God's active love and man's unpredictable response. It may be described in the words of a theologian, W.H. Vanstone: "The activity of God in creation must be precarious. It must proceed by no angular progress—in which each step is a precarious step into the unknown; in which each triumph contains a new potential of tragedy."[7] And further: "In the response of freedom, we do not see the advance of man and society toward some predetermined goal—'the good society,' 'the caring society,' 'the fulfillment of humanity,' 'the emergence of persons as persons'. Our eyes are set upon the concrete and individual crises of human existence.... In and through such situations we see the angular progress of the ever precarious creativity of the love of god.... Man's choice in the endless crises of his existence is the response of freedom—the response upon which love must wait for its triumph or its tragedy. We cannot state in general terms a pattern of response in which appears the triumph of the love of God, nor a pattern in which appears its tragedy: but in the concrete situation of crisis, with its finely balanced possibilities, we can see in which direction triumph lies and in which direction tragedy" (p. 92). Thus no History could be confined to a list of "God's mighty acts," or a list of wise and good men by themselves. Nor is there a progress of Salvation as a kind of millenary plan moving from one five-year fulfillment to another. History is the unpredictable and yet intelligible interplay between divine love and human response, between the eternal ultimate and the ultimate particular.

It has been said that Augustine's is a "theology of history." In the sense of that "history" which Augustine knew from Livy and Tacitus, a factually reliable reporting of past clusters of events, it would never have occurred to him even to attempt a theology of such aimless happenings. On the other hand, one may say that Augustine could hardly have had the intention to conceive a theology of History Universal, since until after his *City of God* became known, there was no such object of study. Orosius, indeed, was the first one to take advantage of Augustine's results, on the basis of something like pre-publication reading. Augustine did speak of "the order of time," but produced never anything like an overall schedule or even the claim of foretelling future developments. Thus his thought stems from no *eidos* of history in the sense of an inherent logic of successive events. Rather, his work projected the *eidos* of man on the canvas of temporality and unpredictable "ultimate particulars," where one can "see" nothing but the "angular progress" of human responses to the "irruptions of the Eternal in time" (Voegelin). In a searching article, "Augustine's City of God and the Modern Historical consciousness," Ernest L. Fortin asks this question: "In view of Augustine's pessimism regarding the perfectibility of human institutions and the structural foundations of society, one is entitled to ask what, if anything, the modern philosophy of history owes to him.... One is still left to wonder in what specific sense Augustine might qualify as the first philosopher of history or the father of modern historical consciousness."[8] Fortin's critical eye looks at Augustine from the standpoint of a) philosophy of history, that is, the attempt to make history intelligible by means of judgments couched in terms of universal concepts, and b) the philosophy of history originating in the Enlightenment. Of the latter, Augustine can be called neither the father nor a favorite son, since from Voltaire to Turgot and from Saint-Simon to Marx, Augustine's insights were emphatically rejected and ignored, and that by self-conscious choice. All the same, philosophy of history presents a general problem transcending modernistic thought. In antiquity, Aristotle's one general statement about history—that it is the realm of singulars—stopped all endeavors to understand this realm through universal concepts. If Augustine did leave us a concept of History Universal, he did not get there by philosophizing about the multitude or succession of singulars. Before proceeding further, it may be worthwhile to ask ourselves what precisely Augustine did, so as to come up with a concept of History. We have already noted that he could not construct a "theology of history" in the sense of embracing the totality of intramundane singular events streaming towards the past. That stream as such cannot be mastered by any theoretical concept. All the same, that is the only meaning that Augustine, in his time, could connect with the word "history."

It seems that Augustine, superbly educated in the humanities, extended already extant conceptual patterns of philosophy and historiography by means of insights stemming from Christian revelation. First, he moved further along the road of historiography, according to which the intelligible unit is the "noble deed," "conspicuous deed," at any rate, Aristotle's "ultimate particular," that which is subject to judgment in the light of the "ultimate universal." It was Aristotle who secured the concept of the *summum bonum* as the *sine qua non* of any goodness of particular action. Augustine moved this concept from an intramundane "happiness" to the "vision of God," highest good both within history and as completed in the eschaton.[9] Secondly, Aristotle's ontology seems to have been Augustine's basis of operation in metaphysical respects.[10] Aristotle's theology was remarkably sparse, more so than Plato's. His identification of God as the Absolute, the Eternally Immutable, was crying out for more. Augustine elaborated Aristotle's theology by the insights supplied him through Hebrew and Christian theology which knew God as "Father of...Jesus Christ, Maker of all things, Judge of all men," (to use the words of the Book of Common Prayer). The unmoved mover turned out to be the Creator, as well as the Redeemer, and also Judge. All this would have still remained in the realm of philosophy, as it did in Plotinus, who undertook similar elaborations. No concept of history could have resulted from such insertions of Christian insights. Thirdly, Augustine perceived a polarity between God's "mighty acts" in history and adequate human responses, both constituting a continuum, although a continuum of relatively few and widely dispersed events. Here the movement of "eternity in time" was a matter of record. Even this chain of divine acts and human responses could not by itself have resulted in a concept of History. It did so only by means of the concept of the 'vision of God' as a goal. The divine-action-human-response nexus, moving purposefully toward an eschatological goal brought into view the whole of History as an intelligible single unit. Thereafter, one could "see" History. What could be thus "seen" could also form the object of study, including philosophical study. That is the sum of Augustine's legacy.

Philosophy, operating with universal concepts, however, could still not make any headway if it addressed itself to the stream of countless singular events. Here intelligibility seemed forever barred not only by the impossibility of finding meaning in a mere aggregate of singulars, but also by the fact that the singulars of future times had not yet occurred. All the same, philosophical efforts to discover typical causation in history did follow from Augustine's discovery of History as an object. One finds them first in Ibn Khaldun and Jean Bodin, who looked into patterns of psychic forces which, being closer to the animal aspects of man, could be posited as both "typical" and "necessary." Thus they arrived at the result of certain cycles in human affairs, a notion which Polybius had prefigured with his "cycle of types of government," and which Vico brought to greater heights with his "natural history" of nations (from which he, significantly, excepted the Jews, God's chosen). Such studies could lead to no more than partial "laws" of typical but merely possible developments. What is more, these "laws" were considered by all three philosophers compatible with the mystery of divine Providence and of human freedom.

A full-fledged philosophy of history emerged only with the invention of the "age," or "phase," of history as the apparent "intelligible unit." This invention was the legacy of Joachim of Flora. The concept of "age" as "phase" must not be confused with the phenomenon of an "epochal consciousness," in the sense of a newness of being, that could be observed in the Hebrew prophets, in Plato and Aristotle, and particularly in the *kerygma* of the early Christian church. The former notion contains not merely the sense of epochal newness, but also the idea that History as a whole consists of a limited number of ages, so that each age can be seen as a "phase," i.e. a "part" of the whole of History. That notion belonged, not to philosophy nor to historiography, but to the myth. Joachim's message of the three ages is uttered wholly in the language of myth rather than theology. His text abounds in such mythical symbols as the tree and its twelve branches, the grafted tree of Christ, the Concordia (parallelity) of relationships in the Old and New Testaments, the tuba representing the preacher of the church as well as the prophets in their time. His "three states" are described as "science, wisdom, and the fullness of knowledge," "bondservice, service of the son, and freedom," "troubles, work, and contemplation," and so on.[11] While the Christian tradition does contain a modicum of mythical elements, it also contains theology ("words adequate to God": St. Basil), and a framework of reason stemming from philosophy. Joachim's effort consists but in the ringing of changes on myths about myths. Still, the concept of three "ages" was launched. Here would-be philosophers of history could find the notion of "units" that were "parts," the ensemble of which formed the "Whole."

After Descartes, philosophers would address themselves to history in search of a) only efficient causes, b) a typology of such causes suitable to explain historical movement, and c) such causes governing the structure and succession of history's "ages." The former interest in the "ultimate particulars" as the intelligible units, faded rapidly. Philosophical study of History concerned itself with impersonal overall structures of "ages" as parts, in the expectation that empirical knowledge of any one part would turn out to be the key to a construction of the whole. Human thoughts and actions were considered derived from the necessity of the structure of each "age" and that of the succession of the "ages." Ultimately, it made little difference whether Marx saw these structures as "modes of production," Hegel as "states of consciousness," or Toynbee as "civilizations." In either case, philosophy of History centered on no more than apparently empirical definition of one or several of its "parts."

It is hardly necessary to point out that this enterprise is as foreign to Augustine as it is to Plato and Aristotle, and to the historiographers as well. All the same, it could not have come about had it not been for Augustine's achievement that enabled men to "see" History for the first time, from which achievement stemmed "History as the symbolic form of our consciousness." Augustine, however, cannot be blamed for the contrived notion of history's "parts" as "intelligible units," which alone accounts for modern philosophy of history. Nothing shall be said here about the perversions of Augustine's *summum bonum* into "absolute knowledge," "classless society," or "Thousand Year Reich." Nor shall we dwell on the secularization of Augustine's divine Providence into an "Absolute Mind," or History by itself. All these developments have made our time one in which the "demons," banned under the sway of a happier balance, have returned. It is thus a matter of no small importance to become fully aware in precisely what symbolic form a consciousness of History can amount to an "illumination of the soul," and which perversion must be characterized as a kind of *fausse conscience.*

NOTES

1. For a modern view doubting the existence of such an object see Sir Herbert Butterfield: *The Whig Interpretation of History* (London, Bell, 1931) and his *Christianity and History* (New York, Scribner's, 1950).

2. K. Loewith: *Meaning in History* (Chicago U.P., 1949), 5.

3. Quoted by Dom Gregory. Dix: *The Shape of the Liturgy* (Westminster, (2)1945), 243.

4. Augustine: *On Christian Doctrine*, II, xxxviii.

5. *OH* IV, 227.

6. R. Guardini: *The Lord* (South Bend, Regnery/Gateway, 1954), 209.

7. W.H. Vanstone: *The Risk of Love* (Oxford U.P., 1978), 6.

8. Review of Politics 41/3, July 1979, 343.

9. *Cf.* K.E. Kirk: *The Vision of God* (London, Longmans Green, (2)1932).

10. *Cf.* R. Schneider: *Seele und Sein; Ontologie bei Augustin und Aristoteles* (Stuttgart, Kohlhammer, 1957).

11. J. von Fiore: *Das Reich des Heiligen Geistes* (München-Planegg, O.W. Barth, 1955.

This Terrible Century

To those of us who are enjoying a life in relative wealth, the educational and artistic offerings of a flourishing culture, and, yes, *in peace*, this century may appear to provide full reason for self-congratulation. To the future historian, however, it may rank as one of the worst centuries of human history. That is, it may so appear to an historian who can discern between good and evil spirits, who is sensitive to the needs of the soul and skillful in reading between the lines of official texts. He may raise the question of why in this century of highly developed culture a new kind of war occurred, the world war; and not just one of them, but one after another. He may wonder at the phenomenon of totalitarianism (again, a novelty in history) and at government that produced by ideology *general slavery*, while formerly only private slavery had occurred. Again, this kind of thing happened not once but three times, with considerable pauses in between, pauses that might have been used for reflection on these novel evils. They were novel in that they stemmed not from a new conception of the state, but rather from a demotion of the state to a mere instrument in the service of ideological adventures of the mind, the entire phenomenon to be called *ideocracy*. Novel also was the fact that human reason was thus distorted not merely in countries where ideological movements set up this new kind of despotism but equally in those countries that appeared to have traveled a road of sanity and sobriety under representative governments. These various points need to be more fully discussed, one by one.

It has taken nearly half a century to develop a deeper and broader understanding of the First World War as this century's worst and key catastrophe. The Great War was spawned by two forces of the nineteenth-century, nationalism and imperialism, that had engendered, among others, four wars before 1914: the Russo-Japanese war (1904-5), the Tripolitan war between Italy and Turkey, (1911); the first Balkan War, (1912); and the second Balkan War, (1913): all of brief duration and manifestly suitable for political settlement.

The outbreak of war between Russia, Austria-Hungary, Germany, and France on August 1, 1914 seemed to all participants to be something of a similar character, so that everybody expected the matter to be over by Christmas. For a while, indeed, it appeared as another of what one might call "conventional" wars. Then, however, it mutated into an unprecedented and unimagined type of warfare: during four years, millions of soldiers existed in trenches and dugouts, endured indescribable artillery duels, every once in a while advanced a few hundred yards of utterly devastated terrain only to lose that gain a few days later. Millions of lives were lost in this seemingly meaningless contention for positions. Millions of survivors found themselves bereft of their sense of meaning. The ensuing cultural impoverishment of the homeland to which they returned manifested itself in all kinds of cultural and political disorder. Socialism and Communism, it is true, already had found considerable acceptance among the working population before World War I, but it did not generate open fighting politics until after the end of that war. Fascism was a direct product of homecoming soldiers in the first five years after the Great War. Nazism found its creator and leader in the resentments and hatreds of a World War I noncommissioned officer who had not learned anything else in life. The following conversation in Dorothy Sayers' *The*

Documents in the Case occurs in the room of a man named Perry, a priest:

> "So here we all are. I never thought you'd stick to it, Perry. Which has made your job the hardest—the War or people like us?"
>
> "The War," said Perry, immediately. "It has taken the heart out of people."
>
> "Yes. It showed things up a bit," said Matthews. "Made it hard to believe in anything."
>
> "No," replied the priest. "Made it easy to believe in everything in a languid sort of way—in you, in me, in Waters, in Hoskyns, in mascots, in spiritualism, in education, in the daily papers—why not? It's easier, and the various things cancel out and so make it unnecessary to take any definite steps in any direction."

World War I terminated four prewar empires: Austria-Hungary, Russia, the Ottoman Empire, and Germany. From their demise arose a number of "succession states": Poland, Czechoslovakia, Hungary, Yugoslavia, Finland, Latvia, Lithuania, Estonia, Albania, Egypt, Palestine, Syria, Lebanon, and so on. To this day most of these nations continue to produce troubles that essentially come from not being prepared for independent political unity; for constituting a unified state. With some trepidation one may call this a new force, to be added to the nineteenth-century forces, of nationalism and imperialism: national political immaturity.

The most destructive novelty, however, were the political ideologies, especially Communism, Fascism, and National Socialism. These three were, first of all, political movements, the movements rooted, however, in a body of ideas that could be mistaken for philosophy, since the ideas transcended the political reality and claimed to apply to being as a whole. Being, of course, is the object of philosophical thought, as it addressed itself to the basic reality of God, nature, and existing things. In other words, to philosophize means to raise questions about the meaning of individual or social existence in the larger reality of what is common to all mankind. Political societies are not monadic, and philosophy proceeds to raise questions about their meaning in terms of a higher, encompassing reality. Early on, in Greek classical philosophy, this meaning was recognized as the "order of the soul."[1] Voegelin here defines "theory" as "an attempt at formulating the meaning of existence by explicating the content of a definite class of experiences." These are experiences of being, such as the love of wisdom, the experience of the just as "right superordination and subordination," the experience of friendship, of death, and of the depth and the height of the soul.[2] Basically, these experiences serve as evidence of what is given, in terms of the cosmos as well as the soul.

Ideology is the name for that kind of disorder which consists in substituting for philosophical questions about what is given a set of assertions about what is not given. What is not given includes the historical future, particularly when one "inquires" about it in order to control the "destiny of mankind." What is given but not accessible to the type of knowing suitable for *things* in this world is the divine reality, above and beyond that of the cosmos and of human history. When speculation of the mind begins to criticize being as such, when it aims not at understanding the "constitution of being" but at its control by the human will, the result is not philosophy but ideology. The Fascist, the National Socialist, and the Communist ideologies were such bastard children of the human mind in the West. Philosophers may have contributed to it. Hegel, for instance, made "states of consciousness" the prime states of history, both past and future, so that his abstractions replace real actors, either men or God. Gobineau was another nineteenth-century thinker, the first to declare race to be man's essence, a claim one should compare with Aristotle's sober ranking of human nature by comparing human being to either animal being, vegetative being, and inorganic being. That difference consisting in reason, he found reason to be the core of human nature. Marx, who was well aware of this philosophical heritage, insisted that labor is man's essence, an assertion which enabled him to describe the division of labor as something that is wrong with being. Marx had to subject humanity to economic determinism in order to make this claim. Freud's reduction of human consciousness to determinism by the subconscious created another premise on which human control over future history could be seemingly secured. All these developments belong to the general sphere of human consciousness of reality and its own nature.

The three ideologies mentioned concerned the sphere of government and public order. In each case we find the creation of a "party" that is unlike all previously existing parties. Political parties of the modern type began to exist in seventeenth-century England. It was not until the French Revolution, however, that one political party claimed to be the possessor of transcending truth and that therefore it could tolerate no disobedience or even criticism. These were the Jacobins. Since they appeared on the historical scene for only a very short time, they were gladly forgotten after their demise. While the Jacobins were a group formed in the vicissitudes of the turbulent French Revolution, with regard to twentieth-century ideologies the respective parties existed long before they actually seized power. In the case of Russia, that meant fifteen years, ten years for Hitler's party, and two or three years in the case of Mussolini's Fascists. These periods of preexistence enabled the three movements to define themselves as something other than previously existing parties. The word, "party," they could not shake, but they would not consent to operate as one of several competing parties. What is more, these ideological groups, or movements, saw themselves not as part of the state, but as ranking above the state and its institutions. In various ways each of these ideological "parties" succeeded in assuming powers to govern that outranked political institutions of any kind, including the state itself. Their leaders did not permit themselves to be classified with any type of ruler known in history. In all three regimes, a previously nonpolitical term was created: *Vozhd, Führer, Duce.* Stalin's prime title was "Secretary of the Communist Party." Mussolini, supposedly under the higher authority of the kind, used the king as his puppet. Hitler, likewise, assumed a somewhat unnamed transcendental character of his position. In all three cases, the result was that, as Camus said, "politics became religion." Now, religion is always worship of something or some being higher than man. Insofar as politics is human order without any direct, divine participation, to confuse or merge it with religion is what Voegelin calls "fallacious," or, in everyday language, impermissible.

Thus we find, first, confusion of philosophical concepts or their derivatives; second, impairment of perception of political institutions and their interrelations; and third, confusion regarding what is worthy to be worshipped and what is not so worthy. The soul that finds itself bereft of the most important means of orientation is a soul subject to incapacity of moral judgment. The capacity of such judgment depends on clarity of the mind regarding ontological premises.

We Americans might now claim a right to congratulate ourselves: we never were tempted by ideology, we never had an ideocratic dictatorship, we never set up a Gulag system, and we never enslaved human minds. But are we distinguished by good order of public and private lives? Let us see what our own newspapers say about this matter:

> "The oft-debated 'social issues'—abortion rights, school prayer, gay rights, and Murphy Brown plot lines—miss the wider calamities of life in the U.S. today. Cold statistics give the essence of the story: In the past three decades, the percentage of children born

outside of marriage has risen fivefold, from 5% to 25%. Today a stunning 63% of black children are born out of wedlock. At the same time, the divorce rate has tripled. The net result is that almost a third of U.S. families now are one-parent households. During the past 30 years, a 560% increase in violent crime, a jump of more than 200% in the teenage suicide rate, and 80% drop in SAT scores."

"The conditions of black ghettos today reveal as much about the disintegration of urban black society as they do about the indifference, hostility or racism of white society. Everybody also knows that other barriers have grown up within the urban black milieu in these last decades that are profoundly debilitating. The effects are manifest in patterns of behavior involving criminality, unwed childbearing, low academic achievement, drug use, and gratuitous violence."

"In Washington D.C., there was a man who drove up to pedestrians, said 'Have a nice day,' and fired a shotgun in their faces. Amy Fisher and Joey Buttafuoco, Mia and Woody, the Glenridge, N.J. gang rape. Michael Griffin and David Dunne. Somalia, Armenia, and Azerbaijan. The World Trade Center bombing. Zoe Baird's and Kimba Wood's nannies. Spotted owl vs. loggers. Judges, journalists, politicians, professors, university presidents, heads of professional associations, foundations, and clergy, have for a long time been afraid to uphold traditional standards. They not only entertained nearly any crackpot idea, theory, or social grievance that entered their ken, but *embraced and legitimized a lot of them*. Where are the people in American life who used routinely to point out that some ideas, some complaints, some movements are in turn weak, insupportable, or false?"

Such reports could be multiplied by the hundreds, but these samples suffice. Who would not recognize our social and cultural existence at this time?

As we turn from journalism to the analysis of scholars, we encounter a different kind of description of our crisis. Eric Voegelin writes of

> [the] apocalyptic enthusiasm for building new worlds that will be old tomorrow, at the expense of old worlds that were new yesterday; its destructive wars and revolutions spaced by temporary stabilizations on ever lower levels of spiritual and intellectual order through natural law, enlightened self-interest, a balance of powers, a balance of profits, the survival of the fittest, and the fear of atomic annihilation in a fit of fitness; its ideological dogmas piled on top of the ecclesiastic and sectarian ones and its resistant skepticism that throws them all equally on the garbage heap of opinion; its great systems built on untenable premises and its shrewd suspicions that the premises are indeed untenable and therefore must never be rationally discussed; with the result, in our time, of having unified mankind into a global madhouse bursting with stupendous vitality.[3]

In the same article Voegelin passes from the heavy sarcasm of the above description to a sober analysis of what is wrong:

> To the people who live in it, the subfield is a closed world. [The 'subfield in the philosopher's larger horizon of reality.'] As a consequence, the point has come into view on which hinges a philosophical understanding of history: that truth experienced is excluded from the subfield, while the larger field is characterized by its inclusion....Truth experienced can be excluded from the horizon of reality but not from reality itself. When it is excluded from the universe of intel-

lectual discourse, its presence in reality makes itself felt in the disturbance of mental operations. In order to save the appearances of reason, the doctrinaire must resort...to such irrational means as leaving premises inarticulate, as the refusal to discuss them, or the invention of devices to obscure them, and the use of fallacies. He does no longer move in the realm of reason but has descended to the underworld of opinion, in Plato's technical sense of *doxa*.

A little later, Voegelin mentions "the persuasive trick of carving history into ascending phases or states of consciousness, for the purpose of placing the carver's consciousness at the top of the ladder," which trick "can be performed only under the assumption that man's consciousness is world-immanent and nothing but that; the fact is that man is capable of apprehending the point of intersection of the timeless with time...."

"The doctrinaire segmentation of history," he says, "has found its climactic expression in the formula: 'We are living in a post-Christian age'...the neat trick of turning the 'post-Christ' of the Christians into the 'post-Christians' of the ideologues."[4] Voegelin's analysis is aimed not only at increased understanding of what it is that constitutes our crises, but also of an awareness of what it is that was lost in the process. "No one is obliged to take part in the spiritual crisis of a society; on the contrary, everyone is obliged to avoid this folly and live his life in order. Our presentation of the phenomenon, therefore, will at the same time furnish the remedy for it through therapeutic analysis."

As David Walsh has observed, Eric Voegelin's work is focused on the question of what, for example, do the

chiliastic visionaries of Puritanism, the rational progressivism of the Enlightenment, the speculative transfiguration of Hegel, the radical activism of Bakunin, the revolutionary messianism of Marx, the religious positivism of Comte, the opaque racism of the National Socialists or the psychoanalytic reductionism of Freud all have in common? The answer is their root inspiration within Gnosticism. In one way or another they arise from a sense of alienation and revolt at the human condition, which they seek to overcome by 'abolishing the constitution of being, with its origin in divine, transcendent being, and replacing it with a world-immanent order of being, the perfection of which lies in the realm of human action.'[5]

These few quotations from Voegelin and Walsh may suffice to indicate what kind of scholarly analysis is capable of penetrating to the root of the crisis and thereby effecting philosophical therapy. They also will enable us to throw some light on the question how it comes that we, the victors in two world wars, the nation that did not need to overthrow any ideological regime, the possessors of an enviable economic system and a normally functioning government, should all the same have to struggle with downright catastrophic symptoms of crisis.

As long as the ideocratic regimes and their totalitarianism existed, the tension of this political polarization sufficed to impose some minimal order on international politics as well as the domestic politics of the democracies. This external compulsion now gone, we find that in the time of the Cold War nothing happened to slow down our own cultural deterioration, so that today its symptoms strike us as undeservedly massive and profound. In other words: what makes this century of ours uniquely terrible is that we, the victors in the war against ideological disorder, the representatives of an exemplary economy and a model type of government, are now becoming aware that we, too, have lost the erstwhile concepts of man, being, meaning, divine reality, and creation. It is from lack of metaphysics that we wallow in fundamental disorientation, unsure of standards and purpose. We who look upon ourselves as strongest in this world of nations cannot help admitting that, as self-reflecting beings we are now blind, deaf, and mute. We are patients needing help, rather than leaders capable of guiding helpless patients. We have suffered a diminution, as well as a distortion of reason which will render us increasingly less able to perceive the requirements of order in our own ranks. As a result, our policies may well appear as increasingly arbitrary acts of power in the world. It is unlikely that these or similar ideologies will begin to rule our political system. Our disorder seems likely to continue as sheer oblivion of norms of order, of insights into what Voegelin calls the "constitution of being," of appropriate language for divine reality and presence in our world.

The work of Eric Voegelin was prompted by the strong experience of ideological totalitarianism. It consists in the in-depth analysis of philosophic and spiritual confusion and obliteration, which analysis, as Voegelin said, has also the character of therapy. Rather than celebrating Voegelin's insight as weapons suited to take care of "them," our ideological enemies, we should gratefully begin to accept them as our own medicine. This presupposes a process of learning to understand Voegelin and his methods of analysis. The purpose of such study would be to be able to "return to the reality of experience which originated the symbols...." Which symbols? The symbols of our own lost order which we ourselves have decided to abandon because the people around us so strongly claimed to find no more meaning in them.

Once we have made up our mind to turn to Voegelin's work, not only for intellectual curiosity but for therapeutic purposes, we will find that other authors are available to the same end. Some may be found in Voegelin's footnotes. Among them we find Stanley L. Jaki. Jaki, a physicist who also has a doctorate in theology, has long been interested in the relation between the teaching of the Bible and the origin of science in Western civilization, including the question of why there was no viable birth of science in Egypt, Babylonia, China, or ancient Greece. Any one of these could boast of astonishing achievements in a few of the sciences, as well as in the techniques derived from them. China had invented the magnet, paper, the stirrup and the horse-harness. The Aztecs built marvels of religious architecture, and possessed a precise calendar. Egypt is renowned not only for its pyramids, but also for its medical knowledge and practices. The Babylonians had a remarkable chemical technique, as well as their famed mathematics.

How can one explain that such beginnings did not develop into an equivalent of the Western enterprise of science? The only way to an answer leads through a close critical analysis of the leading minds in each of these civilizations, a work that Jaki has undertaken with exemplary thoroughness. The result of this study he himself has put in the following paragraph:

> The history of science, with its several stillbirths and only one viable birth, clearly shows that the only cosmology, or view of the cosmos as a whole, that was capable of generating science was a view of which the principal disseminator was the Gospel. It was the gospel that turned into a widely shared conviction the belief in the Father, maker of all things visible and invisible, who created all in the beginning and disposed everything in measure, number, and weight, that is, with a rigorous consistency and rationality. That belief in His creation is the ultimate perspective with respect to origin.... While one's account of the rise and progress of science can fragment the image of science through the application of a fearless though mistaken logic, the same account can turn into a worn-out cliche if the perspective of the Christian origin of science is evaded for some extraneous motivation. Some such motivation must have been at work when the result is the absence of any reference to the Christian faith of so many from Copernicus to Newton.[6]

Of particular interest for Western readers is the question why Aristotle's natural philosophy did not stimulate something of an ancient Galileo. Without trying to follow the complex account that Jaki has produced, let us look at one of his remarks about Aristotle, and Jaki's argument from this particular point:

> Aristotle's seemingly innocuous dictum that 'time itself is regarded as a circle' had indeed been pregnant with momentous implications for the ultimate fortunes of the Greek Logos. For all its brilliance, for all its spectacular initiatives, it remained trapped within a spacious labyrinth where every move and enterprise led in the final analysis back to the same starting point. The possibilities within such a framework had become exhausted within a relatively few generations, and in the end nothing remained except to write commentaries on the great classics of the truly creative phase of the Greek intellectual endeavor.[7]

From there Jaki moves on to Simplicius, "the last great figure of ancient Greek philosophical tradition. His commentaries on Aristotle's cosmology, physics, and metaphysics reveal in stark direction the predicament of the Greek Logos, its lonely wanderings, and its strange shunning of a new light which unexpectedly came to diffuse over the confines of its mighty labyrinth." Jaki later quotes Simplicius "as he held up to ridicule the mind that 'could conceive of such a strange God who first does not act at all, then in a moment becomes the creator of the elements alone, and then again, ceases from acting and hands over to nature the generation of the elements one out of another and the generation of all the rest of the elements.'" Jaki characterizes this passage as "also an implicit reference to the notion of a universe created out of *nothing* and *in time*.... What this implied was the all-important concept of an autonomy which could be accorded to nature only by a rational Creator, remaining forever consistent with His creative plans and decisions."[8] Here is the great problem of many human civilizations, among them the most brilliant ones, such as the ancient Greeks: They saw no possible way out of a universe that was destined ever again to turn upon its own past, returning and returning and returning.

Jaki is no fundamentalist. He considers a "fundamentalist attachment to the perspective of creation just as fatally mistaken as hostility towards a theistic perspective of the cosmos."[9] Nor does his work in any way aim at the removal of the difference between revelation and reason. The two belong to different reaches of human consciousness, as well as to different approaches of our mind. He does argue that the problem of the cosmos belongs to both contexts, and, because it does, it was possible for one civilization to escape from the sadness of eternal return.

Jaki's work, then, essentially demonstrates the enormous consequences of a collaborative side-by-side of Christian faith and Occidental reason. It makes clear that this neighborly togetherness did not make for distortions of either faith or reason. It generated a "robust confidence of an overwhelmingly Christian ambience for which the once-and-for-all process of human and cosmic existence was almost as natural a conviction as the air one breathed."[10] That the same conviction could also generate a temptation "to assume the role of God" is a fact to which Jaki will not close his eyes. Yielding to this temptation, however, results "in a hapless oscillation between two extremes: the mirage of absolute certainty and utter skepticism."[11] Against this kind of derailment, Jaki reminds us, the remedy is "metaphysical realism, the only safe ground between the abysses of an absolute certainty bordering on tautology and a no-certainty-at-all provoking despair."

In conclusion, a warning may be in order that our civilization is not in good shape, furthermore, that awareness of this fact and analysis of the disorder are among the foremost obligations of intellectual leadership. Both require a return to basic questions, such questions as are usually answered at the beginning of things. A thinking person should examine his own underlying assumptions, anxious to discover whether the will to power or deference for being may be at work in his soul. He should also shoulder responsibility for strengthening the metaphysical ground of our discussions about order. It is this kind of turning around that could eventually bring about a degree of sanity to our common existence.

NOTES

1. *Cf.* Eric Voegelin, *The New Science of Politics*, 1952, p. 63 *f.*

2. *Ibid.*

3. "Immortality," *Harvard Theological Review*, vol. 60, no. 3, p. 238.

4. *loc. cit.* p. 257.

5. David Walsh, "Voegelin's Response to the Disorder of the Age," *The Review of Politics*, vol. 46, no. 2, p. 271.

6. *The Origin of Science and the Science of its Origin*, 1978, p. 99 *f.*

7. *Science and Creation*, 1974, p. 130*f.*

8. *Ibid.*

9. *Op. cit.* p. 23.

10. *Science and Creation*, p. 237.

11. *Cosmos and Creator*, p. 141.

The Reality of the Good *

Τhis book is a first-rate intellectual event. The following
story lies behind it: When in the late twenties Hans Jonas
studied at Göttingen under Rudolf Bultmann and Martin
Heidegger, finding the latter's teaching strange and hard to
comprehend, he discovered that ancient gnosticism, about which
Bultmann had instructed him, fitted modern existentialism like
a key in a lock. So, a few years later he published the work that
started modern research on gnosticism, published in a shorter
English version as *The Gnostic Religion* (1958, enlarged edition
1963). In the epilogue to the latter edition he remarked, apropos
of the gnostic denigration of nature as a diabolic creation hostile
to God, that "that which has no nature has no norm." But
modern, nihilistic philosophy struck him as "infinitely more
radical and more desperate than gnostic nihilism ever could be
for all its terror of the world and its defiant contempt of its laws.
That nature does not care, one way or another, is the true abyss.
That only man cares, in his finitude, facing nothing but death,
alone with his contingency and the objective meaninglessness of
his projecting meanings, is a truly unprecedented situation."
While others had commented on the abysmal nature of the crisis
of modernity, Jonas, in despair, set out to do something about it.

* This essay appeared as a review of *The Imperative of Responsibility: In
Search of an Ethics for the Technological Age*, by Hans Jonas (Chicago:
University of Chicago Press, 1984).

In 1966 he published *The Phenomenon of Life: Towards a Philosophical Biology*. Two years later there appeared a paper of his, "Biological Foundations of Individuality," and in 1974, "On the Power and Impotence of Subjectivity," which led to the present volume, first published in Germany under the title, *Das Prinzip Verantwortung*.

The author assesses our situation as extreme in two respects. On the one hand, modern philosophy, from positivism to existentialism, has combined to destroy both the concepts of being and nature. Hence we are doomed to at least a moral nihilism, since "values" (which Jonas refused to consider synonymous with "the good") are no longer "ontologically supported." In other words, for us values, or the good, have no standing in being. We are therefore in dire need of a new philosophy of being. On the other hand, modern technology, combining knowledge and power, is engaged in the business of reshaping both nature and human nature. "Modern technology...an infinite forward thrust of the race...assumes ethical significance by the central place it now occupies in human purpose." While morality has in the past confined its reign to the realm of "action" and has stayed aloof from the realm of "making," it now must invade the latter in the form of public policy. "The changed nature of human action changes the very nature of politics." In the past, moral responsibility focused on man alone, obtaining its philosophical bearings from a vision of nature. Now nature itself has become a human responsibility, so that ethics must seek "not only the human good but also the good of things extra-human."

If this book is an intellectual event of the first order, it is because of Jonas's courage in starting to reconstruct a philosophy of being in the midst of a general philosophical wasteland. True, before him, his former teacher Heidegger loudly called our attention to "being" as he cried out again and again: "How is it with being?" But it is also true that Heidegger's efforts produced no more than a vision of a future "arrival" of being itself, which vision Eric Voegelin characterized as a *parousia*. Heidegger's inability to rescue being from an all-powerful history illustrates the utter devastation of any concept of being by 200 years of modern philosophizing. The destruction philosophers have visited on us has not yet made people lie down in the street, there to perish in despair. Still, we walk on the thinnest of ice in our inability to recapture former visions of truth. Jonas is fully aware of this situation. He goes about this task with utmost circumspection, making sure that every little advance is thoroughly secured. Thus his small book, *Impotence and Power and Subjectivity*, separately published in German, but included as an appendix in the present work, attempts no more than a decisive philosophical refutation of the key arguments that deny the autonomy and power of subjectivity (soul and mind) by positivists, determinists, nihilists. They assert that the context of physical determination is closed; that there cannot be an influence of the mental upon the physical; that there is matter without mind but no mind without matter, so that "the subjective or physical or mental is the concomitant of certain physical occurrences in the brain"; that "soul is the very delusion or make-believe with which reality constantly deceives itself." Jonas characterized the first two arguments as "an idealization" derived from mathematics. So, "what must not be cannot be." The argument pretends to a greater knowledge of nature than we have. "There is no *a priori* certainty that what holds for the whole also holds for all its parts down to the smallest; and what holds for the end result also holds for all intermediate links; and what holds for measurable time intervals also holds for each instant."

More space is devoted to a refutation of the various epiphenominalist arguments. The psychical or mental product, Jonas says, "is not a transitive act of the physical base which goes on functioning as it would anyway, so that the creation of the soul is, in terms of causes, a 'creation from nothing.'" But the defenders of the thesis offer no explanation for this riddle.

Attributing exclusive causality to matter demands the conclusion that mind is impotent. "It follows that all thinking is deception already in itself." But who is deceived? Reality itself? "But no, brains are not deceived. The subject? But this already is a deception as such. And why? Again, no answer, not even that of *l'art pour l'art*." Jonas's negative proofs point to the helplessness of the deniers of subjectivity to explain and solve the difficulties created by their own doctrines. Jonas's verdict: "He who makes nature absurd in order to circumvent one of her riddles has passed sentence on himself and not on her and has forfeited the right to speak any more of laws of nature." From there he proceeds to a mental model that establishes the possibility of a "triggering" of physical effects by infinitesimal amounts of energy originating in the mind. This demonstrates that the power of subjectivity in nature is, at any rate, not a categorical impossibility.

This proof, placed in the appendix of the book, provides that minimum of firm ground from which the author begins to unfold his grand argument. He begins by comparing traditional ethics with the present situation. During all of the past, human experience fell between nature, which appeared abiding, and human works, which kept changing and thus appeared potentially arbitrary. Even then, however, there was consensus that "the arbitrary can never supersede the basic terms of man's being." Man's greatest work, the city, "the whole and sole domain of man's responsibility, must be wedded to morality." Ethics was anthropocentric, but man himself was not an object of reshaping *techne*. "Ethics accordingly was the here and now, of occasions as they arise between men, of the recurrent, typical situations of private and public life," its knowledge of a kind "readily available to all men of good will." Now, however, technology itself is a conglomerate of mighty causes with effects far off in the future. Moreover, it has made both nature and man objects of its reshaping powers and implies threats to the continuation of mankind itself. There arises a human "obligation to ensure a foothold for a moral universe in the physical world."

Jonas points to two key problems of the new situation: morality's focus on the remote future, and the elusive knowledge required by a new ethics. Rephrasing Kant's categorical imperative, he proposes that the time has now come for securing "the conditions for an indefinite continuation of humanity on earth," as addressed to public policy rather than to private conduct. Being concerned wholly with the eventual effects of present action, it commits morality to the time dimension of the future, unlike the traditional ethics which prevailed essentially "between contemporaries." Again, unlike traditional morality, the new situation requires that morality be instructed by expert knowledge. The question is "What insight or value knowledge will present the future in the present?" In the chapter entitled "On Principles and Methods," Jonas calls for a "comparative futurology," a "heuristics of fear," which he calls "a spiritual sort of fear." The knowledge called for, he admits, is "always 'not yet' available"; it is a mere "knowledge of possibilities...adequate for the purposes of a heuristic casuistry." Jonas winds up this introductory part of his book with a series of axiomatic ethical principles regarding the long-term dimension of modern technology: (1) In any action the bad prognosis of its effects must prevail over the good prognosis. (2) "Never must the existence or the essence of man be made a stake in the hazards of action." (3) We are forbidden "to incur the risk of nothingness." (4) In all this we are "not responsible to the future human individuals but the *idea* of Man which...demands the presence of its embodiment in the world." This is "an ontological idea" which leads to the question whether, and in what way, "the concept of value first secured a standing in things and not merely in thought." *Quod est demonstrandum.*

Jonas accomplishes this crucial demonstration through the examples of the hammer, the court of law, walking, and the digestive process. The hammer is an artifact whose purpose precedes its existence, so that the purpose is man's rather than that of the instrument. The law court is also an artifact, but it is but one which requires for its functioning that the same causality which made it is also operative within its living members. In that they must be animated by the end of the court, one can speak of an immanence of the end. Walking is done with the legs, which are given by nature and which animals have as well; thus, we are here drawn not only into the distinction between voluntary and involuntary functions, but also into that nature which is common to men and animals. Legs do not start to walk by themselves without a decision of the will; likewise one may say that "looking is more than passive seeing, listening more than hearing, sniffing more than just smelling, and so on." The provisional conclusion:

> No matter whether the whole linear image of a series [of purposes] is not merely an idealized model to which in reality corresponds an intricate web of many strands: notwithstanding all these unclarities, it is still clear that the action-texture here considered is purposive in the subjective sense, that is, governed by preconceived goals...[and] no such articulated end-means chain can be imputed to the action of animals.

Animals "have their ready-made schemata in the programming of the organism." But if one drives this insight into a general assumption that behind will there are feelings and behind feelings chemical "cues;" if, in other words, "feeling [is] demoted to a mere symptom...then 'purpose,' if it is at all to play an effective and not merely decorative role, must have its seat *first* in *this* causality...and in that case has been allowed an existence outside the psychic realm in general." This leads to the further conclusion "that the distinction between the multipartite ends-means chain of thinking man and the single-step, goal-apprehension of the feeling animal becomes irrelevant in face of the basic question concerning 'power or impotence of subjectivity' in general." Referring to his already-mentioned appendix in which "the proposition, that subjectivity is powerless, is reduced *ad absurdum* in its logical, ontological, and epistemological consequences [and] shown to be unnecessary for the purpose...to preserve the integrity of the laws of nature," Jonas now asserts with utmost confidence that "the 'soul' and hence the 'will' is vindicated as a principle among the principles of nature." "The realm of voluntary bodily movement in man and animal is a locus of real determination by purposes and goals."

Now, focusing on the digestive organs, he first acknowledges and then rejects the contention that "with the evolutionary appearance of subjectivity an entirely new, heterogeneous principle has entered nature." Rather, he holds that "reality, or nature, is one and testifies to itself in what it allows to come forth from it," so that "subjectivity is in some sense a surface phenomenon of nature [and] speaks for the silent interior underneath." Looking backward at the tree of evolutionary descension he finds that subjectivity

> surely disappears somewhere, but sensitivity and appetition as such probably nowhere. Even here, to be sure, we are still dealing with 'subjectivity,' but with one already so diffuse that the concept of an individual, focused subject gradually ceases to apply, and somewhere the series trails off into the complete absence of any such subject. Therefore also into an absence of aim and urge?...On the contrary: it would be incomprehensible that subjective striving in its particularization should have emerged without striving whatever in the emergence itself.

And now to the grand conclusion:

> It is meaningful...to speak of the immanent, if entirely unconscious and involuntary, *purpose* of digestion and its apparatus in the totality of the living body, and to speak of life as the end purpose of just this body....

Purpose is thereby extended beyond all consciousness, human and animal, into the physical world as an innate principle of it.

Opposing a system of nature with purpose and striving innate to it there stands the freedom of the reflective human mind. "It is the prerogative of freedom to be able to say no to the world." In that sense, purpose and striving in nature appear as mere facts that as such have no power to bind our assent. "For this, that is, for real, obligatory affirmation, the concept of the good is needed, which is not identical with the concept of value." Here we find the probably most weighty sentence in the book. Jonas continues: "It is the relationship between goodness and being [*bonum* and *esse*] with whose clarification a theory of value can hope to ground a possibly binding force of values—namely...by grounding the good in being." Here, Jonas comes back to the central effort of such intellectual giants as Augustine and Thomas Aquinas, both of whom sought and found support in Plato and Aristotle. The relation of good to being was once widespread knowledge, not reserved for the philosophical few but current among all who had the minimum of education required by participants in culture. That knowledge was willfully discarded, not by these ordinary people who lived and still live by it, but by the few thinkers whose self-centered ideological intent wanted at all cost to have a "system" even if it costs them the price of lost reality. Jonas most certainly is not one of them. He does admit that "faith in revealed truth can very well supply the foundation for ethics," but then sadly renounces that possibility which "is not there on command...while reason can be set to work upon demand."

One wonders whether Jonas ever gave serious attention to Thomas Aquinas's philosophical identification of goodness with being, and whether, had he turned to it at this juncture, he might not have found his own philosophical principle of the close general link between goodness and being. At any rate, Jonas is induced by his renunciation of faith to pursue no further the "grounding of the good in being" and to concentrate exclusively on his purposed "theory of responsibility," a task of much narrower scope.

To this task Jonas devotes the bulk of the book—175 pages. Since this reviewer's interest was powerfully aroused by Jonas's declared intention to "ground the good in being," may he then be forgiven for saying that, in the end, Jonas accomplishes much less than his beginning promised. First of all, even if we concede to him a successful articulation of a "theory of responsibility," it turns out to be an ethics only for the statesman, applying not to private conduct but solely to public policy. Must we conclude, therefore, that the dangers lurking in public policy are the only evils of life? Those concerned with nuclear war go even further and declare nuclear destruction to be the one and absolute evil, and evil having no origin in the human heart. But let us ask further: how much does Jonas's theory have to say even to the statesman about this responsibility? Earlier in the book he emphasizes both the essence and the existence of man as a moral object. Now he seems to confine himself to the "existence of mankind" alone. As for "grounding the good in being," the sole paradigm he can point to is the acknowledged responsibility of parents for their newborn children. A child's growth, being organic, is indeed "grounded in being," but can this paradigm be simply shifted over to the realm of history? Jonas seems to think so. This involves him in competition with a number of doctrines that have erected the historical future into an exclusive moral object, including not only Marx but also Bloch. Jonas's critique of these doctrines is penetrating and valuable in itself. All the same, his theory of responsibility remains a formula without much substance, and certainly without any ground in being other than the "no" that life says to nothingness.

The value of this book seems to me to lie not in the success of a theory but in the great significance of a philosopher of having begun, in our seemingly hopeless age, a basic philosophical task full of hope and—let us say this at the risk of raising the author's eyebrows—faith. For that achievement not only we, but also those who come after Hans Jonas and find the bottom steps already hewn out, must be deeply grateful.

The Recovery of "The Sacred"?

Great civilizations are the stuff from which historical continuity emanates. Their public institutions are copied far beyond their geographical boundaries, their artifacts treated as standards everywhere, and their letters inspire cliches around the globe. In human geography they function like huge magnets to which all compass needles turn, and in human history as the most visible of "the permanent things," providing endurance in the flux of time. Their influence, power of orientation, and stabilizing effects continue long after the civilization, at its place of origin, has perished or run out of creativity. "Running out of creativity" is a figure of speech that indicates, within a civilization, elements engendering vision and eliciting imitation; in other words, "permanent things" within that "permanent thing" which is a civilization. In mentioning the "perishing" of civilizations, we see that civilizations are permanent only for a while. "Time is killing us," said Ibn Khaldun, while Vico pointed out a cycle, from barbarism to civilization to super-civilization and to a civilized barbarism which, unlike the original barbarism, is unable to create anything. This latter he called the "barbarism of reflection," relating it to the degenerating influence of a class of people characterized by reflection apart from faith.

Our country, in a way, is operating as if it were a whole civilization, let us say, like the Roman civilization of old. Whether it deserves to be called "a civilization," rather than a nation part of a wider civilization, is beside the point. Like Rome, it does provide orientation and relative stability in the world. Like Rome, this country of ours is a concerted effort of human beings held together by common impulses of the heart, the soul, and the mind, and to them these impulses within their civilization come from "permanent things," such things as "the beliefs which we have inherited from our ancestors, though they give no reasons," to use characteristic words that Cicero, in his *Nature of the Gods*, put in the mouth of the conservative Cotta.[1] Similarly, the enduring structure of the family, although confined in each case to a small number of persons, provides the entire civilization with moral and legal standards of sexual relations. And the public laws, both products and pillars of great civilizations, imitate "the ever simultaneous present immutability of God's life."[2] The attraction of a great civilization comes from more than power and wealth.

In all possibility, of all civilizations ours is the most glittering, most astonishing, most inventive, most organized, and most wealth-producing one in human experience. As a network of technology, industry, trade, management, political and private organization, science, education, and services it appears to function with amazing vitality. But at the spiritual, moral, and intellectual core rottenness is visible and expanding. The "faith of our fathers" is not only under external attack, it is also in the process of transforming itself into a narcissist cult of either the human mind, of the self's feelings, or the exotic imagination. The family is endangered not merely by the flood of divorces, the one-parent household, legally protected abortions, but also by such tendencies as that of Congress to promote "federalized child care," while, on the other hand, businesses are offering the purchase, rent, and lease of "children as pets and pets as children."[3] The mission of the family as the guardian of sexual morality is undermined by the schools who, from fear of AIDS, distribute condoms to teenagers. Turning to the judicial system, one notes an "explosion of litigation" as judges, juries, and attorneys vie with each other in pushing damages for tort, accidents, and even products to astronomical figures, producing a mockery of rationalization by forming concepts like "wrongful life," and "negligent infliction of emotional distress." While the law abandons its common-sense limitations, more and more crimes of violence occur without any trace of motive, "just so," for the sake of violence itself.

The sexual revolution combines with drug fever to degrade life's meaning to a series of "highs," by whatever means; the resultant "subculture" manifests itself by a studied craziness of dress, body painting, hairdo, language patterns, poetry, and music. The word, "subculture," is in quotation marks because it in itself manifests a widespread inability to distinguish civilization from barbarism, about which distinction there used to be little doubt, even earlier in this century. Another manifestation of the barbarity masquerading as "subculture" is commitment to political causes of great variety which have in common hostility to one's country, family, and tradition. The "untrammeled freedom" claimed by each individual results also in an identity problem that seems to be without precedent in world history.

It is not that we are wholly without people who are seriously concerned about such developments and consider it their duty to stem the obnoxious tide. However, as they attempt to do so while categorically excluding any traditional or even metaphysical authority, they find themselves drifting. In vain, they sit at their desks seeking to produce "values" by a sheer effort of the unaided mind. What they have to offer on the market carries no weight of obligation, which fits an idea-market consisting of an emotional babble of value-idioms, none of them more than a clever guess.

Then there are laws of dissolution. In music, the serialist says: "Thou shalt not use any note more than once, lest it become a tonal center." In Cubist painting the law is: "Thou shalt not leave the object intact." In literature: "Thou shalt have no hero to your story," which is the first commandment followed by the other one like unto it: "Thou shalt not portray any personal character, because there is not truth in any character except that of the ideology to which the person is committed." Regarding films the law forbids the depiction of reality, since it is nothing but illusions, so that only irrational dreams or actions deserve to be called real. In sexual relations, "normal" is taboo. Moral feelings are permitted, even emphasized, provided that God remains beyond the pale. Patriotism is allowed, but only in the form of a total critique of one's country. These laws of dissolution have become the hallmark of institutions of higher learning, particularly the most prestigious ones. There they are crowned by a law that declares inadmissible any criticism of this teaching for its premises. The process of dissolution, as can be seen, is not without its own discipline.

In daily life motivation is either confused or trivial, because there is no vision. To rediscover that vision which used to orient us in nature, history, and faith we must ask philosophers and theologians. And yet, they also have submitted themselves to laws of dissolution forbidding such concepts as being, natural law, divine grace, and truth. The entire tradition of Jesus Christ, his birth, life, sayings, and above all his death and resurrection have been pried apart piece by piece and severed from any conviction. Philosophy as well as theology used to begin with something that was implicitly believed by all. That, in modern times, has given way to systemic doubt, analysis, which turned into the spirit of criticism and, eventually, into the mentality of nihilism. If process first took the place of being, process was then deprived of direction so that, in turn, it yielded to any orgy of meaningless but vehement change, the vehemence taking the place of what Karl Marx called "radical," the root of things.

What is happening to us is a barbarism of the spirit on the height of intensively intellectual civilization. "Barbarism of reflection," Vico called it. His description of this state, written in the first half of the eighteenth century, strikes us today as astonishingly fitting our crisis:

> Such peoples, like so many beasts, have fallen into the custom of each man thinking only of his own private interests and have reached the extreme of delicacy, or better of pride, in which they bristle and lash out at the slightest displeasure. Thus no matter how great the throng and press of their bodies, they live like wild beasts in a deep solitude of spirit and will, scarcely any two being able to agree since each follows his own pleasure or caprice....They shall turn their cities into forests and the forests into dens and lairs of men. In this way, through long centuries of barbarism, rust will consume the misbegotten subtleties of malicious wits that have turned them into beasts made more inhuman by the barbarism of reflection....[4]

Two and a half centuries before our time, Vico saw the sway of mindless violence, intellectual dissolution, deep loneliness in the midst of crowds, and the disordered existence that attends the hyperintellectual stage of great civilizations—the stage where the reflective mind no longer reflects on reality but centers on itself—overreaches its own limits in an arrogance of postulated self-creation. What results is called "lifestyle;" a "style" of vice for the masses, and a style of nihilism for the educated.

Apart from mind and spirit, one cannot speak of misery in our time. There is great and widely distributed wealth, still much opportunity and social mobility, education on an unprecedented scale, by and large international peace in spite of deep tensions, and a universal attitude of shallow optimism. All the same, behind the mask of "fun" there is no radiance of happiness. Materially we are comfortable, but there is great spiritual restlessness. People look for new cults, although it may also be true that they are not looking for meaning. In fact, the quest for exotic, bizarre cults, cults of the obscure and the forbidden, reveal that the spiritual restlessness is a search for still further out, not yet imagined degrees of untrammeled human freedom. All the same, it is the spirit rather than the intellect that feels unhappy and neglected. Even the intellect, in some cases, seems to acknowledge that without spiritual vision there can be no under-standing that deserves the medieval respect for *intellectus*, as distinct from *ratio*. All of which combines to overwhelming evidence that what we need is something we have lost, the good of "permanent things," that which is higher in rank than what we buy and sell among ourselves, and also higher than anything that most colleges have to teach nowadays.

Which brings up the question of whether it is possible to recapture spiritual anchors and foundations once we have lost them, or, must we say with Lewis Carroll, "all the king's horses and all the king's men couldn't put Humpty Dumpty together again"? Before Lewis Carroll coined that metaphor, Edmund Burke thought of another, that of the father whom his daughters cut into pieces which they boiled in the hope of thus obtaining a rejuvenated father-person. (I hope the reader will note my "inclusive language.")

"The Sacred" is the topic given to me for this piece. It is a concept of religion, not one religion but nearly all religions, as demonstrated in the comprehensive work of Mircea Eliade, through which the distinction between "the sacred and the profane" runs like a red thread. "Religion" is a similar concept, and a late one at that. It refers to the ensemble of myths, symbols, rituals, thoughts, and affects held in common by a multitude who, through this common treasure, become a people. In other words, religion is not something like an object that we use or refrain from using, but we are part of religion which in turn makes us what we are and who we are, both communally and personally. So then, where there are no people united by such beliefs there is no religion; where there is no religion there is no united community. A religion's symbols can be described but mean nothing to the observer whose inner life is not touched and shaped by this symbol. Even Mircea Eliade's work communicates no religious spirit to the reader; it is an astonishingly comprehensive survey of religious phenomena, carefully and painstakingly recorded by a positivist scholar. So is the similar but earlier book by Rudolf Otto, *The Idea of the Holy* (1917), the very use of holy as a noun betraying the author's attitude of looking at it from without. Still, both Otto and Eliade represent the efforts of professional academics to "recover" a missing dimension of their lives. They do it by recording how certain symbols filled people of the past with awe, fear, hope, or trust, these same symbols that for us have sunk to the role of mere souvenirs with which we may at best be linked by a certain amount of nostalgia. They take the symbols in their hands, as it were, fondly, shyly, feelingly, like a middle-aged woman who finds the dolls in the attic that were once her childhood's delight. In vain: no amount of adult affection can bring back the old magic—the dolls are now souvenirs. So do religious symbols that no longer represent live experiences of living people, experiences that form the umbilical cord between human souls and the higher reality shining through the symbol. But "The Sacred" is not even a symbol, so it remains at best a thought of a lost way of life but without power in itself to relink us to the lost reality.

By way of a concrete example, let us look at Robert N. Bellah's *Beyond Belief*. Bellah speaks of himself as a man who has recovered Christian faith and would help others recover theirs. He emphatically chooses the method by focusing on the symbols, for "in both scientific and religious culture all we have finally are symbols"—spoken as a sociologist to whom science and religion are equally "culture."[5] Thus, he looks at symbols from a cool distance wondering "how much transcendence it can be made to carry for those who have chosen this particular shape to

represent the pattern of their religiousness."[6] "Transcendence"
here appears to be something like a weighty mass, "religiousness"
a pattern chosen among others for no particular reason, the
whole process a value-free option. "Religious symbol systems"
seem to be lying around, ready to be "appropriated." Bellah
reports about one of many experiments of "appropriation," this
one an Anglican service at Canterbury House in Ann Arbor,
Michigan. In this event, symbols of Christian worship were
deliberately mixed with symbols of contemporary counterculture. Bellah reports: "The conventional service today lacks au-
thenticity because it has no surprises; it is not a point at which the
world of everyday is broken through but only a particularly cozy
corner of it. Certainly the Canterbury House service contained
the possibility of opening up 'new experiences.'"[7]

It would seem that by "experiences" Bellah meant anything
characterized by "strong feelings," psychological "excitement,"
in other words, wholly subjective agitation. Now religious symbols have their origin in profound experience but experiences of
participation in non-subjective reality. Here, Jaroslav Pelikan
remarks about the generation of Christian symbols of faith: "The
time is fulfilled...in these last days": it is obvious from these and
other statements of the early generation of Christian believers
that as they carried out the task of finding a language that would
not collapse under the weight of what they believed to be the
significance of the coming of Jesus, they found it necessary to
invent a grammar of history."[8] The original event was the
encounter with Jesus in which there was formed the belief in
Jesus's divinity. Thomas the Twin said it spontaneously: "My
Lord and my God." This experience, shared by a few thousand
Christians, led to common worship practices in which there
developed a suitable liturgical language. From the early Christians who had known Jesus, the experience passed on through
centuries chiefly by personal contagion, as it were; suffering
losses of intensity, then gaining a new vigor, but always centering

on Jesus Christ "come down from heaven," and the divine Father to whom Jesus had always pointed, the Unseen Beyond whose pull was the very crux of the experience.

Bellah, too, speaks of "contemporary religious consciousness" as having a "strong note of innerness. There is an intense preoccupation with authentic personal experience...with the self."[9] Preoccupation with self is, of course, precisely that in which modern psychology and sociology radically differ from Christianity. On this premise Bellah bases his description of "the most significant religious movement of our time," in which "Christians can join with non-Christians in the emerging value-consensus, in criticizing existing values...and insisting that values to which societies are committed be actualized for all social groups."[10] He is here speaking of the modern trans-national protest movement characteristic of Western civilization, for which he claims a "possibility to recognize the operation of the holy spirit [*sic*], to use Christian symbolism."[11] In all this, he sees "social science beginning, faintly and crudely, to be able to cope with the richness of reality as religion has seen it.... In particular some social scientists have come to feel that there are profound depths in the religious symbols that we have scarcely begun to fathom and that we have much to learn from."[12]

Here is the core of the matter. What Bellah defines as "recovery" is really an appreciation of "the depths of symbols," an essentially aesthetic evaluation. The symbols are appreciated also for their utility, for they "express the feelings, values, and hopes of subjects," and "regulate the flow of interaction between subjects and objects" or "attempt to sum up the whole subject-object complex or even point to the context or ground of that whole."[13] Eventually, Bellah makes his most extreme statement: "To put it bluntly, religion is true." The term "religion" here, like "the sacred," is no symbol but an abstraction, so what can be the meaning of a statement that an abstraction is "true"? The sociologist who forgets his value-neutrality long enough to admit "the value of religion" and also claims to "teach religion" rather than "just about religion,"[14] is, in spite of his sense of daring, still worlds away from a live experience of ineffable divinity and the turning-around of the soul which occurs in that experience. With the methods of philosophy rather than sociology, Henri Bergson referred to the "opening of the soul" and what it is open to as the second, and more important source of morality and religion, the first one being society's pressure.[15]

W hy did Mr. Bellah not succeed in making the movement for the sake of which he wrote his book? Wolfgang Smith has something to say about that, in his *Cosmos and Transcendence*:

> The crossing of boundaries turns out to be a rather rare occurrence; we must not let ourselves be fooled. It is true, for example, that in modern times there has been an unprecedented interest in the study of history; and yet one finds that it is almost invariably a case of history truncated by the mental horizon of our age and colored by the humanistic sentiments of our civilization. The Zeitgeist is indeed a force to be reckoned with, and it is never easy to swim against the stream.[16]

The Zeitgeist of our age is no mere fad; it is powerfully held in place by three pillars, each the established dogma of an academically dominant science. First, it is the impersonal and mechanical idea of the universe left to us by Newton. As Edwin Burtt described it:

> When Newton's conception of the world was gradually shorn of its religious relations, the ultimate justification for absolute space and time as he had portrayed them disappeared, and the entities were left empty but still absolute [and] unquestionably assumed as an infinite theatre in which, and an unchangeable entity against which, the world machine continued its clock-like movements. From accidents of God they

became sheer, fixed, geometrical measure for the motion of masses. And this loss of their divinity completed the de-spiritualization of nature.[17]

The consequence of "the elimination of God from the scene"
was the need to do the same for "these residual souls of men,
irregularly scattered among the atoms of mass that swam me-
chanically among the ethereal vapors in time and space.... They,
too, must be reduced to mechanical products and parts of the
self-regulating clock."[18] This image of the physical universe has
been "shattered" by the physics of Planck, Einstein, Heisenberg,
and Schrödinger, and yet, says Wolfgang Smith, the idea remains with us as "an implicitly assumed background, a mental
presupposition that serves to shape and define the general
scientific outlook."[19]

The second pillar of the Zeitgeist is the vast structure of
psychoanalysis and psychiatry; the legacy of Freud and Jung. It
places ultimate belief in the unconscious and uses this belief as a
battering ram against religion which alone, in Freud's own
words, is to be "taken seriously as an enemy." Even though where
there once was only Freud and Jung there is now a pluralism of
psychoanalytical schools; "once the therapeutic mentality becomes dominant within a culture, it is no longer necessary to
vituperate against Christianity," says Wolfgang Smith. Using
the language of Philipp Rieff, he argues that "the present ferment
in the Roman Catholic Church is less a new theology than a
move toward more sophisticated accommodations with the
negative communities of the therapeutics," and ends by quoting
Rieff as saying: "The Sacralist yields to the analysis as the
therapeutic functionary of modern culture."[20] The third pillar is
the dogma central to the social sciences, which says that quantification is the only permissible method of even the sciences of
man and society, that facts differ radically from values and only
facts must be admitted to scientific analysis. This eliminates
from the science of man any theory encompassing transcen-

dence, values, and divinity. There is great affinity between this reduced reality of man and the reduced reality of the mechanical world view left by Newton. The name for this dogmatic reduction is Positivism, a term coined by Auguste Comte as a bar against metaphysics, and academically implanted by Levy-Brühl, Dürkheim, and Max Weber. A perceptive commentator of our time aptly calls it, "operationalism." With one, again dogmatic, exception (equality) it relativizes all values, elevates all facts to the same absoluteness of relevance, and is as intolerant of the slightest trace of religious belief as the Inquisition was against heresy. Such traces are suppressed as impermissible even in conversation and in the classroom.

The modern Zeitgeist, then, is the combined hostility to religion on the part of three academic and intellectual power-structures, each claiming metaphysical authority without any metaphysical conviction: Physics, Psychoanalysis, Positivism,—the three "P's." Chesterton called this "the Mind moving in a perfect circle....There is such a thing as a small and cramped eternity...a combination between a logical completeness and a spiritual contraction."[21] We do live in an age of logical and technical completeness combined with spiritual contraction. This does not mean that all spiritual yearnings have withered away. It does mean, rather, that most spiritual yearnings seek and find counterfeit spiritualities widely available, the inner emptiness being filled with nothing of substance. Our question is, what is one to do when "permanent things" no longer are visible, when nothing more substantial than each moment's "fun" is experienced as that common something that binds individuals into a whole, or when such words as "truth," "man," "soul," "nature are no longer received as valid coin? We are meeting here under the auspices of words like "renewal" and "recovery," implying a suggestion that some definable and organizable effort of mind and heart will lead us back to solid ground where we would learn again to do right things, think right things, and feel right things.

We have seen from the Bellah book that, were such an effort defined as deliberate reattachment to certain historic symptoms, deliberate feelings of awe (as before "The Sacred"), strenuous study of metaphysical treatises, it would not avail. Such words sound like trumpets, but should we not remember that they sound "under the rubble," within the wasteland that is our present habitat? The rule of the Zeitgeist is nihilistic but it has the logic of contraction, and that logic masses enormous weights of power. If I may be allowed to quote myself, the concepts required for any recovery

> have been not merely undermined but downright eliminated by modern philosophy, psychology, and anthropology. That means that an attempt to return to the natural law of Thomas Aquinas, for instance, would be tantamount to fetching from afar a text written in a language "not understanded by the people." We would recover no more than the words. Our contemporaries would not be mentally and spiritually equipped to read these words with sensitivity or even with interest. As for us, who might seek to "return to natural law" by nothing more than reprinting ancient texts, we would stand convicted of laziness.[22]

Metaphysical words, symbols, and even myths are no more than the "outward and visible signs" behind which one means an "inward and spiritual grace." Even this latter is a symbolic expression for the ultimate inner experience that at all times has been the mode in which human souls, hearts, and minds have encountered higher and ineffable reality. That kind of experience alone is also for us the road of "renewal" and "recovery," provided one does not confuse it with any "experience"; with, for instance, the "experiences" one expects to result from a cleverly arranged social happening, even if that happening "happens" to include a liturgical service. In that sense, the dime-a-dozen experiences for which modern "life-styles" are angling every day remain empty and fleeting. The experiences large with fruit are those capable of engendering metaphysical insights. For with regard to metaphysics the chief question to ask is not, "What do the texts say?", "What does metaphysics teach?", but rather, "How is metaphysics possible?" In the same article of mine above quoted I went on to point to the experiences of Solzhenitsyn and other inmates of the Gulag Archipelago who, in the face of complete individual annihilation, encountered divine reality and the reality of goodness. These Russian labor camp experiences must be rated as milestone events of our age.

Were this kind of experience all we could discover, we might feel compelled to wish for ourselves a totalitarian regime so that, in its extremities of inhumanity, we could recover our own humanity. That wish would be as inadmissible as the spiritual extreme in which some early Christians actively sought to bring upon themselves a martyr's death, only to be roundly condemned by the Church. Thus, we must keep our eyes open to somewhat comparable experiences that are possible under our cultural circumstances. One of these has occurred among psychiatrists, proceeding with the very methods of their discipline and under the conviction that evil is nothing but a variety of psychic disease implying no fault, who came face to face with the unexpected reality of evil in human will. As one of them relates:

> I knew practically nothing about radical human evil. I did not believe in the existence of either the devil or the phenomenon of possession. I had never attended an exorcism. The very name of evil was absent from my professional vocabulary. I had received no training on the subject. It was not a recognized field of study for a psychiatrist or, for that matter, any supposedly scientific person. I had been taught that all psychopathology could be explained in terms of known diseases or psychodynamics, and was properly labeled and

encompassed in the standard *Diagnostic and Statistical Manual.* The fact that American psychiatry almost totally ignored even the basic reality of the human will had not yet struck me as ridiculous.[23]

Through one or two of his cases Dr. Peck was finally driven to the recognition of the key role of the human will and the choice of evil as a real possibility of that will. Dr. Peck is now a psychiatrist turned Christian by the consistent application of psychiatric methods which led him to "shatter" the Freudian and Jungian psychoanalytical world, just as Planck and Einstein, through the consistent application of Newtonian method, came to "shatter" Newton's physical universe. Other psychiatrists, those specializing in Multiple Personality Dissociation, have experienced similar encounters inducing them to accept Christian beliefs.

In the case of the Soviet Gulag inmates and the American psychiatrists, the common element is the utterly shattering encounter with radical evil, an encounter that in the forties also brought a good many German intellectuals back to the Christian faith. What about positive experiences, experiences of at least some condition of goodness? Are none of these to be reported? They are, but they come in curiously unrelated forms. A contemporary Estonian composer, Arvo Pärt, had early in life committed himself to twelve-tone serialism which he found to be a part of T.S. Eliot's Wasteland. His way from "under the rubble" led him through the equivalent of the musician's "abyss," through complete silence, musical silence, mental silence, spiritual silence, silence observed for years, silence as the soul's recovery-regime from absolute lostness. As he began to emerge, cautiously sounding first one note, then a repetition of that note, he remained committed to silence as the point of beginning, and allowed no notes "unworthy of the underlying silence." The emerging music turned out to be strongly spiritual, and his latest composition is a Passion according to St. John. One wonders whether Pärt had ever heard of Max Picard's 1948 book on silence, but, in any case, two remarkable persons found an original and viable way of personal renewal.

We are not the first ones to raise the question of how to attain "renewal" and "recovery." I would like to conclude by referring to three thinkers who answered this question in an identical way. First, Eric Voegelin, who more than any other contemporary thinker has thrown light on the link between metaphysics and mystic-philosophical experience repeated frequently the basic importance of the "primary experience of the cosmos," an experience present at the origin of myth, present as the philosopher's myth of classical Greek philosophy, and never to be neglected or ignored. Second, a contemporary scientist and philosopher, Wolfgang Smith, speaking about the "twin realms of mathematicized objectivity and an illusory subjectivity" which "together...have in effect swallowed up the entire locus of reality," so that "beyond we see nothing; we cannot—our premises do not permit it," gives this advice: "What then is out there that could possibly be seen? And by what means? The answer is surprisingly simple: What is to be seen is the God-made world, and this seeing—this prodigy—is to be accomplished through the God-given instruments consisting of the five senses and the mind."[24] Third, it gives me great personal pleasure to turn, for another, almost identical answer, to G.K. Chesterton. He would not be Chesterton if his answer were to start at the point we would never have thought of by ourselves: Elfland, the realm of fairy tales, enchanted castles and animals, witches, and talking trees. This land is "not a necessity...we do not count on it, we bet on it." Chesterton describes his first two experiences, indefensible and indisputable: "The world was a shock, but it was not merely shocking; existence was a surprise; but it was a pleasant surprise." What began with the fairy tales of childhood became the basic faith underlying the adult's life:

> I felt that life itself is as bright as a diamond, but as
> brittle as a window pane....The wonder has a positive
> element of praise...and this pointed a profound emo-
> tion always present and subconscious; that this world
> of ours has some purpose; and if there is a purpose,
> there is a person.

The resulting attitude toward the world is describable as the
opposite of house-hunting:

> No man is in that position. A man belongs to this
> world before he begins to ask if it is nice to belong to
> it. He has fought for the flag, and often won heroic
> victories for the flag long before he has ever enlisted.
> To put shortly what seems the essential matter, he has
> a loyalty long before he has any admiration.[25]

What Chesterton describes is "faith," but not in the sense we
use when speaking of someone as a Christian, a Jew, or a Muslim.
Of his Christian faith Chesterton has little to say in *Orthodoxy*,
instead he has that reserved for *The Everlasting Man*. But, and
here we may return to Voegelin, it is that basic Chestertonian
faith which not only all higher religion but all higher thought
presupposes, as a given. When Anselm composed his *Proslogion*
he saw himself engaged in *fides quaerens intellectum*, i.e., in the
movement from a basic and given faith to the intellect's fuller
understanding. For without that basic faith, there is nothing to
talk about, or even to think about. So that the cosmos, always
accessible by means of spontaneous reflection on simple sense
impressions, can thus always move us to say: "Why,—there is,
indeed, *something* rather than nothing!" "Why—what there is
comes, and goes, and moves in its way and no other!" So there is,
first, the actuality of given existence, fact eliciting admiration
and praise. Such faith underlies all human experience, as St. Paul
pointed out in the first chapter of his letter to the Romans
(19:21). The soul that finds itself moved by given reality knows
itself to be a part, and its movement to be participation.

I end with a final quotation, from a book published in the same decade as Chesterton's *Orthodoxy*: William James's *The Varieties of Religious Experience*. Like Dr. Peck, James approached religious experience as a psychologist, a man of modern science, but he reported with utter veracity and an open mind on what he found. Having quoted verbally a great number of different religious experiences, he comments:

> Such is the human ontological imagination, and such is the convincingness of what it brings to birth. Unpicturable beings are realized, and realized with an intensity almost like that of an hallucination. They determine our vital attitude as decisively as the vital attitude of lovers is determined by the habitual sense, by which each is haunted, of the other being in the world.... They are as convincing to those who have them as any direct sensible experience can be, and they are, as a rule, much more convincing than results established by mere logic ever are.[26]

James speaks of "the human ontological imagination." "Ontological," as is well known, functions as almost a synonym with "metaphysical." James gives us example after example of experiences that "make metaphysics possible." Whether he shared the ensuing convictions or not is beside the point. The experiences he described did occur to men and women of about a hundred years ago, people living in our modern times and under its tyrannous Zeitgeist. When I said, earlier, that the road of renewal and recovery led not through an intentional focus on symbols and ancient texts but through relevant inner experiences, I became liable to provide an answer to the possible question: "But—are such experiences still possible in our days?" I hope to have provided at least some evidence that will preclude a simple "No" as an answer to that question.

NOTES

1. Marcus Tullius Cicero, *Nature of the Gods* (New York: Penguin Books, 1972), 194-95.

2. Boethius, *The Consolation of Philosophy* (New York: Carlton House, 1976).

3. *Fidelity*, vol. 7, no. 8 (August 1988).

4. Giambattista Vico, *The New Science* (Ithaca, N.Y.: Cornell University Press, 1968) 424.

5. Robert N. Bellah, *Beyond Belief* (New York: Harper & Row, 1970), 246.

6. *Ibid.*, 204.

7. *Ibid.*, 215.

8. Jaroslav Pelikan, *Jesus Through the Centuries* (New Haven, Conn.: Yale University Press, 1985), 21-22.

9. Bellah, *Beyond Belief*, 224.

10. *Ibid.*, 226.

11. *Ibid.*, 228.

12. *Ibid.*, 245.

13. *Ibid.*, 252.

14. *Ibid.*, 257.

15. Henri Louis Bergson, *The Two Sources of Morality and Religion* (New York: Henry Holt and Company, 1935).

16. Wolfgang Smith, *Cosmos and Transcendence: Breaking Through the Barrier of Scientific Belief* (La Salle, Ill: Sherwood Sugden, 1984), 134.

17. Edwin Burtt, *The Metaphysical Foundation of Modern Physical Science*, rev. ed. (1955), 262.

18. *Ibid.*, 300.

19. Smith, *Cosmos and Transcendence*, 25.

20. Philipp Rieff, *The Triumph of the Therapeutic* (New York: Harper & Row, 1968), 77.

21. G.K. Chesterton, *Orthodoxy* (London: John Lane, 1908), 31-32.

22. Gerhart Niemeyer, "What Price Natural Law," *Aftersight and Foresight* (Lanham, Md.: University Press of America and Intercollegiate Studies Institute, 1988), 261.

23. M. Scott Peck, *People of the Lie* (New York: Simon and Schuster, 1983), 178.

24. Smith, *Cosmos and Transcendence*, 135.

25. Chesterton, *Orthodoxy*, 96, 99, 108, 118.

26. William James, *The Varieties of Religious Experience* (New York: New American Library of World Literature, 1958), Lecture III.

Recovering History and Redeeming the Time

During the first half of our century, Basil Willey provided students of literature with four admirable background analyses: *The Seventeenth Century Background, The Eighteenth Century Background*, then, having grown "tired" of *"background,"* *Nineteenth Century Studies, and More Nineteenth Century Studies,* published between 1934 and 1956. These books are concerned with what he calls "religious and moral ideas," and, later, "the loss of faith." This emphasis sounds astonishing to those of us who live at the end of the century, but it would have appeared wholly natural to people of the last century, who might have remembered that "theory" once meant "explication of experiences of the transcendent in language symbols" (Eric Voegelin, in *The Philosophy of Order,* Opitz and Sebba, eds., Stuttgart, 1981, 82). Voegelin continued: "The knowledge of the essence of man-in the Platonic and Christian sense-reaches recognition in these experiences.... A science of man and society exists insofar as this theory has been developed." Basil Willey would hardly have used words of such precision to state the problem to portray his "backgrounds", but he must have seen it in similar terms.

It may not be superfluous to dwell for a moment on Willey's two books on the nineteenth century. The first contains essays on Coleridge, Thomas Arnold, Newman and the Oxford Movement, Thomas Carlyle, Bentham, John Stuart Mill, Auguste Comte, George Eliot and, in the context of her life, Hennell, David Strauss, Feuerbach, and concluding with Matthew Arnold. We note his basic inclination to stay with English thinkers, but Willey does include a Frenchman, Comte, and two Germans, David Strauss and Feuerbach, both "Left" Hegelians. Still, the book's absence of Hegel, Marx, and Nietzsche is cause for wonder. Willey called this enquiry "preliminary" and inadequate to "the vastness of the subject," hence the follow-up. This one deals with Francis Newman, Tennyson, J.A. Froude, and a number of mid-century essayists whom he groups together under the title, "Septem Contra Christum," Mark Rutherford, and John Morley. No continental thinker this time—both volumes speak of the deep reaction against the eighteenth century, "that terrible century," as the Romantics called it. They had had enough of atheist scoffing and blaspheming, of contempt for Christian tradition, institutions, and symbolism. All the same, they did not return to the past. Two or three generations strongly interested in religion pursue it as if they had a personal title to recast the faith in the image of their subjective feelings about life, nature, and the "I." The individual begins to adore the wonder of its mind and its powers to subjugate the world. The self's creative energies appear as the equivalent of miracles. While the great English poets of this century thirsted for the supernatural, J. Hillis Miller could write a book portraying five of them, under the title, *The Disappearance of God.* Willey's awareness of the nineteenth century "crisis of faith" is correct, but hardly discerning. His analytical powers fall short of his intuitive appraisal of the situation. If we compare his picture of the century with, for instance, Mario Praz' *The Romantic Agony,* or Hans Urs von Balthasar's *Prometheus,* we miss the cutting edge of a deeply probing mind.

With caution, we may mention the problem of a "Twentieth Century Background." Too many features of our century are without precedent in the three preceding ones: three huge and terrifying historical events have left their trauma on all thinking people: the First World War, the Russian Revolution, Hitler's mass-murderous regime. Equally terrifying developments have occurred in the realm of the mind. Irrational and subversive "causes" have made themselves politically dominant in two large nations, socially dominant in scores of medium-sized ones, and fully respectable among the intellectuals of the rest. Between these "causes" and their opponents rational debate is an impossibility; no basic experiences serve them as common patrimony; language is but a means to manipulate with hostile intent. A combative animus manifests itself not only in regular warfare, but also in institutionalized murder. Furthermore, this situation belongs not to the relation between states as states: the "causes" are carried by mass movements transcending national boundaries as well as national interests; they are bodies vaguely resembling churches but worshipping no god, and political "parties" are their localized shock-troops. The twentieth century consciousness—one would have to say, "of Western intellectuals"— has brought forth demons of modernity, utterly dissimilar to the demons of bygone ages. Given their presence, politics is no longer a terrain familiar to rational inquiry that centers in justice and prudence. Even the problem of God appears distorted during an age in which a cause centered on overt anti-theism can be categorized as a religion" (as by R.C. Zaehner in his *Concordant Discord: The Interdependence of Faiths, 1970).*

The twentieth century, then, has elicited questions of deep confusion: "What is this that is happening to us?" "How could it possibly come about?" "What or who has caused it?" "How can one understand our situation?" Scholars, of course, were asking such questions long before the general public did, when, to their own puzzlement the philosophical tools their education had equipped them with turned out to be inapplicable. Let us listen to Eric Voegelin as he describes his own bafflement, early in the century:

> [The] curious default of the school philosophies in the
> face of an overwhelming political reality had attracted
> my attention ever since I was a graduate student in the
> 1920s. The default was curious because it assumed the
> form not of a lack but of a superabundance of theories
> of consciousness and methodologies of the sciences.
> And I had to work through quite a few of them as part
> of my formal training, such as the neoKantianism of
> the Marburg school, the value-free science of Max
> Weber, the positivism of the Viennese school, of
> Wittgenstein, and of Bertrand Russell, the legal posi-
> tivism of Kelsen's Pure Theory of Law, the phenom-
> enology of Husserl, and, of course, Marx and Freud.
> But when in the course of my readings in the history of
> ideas I had to raise the question, why do important
> thinkers like Comte and Marx refuse to apperceive
> what they apperceive quite well, why do they expressly
> prohibit anybody to ask questions concerning the
> sectors of reality they have excluded from their per-
> sonal horizon? Why do they want to imprison them-
> selves in their restricted horizon and to dogmatize
> their prison reality as the universal truth? and why do
> they want to lock up all mankind in the prison of their
> making,—my formidable equipment did not provide
> an answer, though obviously an answer was needed if
> one wanted to understand the mass movements that
> threatened, and still threaten, to engulf Western civi-
> lization in their prison culture *(Anamnesis,* tr. Gerhart
> Niemeyer, 1978, 3 ff.).

Similar passages could be added to this one. A remarkable
example is found in the Epilogue to Hans Jonas's *The Gnostic
Religion (2nd* ed., 1963). Jonas, Voegelin, Quispel, Cochran,
and others belong to that select few whose scholarly energies

combined to overcome the impasse at least partially. Through
them there occurred a reconstruction of theory, in spite of the
positivistic ban on theory. Eric Voegelin's first book which broke
the ban was called *The New Science of Politics*. Its title called
attention to the new science that had gradually grown in such
fields as philosophical anthropology, classics, orientology, biblical studies, comparative religion, literary criticism. Speaking of
this he remarks: "For two generations, now, the sciences of man
and society are engaged in a process of retheoretization. The new
development, slow at first, gained momentum after the first
World War; and today it is moving at a breathtaking speed" *(The
New Science of Politics*, 1952, 3).

The relevance of this development to the "Twentieth Century
Background" is as follows: the process of retheoretization provides, at long last, standards of criticism with the help of which
the demons of our time can be properly analyzed as products of
modem consciousness. The convergence of several sciences in
this regeneration of theory makes possible an adequate criticism
of the academic school systems as well as of the ideologies of the
twentieth century. Finally, the astonishing expansion of historical knowledge, the opening of newly widened access to sources
in many civilizations, a deepened understanding of classical
Greek philosophy as well as of Christian philosophy, combine to
form a body of knowledge that has therapeutic character, in that
it is an antidote to the pneumopathology, the spiritual sickness
of our time. Without this "new science" no background study of
our century would be possible. No "religious or moral" questions
could be identified, and no "loss of faith" detected. Still, the "new
science" is one side of a broad academic controversy, in that
positivists, marxists, relativists, futurists, and activists want to
have no part of it, even refuse to admit its existence and to enter
into conversation with it. The "background" thus is itself split by
academic warfare so that the critic cannot avoid having to take
sides. Such "side-taking" should not be misconstrued as subjec-

tive like or dislike, however, is inescapable in the course of strict theoretical criticism. Thus, writing about the "background" of the twentieth century has become a matter of passionate divisions, to the point of destroying reputations and killing by silence.

So much for Basil Willey's problem. Marion Montgomery's work to some extent also intends the background but does not confine itself to that scope. Montgomery has achieved a view of history, not history as circumscribed by institutions, elections, migrations, and wars, but by mind and soul in the American past. That might be a dry-as-dust history of ideas, but not in Marion Montgomery's work. He moves in historical dimensions while he "pursues the study of the human heart." That entails touching on the absolute while comprehending what is contingent. Even that kind of enterprise could be undertaken in an abstract and dogmatic way, but Montgomery is interested in living encounter rather than general propositions. A tender providence has furnished him a fruitful starting point: the figure of Flannery O'Connor. This great American writer had a slender body of work wrought under great difficulties in her short life of thirty-nine years, while an incurable disease permitted her only three daily hours of creative energy. The one propositional concept about her that Montgomery allows himself is that of "prophetic writer," a title that comes to one's lips readily when confronted with this unique literary phenomenon: a writer of unshakable Catholic faith with a great talent for the grotesque, writing about "Christ-haunted" people and their tragic situations, with profound humor.

She defies comparison. Still, the mind wanders from her to another great writer who likewise depicted human souls in grotesque deformations caused by loss of faith. Dostoevsky remarked in his notebook: "Repudiate Christ,—and the human mind can arrive at the most astounding conclusions" (quoted in Henri de Lubac, *The Drama of Atheist Humanism*, 1963, 184).

He, too, was a single person contending with a powerful antitheist Spirit of the Time. Unlike O'Connor, he himself had once been an adept of that Spirit but converted to the Christian faith in prison. It is worth our while to dwell on a strange incident when Dostoevsky, in 1867, stood in Basle before a Holbein painting showing the ghastly pale corpse of Jesus lying flat against a dark background. His wife found him there, after twenty minutes, his face ashen with a deep fear. Later the writer places this picture on the wall of Rogozhin's house, in his novel *The Idiot.* There he obviously describes his own erstwhile experience in the words: "One cannot help saying to oneself, if death is such a terrible thing, if the laws of nature are so strong, how can one triumph over them?...When you look back at this picture, you can imagine nature as a huge beast, dumb and implacable.... Or, an enormous machine of modem construction...which had stupidly caught, crushed, and swallowed a great Being, a Being beyond all price...." Lubac comments on this passage as follows: "Let us recall the date of Dostoevsky's visit to the gallery in Basle: 1867. In that second part of the nineteenth century everything conspired to intensify the rivalry in which universal Necessity has always competed with the living God. German metaphysics and French positivism led to the construction of that prison whose bars were one day to be shaken by Bergson, from which Claudel, like Saint Peter of old, was to be miraculously freed.... At the moment when he set eyes upon Holbein's painting, the whole burden of the century suddenly weighed upon the soul of Fyodor Mikhailovich.... It had shaken him to the heart" *(Ibid.,* 175).

So that we get a clear idea of what it means to be alone, confronted with a hostile Spirit of the Time, let us briefly recall Thomas Aquinas, having returned victorious from his last combat with Siger of Brabant. In the words of Chesterton: "This particular quarrel was the one point, as we may say, in which his outer and his inner life had crossed and coincided; he realized how he had longed from childhood to call up all allies in the battle for Christ; how he had long afterward called up Aristotle as an ally; and now in that last nightmare of sophistry, he had for the first time truly realized that some might really wish Christ to go down before Aristotle. He never recovered from the shock. He won his battle, because he was the best brain of his time, but he could not forget such an inversion of the whole idea and purpose of his life...in the abyss of anarchy opened by Siger's sophistry of the Double Mind of Man, he had seen the possibility of the perishing of all idea of religion, and even of all idea of truth" *(Saint Thomas Aquinas,* 1956, 141 f.).

Dostoevsky had always longed to create a literary character who would portray the perfection of human virtue, a man wholly living in God's presence. He never succeeded. But at all times he could produce images of the demons that threatened to destroy humanity in his century. As he said, he had produced a stronger case for atheism than the atheists themselves. Still, he was the one man who, by the power of his writing, stopped the seemingly irresistible nineteenth century advance of untruth. His stories make grim reading. Flannery O'Connor, by contrast, seems always to be of good cheer: in the face of her disease, of the disappearance of God as well as man, from literature, of the political convulsions of the times. Unlike Dostoevsky she is not "tormented" by God. There is no manifestation of inner conflicts. *Salva facta est.* She is a "realist of distances," because the onslaught of lupus brought her face-to-face with death, and, from that vantage point, in "reflective distance," she can write with an indestructable sense of humor.

"Prophetic poets" bring to our mind the image of Elijah, crushed to the point of hopelessness by the power of King Ahab and his Ba'al-worshipping queen Jezebel, who had erected a temple to her idol and flooded the country with hordes of its prophets. Elijah, having to flee for his life, is sitting in utter discouragement under a tree wishing to die. To God's question, he replies: "I have been very jealous for the Lord God of hosts:

for the children of Israel have forsaken thy covenant...and I, even I only, am left; and they seek my life, to take it away." But God curtly dismisses such self-pity, and, with the words," I have left myself seven thousand souls who have not bent the knee to Ba'al," he sends Elijah forth on this prophetic mission.

If we use the word "prophet" in its conventional meaning, and accept the three examples I mentioned as representative, one might venture a general statement that a prophet is a figure wholly absorbed with concern for the relation of God with man, not so much in particular instances but rather in the public teaching and dominant patterns of a society. By force of this situation, he is a solitary figure, standing his ground against attitudes and ways of acting that have become popular. He is also one who proclaims truth unselfconsciously, much as a man fighting in a great historical battle utterly forgets about his own life. We call prophetic men who have stood the ground of truth in historical watershed situations, from which streams run down in opposite directions: streams of living water to the one side, and streams of blood to the other. It makes little difference whether the figure was what the Bible calls a man of God, or a philosopher, or a writer and poet. Nor does it matter whether he is engaged in a contest between false and true prophecy, or deformed noetic thought and divinely formed consciousness, or egocentric poetic imagination and god-open consciousness. In either case, the awareness of reality is at stake, and with it, the order of human lives. A crisis of falsehood befalling an entire culture is an even greater historical catastrophe than a battle of the character of Poitiers or Issus. We find ourselves between a body of literature and writing that attests to the absence of God, the unreality of the human person, the authority of the unconscious, the vision of "life-creating" violent revolution, the guilt of environment, the primacy of sex over other activities, and, on the other side, storytelling like that of Flannery O'Connor, Eudora Welty, or Walker Percy. Taking in the character of our predicament, one may well mumble the words of *Revelation:* "And there was war in heaven." Numerical criteria are irrelevant: the prophet is always one against the innumerable many. Dostoevsky and O'Connor also might have said: I, even I alone, am left" Yet had they done so, an angel would have disallowed their self pity and just fed them, "because the journey is too great for thee." And then God's words would have come, "I have left myself seven thousand souls who have not bowed the knee to Ba'al."

The "foreground," if it is contemporary literature, shows a gulf existing between the works proclaiming reality and those describing illusions as if they were truth. We need not count members on one side and the other, nor measure the quantity of works. Thus Marion Montgomery focuses on Flannery O'Connor as the whole of "foreground." He helps us look at her country-boys, conceited intellectuals, sweet or crabby old ladies, adolescent eccentrics—all of it alive, humorous, and deeply mysterious. The brief and full life of this modern, Catholic and yet utterly un-"Catholic" writer, devastated by lupus, unsentimental, unselfconscious, unconventional, unconfused, and undaunted—it is something one would not have expected in our time: a unique and prophetic figure. From God's point of view, it is she who is eminently in the "foreground." It so happened that this highly intelligent, although self-educated, lady reviewed a great number of books for the *Bulletin* published by her diocese, and that in these reviews she herself, rather than a critic, introduces us to the "background." It is a background divided, as is the foreground, as if by "war in heaven." So she read those philosophers whose deformed teaching spoke to us of the absence of God and the non-being of man. On the other hand, Miss O'Connor found a master interpreter of the crisis of our time, Eric Voegelin, whose books she covered with her marginal notes. She made herself knowledgeable of the dominant thinkers; Martin Heidegger, Jean-Paul Sartre, Auguste Comte, Friedrich Nietzsche, Karl Marx, and Sigmund Freud. On the other side, she discovered Von Hügel, Maritain, Guardini, Eliade, Teilhard de Chardin, and Gilson. There were, in battle order, the two sides of that "civil war," as Montgomery puts it, sprung of "an untenable antithesis between 'Science' and 'Humanities.'"

I find myself still talking about "background," thereby misleading my readers. For Montgomery's work must not be compared with Basil Willey's studies, even though his subtitle, *The Prophetic Poet and the Spirit of the Age,* might suggest that it is. The relevant comparison, rather, is with another prophetic poet of our time, Aleksandr Solzhenitsyn. Solzhenitsyn saw that Russia's problem was that of the missing history. Since 1917 the history of the Communist Party has replaced Russia's national history, and for the preceding period, the truth is distorted. His early and first concern was to recapture Russia's history, of which he has now written several volumes. Like Solzhenitsyn, Montgomery has essentially undertaken a work of supplying America's history in so far as it had been missing. "We have lost the capacity for careful thought, for the most part," he observes, "an effect and a cause accompanying the spiritual incapacity to accommodate what our intellect has boldly "pried off" from the created world." Marx had stripped all reality except that of economic production and class revolution, Freud all but the unconscious production of sexual drives, Sartre the entire cosmos with God to boot, and the futurists the historical past. "A people without a history," remarked T.S. Eliot, "is not redeemed from time, for history is a pattern of timeless moments." The comparison of Russia's case with ours is thus not as farfetched as it might seem. To reduce Russia, indeed, the entire world, to a history of Russia's Communist Party presupposes a preceding process of vast destruction in man's consciousness of reality. In our case, this destruction has been wrought, not by the Communist Party, but by writers, philosophers, poets, and teachers engaged in "prying off entire complexes from the created world." In general, one may say, these are the higher realities, once the findings of the newly discovered mind, and the experiences of the spirit rising above self-regard and self-preservation. These experiences and their records have been "pried off" from our history and our ken. With them we have largely lost the capacity for those "timeless moments" of which Eliot speaks, and thus for the order of being. Montgomery seeks to retrace our steps and to look for the places and the times where and when the losses occurred, and what they involved. Eric Voegelin's guiding principle, "The order of history is the history of order," seems to have inspired Montgomery, too.

A word may be in order about Eric Voegelin's work. Earlier in this century, Western minds were struck and moved by two great studies of history: Spengler's *The Decline of the West,* and Toynbee's *Study of History.* Both looked at the succession of empirical phenomena: leaders, peoples, migrations, conquests, collisions, empires, cultures, declines, and collapses, seeking to derive a universal meaning from such streams of singularities. In both cases the aim was a meaning of history, i.e. of all that has happened (and will yet happen?), not excluding any detail. Moreover, the meaning of history was expected to be realized in history itself. These two works, appearing against the nineteenth century background of Hegel, Marx, and Comte, generated a lively interest in historical speculation and strong motivation for a futurist activism.

Eric Voegelin began his *Order and History,* a similarly salient work, at mid-century. From the outset, however, his subject was the order of human existence in history, order understood in terms of man's participation in the "constitution of being" and in divine grace. Still, even Voegelin believed at first that history could be imagined as a kind of single line running from a beginning to a meaningful end. The empirical materials on which he worked were not as obstreperously resistant to philosophy as those of Spengler and Toynbee. He distinguished three "leaps in being," occurring when the human soul differentiates from a compactly mythical image of reality and discovers in itself experiences of participation in the divine from which are developed visions of absolute justice and goodness. He described in the first three volumes of *Order and History* the "leap" made by Israel, and that other by Socrates, Plato, and Aristotle. He also mentioned Christianity as a third "leap," to be examined later. When, after a hiatus of fifteen years, he published Volume IV, however, it dealt with *The Ecumenic Age* and the varieties of structured order emerging under its pressures. As a result of his research for this volume, he concluded that it proved "impossible to align the empirical types in anything like a course," and that it was necessary to abandon the unilinear image of history. He did not abandon his guiding principle that "the order of history was the history of order," for the application of this principle had led precisely to this change of conception. The new concept demanded "that analysis had to move backward and forward and sideways, in order to follow empirically patterns of meaning as they revealed them selves in the self-interpretation of persons and societies in history" *(OH,* Volume IV, 57). We note that Voegelin speaks of "order in history" rather than "the order *of* history."

At this writing, twelve years have passed. Eric Voegelin has gone even further in deemphasizing temporal succession as carrying universal meaning. What he had formerly arranged in "before and after" he now tends to see as perennial tension between opposed possibilities of consciousness. Thus he moves philosophy of consciousness onto the same level as philosophy of history, both in closest contact. Voegelin's last volume of *Order and History* has much to say about the paradox of consciousness that is capable of experiencing the absolute but must speak of its experiences in the language of things in this world. Both the language that communicates such experiences, and the imagination that gropes for adequate symbols, have this paradoxical structure. Here possibilities of truth and error, of attainment and failure, lie close to each other. Any language "adequate to God" entails a certain amount of human assertion. This assertive element in imagination also "offers imagining man escapes of a sort from the reality by which it is governed" ("Reflective Distance vs. Reflective Identity," volume V of *OH*). When reflecting man keeps the proper "reflective distance," imaginative language may attain the luminosity of truth. Right next door, however, is the possibility that the assertive aspect of imagination be "heightened to self-assertion," in which case "it may end up in the illusion of the inquirer becoming master, or even creator, of reality. This imaginative perversion of participatory imagination into an autonomously creative power has remained a constant in history." In other words, the soul, even when attaining its highest reach, may respond with a "yes" to divine reality, but just as often with a "no." Or, when experiencing the inner "pull," man may respond either to the pull of the "thingly beyond" or to "the divine Beyond of the *nous.*" Voegelin continues: "The movements are not equal but distinguished as either a movement to a state of existence from which, as it were, 'God is absent,' or an immortalizing movement toward likeness with God."

While the excursion into Voegelin has been long, it is not extraneous to the matter under discussion. Marion Montgomery is dealing with matters of history in America in just the way Voegelin does. He moves backward and forward and sideways, returning to a place he has visited before to look at it in a different light. He is not primarily interested in the chronological order of the matters he deals with, but with the responses of the human heart to "the drawing of this Love and the calling of this Voice." It is the spectrum of various responses that he explores as he probes the Puritans' vision, that of Edgar Allan Poe, the symbols regarding Nature in America's North and South, Emerson's addresses to America's youth, and Hawthorne's gnawing misgivings about what had gone wrong in the process. Montgomery knows that no labels saying "true" or "false" are attached to one or the other response, so he moves back and forth, often several times over the same ground, probing, comparing, weighing. Voegelin said: "Only the process comprehending the steps, when moved into reflective distance, will let the truth of existence become luminous by letting the symbols illuminate each other." Marion Montgomery, often repeating Flannery O'Connor's characterization of herself as a"realist of distances," himself keeps the "reflective distance" that is proper to the human mind when dealing with problems of participation. As he moves from poet to poet, and thinker to thinker, often combining responses widely separated by time and space, he does "allow the symbols to illuminate each other." He avoids any merely subjective distinction of friend from foe. He does not draw battle lines. He takes into account that a human failure in the quest for truth permits no certain inference of deliberate ill-will, notwithstanding the fact that an explicit will to "do without God" was voiced by a number of thinkers, in the nineteenth century and ours. Montgomery proceeds on the premise that the process of human consciousness moves in an area of freedom the nature of which is not always recognized before it is too late.

Enough has been said to illuminate Montgomery's warning that his undertaking carries dangers both to the author and the reader. It seeks to elicit the reader's own response to "timeless moments" of the past. The reader is invited to allow his own formation by the "mutual illumination of symbols." The work as a whole, therefore, has the intent of a spiritual therapy, Montgomery's own version of St. Paul's "redeeming the time." A deep understanding of America's spiritual and intellectual history is meant to attune present consciousness to the truth of existence, yet it does not come in the form of a sermon. Nor has religious dogmatism guided Montgomery's pen. His offering is a peculiarly apperceptive analysis of the interpenetration of literary and philosophical materials, and the offering calls for the reader's active sharing in awareness of his heritage. Thus it is not a work of easy reading or literary entertainment. Yet for those who are willing to live with it for a while, it holds unexpected encounters with minds of depth and imagination, adventures of a very special kind, and the one who rides out to meet adventures may be the one selected to find the Holy Grail.

God and Man,
World and Society

Reconstituting Political Theory *

One of the most striking insights of Eric Voegelin's *New Science of Politics* (1952) was thus stated: "...the essence of modernity (should be recognized as) the growth of gnosticism," meaning by gnosticism a type of religion that places some elect men, by virtue of a special knowledge (gnosis), into a savior's role against a world experienced as totally alien and corrupted. This, Voegelin demonstrated, is the structure not only of the various gnostic religions of the first three centuries of our era, but also of the numerous revolutionary ideologies, which have arisen in Western civilization since the end of the eighteenth century and have resulted in a "redivinization" of politics, i.e. a fusion of politics and salvation which the Christian order fundamentally separated from one another. The modern gnostic identifies transcendence, political action, and its hoped-for result, a transformed social order, and this identification of transcendence and political immanence means that some men or groups see themselves in a quasi-divine position as redeemers of mankind. Voegelin contrasted with such ideological idea systems the science of politics that had been created by Plato and had continued in our civilization until last century's positivistic destruction: a critical examination of public existence by the

* This is a review of Eric Voegelin's *Science, Politics, and Gnosticism,* (Chicago: Henry Regnery Co., Gateway Edition, 1968).

philosophical consciousness oriented in love toward the divine ground of being. On the basis of this and related distinctions, Voegelin deciphered a new periodization of history in his *magnum opus, Order and History*. Philosophy was a latecomer, finding everywhere societies in existence and order based on varieties of cosmological myths. These myths, through which men symbolized their experience of the ground of being in stories about gods and goddesses, nature and nature's forces, creation, death, and regeneration, society, man, and proper action, did not differentiate between god and man, nature and society, existence and action. Everything was packed tightly together in the same set of myths. At a certain time, however, a process of differentiation began, more or less simultaneously on various parts of the globe. Israel differentiated the element of righteousness as the will of a God who stood over against his people. Greek philosophy discovered the manifestations of transcendent order in the experience of the human soul, with other differentiations being achieved by the Buddha, Lao tsu, Confucius, and Zoroaster. Thus Voegelin sees philosophy in a historical perspective, a new way of life consisting not so much in knowing sets of propositions but rather in the lucidity of consciousness regarding man's participation in the divine transcendence, and in the "Socratic practice of dying so that a man may measure up at the Last Judgment" (39). Later, the combination of Christian revelation with philosophy attained an optimum of rationality is that the discipline of noetic consciousness allied itself with the illumination of being by faith.

The present historical situation is dominated by ideologies which separate man from the source of order by postulating the loss or the death of God. Positivism banned philosophical inquiry into the ground of being from what has become a willfully reduced notion of alleged "science," actually an arbitrary imposition of the natural science model on things human, and as a result our civilization found itself deprived of "conceptual tools with which to grasp the horror that was upon her. There was a scholarly study of the Christian churches and sects; there was a science of government, cast in the categories of the sovereign nation-state and its institutions; there were the beginnings of a sociology of power and political authority; but there was no science of the non-Christian, non-national intellectual, and mass movements into which the Europe of the Christian nation-states was in the process of breaking up" (5). Voegelin's effort has been to remedy this situation, but he has not confined it merely to creating a science of modern ideologies. He could not distinguish ideology from political philosophy until he had reestablished a true understanding of the classical *episteme politike*, as well as achieved a philosophical rather than an ideological construction of history.

The book under review bears the subtitle "Two Essays." Actually, there are three: Voegelin's 1958 inaugural lecture at the University of Munich, a second essay on "The Murder of God," and an article "Ersatz Religion" which was not contained in the German original but published in 1960 in *Wort und Wahrheit* and in English translation in *Politeia*, a student-directed periodical at Princeton and Rutgers, the issues of which were hard to come by. The first two of these essays are superbly translated by William J. Fitzpatrick, the former faculty adviser of *Politeia*. In his "Forward to the American Edition" Voegelin states the book's purpose: "To draw more clearly the lines that separate political gnosticism from a philosophy of politics," and, to this end, focus on "the death of God...the cardinal issue of gnosis, both ancient and modern." He does this in the first essay through studies of Marx, Nietzsche, and Heidegger, and in the second through a comparison of the medieval Golem legend with the "death of God" passages of Nietzsche and Hegel. The third essay dwells first on the chief case of medieval gnosticism, Joachim of Flora, and demonstrates the similarity of his pattern of symbols with such modern ideologies as progressivism, positivism, Marxism, psychoanalysis, communism, fascism, and national socialism. All of these, Voegelin finds, have this structure in common: they represent metaphysical discontent, attribute evil to the world rather than to us human beings, believe that salvation from this evil world is possible, expect that the order of being will be changed in a historical process, assume that this change is to be brought about by human action, and look on their ideological "knowledge" of the method of change as the message of salvation to mankind. Voegelin's achievement is to have demonstrated the profound irrationality of such beliefs from which stem the sundry disorders that beset our time.

Genuine science, by contrast, deals with everyday problems of order but is "ontologically oriented," concerned with insights into being, and characterized by an openness of the inquirer's soul toward the ground of being. Gnostic ideology consists of power-motivated idea systems. It begins with willful assumptions and insists on system-building, refusing even to consider questions that cannot fit into the system as a whole. Thus arises the "prohibition of questioning" of which Voegelin presents telling examples of Marx, Comte, and Nietzsche. To man's genuinely curious question about his origin and his Creator, Marx replies: "Do not think, do not question me,...for the socialist man (such a question) becomes a practical impossibility." (*Economic and Philosophical Manuscripts of 1844.*) This enforcement of the system by intellectual despotism induces Voegelin to call Marx "an intellectual swindler" (28). Nietzsche expressed his will to power as a "suddenly erupting resolve for ignorance, for arbitrary occlusion...a kind of defensive stand against much that is knowable." This is pushed further into a "not unscrupulous readiness of the spirit to deceive other spirits," and ultimately to self-deception in "a kind of cruelty of the intellectual conscience." (No. 230, *Beyond Good and Evil.*) A profound analysis of the underlying psychology leads Voegelin to conclude: "Gnosis desires dominion over being; in order to seize control of being the gnostic constructs his system. The building of systems is a gnostic form of reasoning, not a philosophical one" (42). It is the opposite of the "open soul" attitude of the "lover of wisdom." In Heidegger, the gnostic attitude manifests itself in the construction of being as something approaching us from the future, "somewhat in the way a ruler makes an appearance" (46), which leads Heidegger to ignore the experiences of friendship, love, faith, and hope, "the ontic events — described by the Hellenic philosophers — wherein the soul participates in transcendent being and allows itself to be ordered by it" (47). Thus in modern times we have idea structures that dress themselves in the apparent mantle of philosophy even to the point of occupying philosopher's chairs, without being philosophy and which, on the contrary, look on idea systems as instruments of salvation and means to dominate (39).

Now to the "issue of God." The mention of this word by a serious philosopher of political order strikes some people in our time like an obscenity; this is the result of what Voegelin has called, in the *New Science*, the positivistic "taboo on theory." When philosophy differentiated, from the entire compact picture of being as represented by the myth, a world-immanent "nature," the result was the concept of a transcendent God, and man's relation to transcendence became a problem in the reflection on which man came to understand his own nature. Man's inquiry into human participation in the divine ground of being has been the source of order of all human societies, not excluding the ones which the organized body of Communism now occupies and used for its own purposes. Where man cuts himself off from this source of order, something else has to replace it; in the nature of things this could be only a material factor (economics, race) or a human program of self-salvation raised to the rank of an absolute. In either case, man deifies something contingent and non-divine, as a result of which he falls subject to the demons arising from a humanity without grace.

Thus, the denial or the "death" of God is indeed the central issue in an understanding of our time; this is the conclusion which even the agnostic Camus could not escape as he undertook, in *The Rebel*, "the attempt to understand the times in which we live." Characteristically, today many people face "the issue of God" as a purely personal agony, as they struggle with what they believe is a subjective incapacity to believe, but what actually is the powerful contemporary influence of godless ideologies. All the same, their sensitivity on a personal problem creates for them a real difficulty in accepting a scholarly inquiry into the "issue of God" as an integral element, negative or positive, in political order. They support the positivistic "taboo on theory" as a kind of personal immunity from inquiries that are subjectively painful. In the realm of scholarship, fortunately, such obstacles have been overcome. A number of outstanding scholars, some of which incidentally happen to be agnostics personally, have created conceptual tools with the help of which "the issue of God" can once again be scientifically approached. Voegelin mentions particularly Hans Jonas, Hans Urs von Balthasar, Gilles Quispel, and Jacob Taubes. They, together with himself, have helped to make genuine political theory once again possible, for the first time after the positivistic destruction. Now the political philosopher can "trace the phenomenon back to its ontic roots and — reduce it to ontological type concepts...(which, says Voegelin) is the task of science" (114).

The meaning of the book's title is now clear. The work, small as it is, constitutes a most important contribution to Voegelin's rehabilitation of the *episteme politike*, precisely because it focuses on "the issue of God" as the central problem of the dividing line between political rationality and irrationality. After the *New Science* many positivistic critics of Voegelin rejected him for what they considered a left-handed attempt to "reintroduce religion" into political thinking. In this book Voegelin makes it clear that his intent is not preachment but the reconstitution of the full range of political theory from which to exclude God would be dishonest, unscholarly willfulness. It may occur to some readers that Voegelin's verdicts on Marx ("an intellectual swindler"), Hegel ("the golem celebrating a ghastly ritual on the grave of the murdered God"), and Nietzsche ("demonic mendacity") are harsh to the point of name-calling. Actually, Voegelin has shown in many different ways that stamps of approval or disapproval are the last things on his mind, in dealing with idea structures, that employ the outward forms of rational inquiry for a basically irrational or anti-rational discourse. Such thinkers, by their own admission, have rejected the common universe of reason. This forces Voegelin, having demonstrated the underlying irrationality, into an inquiry concerning the psychology of the gnostics, whence the statements that sound like name-calling. He does this, in the case of the spiritually sensitive Nietzsche, with profound compassion, albeit without pulling any punches. At any rate, such judgments serve above all to separate ideological from philosophical thinking. About the ultimate movement from gnostic disorder to a reconstructed political order, Voegelin is strongly optimistic. For "we are living," he says, "in one of the great epochs of western science" (6), by which he means above all the science of things human and spiritual. In this upward movement from the brink of the abyss, one of the brightest shining names must be that of Voegelin himself.

Faith and Reason in
Eric Voegelin

My title is not arbitrary. It was the first title proposed to me by the chairman. The present, official title, "Religion and its Place in Political Philosophy," is a different theme. Furthermore, the fact that Voegelin's essay, "The Gospel and Culture," was assigned as reading for all, points yet to another topic: "Eric Voegelin and Christianity." With the chairman's permission, I shall address my remarks to the first of these three possible topics, hoping that I shall travel no further away than a stone's throw from the other members of the panel.

In his correspondence with Leo Strauss, Eric Voegelin stated that "the cosmos and God are given." Strauss disagreed. At first it seemed that Strauss was using the terms "religion," "faith," and "God," in their colloquial meaning. When that was clarified, both men at one point found that they were "not far from each other." At the end, though, Strauss's statement that "Jerusalem" and "Athens" were incompatible with one another seemed to put a full stop to any further discussion.

What did Voegelin mean when he said, "cosmos and God are given"? He certainly was not speaking of any truth concerning either. Later, he preferred the formula, "the cosmos is man's primary experience." "Primary," because it is unavoidable. "Experience," in the sense of inescapable wonderment. Wonderment about the visible cosmos would entail various sorts of surmise about some higher reality in, and beyond the mysterious manifestations of, let us say, "life." Thus, if cosmos is given, so is God. From this wonderment arose the manifold of myths, man's first type of order of his existence. According to Eliade, the gist of that order is represented by the formula: "Thus the gods have acted, thus we too must act"; not more than the early distinction between the sacred and the profane.

Voegelin's greatest achievement, in my view, is to have established the link between reason, faith, and revelation in Greek classical philosophy. Concerning faith and revelation, he says the following: "...a plurality of experiences in which transcendence comes into grasp. In Faith and Revelation levels of transcendence beyond the Truth of Being become accessible— but the symbolism of faith and Revelation retains the qualities of 'likeliness' that characterizes both Doxa and Myth, as distinguished from the Ananke of the Logos. Revelation does not abolish the truth of Being. Hence, with the entrance of Revelation into history we enter into the history of permanent rivalry between the two sources of truth" (*Order and History*, vol. II, *The Greek Polis*, p. 119). We notice that the passage distinguishes not two but three sources of truth. The "Ananke of the Logos" refers surely to the strictness of discursive logic as the mind discovers the intelligibility of the realm that the Chinese call "the 10,000 things." What philosophers discover, however, is not exhausted by the knowledge of things, not even by their essences. They also discover the mind's reaching for the Beyond of all things.

For a suitable illustration, let us look in Plato's *Republic*, Book VI, where "The Good" is the subject matter. Here are Plato's words: "This, then, which gives to the objects of knowledge their truth and to him who knows them his power of knowing, is the Form and essential nature of Goodness. It is the cause of knowledge and truth; and so, while you may think of it as an object of knowledge, you will do well to regard it as something beyond truth and knowledge....[Objects of knowledge] derive from the Good not only their power of being known, but their very being and reality; and Goodness is not the same thing as being and reality, but even beyond being, surpassing it in dignity and power" (508e-509b). Mention is made of "objects of knowledge" and "their power of being known." Still higher, though, we must look for "The Good" which not only brings the object-things into being but also is the cause for the mind's knowledge of them. That *realissimum* surpasses the reality of things in "dignity and power." Still, Plato does speak about that Beyond with a certain amount of precision. He calls it "The Good," or "Goodness." Surely, one experiences a relation to the Good which is called "love." Plato is here moving in the realm of that highest divinity from which all reality originates. What is the meaning of the name "Goodness" which he attributes to it? Could it be that this *realissimum*, "beyond truth and knowledge," can yet be reached by the power of knowing that belongs to love, rather than that which belongs to the intellect? If so, Plato would articulate here the experience of all mystics, that love is capable of higher knowledge than mind. Here is the imagery found in *The Cloud of Unknowing* (14th century): "Lift up thine heart unto God with a meek stirring of love; and mean himself and none of his goods...when thou doest it, thou findest but a darkness, and as it were a *cloud of unknowing*, thou knowest not what, saving that thou feelest in thy will a naked intent unto God.... For if ever thou shalt see him or feel him...it must always be in this cloud and this darkness...all reasonable creatures...have in them...one principal power, the which is called a knowing power, and another principal working power, the which is called a loving power. Of the two powers, to [the] knowing power, God, who is the maker of them is evermore incomprehensible; but the second, [the] loving power, he is...all comprehensible to the full" (chs. 3 and 4). Eric Voegelin had the highest esteem for this book which seemed to him to represent the chief direction of his own scholarly efforts (Cf. Ellis Sandoz, *The Voegelinian Revolution*, 1981, p. 180). About this book Eric Voegelin said:

"From my first contact with such works as *The Cloud of Unknowing*, to my more recent understanding of the mystical problem...the great issue [has been]: not to stop at what may be called classical mysticism, but to restore the problem of the Metaxy for society and history" (*Order and History*, vol. v., p. 12).

Without any conclusions at this point, let us return to Voegelin's analysis of the Pre-Socratic philosophers. In the context of Heraclitus, Voegelin remarks: "The tension between the experience of the flow of 'things' and the experience of a direction in the soul toward the divine 'All-Wise,' as well as the tension between the symbols expressing these experiences, will remain from now on" (*op. cit.*, p. 236). If we relate this to Voegelin's analysis of Parmenides, we learn that the way to the highest truth is the way through traditional thinking about the cosmos, what Parmenides listed under his "delusions." "In Revelation the Doxa has expanded into a truth beyond the Truth and Delusion of Parmenides. In order to arrive at this higher Truth, however, man had to discover the cognition of faith; and the way of Pistis (Faith) is not the way of the Logos that speculates on the experience of 'Is!'" (p. 218).

At this point one might ask the question whether "faith" would not apply to a range of phenomena with a variety of relations to "the logos." To begin with, there is Parmenides's *Doxa*, the traditional opinions about the cosmos, the "given" from which he started. Would not the "likeliness" of Plato's "Goodness" be a quite different kind of faith, one not before and below, but above "the logos"? Then one might think of the strong faith in the rationality of the universe, on the basis of which Einstein, Planck, and Schrödinger resolutely opposed the Copenhagen Indeterminists. Neither Einstein nor Planck were "religious" in Strauss's sense. Could not one conceive of their "faith" in the intelligibility of "the given," as a bridge spanning the entire distance between "the primary experience of the cosmos" and Plato's "The Good"?

Still more different would be what St. Paul called "the life of faith" of a devout Christian. Its foremost character would be strength, confidence, and joy drawn from "the substance of things hoped for, the evidence of things not seen" (Heb. 11:1). There is something like an entire edifice of convictions, many of them subject to the "ananke of the logos," and others, recollections of the historical life of Jesus Christ, "sent by God the Father," "born under Caesar Augustus," "suffered under Pontius Pilatus," "crucified, dead, and buried," who "on the third day rose again from the dead" and "ascended into heaven." These symbols are utterly different from the kind of "likeliness" of, say, the myth of Krishna's periodical incarnations, wrapped in a life story complete with details of Krishna's childhood. Rather, it is a recollection of events that occurred in history, to be sure with a meaning that far surpasses the "knowledge of things," but which the faithful find to be fully in reach of the cognitive power of love. This is a type of life, characterizing a civilization, that seems to be governed by "reasons of the heart" which, in Pascal's words, differ from those of reason itself. Does Pascal's distinction amount to classifying these motives under "irrationality," or "incompatibility with the light of reason"?

Voegelin is the first philosopher who has introduced us, with his precise analytical language, into these complexities of experience, symbols and concepts, faith, revelation, cognition of mind and cognition of love. Not only we, but many generations to come will never be done with finding more reasons for gratitude to him for this. I should like to be remembered for having said this, because I shall now move to certain critical remarks about Voegelin's pertinent concepts.

The first concept is usually formulated by Voegelin in the words, "The fact of theophany is its content." Theophany means, of course, a manifestation of God. The fact that God allows himself to be manifested would, one admits, be sufficient content of such an event. Still, I do not believe that the concept fits the theophany of Jesus Christ. There is a whole story of his life and death, defined in terms of time, place, situation, words, and action. It is true that Jesus dwelt, again and again, on the truth that the Father had sent him and that he was doing the Father's will, as the central meaning of his incarnation. But Jesus's life and especially his death, go beyond what would be a pattern "fitting" any conceivable number of "sons of God." Jesus said to his disciples that his blood would be shed "for you and for many, for the forgiveness of sins." This is a content of his incarnation beyond the mere manifestation of God. Furthermore, Voegelin applies to the story the formula of a "saving tale," derived from Plato. Jesus's story, however, culminates in a saving deed, rather than in a tale.

My other criticism is of the elimination of the Resurrection by reducing the resurrection experiences of the disciples to the type of Paul's vision (*Order and History*, vol. IV, *The Ecumenic Age*, p. 244). Voegelin slips this concept to us in the form of a clause which says, "Paul, who knew something about visions, classified (those of the disciples) as of the same type as his own." Two relevant passages in the *Acts of the Apostles* indicate that he did nothing of the kind. When Paul, as a prisoner, had a conversation with Agrippa, he said: "Therefore, King Agrippa, I was not disobedient to the heavenly vision" (AA 26:19). On the other hand, Peter, in his first sermon on the Day of Pentecost, put it differently: "This Jesus God raised up, of which we are all witnesses" (AA 2:32). Being "witness" and "loyal to a heavenly vision" are not different ways of speaking of the same kind of experience.

Finally, I should like to return to a point passed over quickly: what did Voegelin mean when, in the analysis of Parmenides, he spoke of "Doxa as Revelation"? "Doxa" here refers to the second part of Parmenides's vision, where he is dealing with "delusions" incompatible with is own experience of "Is!" The delusions turn out to be Parmenides's own cosmology, including the pantheon of gods. Voegelin comments on the vision itself that "being cannot reveal itself but must be revealed by a goddess." He finds this particular revelation having a peculiar structure: "it has neither soul, nor will, nor creative power" (*Order and History*, vol. II, p. 218). Plato, in his late myth in the Timaeus, fills one of the gaps left by Parmenides in that he supplies the figure of the demiurge, "the mediator between Being and the cosmos...expressing the incarnation of Being in the physical cosmos...but also in the order of society and history" (*loc. cit.* p. 117). Then Voegelin meditates on the further developments that "would proceed in the direction beyond Plato," *viz.* "an expansion of the Doxa to include the revelatory sphere itself." And he adds: "This final step was taken, not within Hellenic philosophy, although its logic was immanent in its course, but only in the Hebrew-Christian revelation" (*loc. cit.*, p. 218).

In difficult yet precise language, Voegelin here deals with the tension between faith and revelation. "Faith," he says, is the realm of "likeliness," where "the articulation of the experience (of the cosmos) can be more or less adequate, complete and consistent,...more or less true,...a specifically contingent truth as compared with the strict truth of the Logos," albeit still an articulation of truth. When this, called Doxa by Parmenides, had been included in Revelation, as in the Hebrew-Christian doctrine of Creation, the former Doxa had turned "into a Truth beyond the Truth and Delusion of Parmenides,...a higher Truth" (*ibid*). Revelation is a process occurring in the mind. A "higher truth" obviously calls for "a higher mind," compared with the mind concerned with finding a way over a mountain, or with figuring out the ingredients of a particularly tasty dish. It must be a mind excelling in collection, openness, and receptivity, in that it experiences "Revelation," in which God rather than man takes the initiative. Revelation must be preceded by theophany, since there can be no "cognition" of God as one never even dreamed of, but rather there can be only a re-cognition of a *realissimum* previously encountered. Although Revelation occurs in the mind, it may not take the form of language. Even if it does take that form, it may be of such brief duration as to keep the mind from repeating it afterwards. Finally, the "intellect," as Voegelin reminds us, "could take the offensive and substitute the truth of speculation for the truth of faith, as it has happened in the modern gnostic movements of Progressivism, Hegelianism, Comtism, and Marxism" (*loc. cit.* p. 219). Faith, in this further, and maybe final, meaning is the mode of the mind acknowledging the limits of its creatureliness and mortality. All this Voegelin sums up in one sentence when he speaks of philosophizing as *fides quaerens intellectum.*

Christian Faith, and Religion, in Eric Voegelin's Work

The gentle reader may be wondering whether there is a reason that the word "Christianity" is missing in this essay's title. There is, indeed. According to the Oxford English Dictionary, *Christianity* is a term used with several meanings: (1) the whole body of Christians; (2) the religion of Christ, the Christian faith; (3) the state or fact of being a Christian; (4) ecclesiastic jurisdiction. Since discussing Eric Voegelin's views on these and related realities demands that we distinguish and conceptualize with great philosophical discipline, we would do well to avoid such ambiguous notions. We begin, then, by noting that Voegelin's thoughts about Christian faith are separate from his position on Christian religion, or any organized religion, and we shall focus our attention first on the Christian faith, in Voegelin's work. Moreover, for the purpose of this article, we are not focusing on all parts of Voegelin's work that deal with the nexus between faith and reason, or religion and philosophy. One can deal with these questions objectively. We are more interested with passages from which some inferences may be possible about Voegelin's own experiences, and beliefs, regarding Jesus Christ and his Church. Therefore, while fully acknowledging the great power of such texts as "The Gospel and Culture," "Immortality: Experience and Symbol," "Response to Professor Altizer's "A New History and a New but Ancient God,"[1] also "The Beginning and the Beyond: A Meditation on Truth,"[2] I shall concentrate on the three *loci classici* relevant to the problem of Voegelin's subjective beliefs: Voegelin's letter to Alfred Schuetz of September 1943; Voegelin's letter to Alfred Schuetz of January 1953 (together with the letter from Schuetz of November 1952, to which this is Voegelin's response); and the final paragraph of *Israel and Revelation (*volume I., *Order and History).* The later essays, "Immortality," and "The Gospel and Culture" contain no new texts relevant to our question.

The September 1943 letter to Schuetz is found in the German version[3] while the American version[4] has a chapter, "Remembrance of Things Past" that was specially written for this book. Here Voegelin mentions his motives at the time of the letters:

> The answer I attempted in 1943 emerged from long years of occupation with Husserl's phenomenology, and equally long years of discussion with Alfred Schuetz about its merits and limitations.... Our discussions came to a head when, in the summer of 1943, I was at last able to obtain a copy of Husserl's *Krise der Europaeischen Wissenschaften....* In this essay, Husserl elaborated on the motivations of his own work by placing it in the context of a philosophical history. In his conception, the history of man's reason had three phases: (1) a prehistory, of no particular interest to the philosopher, ending with the Greek foundation of philosophy; (2) a phase beginning with the Greek *Urstiftung,* the primordial foundation of philosophy, that was interrupted by the Christian thinkers but then renewed by Descartes, and reached up to Husserl; and (3) a last phase, beginning with the *apodiktische Anfang,* the 'apodictic beginning' set by his own work, and going on forever into the future within the 'horizon of apodictic continuation' of his phenomenology.... I was horrified because I could not help recognizing the all-too familiar type of phase construction

in which had indulged the Enlightenment philosophers and after them, Comte, Hegel, and Marx...with
the purpose of abolishing a 'past history' of mankind
and letting the 'true history' begin with the respective
author's own work. I had to recognize it as one of the
violently restrictive visions of existence that, on the
level of pragmatic action, surrounded me from all
sides...in the form of Communism, National Socialism, Fascism, and the Second World War.

Voegelin's decision is put separately, in a two-sentence paragraph: "Something had to be done. I had to get out of that
'apodictic horizon' as fast as possible."[5]

The problem, here, is *history*. Voegelin's letter of September
1943 was his first step of the "getting out" he mentions above. He
dwells on the manhandling of history: "(Husserl's) relevant
history of mankind consists of the Greek antiquity and the
modern time since the Renaissance. Hellenism, Christendom,
the Middle Ages—an unimportant period of more than two
thousand years are a superfluous interlude; the Indians and the
Chinese (Husserl puts them in quotation marks) are a slightly
ridiculous curio at the periphery of the earth-disk, in the center
of which stands Western man—man as such."[6] Here we have one
of the two or three powerful motives for Voegelin's philosophy
of order: his sarcastic language indicates blazing anger at a view
that excludes from the history of the human mind more than two
thousand years as if they had never happened. That period
embraced such men as Dionysius the Areopagite, John Scotus
Erigena, Anselm of Canterbury, Siger of Brabant, Thomas
Aquinas. In his work Voegelin did indeed bring these men, their
historical period and their thought, to our attention.

In that same letter, however, he begins this endeavor by
showing that Descartes, Husserl's *Urstifter,* the primordial founder
of philosophical newness, or new philosophy, had some of his
roots in the Christian Middle Ages.

'The meditation of Descartes,' he said, 'is not as

staggeringly new as Husserl believes. Descartes's meditation is in principle a Christian meditation in the traditional style; one can even classify it more precisely as a meditation of the Augustinian type, as it has been conducted hundreds of times in the history of the Christian spirit since Augustine. The anonymous author of the *Cloud of Unknowing* has formulated the classical theme of meditation as well as any other thinker: 'It is needful for thee to bury in a cloud of forgetting all creatures that intent to God ever God made, that thou mayest direct thine intent to God Himself.' The annihilation of the world's content *per gradus* from the bodily world to the soul's and so to attain the point of transcendence at which the soul, in Augustine's words, can turn its *intentio* to God,—that is the purpose of meditation."[7]

He adds later: "In the transcendence of the Augustinian *intentio* the I is certain of God and of itself (not in a dogmatic sense, but in the mystical sense of transcendence into the ground)."[8] Similarly Voegelin, in the *New Science of Politics* (1952), shows that not only Descartes but also Hobbes wanted to be a Christian thinker:

'Into this somewhat empty vessel of a political society Hobbes pours the Western-Christian civilizational content by letting it pass through the bottleneck of sanction by the sovereign representative.' He speaks of Hobbes' 'intention of establishing Christianity...as an English *theologia civilis* in the Varronic sense.' The attempt is flawed, though: 'When (Hobbes) treats Christianity under the aspect of its substantial identity with the dictate of reason, he shows himself as oddly insensitive to its meaning as a truth of the soul as were the Patres to the meaning of the Roman gods as a truth of society.'[9]

Eric Voegelin has not left any autobiographical statements about his religious faith. We can therefore do no better than to examine his language, as he deals in general with Christian religion. In the above texts, he:

(a) corrects Husserl by pointing out that Descartes's (Third) Meditation is a classical example of a Christian meditation.

(b) quotes, with strong approval, the *Cloud of Unknowing, a* fourteenth-century work by an unknown author which is the probably most eminent text of Christian mysticism.

(c) acclaims the ideas of St. Augustine, the highest ranking Christian thinker of antiquity.

(d) uses a spiritual and a philosophical concept bespeaking a close relation between man and God when he speaks of the human 'certainty of God and of itself (not in a dogmatic sense but in the mystical sense of transcendence into the ground of being).'

(e) calls Christian faith "a truth of the soul."

This is Christian language, and the only thing that keeps us from attributing Christian faith to Voegelin's works is that at no point does he use such language in an autobiographical context. Is one not moved to the conclusion that the author of these remarks, if he is not himself a Christian, is at any rate no despiser of Christian belief, as were the protagonists of the Enlightenment? Later, in volume IV of *Order and History*, Voegelin begins to speak of "the Beginning" and "the Beyond" as the dimensions of non-thingly reality (in contrast to the cosmos), and insists, in this context, that the myth is the only symbol available to man when he needs to speak about experiences of divine presence. So necessary is then the myth that to destroy a myth should be considered a criminal activity.

These insights into experiences of divine presence, and the human countermovement they require, must be borne in mind as we turn to Voegelin's letter to Schuetz of January 1953.[10] In 1952, Voegelin's *New Science of Politics* was published. Schuetz's reaction was wholly negative: I thought that you merely wanted to trace the immanent evolution of the transformation into immanence within Christian philosophy and from the Christian viewpoint. But further reading showed me—perhaps mistakenly-that you take your stand wholly on Christian doctrine."[11] Schuetz's objection then probes even deeper: "(In the New Science) it is clearly stated that the origin of gnosticism finds its explanation in the vacuum that Christianity, in the course of dedivinization, created by eliminating civil theology.... You then say that gnostic experiment in civil theology is fraught with various dangers. The first is the tendency of gnosticism to replace, rather than complement, the truth of the soul. When gnosticism became openly anti-Christian, the truth of the open soul was destroyed wherever gnostic movements spread.... Here I simply cannot follow you. Why should not a gnostic philosophy make possible an open soul and access to the existential truth?... Why there cannot be, or have been, a metaphysics that preserves the open soul even without Christian eschatology?"[12]

Voegelin replied: "Essentially my concern with Christianity has no religious grounds at all." Here he seems to say, "but I am not a Christian!" As for his work, he continues to point to the "impossible" omission "of the 1500 years of Christian thought and Christian politics" in historiography and philosophy. "Whatever one may think of Christianity, it cannot be treated as negligible." Then Voegelin enumerates three "very significant achievements which should not be neglected." And this philosopher, who has just remonstrated that his work "has no religious grounds," takes several pages to praise, in the most concrete detail, "Christology," the "Trinity," and "Mariology," clearly the centermost Christian dogmas. One should bear in mind that Voegelin's distaste for dogma has been stated often and with vigor. One cannot help feeling that a strong personal conviction has manifested itself here.

The next item, in Voegelin's mind, anno 1943, is the problem of the myth. Again, Voegelin's anger was excited by the modern tendency to read Plato without Plato's "deliberate myths." He moves into the problem through the chapter "On the Theory of Consciousness" which he wrote soon after the September letter.

> Since processes transcending consciousness are not experienceable from within and since for purposes of characterizing their structures we have no other symbols available than those developed on the occasion of other finite experiences, there result conflicts of expression. These are, if not the only one, still the most important root of the formation of myths. A mythical symbol is a finite symbol supposed to provide 'transparence' for a transfinite process. Examples: a myth of creation, which renders transparent the problem of the beginning of a transfinite process of the world; an immaculate conception, which mediates the experience of a transfinite spiritual beginning, an anthropomorphic image of God, which finitizes an experience of transcendence; speculations about the preexistence or post-existence of the soul, which provide a finite formula for the beyond of birth and death; the fall and original sin, which illuminate the mystery of finite existence through procreation and death, and so on.[13]

In other words, the areas of non-thingly reality which Voegelin mentions can be intellectually ordered only by myths, but these myths have a decidedly rational function in that they provide an acceptable order through views of ultimate realities, which in turn makes possible rational thought on realities of nature and society.

None of the quoted passages from Voegelin's works amounts to a confession of Christian faith on the part of Eric Voegelin. Yet, if one remembers that these are scholarly texts (even the letters) one must be profoundly astonished at the inner freedom with which Voegelin can speak of God and Christian dogmas.

Let us remember the type of statements which for more than a century have defined the attitude of scholars toward such realities: "No intelligent man in this age of the world will for a moment maintain that there is any truth in Christianity"; "The attitude of the college, toward the modern spirit of inquiry, proposes to be guided by reason rather than by faith"; "It is all a 'mere prejudice,' so we might as well rid ourselves of prejudice as of religion." (I take the quotations, which are fully representative, from an article in *First Things*.[14]) Against this general background, Voegelin's manner of speaking about Christianity sounds almost like a Christian sermon. All the same, it is no personal confession of faith. If it were that, it would look out of place in a scholarly work and have had no effect whatever on contemporary scholarship. What is does convey is Voegelin's denial of a hostile quarrel between faith and reason. Christian dogmas are myths but so is a concept of the "I." Consciousness is capable of transcending itself and nature, and concepts regarding "the transcendence" are needed for the fundamental "certainties" which undergird judgments about immediate and concrete realities.

There does seem to be a restless curiosity regarding Voegelin's personal faith which is likely to obscure a full awareness of Voegelin's enormous achievement in having restored to science the ability rationally to look on God, myths, and dogmas of faith. The great letters between Schuetz and Voegelin obviously are based on the assumptions of scholarly search and findings, the limit of which bars such content and form as would be germane to a sermon. Thus, if Voegelin, particularly in the 1953 letter to Schuetz, appears to treat Christian faith with the full understanding of one who shares it, one may at times wonder whether professional detachment has not put any permanent obstacles in the way of faith. One should remember Goethe who, without being a Christian, could say: "Let the natural sciences grow in ever wider expansion and profundity, and the human mind enlarge itself as much as it wants, it will never get any higher than the loftiness and ethical culture of Christianity, as it glistens and shines in the Gospels!"[15]

The last paragraph of *Israel and Revelation*, however, looks somewhat different in this respect. Its relevant part reads as follows:

> A prayer of such intenseness as the *Nunc dimittis* of Luke 2:29-34 cannot be explained as literary reminiscence; it belongs to the tradition of the Deutero-Isaiah. And the preoccupation with the problem of the Suffering Servant is attested by the story of Acts 8: The Ethiopian eunuch of the queen, sitting on his cart and reading Isaiah, ponders on the passage: "Like a sheep he was led away to the slaughter." He inquires of Philip: "Tell me, of whom is the prophet speaking? of himself, or of someone else?" Then Philip began, reports the historian of the Apostles, and starting from this passage he told him the good news about Jesus."[16]

Voegelin, habitually, used the King James version of the translated Bible. When we check there the "History of the Apostles," we find these words: "Then Philip opened his mouth, and beginning at this Scripture, preached Jesus to him" (Acts 8: 35). Should we conclude then that "the good news" was Voegelin's own initiative, or that he, at this point, was working with a different translation? Both are possible. If the former should be the truth, we would have here another manifestation-which, indeed, would be a very important one-of Voegelin's own feelings. One might then be inclined to ask: "Of whom does Voegelin speak, of himself or of some other man?"

We have covered the three areas in Voegelin's work which I have characterized as *loci classici* regarding the topic of the Christian faith in Voegelin's writings. Volume four of *Order and History*, however, contains Voegelin's treatment of the Fourth Gospel (in the "Introduction"), and the Letters of St. Paul, in chapter five. We must briefly look at these passages, for volume four (The Ecumenic Age) occupies a place of its own, prominent not only among the five volumes but among all other books of Voegelin. The "Introduction" is a fifty-eight page essay that essentially corrects all hitherto conceived views of the history of philosophy, including that of Eric Voegelin himself. It covers the vast stretch of time from the beginning of the Persian Empire until the end of the Roman Empire, a period of imperial conquest and the syncretistic spirituality that developed under its political pressures. Voegelin has characterized it as a period in which the awareness of divine order generally contracted into personal experience, while the creator-god evolved into the redeemer-god. If we have not dealt with these passages before, it is because Voegelin's emphasis here is more on his own theoretical concepts than on the content of the Christian faith. He has named this entire process "the loss of balance between the Beginning and the Beyond."

Voegelin clearly saw the difficulties emerging from this development, since "there is no language in the abstract by which men can refer to the hierophanic events of the noetic and pneumatic differentiations, but only the concrete language created in the articulation of the event." The mystic experiences are the real core, the language articulating the experiences must be taken at face value; the difficulties begin with the creation of language to meet other needs, either those of institutionalized religion, or those of a political whole. The difficulties left their permanent results in history: "A new intellectual game with imaginary realities in an imaginary realm of thought, the game of propositional metaphysics, has been opened with world-historic consequences that reach into our own present."

Among other consequences was the creation of the term *religio* by Cicero, also the "further development of Scripture, as when (Israel) superimposed the word of Scripture over the word of god." Voegelin is fully aware that this superimposition was practically needed for protection "against the pressure of competing wisdom in the multi-civilizational society." The undesired legacy, however, is, in Voegelin's eyes, "the separation of symbol from the concrete experience of God (which) can degenerate into a word of man that one can believe or not." Finally, Voegelin notes "the expansion of the Word from the immediate experience of the Beyond to the mediated experience of the Beginning," through which, Voegelin observes, there could, and did, develop a misunderstanding of man's "imaginative ability...as a power to bring the Beginning under the control of consciousness."

In these brief remarks about the character of Voegelin's great "Introduction" to volume four one can discern Voegelin's acknowledgment of the experience of God and its inevitable link with rational reasoning. One feels that Voegelin understands because he shares this experience. It is the sharing, by one present mystic, of the experiences of other mystics. It is the awareness of the reality of God's presence, in variegated forms, across centuries and millennia. It is the emphasis, by a mystic philosopher of today, of the full height and width of the reality human consciousness has tried to comprehend. This is all that can be said about Voegelin's faith, in the context of the "Introduction" to *The Ecumenic Age*. If this strikes the gentle reader as too abstract, let him acknowledge that Voegelin, at no time and no place, has ever critically diminished the full reality of Jesus Christ.

There is, besides the Introduction, another place in volume four of *Order and History*, where Voegelin deals with Christianity: chapter five, "The Pauline Vision of the Resurrected." It so happens that I wrote an extensive critique of volume four,[17] of which the part dealing with chapter five, has been widely reproduced. Even though my criticism, were it written today, would be somewhat milder, I shall simply reproduce the 1976 text:

> The treatment strikes me as unsatisfactory on a number of counts. The title is misleading, since 'the vision' is the entire 'speculation' of St. Paul as analyzed by

Voegelin, leaving out of consideration the single, brief vision on the road to Damascus which was Paul's encounter with the person of Jesus Christ.... Apart from the problems of 'the historical Jesus,' the facticity of Jesus himself separates Christian theology as a type from all myths and philosophical speculations. Since Voegelin points out that Plato's myth was an *alethinos* logos, a true story, he should have allowed a special category also for St. Paul's story.... Christianity...was born from spiritual amazement about a particular person Jesus, his deeds, teachings, and such claims as that men in order to gain their lives must lose them for his sake, that it will be he whom men will face in the ultimate judgments, that there will be a new covenant with God in his blood, that he would die to free humanity from sin, that he alone had full knowledge of the Father. Christian theology, then stems...from the question which Jesus himself put: 'Who do you say I am?'...Voegelin allows that Paul shows that man is a creature in whom God can incarnate himself. St. Paul, however, reflects on what it means that God did incarnate himself in one particular man at one particular time. His speculations are about the consequences of this 'mighty deed' of God, not about the processes of consciousness, which is why general speculations and myths about 'Heaven and Earth' are assimilable to Christian dogma, but the reverse is not true.

This may be the proper place for some personal episodes which would not be mentioned if Eric Voegelin's language on these occasions might not possibly throw some light on the question of this article. When the above quoted critique of volume IV appeared, an American professor and friend of Voegelin's attacked me, in Voegelin's presence. Voegelin rejected his sharp words, saying: "Let it be; this is a personal problem." Could Voegelin have meant that his personal problem was an inability to embrace the Christian faith with a personal surrender? Furthermore when I, four years later, was ordained a priest in the Episcopal Church, Voegelin called me and congratulated me with some remarks among which the word, "admiration," was particularly striking. If he "admired" my ordination would that not be the reaction of someone who recognizes that he, personally, could not have taken such a step? Finally, ever since I got to know Voegelin, in 1947, I have heard him speak of himself as "a Christian," later with the qualification, "a pre-Reformation Christian," and still later, as a "pre-Nicaean Christian." The meaning of "pre-Reformation Christian" is clear. "Pre-Nicaean" can only be a Christian of the age in which great dogmas were evolved without the action of any church council. This last qualification expresses Voegelin's uneasiness about "propositional metaphysics," and "propositional theology." Human knowledge of things can, and must be put in the form of propositions. Regarding that reality which consists not of things, however, insights stem from inner-based experiences and can be represented only by language the experience itself has generated or, otherwise, by a kind of myth assimilable to other symbols of faith and knowledge. The temptation to mistake such insight for a proposition about things must be strongly resisted.

Let us now see to what conclusions the above findings may justifiably lead us. First, "the problem of God" does not seem to Voegelin to be more-or-less of a problem than the reality of one's neighbor. The divine reality as such neither requires nor is comprehensible though analytical argument: "Drawing on Israelite, Christian, and Hellenic sources, the symbolization of the structure can be concentrated in the formula: The divine reality, the theotes of Colossians 2:9—that moves man's consciousness from the Beyond of all cosmic contents, from the *epekeina* in Plato's sense-also creates and sustains the cosmos from its Beginning, from the *bereshit* in the sense of Genesis 1:1."[18] In other words, not the reality as such but rather the symbolization of the reality contains difficulties. Attention is drawn to the fact that this reality is not subject to discovery, or verification by the senses, like things are. It is a matter of inner *experience*. If not by all, the experience by some has found acceptance as epiphany by the many. "In this [i.e., the Israelite background] environment, the primary experience of the cosmos has been shaken at an early date by Moses' experience and symbolization of divine reality as the 'I am' of the Thornbush Episode. The experience brings the deeper stratum of divine reality, its absolute Being, into imme- diate view."[19] This reality content of the inner experience also applies to Christian faith: "The god who spoke to Moses in the Thornbush now speaks through the mouth of man to other men.... The 'I am' in Jesus, on the other hand, reveals itself as the living presence of the word in a man... (it will) for every man who responds to its appeal, dissolve the darkness and absurdity of existence into the luminous consciousness of participating in the divine word."[20] Voegelin puts himself into sharp contrast with so many contemporary philosophers or historians who seek to put Christianity on the same plane as other great religions by not mentioning Jesus as the core of Christian faith. Even here does Voegelin not mean to say: "I believe." Yet, in all his work he has not with such deep and correct understanding presented the substance of any other religion. One should also insist that here, as in all other similar passages, there is no trace of a nominalistic, psychoanalytical, or sociological explanation of this, or other spiritual phenomena, in Voegelin.

Nor does he leave the matter as a series of historical phenom- ena of which each may be as good as any other. In other words, there is spiritual truth, even though it cannot be something found attained by measurement or experiment. Light on this problem can be found in philosophy as well as in religion: "(Plato) is aware of the limits set to the philosopher's exploration of reality by the divine mystery of the noetic height and the apeirontic depth. Since the philosopher cannot transcend these limits but has to move in the In-Between...the meaning of his work depends on an ambiance of insight concerning the divine presence and operation in the cosmos that only the myth can provide. Plato's answer to the predicament is the creation of the *alethinos logos,* the story of the gods that can claim to be true if it fits the cognitive consciousness of order created in the soul of man by the erotic tension toward the divine Beyond."[21] Voegelin's insight here is cast in the form of his own concepts, of which one can only say, "why have they been missing for so long?" The first one, the "In-Between," of course stems from Plato's *Symposium,* but no thinker before Voegelin has tried to give it common coinage. "In-Between" is certainly the character of human existence where it is matter of spiritual experience, and awareness of this fact will then justify of truth as "the myth." Clearly, Voegelin sees such symbols of reason and faith as a continuum. Again, there are myths conveying truth, and there are other myths, for example, the Nazi myth of race as the key to human character. The criterion of mythical truth is provided by a consciousness filled with the loving tension toward God. Who, understanding this Platonic formula, could reject it by the argument that it did not come from the Bible? Possibly one might object that "the loving tension toward God" is an inner phenomenon that cannot be tested by other people. But Voegelin provides also an outside criterion present in public soul life: "The immediate presence of the movements in the In-Between requires the revelatory language of consciousness. This is the language of seeking, searching and questioning, of ignorance and knowledge concerning the divine ground, of fertility, absurdity, anxiety, and alienation of existences, of being moved to see and question, of being drawn toward the ground, of turning around, illumination, and re-birth."[22]   In other words, the experiences and the language of symbolization alike are right if both fit the "In-Between" situation of man.   Any language that ignores this condition, as it trumpets certainties and denies ignorance and conversion, cannot be a voice from the "In-Between" human soul.

Those who still, at this point, are impatiently waiting for a judgment on Voegelin's personal confession of faith should be sent to the four o'clock session of tattling and gossiping, where they will undoubtedly hear something that for a time will satisfy their idle curiosity.

NOTES

1. See *The Collected Works of Eric Voegelin,* vol. 12, *Published Essays, 19661985,* ed. Ellis Sandoz (Baton Rouge: Louisiana State University Press, 1990).

2. *Collected Works of Eric Voegelin, vol.28, What Is History? and Other Late Unpublished Writings,* ed. Thomas A. Hollweck and Paul Carhigella (Baton Rouge: Louisiana State University Press, 1990), pp. 173-232.

3. *Anamnesis: Zur Theorie der Geschichte und Politik* (Munich: R. Piper, 1966).

4. *Anamnesis,* trans. and ed. Gerhart Niemeyer (Columbia, MO: University of Missouri Press, 1990)

5. *Anamnesis* (English), pp.9-10.

6. *Ananamnesis* (German), p. 22

7. *Ibid.,* p. 33

8. *Ibid.* p. 35

9. *The New Science of Politics* (Chicago: University of Chicago Press, 1952), pp. 154-56.

10. "On Christianity," in *The Philosophy of order: Essays on History, Consciousness, and Politics,* ed. Peter J. Opitz and Gregor Sebba (Stuttgart: Klett-Cotta, 1981),1981, pp. 449-57.

11. Alfred Schuetz to Eric Voegelin, November 1952, *ibid.,* p. 443.

12. *Ibid.,* p. 446.

13. *Anamnesis* (English), p. 21 f.

14. George M. Marsden "God and Man at Yale (1880)," *First Things* 42 (April 1994), 39-42.

15. *Eckermann's Conversations with Goethe,* trans. R. 0. Moon (London: Morgan, Laird and Company, Ltd., 1950), 11 March 1832, p. 615.

16. *Order and History, vol. 1, Israel and Revelation* (Baton Rouge: Louisiana State University Press, 1956), p. 515.

17 "Eric Voegelin's Philosophy and the Drama of Mankind," *Modern Age* 22 (1976): 22-39.

18. *Order and History,* vol. IV, *The Ecumenic Age* (Baton Rouge: Louisiana State University Press, 1974), p. 9.

19. *Ibid.,* p. 12.

20. *Ibid.,* p. 14.

21. *Ibid., p.* 11.

22. *Ibid.,* pp. 17-18.

God and Man,
World and Society:
The Last Work of Eric Voegelin

Voegelin's magnum opus (*Order and History*) was concluded with volume five, a slim book of only two chapters (*In Search of Order* [Baton Rouge: Louisiana State University Press, 1987. Pp. 120.]). The original plan called for six volumes, of which three were published in 1956-57. The fourth was to be on "Empire and Christianity." Instead, volume four, titled *The Ecumenical Age* and published in 1974, took a direction other than announced. Between it and volume five, a number of great and important essays were written: "Equivalences of Experience and Symbolization in History," "The Beginning and the Beyond," "Wisdom and the Magic of the Extreme." That last volume of *Order and History* cannot be fully appreciated and understood without taking into account what Voegelin said in volume four as well as in these great essays, two of which bear the subtitle, "Meditation."

How far back must one go to understand Voegelin's work as a whole? A number of Voegelin's books were published in German before Voegelin came to this country. There is a monumental, as yet unpublished, history of political ideas which was all but completed when, around 1948, he decided that accounting for the succession of ideas was a less-worthy enterprise than another one, which he announced with the *Programmschrift, The New Science of Politics* (1952). This study's first fruits were those first three volumes of *Order and History*.

The next book, however, was not volume four, but *Anamnesis*(in German, 1966) which, as the title indicated, focused chiefly on problems of consciousness. Volume four did not appear until 1974, not only dealing with materials other than one would have expected from the originally announced title, but also breaking with Voegelin's concept of history that prevailed in volumes one, two and three. By "Ecumenical Empires" Voegelin meant the enormous varieties of different faiths, gods, cultures, gathered under a single ruler, from 550 B.C. to 547 A.D. They were characterized by novel problems of self-understanding, not only on the side of the rulers but also on that of the conquered communities, peculiar problems of consciousness of "exodus" and alienation. Voegelin let it be known then that volume five would be the last one of the series. There was much speculation of what is might contain, and one expected that most of the important essays then published would be gathered in the concluding volume. Voegelin himself did consider this possibility but eventually decided against it. Instead, in the last three years of his life, he wrote the two chapters which now make up volume five, and of which he said that they were "the key to all his other works" (*In Search of Order*, Foreword by Lissy Voegelin). During the last ten or so days of his life, having returned home from the hospital, Voegelin still wrote an essay published in the *Journal of the American Academy of Religion* (53: 569-84): "*Quod Deus Dicitur*," which proves that to the very end he was in full power of creative work. One cannot assume, therefore, that he failed to add more chapters, or more materials, to the two already written, "The Beginning of the Beginning," and "Reflective Distance vs. Reflective Identity," from sheer weakness. Again and again he insisted, "This will be Volume V." We must then look on this last brief book as the completing movement of a truly astonishing effort of mind, soul, and spirit by which Voegelin has restored to the science of human order adequate concepts of God, man, history, and consciousness.

Ask not, "what is Voegelin's philosophy?", meaning, "what is Voegelin's philosophical system?" Philosophers's "systems" in modern times have been one of the chief causes of man's loss of reality, as bodies of abstract propositions were mistaken for reality itself. Voegelin eschewed both abstract propositions and closed systems. He bade us recapture "wonderment" about the cosmos, the human mind, and the Beyond not by means of speculation but by looking in the works of great mystic philosophers. Textbooks about them were useless as they treated these works as mere past phenomena, belonging to the "history of ideas." Voegelin approached them, not as "contributions" to later thought but as events past but still present, belonging to kindred events in our time and others still to come. Voegelin, in other words, took his departure not from abstractions but from concretenesses, which is why, again and again, he spoke of his methods as "empirical." He proceeded in terms of what he could find, as whatever time and whatever place, letting the story emerge from the writings. In fact, the writings yielded two versions of a story: one of a human person finding himself being "drawn," "pulled," or "compelled" by a divine Beyond and thereby "converted," meaning "turned around" from nearsightedness to farsightedness, from "opinion" to "truth," from "darkness" to "light." Such experiences created a cleavage between "before" and "after," and thus an experience of history. In these kind of experiences Voegelin found the sources of human order, so that he could coin the governing principle: "The order of history is the history of order."

Still a mere catalogue of such events could never add up to an "order of history." Voegelin's comments, though always deferring to the texts, provide the perspective of coherence. He points out "constants" whenever they appear. "Cosmogony" is one such constant which will keep popping up with a variety of contents. Another is "historio-genesis," the insistence on tracing one's people, dynasty, even savior, to the beginning, the root of ultimate authority. A third constant is "the question," or as Aristotle related, "every man's" desire to know. From Plato Voegelin takes the constant of the "in-between" (*metaxy*), in which occurs the interplay between God and man, since it is neither existent nor nonexistent. Another constant is the "tension toward God,"—still another the paradox of consciousness. The reader who may find himself bewildered by the multitude of texts, sometimes of authors unheard of before, does well to pay close attention to these concepts, for here is the structure of Voegelin's vision. It is a vision of the "constitution of being," and the "essence of existing things" by mystic philosophers experiencing the "constitution" of their own existence in the appeal and response between the divine Beyond and the questioning human mind. This relation they called *ratio*, wisdom, truth. Voegelin's close analysis of these processes has made possible the discernment, among concepts and symbols, of admissible and inadmissible ways of conceiving "reality" and "order," without drawing the criteria of admissibility from anything like a dogmatic orthodoxy.

Because of Voegelin's insistence to work not with his own abstractions but with the experiences underlying the great philosophic texts, he has been called a Platonist, an Aristotelian, a Neo-Platonist, and a Hegelian. It is true that his discovery of Plato's noetic meditation was what made him discontinue his universal history of ideas and begin his search for the "history of order," and that he turned to Plato again and again, until the second chapter of volume five. Still, he also turned to Aristotle, as well as to Hegel. In all three cases, however, he went beyond what he found and carried the quest into regions and depths not found in the original. In the case of Hegel, his admiration was offset by his profound rejection of Hegel's "reflective identity" and "imaginative oblivion"—the chief example of inadmissible "games played with the concept of being." No such fault could be traced to Plato who remained for him a living past speaking truth to a living present, which, however, does not make Voegelin a Platonist. Still, the story begins with Plato's *Republic*, with the myth of men in darkness, chained to a rocky wall while observing shadows of things passing by above, in an otherwise unseen light. At one point, "one of them is set free and forced suddenly to stand up, turn his head and walk with eyes lifted to the light," eventually "someone would drag him up forcefully the steep and rugged ascent until he had hauled him into the sunlight...." The form of the myth which Plato uses here makes clear that the process of truth is initiated and carried through not by the philosopher himself but by "someone" who forces and drags him until he is face-to-face with reality. On what occasions does Plato use other myths? When speaking of everything: all topics transcending the imagery fashioned from the sense experience of things in this world.

Commenting on Plato's myths, Voegelin says: "Man is not a self-created, autonomous being...he is not a divine *causa sui*; from the experience of his life in precarious existence between birth and death there rather rises the wondering question about the ultimate ground....The question is inherent in the experience from which it rises; the *zoon noun echon* that experiences itself as a living being is at the same time conscious of the questionable character attaching to this status. Man, when he experiences himself as existent, discovers his specific humanity as that of the questioner for the where-from and the where-to, for the ground and the sense of his existence" (*Anamnesis*, English translation, 1978, p. 92). Voegelin points to the wealth of symbols, describing the state of unrest, the quest, and its results: "wondering *thaumazein*; seeking, searching *zetein*; search *zetesis*; questioning *aporein, diaporein*." There is further, the pull (*helkein*) of reason and the counterpulls (*anthelkein*) of the passions. There is the realization that "the whole realm of the spiritual is halfway indeed between (*metaxy*) god and man.... Man exists in the tension between mortality and immortality, between the apeirontic depth and the noetic height. The *apeiron* and the *nous* reach into his *psyche* and he participates in them, but he is not identical with, or in control of, either the one or the other" (*ibid.*, p. 102).

As Voegelin thus comments, Plato strays further and further from the world of things and sense experience, as he has Socrates say: "In like manner you are to say that the objects of knowledge not only receive from the presence of the good their being known, but their very existence and essence is derived from it, though the good itself is not essence but still transcends essence in dignity and "surpassing power"—which makes Glaucon throw up his hands: "heaven save us, hyperbole can no further go!" and Socrates replies: "The fault is yours for compelling me to utter my thoughts about it" (*Republic* 509b). Or, in the *Phaedrus*, where Plato quotes Socrates: "But at such times as (the gods) go to their feasting and banquet, behold they climb the steep ascent even to the summit of the arch that supports the heavens (and they) stand upon the back of the world, and they look upon the regions without.... It is there that true being dwells, without color or shape, that cannot be touched; reason alone, the soul's pilot, can behold it, and all true knowledge is knowledge thereof..." (247c). Here is where Voegelin has found the text for his concept of *the Beyond*.

Let us now briefly look at a manuscript written in the middle of the 1970s to see what Voegelin has to say about the same topic: "I shall begin from the Beginning, from the cosmos as it impressed itself on man by the splendor of its existence, by the movement of the starry heavens, by the intelligibility of its order, and by its lasting as the habitat of man. The man who receives the impression, in his turn, is endowed with an intellect both questioning and imaginative. He can respond to the impression by recognizing the divine mystery of a reality in which he is a knowing partner, although it is not of his making. In this experience of the cosmos neither the impression nor the reception is dully factual. It rather is alive with the meaning of a spiritual event, for the impression is revelatory of the divine mystery, while the reception responds to the revelatory component by cognition of faith. This is the experience to which St. Paul refers in Romans 1:18-23, when he chides his contemporaries for not recognizing the truth of God revealed in the cosmos" ("The Beginning and Beyond"). Voegelin continues on the next page: "An experience that is structured in the manner just adumbrated cannot be adequately described in terms of object and subject, with reality playing the role of the object and man that of the subject of cognition. It rather is to be described as a process within reality that comprehends both the cosmos with its divine mystery and the man with his mind in which the mystery becomes cognitively luminous. Within that comprehensive reality, the experience is luminous to itself as a divine-human movement and countermovement, as a movement of revelatory appeal from the divine and a countermovement of apperceptive and imaginative response from the human side."

This latter comment by Voegelin is remarkable for the way in which he speaks of the philosopher's luminosity by way of "revelation," "faith," "appeal," and "response." We are enabled to see the Greek "discovery of the mind" as the mystic experience of the philosophers and the discovery of God beyond the cosmic gods, and beyond man's searching mind. This is the event of order in history: "When the meditation reaches the luminosity of self-reflection, the quest of the unknown god is enriched by the awareness of the hitherto unknown man who now discovers himself as the knower of the unknown" (*ibid.*, p. 50). The event, Voegelin adds, is unnecessarily obscured by the term "transcendence" when that word suggests a clean separation between two realities. "In the first place, there is no 'transcendent reality' other than the Beyond experienced in [the soul's] 'rise.' If it is torn out of the experiential context, it suffers the intentionalist reduction to an object in whose existence one can believe or not..." and also, "the experience becomes unrecognizable as an advance of the *cognito fidei* from the intra-cosmic *fides* to the *fides* of the Beyond." Voegelin insists that Plato "does not transcend the 'cosmos,' or the 'world' as if they were given objects, but engaged within reality in a movement that will let a compact, and therefore comparatively opaque, image of Being become transparent for the truth of the Beyond. As a cognitive event, the act is a man's exodus, in response to a divine appeal, from opaque to luminous Being...." The "here" is not separate reality from the "beyond," rather, "there is still the cosmos with the mystery of Becoming and Perishing, there are still gods and men, and there is still the world of matter, plants, animals, and artifacts, external to the body in which the consciousness of man is rooted.... Nevertheless, something has happened that affects the truth of the cosmological *fides*. For the noetic act has reflectively discovered itself as the response to an appeal from the immortal, and immortalizing, divine reality 'beyond the cosmos.'" This, second of two versions of a story mentioned above, I believe to be a statement one can understand as representing the core of Voegelin's work. Here is Voegelin's insistence on the concept of man as a being responding to God's appeal, of the human soul as that which can sense the appeal, and of the language symbols for this entire process. Man's order of existence flows from the luminosity thus gained, and all this without any need to attempt a formal "proof" of God's existence.

One may say that Voegelin gave us a new Plato and a new Aristotle, through his probing exegesis of the texts, probing for the underlying experiences. Voegelin is the modern philosopher of experience as the root of philosophic cognition. He himself has remarked that ever since Locke various thinkers have endeavored to bring experience once again into the purview of philosophy, but with little success, until Hegel. Hegel did, indeed, philosophize from the experience of transcendent reality, but he unfortunately also perverted it by "imaginative oblivion."

After Hegel, inner experience had been thoroughly psychologized, and philosophy had become sick unto death from the positivist virus. In that wasteland situation, Voegelin has shown how one can speak of mystical philosophic experience without preaching: he has led his reader's alongside Plato's spiritual journey, so that Plato has become, as it were, our contemporary, and we his. In the process, Voegelin has demonstrated the revelatory root of philosophy, to the extent of speaking of philosophy, religion, and myth as "equivalents," and of the problems of experience and its symbolic manifestation as "the problem of universal humanity." Voegelin sees the problem of God as the one dominating the reflective mind, and the enduring source of public order. By contrast, speculation on divinity apart from that inner experience leads to disorder; the mind is spurred by the lust for power instead of the desire for knowledge causes disorder; the mind that fences God into the limits of abstract propositions causes disorder; the mind fusing itself into a pretended identity with the divine causes disorder; the mind fancying itself to be "its own place" causes disorder. As Voegelin also restored the concept of the soul, he led us to the reality of "man," as well as to that relationship in which man's mind deserves the name of *ratio*, reason or wisdom.

Nor was this done in the manner of giving a lesson: "Why don't you look at Plato and see what *he* did?" Voegelin himself entered into the revelatory experiences of the past with his whole soul and then, on his own, continued the journey. That is why there is no "Voegelinian philosophy" as there was a Hobbesian, Kantian, Hegelian philosophy, all of these closed "systems" taking the place of living reality. Through him, philosophy received again the meaning that Plato conferred on it: It is a way of life rather than an accumulation of propositions. It is life in openness to reality, the life—as Bergson said—of the "open soul" capable of being filled with love for all that is, through the love of God.

In the last ten or fifteen years of his life, Voegelin gave increasing attention to the problem of consciousness as it deals with ineffable reality rather than with objects. Ever since Descartes, consciousness has been discussed by philosophers within a reduced horizon. Descartes saw himself as "a substance whose essence consists in thinking" and added that thinking is "entirely distinct of the body (and) would not cease to exist if there were no body." To this disembodied reality he had given the task of "reforming" its thoughts and to put them on a ground "that entirely belongs to me." From this ground consciousness appeared not only as utter subjectivity, but also as a sovereign subject dominating the world of bodies as its object. In the process, the external world itself was purged of everything that was not controllable by consciousness in the way mathematics is. From such premises there arose the open problems that drove modern philosophy to materialism, idealism, positivism and, ultimately, nihilism.

Having carefully worked out his differences with this tradition, in a critique of Max Weber and one of Husserl, Voegelin did not begin with epistemology which, he said, does not exhaust the scope of philosophy, and is neither an independent theme nor a sphere in which all other philosophical problems are rooted, in the sense that a "founding epistemology would amount to founding a philosophy" (*Anamnesis* [1966], p. 22). There can be no awareness of consciousness in the abstract, apart from concrete experiences and their linguistic articulation. Such historio-empirical observation, however, does not have the purpose of establishing one's own "precious position" as the culmination of history. The point is, rather, to penetrate the noetic formation of the great thinkers of the past to "its point of transcendence, with the end of training and clarifying one's own awareness of experienced transcendence." In this sense, historical comprehending description is "a catharsis, a '*purificatio*' of the mystical kind, with the aim of personal *illuminatio* and *unio mystica*.... In this way it can lead to a philosophy of history" (*ibid.*, p. 31).

Voegelin begins where Husserl had left off: "The positive starting point for the description of the structure of consciousness should be sought in the phenomenon of attention and the turning of attention to something. Consciousness seems to be a center of energy which can be directed to the various dimensions of consciousness in order to start processes of its constitution" (*ibid.*, p. 43). Accepting Husserl's accomplishments on "intention," Voegelin calls this "intentionality," the deliberate aim-taking of consciousness at an object. The object, of course, would be found in what we loosely call "reality," the complex of things, processes, forces, events, actions, strivings, and attractions of which our own existence is a part. "Intentionality" is the element of desire, purpose, or volition in the processes of consciousness. Now, to find this element in Voegelin's empirical materials, Plato mentioned two concrete forces his consciousness experienced: *zetein* and *helkein* (the first, questioning and searching; the second, being drawn or moved). Only the first of these can be strictly called "intentional," aiming at object. The experience of being drawn, by contrast, has the character of a mystery, and a mystery is not an object. Of these two forces Voegelin remarks that they are "neither speculative assumption, nor do they operate as a blind a priori"—in other words, they should not be thought of as quasi-mechanical constants.

The philosopher who experiences these forces is reflecting not only on objects and mysteries, but also on his own consciousness. In this respect he represents a higher level of conscious mind than the poetic myth-maker who precedes him in historical time. Plato's self-reflection also lead him to the conclusion that there is a problem of balance. For "neither must the desire to know reality as the intended object degenerate to an intentionalist desire to know the mystery of the horizon; nor must the consciousness of the omnipresent mystery thwart the desire to know by assuming objects this side of the horizon to belong to the

sphere of the mystery" ("Wisdom and the Magic of the Extreme," *Southern Review* 17:245). The self-reflection of consciousness thus recognized a tension and a requirement of
balance; this balance Voegelin calls the "third structure" of
consciousness, all three being constants.

In no area of his work has Voegelin produced as many
interpreting concepts as in the field of consciousness, and it is this
group of concepts that makes up his philosophy of consciousness.
The most important one is probably "the paradox of consciousness." On the one hand, consciousness is located in human
beings "in their bodily existence." In that respect one may say that
the subject is "being conscious of something," "thinking of
something," and so on, which is metaphorical language about
both reality and consciousness. Voegelin, as we have seen, calls
this structure "intentionality," and the corresponding structure
of reality, "thing-reality." But inasmuch as consciousness is real,
and thus part of a larger reality, reality is not so much an object
of consciousness but "something in which consciousness occurs"
(*In Search of Order*, p. 15). This latter way of perceiving consciousness, however, occurs in history only at the time when, at
least in some cases, a self-reflective human consciousness, finds
itself moved by the larger reality of which it is a part. That
occurrence is called "becoming luminous" for an otherwise
mysterious truth. Thus Voegelin notes, in consciousness, not
only intentionality but also luminosity. In the latter event,
consciousness discovers that it is participating in a reality in
which it has partners comprehended by that reality. By virtue of
this structure, consciousness belongs, "not to man in his bodily
existence, but to the reality in which man, the other partners in
the community of being, and the participatory relations among
them occur" (*ibid.*, p. 16). This "between"-structure Voegelin
calls, as we have seen, *metaxy.* He continues, "to denote the
reality that comprehends the partners in being, that is, God and
the world, man and society, no technical term has been devel-

oped." Following the habit by which we say, for example, "it rains," Voegelin proposes the name "It-reality," to distinguish it from the "thing-reality." Voegelin concludes: "Consciousness, then, is a subject intending reality as its object, but at the same time something in a comprehending reality; and reality is the object of consciousness, but at the same time the subject of which consciousness is to be predicated." What is more, language itself has the same paradoxical structure, containing terms referring to things to their concrete existence, and other words pointing to meanings in a wider sense. All of which—Voegelin calls in consciousness-reality-language—constitutes a single paradoxical structure within which we ask questions and search for answers.

What kind of questions? Well, the obvious ones which are also basic: the Beginning and the Beyond, wherefrom and whereto? They are questions both about Being and our way of living, as well as about the things around us, and "every man desires to know" about them, for no thinking being can live as a thinking being without such questions occurring to him. Voegelin's philosophy of consciousness has explored in precise detail the difficulties of this process. Foremost among them is the fact that the questions are asking, in the language pertaining to things, about a reality which does not have the character of object because we ourselves are part of it. We cannot use thing-related language but must realize that it pertains not to nonobjective reality. Thomas Aquinas was fully aware of this when insisting that our vocabulary of things can be no more than an analogy. Still, in our time, Husserl once more made "intention," that is, attention to thingly object—the one and only mode of consciousness—so that Voegelin's work must be called an important breakthrough in this field.

Two more concepts regarding consciousness should be mentioned: Imagination, and Reflective Distance. "Truth," Voegelin remarks, "is not, as the surface language suggests, a something lying around to be accepted, rejected, or resisted; imagining truth' as a thing would deform the structure of consciousness in the same manner as does transformation of the symbols 'reality' and 'Beyond' into things for purpose of manipulations....The symbols arise from the human response to the appeal of reality, and the response is burdened by its character as an event in the reality to which it responds." Of this event, Voegelin finds that it is "imaginative in the sense that man can find the way from his participatory experience of reality to its expression through symbols" (*ibid*, p. 37). Here, too, he discovers paradox: "Imagination...belongs both to human consciousness in its bodily location and to the reality that comprehends bodily located man as a partner in the community of being. There is no truth symbolized without man's imaginative power to find the symbols that will express his response to the appeal of reality; but there is no truth to be symbolized without the comprehending It-reality." Still, imagination is a kind of neutral force in this process, of which Voegelin says that it even offers imagining man "escapes," of a sort, from reality. His experience can be a creatively forming force, but it also can be deformed "if the creative partner imagines himself to be the sole creator of truth." Similarly, when "the reality that reveals itself in imaginative truth" is misread as a "truth that reveals reality," as did the Baccalaureus in Goethe's *Faust* who said: "The world, it was not before *I* created it." This kin of imaginative perversion "is not a mistake in a syllogism or a system, to be thrown out for good once it is discovered, but a potential in a paradoxic play of forces in reality as it moves toward its truth." In other words, imagination is assertive and can pervert to the point of self-assertiveness.

Finally: Reflective Distance. When introducing this concept, Voegelin lists the symbols with which he has so far worked: "The tension of the metaxy, the poles of the tension, the things and their Beyond, thing-reality and It-reality, the human and the divine, intentionality and luminosity, the paradox of consciousness-reality-language, and the complex of participation-asser-tion-selfassertion." This is a good point at which to stop and muse, remembering what precisely occurs in a consciousness as it begins to wonder at what has been going on within it, and within participation. Such wondering awareness of itself is the dimension of consciousness Voegelin calls "reflectively distanc-ing remembrance" (*ibid*, p. 41). Volume five here picks up the thread from "Mystery and the Magic of the Extreme": "The conception of truth as a growth of luminosity in the process of reality imposes respect on the thinker and the present; he must respect his past as much as he respects his present that will be past for a future present.... Plato was aware of the reflective distance between his existence as an event of participatory consciousness, and the exegesis of the event through the symbols he developed in his work.... I have therefore chosen the phrase 'reflective distance' as a technical term to denote Plato's awareness of the problem. It is meant to bring to conceptual clarity the difference between reality becoming reflectively luminous in consciousness and the collapse of reflective luminosity into self-reflective identity" (p. 260f). These quotations will make clear the meaning of the title Voegelin gave to the second chapter of volume five: "Reflective Distance vs. Reflective Identity," the first represent-ing Plato, the second, Hegel, whose "imaginative oblivion" Voegelin analyzes with unprecedented precision. Imaginative oblivion has power to wipe out of cultural existence the symbols of truth created by past thinkers and to nourish an illusion that one's own imaginative moves constitute an absolute beginning, in the form of "the new age," "the new world," of "the new man."

In his Introduction to volume five of *Order and History*, Ellis Sandoz recalls Voegelin having said to him: "From my first contact with such works as *The Cloud of Unknowing*, to my more recent understanding of the mystical problem...the great issue has been: not to stop at what may be called classical mysticism, but to restore the problem of the Metaxy for society and history

(p. 12). We have just briefly surveyed what Voegelin did in this regard, his philosophy of consciousness that is not spinning on itself but is "consciousness of something," and, using the words of Karl Barth, "the ultimate and decisive capacity for the *intellectus fidei* which does not belong to human reason acting on its own."

We have sought to convey the meaning of Voegelin's work by talking, first, on man's meditative response the divine appeal, and second, on the intricacies of Voegelin's philosophy of consciousness. By way of conclusion, let us look at his philosophy of history. There can be no question that, at first, Eric Voegelin saw history similarly to the Romantic thinkers, that is, as a unilinear movement. He differed from others, from the beginning, by seeing the order of history as a "history of order." Thus in the *New Science of Politics*, he speaks of a succession of truths in which human societies have understood themselves: first, cosmological truth, next, anthropological truth, and finally, soteriological truth (p. 77). Later in the book, he talks of a "civilizational cycle of world-historic proportions...transcending the cycle of the single civilizations. The acme of this cycle would be marked by the appearance of Christ; the pre-Christian high civilizations would form its ascending branch; the modern, Gnostic civilizations would form its descending path" (p. 164). In the first three volumes of *Order and History* he added the concept of "leaps in being," each leap marked by a spiritual outburst and a differentiation of what was previously a compact bundle of several elements of order. The first differentiations occurred during a period lasting altogether some five hundred years, when the Hebrew prophets, the first Greek philosophers, the Buddha, Confucius, Lao-tsu, and Zoroaster were living. What happened, then, in Israel was the differentiation of righteousness; in Greece, the differentiation of the soul and its noetic experiences.

There can be no question that in volume four of *Order and History* Voegelin broke with this idea, without, however, abandoning his leading principle, "The order of history is the history of order." As he pursued this principle into more and more cultures and civilizations, finding ever new historical materials, it became clear to him that these materials just would not permit their arrangement on any line, straight or crooked. What happened, and conveyed order to history, was man's response to the divine appeal in a great variety of manners but with the same universal meaning. Voegelin's emphasis shifted from the symbol of "leap" to the symbol of The Story. The story of Genesis, which he analyzes at the beginning of volume five, may serve as a representative example. No human being was present as an observer, yet it is a story written by a human being, or a group of them. It is not told in the first-person singular, nor in the third-person singular about a human being. So Voegelin can say, "The event of the quest is part of a story told by the It, and yet a story told by a human questioner, if he wants to articulate the consciousness of his quest as an act of participation in the comprehending story" (p. 24). In biblico-critical terms this is the "Beginning" of the Priestly document which also comprises the story of Israel, the Patriarchs, the monarchy and more, in other words, the history of man "continuing the creational process of order in reality." Continues Voegelin: "The story is the symbolic form the questioner has to adopt necessarily when he gives an account of his quest of wresting, by the response of his human search to a divine movement, the truth of reality from a reality pregnant with truth but not yet revealed." The experience itself is common to humans who are in any way sensitive to wonderment with this world, its forms, energies, beauties, and varieties of things, all of which looks as if it wanted to convey to us a message. The "great quests for truth" are events of deciphering this yet unspoken message of the It-reality.

These events, however, "do not occur in a vacuum. They occur in social fields, constituted by older experiences of order and symbolizations of their truth, now experienced by the questioner to have fallen into disorder and decline. The quest for truth is a movement of resistance to the prevalent disorder; it is an effort to attune the concretely disordered existence again to the truth of the It-reality, and attempt to create a new field of existential order in competition with the fields whose claim has become doubtful" (p. 25). How do such "stories" create order? Voegelin says, when the story "speaks with an authority commonly present in everybody's consciousness, however inarticulate, deformed, or suppressed the consciousness in the concrete case may be." Otherwise put, the story will remain but a private utterance remaining idiosyncratic to a particular author unless the author, "in the course of his quest, finds the word that indeed speaks what is common to man's existence as a partner in the comprehending reality" (p. 26). What Voegelin has described here is not merely the paradoxic structure of consciousness but of truth: Truth is (a) a human narrative cast in the language of intentionality, or "thingness"; (b) a story not only about but of, the It-reality, an event "in which the It-reality becomes luminous for its truth." These two aspects must not be separated which they would be if passed off "as a narrative told either by a revelatory God or by an intelligent human being." It is both, Voegelin insists, and "it has this paradoxic character inasmuch as it is not a plain narration of things, but at the same time a symbolism" of the human beginning of order as an act of participation in the divine Beginning. Now to the properly historical dimension.

The story would be unthinkable, unexperienceable, and incomprehensible if, by any chance, it could be told by a human being apart not only from the social world with its history but also from Creation of which the entire social world is a part. To this proposition, it seems to me, nobody can deny assent. Voegelin puts this commonsense insight now in the form of a concept: "The story cannot begin unless it starts in the middle." That means that each story is preceded by other stories with which it is in some relation concerning truth or untruth. It also means that "the Platonic metaxy cannot be the last word in the matter; if it were, we would not have to engage in a quest of our own but could simply reprint Plato's dialogues; the mere fact that we refer to the Platonic analysis in the context of our own forcefully suggests that the problems surrounding 'the middle' are not exhausted by the symbolism of the metaxy" (p. 28). And now, Voegelin's conclusion, containing in a nutshell, his new philosophy of history: "In the pursuit of questioning, thus, we encounter a plurality of middles, validating a plurality of quests, telling a plurality of stories, all having valid beginnings."

Does this sentence suggest a number of different realities, or a number of mere episodes of telling the same "comprehending It-story"? Voegelin curtly dismisses the first suggestion as having no basis in human experience. What, then, of the second possibility? Voegelin comments with a somewhat enigmatic sentence: "The questioner, when he renders the account of his participatory quest, is conscious of a Beginning beyond the beginning and of an End beyond the end of his story" (p. 29). The sentence, enigmatic by design, still clearly points to the enigmatic present conscious of a Beginning and an End which Plato, for instance, discovered when struggling to articulate his experience of the It-reality and in the process became aware of the quest itself. Plato experienced the formative presence of the Nous as a divine Beyond, but he also described this divine Beyond as the Beyond experience of the gods themselves. What Plato conveyed in his complex and tentative language is the insight that "the Beyond is not a thing beyond the things, but the experienced presence of the formative It-reality in all things" (p. 30).

Voegelin's name for this presence is "parousia." He then continues: "The Parousia of the Beyond, experienced in the present of the quest, imposes on the dimension of external time, with its past, present, and future, the dimension of divine presence." Of these time dimensions of history, Voegelin says, "The past is not simply the past, nor the future simply the future, for both past and future participate in the presence of the same divine-immortal Beyond that is experienced in the present of the questioner's participatory meditation," which he also calls an "indelible present," a present that cannot and will not simply pass down into the abyss of oblivion. So now he concludes: "We have to speak, therefore, of a flux of presence endowing all the phases—past, present, and future—of external time with the structural dimension of an indelible present" (p. 31). When the Beyond is fully understood as a non-thing, the being things (other than the gods) can be fully understood in their thingness. They acquire "a nature," this nature understood in their thingness, "as the form they have received as their own through the formative presence of the Beyond." Voegelin adds that this nature of the things can in turn become an autonomous matter of exploration, "so autonomous indeed that its origin in the formative presence of the Beyond can be forgotten and a capitalized Nature will assume the functions of the It-reality." With this remark we have returned from history to nature, but in the context of things in the thing-reality and their participation in the formative It-reality, which is Voegelin's central insight. All of Voegelin's works in the last ten or fifteen years of his life are full of statements about this combination, but there are eight pages in volume five, from page 23 to page 31, which contain the essence of Voegelin's new philosophy of history as order and consciousness as its history. They are held together by the symbol of The Story, or The True Story.

One final remark remains to be made, about progress. The very essence of The Story of each of the spiritual outbursts that occur from time to time, all over the world, is progress from ignorance to knowledge, from darkness to luminosity. But as a whole, history cannot be construed as a single progressive motion. "History," Voegelin says at the end of his "Wisdom and the Magic of the Extreme," "turns out to be a process not only of truth becoming luminous, but also of truth becoming deformed and lost by the very forces of imagination and language which let the truth break forth into image and word. The imaginative response can issue into the untruth of a Second Reality...when visionary symbols are subjected to the deformative process of doctrinization and literalization." He is speaking about our age, of a "public unconscious...that proves remarkably resistant to the appeal of noetic balance....The pleromative presence of truth in the second Christs of the nineteenth century, of the Fourier, Saint-Simon, Comte, Hegel, (and) Marx, is followed by its pleromatic fulfillment through the executioners of the twentieth century" (p. 285f). In other words, there is a history of deformations parallel to the history of creative formations. Voegelin's philosophy includes the one with the other, but not with a shoulder-shrugging "That's the way it is," but rather with an energetic resolution to lay bare the antinoetic motions of self-assertive imagination and will-to-power that result in an epidemic "disease of the spirit," as well as the grave political disorders that ensue. Voegelin's achievements in the analysis of "deformation" are no less a title to a philosopher's distinction than his exegetic and symbolic explorations of the mysteries of order.

Beyond Institutions of Power and Patterns of Profit

T*he following form the premises of this essay:*

1. Totalitarianism-in-reform is an entire period during which both the countries emerging from Communist dictatorship and Western countries face unprecedented difficulties. Any help given in this situation, no matter by which, should be also of unprecedented quality.

2. Political institutions cannot be successfully transferred from one country to another unless there is a shared tradition.

3. The Communist ideology enslaved Eastern countries but was created in the West, and the intellectual and spiritual background which made this creation possible still continues.

4. Western governments and business firms have offered limited help, soley to financial transfers, investments, and technical instruction.

We are talking of *Schicksalsgemeinschaft*, i.e., an historical situation encompassing Western with East European countries in a pattern of common concerns. The word itself admits of diverse interpretations. If understood as, "Europe and the United States," the focus would remain on problems of NATO. If read as "The democratic and industrialized West and the European nations emerging from Communist dictatorship," neither the problems nor the remedies are as yet fully clear. I submit that intellectual and psychological aid should be considered at least as important as material and organizational help. As we seek to understand and properly meet the situation I suggest help. As we seek to understand and properly meet the situation I suggest that, for the sake of brevity, we use the word "Atlantia" for the industrial and democratic West, and "Eucentria" for the formerly Communist nations.

The plight of "Eucentria" seems to be deeper, culturally and personally more devastated, than was the case in Germany and Italy after war had removed their ideological regimes. Historians will eventually solve this puzzle. But the facts are undeniable. In a recent report on what was then East Germany ("Letter from Germany," *The New Yorker*, June 18, 1990), Jane Kramer tells us of a mother commenting on her children and her friends, that she knows of only three kinds of people, "Children of the war, children of the state (she obviously meant the Communist regime), and children of rock," all three crippled for normal life, and her own son, belonging to the third category, a suicide. It is interesting that she sees the Communist ideology as only one of the causes, another being the cultural emanation from the Western subculture, which suggests that "Atlantia," too, may need help, within the *Schicksalsgemeinschaft*.

I am braced for vigorous objections: "Why should *we* seek help rather than giving it? Are we not strong both economically and technologically? Have we not just won a war in the most convincing manner? What *are* we lacking?" Well, one should not be long with some answers: "How about sexual morality? How about a viable concept of man which is missing? The rising crime rate, the flood of excessive litigation? How about leading universities dropping the study of Western civilization? How about teachers of constitutional law desperately but in vain looking for a moral foundation of their thinking? And the arts, their products testifying to an underlying nihilism?" John Silber has said: "When we speak of a 'Me-Generation,' we mean a generation of the ego—the ego without limitation, the parasitic ego that totally ignores the conditions on which its existence no less than its fulfillment depends. For some extreme individuals, not even their imagination can transcend their pursuit of what feels good for them." Later, he adds: "One frequently hears the claim that only women can understand women, that only homosexuals can understand homosexuals, that only blacks can understand blacks. All share an epistemology which denies the transcendence on which knowledge and even the assertion of the limitation of knowledge depend" (*The Intercollegiate Review*, Fall 1990, p. 40). This absence of adequate epistemology, of course, results from a lack of philosophy of being and metaphysics. In this intellectual vacuum a new ideology is being thought up by the intellectuals. It is called "Political Correctness," and is busy inventing a whole new series of sins while dropping the old list. We hear of the sins of *eurocentrism, heterosexism, essentialism.* As one professor of a reputable Eastern college relates: "Ah yes, we are compelled to be politically correct and ever so multicultural. A multicultural committee has been established to review curriculum, and multicultural reeducation camps have been slated for the summer. They hope the 'eurocentric and heterosexist' faculty members will enter seminar only to emerge clean...ever so clean" (From a private letter).

Again, I am hearing objections: "How can you speak thus about a society blessed with an orderly democratic government, human rights, prosperity, and progress—how could such a society be described in terms of ignorance and mental poverty?" With a kind of desperate courage I shall go even further and submit that our intellectual institutions are steeped in the same kind of mentality that first made Communist ideology possible. Nor do I mean the unmovable socialist professors who continue to build socialist university departments, as if nothing had happened in the European East. What I am describing is a much more universal disposition of our educated public to *sacralize* politics.

All modern ideologies aim at a kind of salvation, appropriating the Christian symbol but drawing it from heaven into this world of history and politics. That transposition radically changes the meaning of "salvation." As Christians believe, mankind needs to be saved from the evil generated by the human will "moving against its divine original" (Charles Williams, *The Forgiveness of Sins*), the Savior being God himself. Salvation conceived as an exclusively human political enterprise, however, must replace the Christian hope with an historical goal. It can envisage only liberation from anything that might limit human freedom and impede total human equality, which means salvation from a superior God, from any higher norms and destiny. The attempt to transpose a vision of divine perfection into human history is an extremely dangerous fallacy. Around it there will form any number of social and political "causes," each operating under the illusion of its own superhuman importance, so that all values other than its own goals can and will be shoved out of the way. This illusion, elevated to the place formerly held by Christian hope, is the disease at the heart of Western culture. Christian supernatural hope was the central energy that created Western culture and its Eastern sibling. Secularization occurred in three historical impulses: The Enlightenment, the French Revolution, and German Romantic philosophy with Hegel, Feuerbach, Marx. The replacement of Christian hope by a goal of history generated no culture, only a counterculture. This general condition accounts for the numerous manifestation of basic disorientation, and such disorientation is apt to render large masses vulnerable to this or that claim of political "totality." How can this condition coexist with economic and technological excellence? I can only point to the work of Eric Voegelin, who with painstaking analysis has shown that "the death of the spirit is the price of progress." As to the question of the future, Voegelin merely says: "A civilization can, indeed, advance and decline at the same time, but not forever" (*The New Science of Politics*, 1952, p. 131 f.).

Perhaps I have said enough to lend plausibility to my conviction that the erstwhile overthrow of Fascism and Nazism and the present bankruptcy of Communism have not brought about the end of the West's cultural crisis. Hence "Eucentria" and "Atlantia" find themselves sharing the same crisis, in a way, together, even though in different manners. The West's impotence in matters of spirit is the counterpart of "Eucentria's" impotence to move from a command to a market economy. They need help, but so do we. We have the skills and tools that can be useful to them. What have they to touch the poverty of our philosophy? They do have something over us, the suffering, through generations, of the worst degradation of the human soul, the lowest fettering of the human mind. There were persons among them who endured in patience; they now feel thoroughly purged, in all their being. There were others, even in Soviet labor camps, who in moments of all but total annihilation rediscovered metaphysical reality, moral and spiritual order, regained their orientation in life. Since I spoke of the nihilism underlying the arts, I should like to mention the Estonian composer Arvo Pärt. For many years he was imprisoned in what was to him a *Wasteland*, the twelve-tone system of music. To gain freedom, he reduced himself to complete silence, not only as a composer, but as a human being. Patiently he waited for reality to reopen. At first, there was only one note, to which he listened long, eventually repeating it, in various rhythms. At length, he recovered his art, with the help of Gregorian chant and its marvelous simplicity. Even now, he insists that his composing is obedient to the underlying silence. Arvo Pärt has given us the most spiritual modern music in the world.

These cases must be seen in their concreteness, but also as a sign that, after long times "under the rubble," some kind of return to the reality of being, virtue, authority, and order, can be possible. Those cases in East Europe are both paradigmatic and constitutive. It looks as if obedient suffering under totalitarian falsehood has put some of the victims in a position where they can give us help in our poverty of the spirit. Plato had some words relevant to the situation: "You agree that the Sun not only makes the things we see visible, but also brings them into existence and gives them growth and nourishment...and so with objects of knowledge. These derive from the Good not only their power of being known, but their very being and reality, and Goodness is not the same thing as being, but even beyond being, surpassing it in dignity and power" (*Republic*, VI, 509). Between material help, no matter how urgently needed, and goods of the mind and the spirit, it is the latter that "surpass in dignity and power."

After Lenin—
Who Helps Whom?

Halfway through the Moscow coup of August 1991, a crack might have been heard. What had cracked was a thin, yet exceedingly strong vault above the entire Soviet Union, invisible but still depriving people of air and light, as it were. It was the oppressive presence of total power yielded by people who, even though they were natives to the land, appeared alien. They claimed ultimate authority over the lives, emotions, and activities of all individual persons, threatening them with unpredictable, terrifying punishment, a power unprecedented in history. The relatively small number of persons who constituted that vault were held together by a semi-rational ideology that equipped them with a narrow single-mindedness, which was precisely what made the strong vault brittle. When in those August days two tank units had taken up defensive position around Yeltsin's "White House," the forces of the putschists did not dare to move. That was the end:

> Humpty-Dumpty sat on a wall:
> Humpty-Dumpty had a great fall.
> All the king's horses and all the king's men
> Could not put Humpty-Dumpty together again.

The suddenness of this end is of great historic importance. There were no opposition parties in the Soviet Union, indeed, there were not even informal dissident groups who had time to prepare themselves. Modern totalitarian regimes have brought about an atomization of the subject populace. Thus, what "popped out" from "under the rubble" were people who for the first time were standing, in full sight of one another, yet having no intellectual horizon in common. People who had not even been allowed to be responsible for their families or education were suddenly faced with citizens' responsibilities. What is more, the collapse of Communist political rule included the disappearance of any rule over the economy.

That is one half of the situation. The other half consisted of nations who, for at least sixty years, had felt threatened by a fully armed Soviet power which had committed itself to set up communist dictatorships anywhere in the world where the opportunity presented itself. And this expansionist commitment of the Soviet power was backed by heavy nuclear armaments. Totalitarianism, for all its irrationality of visions and motives, had a structure that managed to maintain itself with very little change. In that sense, it figured in international relations like a constant factor. The West, organizing itself in NATO as a defensive alliance, also threatened the Soviet Union through its nuclear weapons so that there arose a kind of balance, openly named "mutually assured destruction." Even if it was the old balance of power, it was a kind of balance. Let us call it a "balance of horrors," neither war nor peace, but a kind of perverse order of evils. So the sudden collapse of Communist power left the people of the Soviet Union in a grizzly puzzlement of indecision; it also left the Western powers bereft of the principle that for generations had guided their foreign policies, and thus, likewise, without ideas that can rule actions.

The fact is that the West had for most of this century experienced a profound void of ideas; a void that was philosophical, theological, as well as political. The grim irony of this situation prescribed that the void of ideas should be concealed, as it were, by the Communist threat. The void itself had been brought about by the unproductiveness of the modern critiques. Thus we have, in this century, only two main philosophical movements, Existentialism and Logical Positivism, both of which were hostile to the concept of Being. In fact Existentialism's militancy rejected any evidence of Being, and thus reduced human existence to an equally militant subjectivism. Positivism replaced Being with the totality of "atomic facts," each fact a monad. In theology, the critical movement, once intended to achieve more knowledge about the Biblical texts, had changed course and now began to criticize the core of the Christian faith itself. A third critical wave aimed at the moral order, attacking it as "oppressive," created by some group's ulterior motives.

As early as 1930 the void could be felt. As one of many examples, let me mention James Burnham, a philosophy professor also interested in world politics. Requiring a "theory" by which he could analyze what was going on, he found nothing available except Marxism, and decided for the Trotskyite branch. Realizing, after a few years, that this commitment obligated him to believe and apply dialectical materialism, he severed his connections with Trotsky, but then turned toward the young American conservatism, which found its basic unity, again, in anti-Communism. Thus Communism, directly or indirectly, enabled people in the West to do their public thinking, which legitimized their public existence. A direct influence can also be linked to the nearly universal socialist tendency in dealing with domestic problems. That the West had little to say by itself, about itself, became clear in the decade before World War II, when England and France had come to the end of their policies concerning with defeated Germany and turned out to be vacillating, ambiguous, and irresolute in their actions vis-a-vis Japan, Mussolini, Hitler, the Spanish Civil War.

Faced now with the debacle of Soviet Communism and the ensuing crisis of the socialist idea, the West has at its disposal money, economic productiveness, and managerial skills, but nothing at all in the field of ideas, philosophical or political.

There are many cases of people emerging from the Communist despotism who, finding in the surrounding West a void of ideas, fall into a condition of *Angst*, as Vaclav Havel calls it. Tatyana Goricheva reports of her deep disappointment with Western "nihilism" which, she observed, causes a lack of freedom and even the incapacity to desire freedom. These are just two among many similar voices expressing Eastern expectations of finding in the West not just material wealth but also sound basic thinking.

The loss of such concepts as "being" and "man" had not wholly escaped the attention of philosophers. Thus Heidegger, as early as the 'twenties, based *Sein und Zeit* on the core question, "How is it with Being?" (translated, for reasons of internal consistency, as "How does it stand with Being?"). If Existentialism at first struck Western civilization with the force of a whirlwind, that was because it asked the main questions which had not been asked for centuries. Heidegger's chief concerns thus appeared closer to people's *angst* experiences. What Heidegger then delivered, however, failed to fulfill the promise implied in his questions. He obtained concepts and proofs chiefly by semantic manipulations. In Greek and German he traced words and syllables to their most ancient meanings, sometimes to Sanskrit. Then he set up an abiding contention between primordial and current word-senses and created a novel kind of myth consisting of linguistic conflicts. The primordial component provided an apparent depth of meaning to which it seemed possible to attach higher rank.

As I wish to compare and contrast at least two philosophers of midcentury with Eric Voegelin's work, I have chosen a work by Heidegger published around 1950, *An Introduction to Metaphysics* (Anchor Book 1961, German original 1953). Here we find something like the following passage:

> But disaster and the possibility of disaster do not occur only at the end, when a single act of power fails, when

the violent one makes a false move; no, this disaster is fundamental, it governs and waits in the conflict between violence and overpowering. Violence against the preponderant power of being *must* shatter against being, if being rules in its essence, as *physis*, as emerging power.... But this necessity as disaster can only subsist insofar as what must shatter is driven into such a being-there. Man is forced into such a being-there, hurled into the affliction *(Not)* of such being, because the overpowering as such, in order to appear in its power, *requires* a place, a scene of disclosure. The essence of being-human opens up to us only when understood through this need compelled by being itself. The being-there of historical man means: to be posited at the breach into which the preponderant power of being bursts in its appearing, in order that this breach itself should shatter against being (*op. cit.* p. 136 f).

The difficulties of the language can by no means be attributed to the translator; rather they stem from the combination of un-heard-of-word-meanings with the hypostatization of the resulting concepts. Heidegger's promise remained unfulfilled. In the famous *Der Spiegel*-interview, a few years before his death, Heidegger considered the situation so "desperate," that "nothing but a new god" could bring help. In other words, the appearance of another pagan divinity is the last and best hope of "Being."

As a second work on ontology I have chosen Nicolai Hartmann, *The New Ways of Ontology*, (Chicago 1953, German original, 1949). Like Heidegger, Hartmann insists that "among historically recorded systems of philosophy there is none for which the domain of being, taken in strict universality, is not essential" (p. 5). The old ontology, with its deductive methods, however, is gone forever. "The critical epistemology of the modern age from Descartes down to Kant did not succeed in completely replacing the old ontology with a new doctrine of equal value. But it had so thoroughly destroyed its suppositions that a metaphysics erected on the old basis was no longer possible" (p. 9). Hartmann attempts a new beginning by creating a system of categories, many of them new. "Ontology is not concerned with knowledge, much less with judgments, but with the object of knowledge in so far as this object is at the same time 'transobjective.'" "(It follows that) the principles of being...are just as indifferent to the dividing line between the knowable and the unknowable as the being whose principles they are." Hence Hartmann's categories "are drawn from the content of knowledge such as it has emerged from the whole field of scientific research" (p. 18). "In so far as we can gain any knowledge of categories, we do not gain it by a priori methods nor by raising principles of reasons into consciousness, but rather through an analysis of objects...in this way we grasp in the first place ontological categories only, not cognitive categories as such...it follows that epistemology, taken by itself, in regard to the problem of categories, is not independent but presupposes an ontological understanding of the whole field of objects.... Moreover it follows that epistemology...cannot be a fundamental philosophy.... Rather it needs an ontological foundation" (p. 19).

Hartmann arrives at four realms of being: the spatial, outer world; a non-spatial inner world intelligible to consciousness; both of these divided into strata: the spatial world into a stratum of inanimate things with physical processes, and a stratum of animate beings. The non-spatial, "first understood as the inwardness of consciousness," divides into the stratum of the psychic and the stratum of the spiritual. Hartmann counsels what he calls "modal analysis," a procedure prominently employed by Michael Oakeshott. Hartmann concludes: "Every one of these strata has its own peculiar ontological categories which nowhere simply coincide with those of the other strata." Hence, concretely speaking, "no man alone embraces all four strata of being. It is the same with society, and the historical process.... On the other hand, it is entirely possible if there are strata of being which cut across the strata of actual structures and if, accordingly, the more strata the actual structures possess, the higher they are" (p. 51).

These all-too-brief remarks merely intend to show that a degenerate civilization need not be endured as if it were a verdict on philosophy as such. This point receives much strength from the astonishing success of Jacques Maritain and Etienne Gilson in having brought to new life the philosophy of Thomas Aquinas, indeed the whole of Christian philosophical endeavor. G.K. Chesterton and Hilaire Belloc, along with C.S. Lewis and Charles Williams, have equally done admirable work of critical reason joined to Christian faith, largely in essay form.

Eric Voegelin—to whom we are now turning—has insisted that his ideas are not new. In a profound sense, this is true. All the same, Voegelin's identification and intellectual penetration of problems strikes the reader as something he has not yet encountered. His concept of being is startling, to say the least: Instead of a colorless universal as the root of everything Voegelin assumes a community of transcendental and immanent partners, evidenced by human experience. Man's place in this community, and knowledge of himself, depend on his conscious experience of participation. While the whole remains unknowable, considerable knowledge can be obtained through inner experience, the "aggregate of experiences to which (theory) must permanently refer for empirical control" (*The New Science of Politics*, p. 64). Moreover, Voegelin assumes that the symbolization of that experience has a history, so that there is not only "a drama of life," but meaning in history not necessarily progressive, and as history inseparable from the whole. A basic ignorance of the whole abides, but since it is not blind ignorance, it can be called, with Cusanus, *docta ignorantia*. As Voegelin makes each of these statements on the basis of well-documented human experience, his can be called an empirical philosophy.

Voegelin's *Programmschrift*, *The New Science of Politics*, appeared in 1952, but the first coherent outline of his philosophy of being is found in the Introduction to volume I of *Order and History*, dated 1956. Here is the first paragraph: "God and man, world and society form a primordial community of being. The community with its quaternian structure is, and is not, a datum of human experience. It is a datum in so far as it is known by virtue of his participation in the mystery of its being. It is not a datum of experience as it is given in the manner of an object of the external world but is knowable only from the perspective of participation in it." Experience is the material to be understood, but the "perspective of participation" is the direction in which experience occurs, and in which mankind has found various modes of insight into reality and principles of existence. The "perspective of participation" may disturb Voegelin's readers, and he himself is the first to admit its disturbing character, for it may invite the image of man as a self-contained spectator. "But man is not a self-contained spectator," says Voegelin. "He is an actor, playing a part in a drama of being and, through the brute fact of his existence, committed to play without knowing what it is." All the same, Voegelin adds, "Participation in being...is not a partial involvement of man; he is engaged with the whole of his existence, for participation is existence itself. There is no vantage point outside existence from which its meaning can be viewed." That means, of course, that "the role of existence must be played in uncertainty of its meaning, as an adventure of decision on the edge of freedom and necessity." Here, obviously, is something like Hartmann's categories, but they are not emerging piecemeal or without an inkling of the whole. Still, the condition of ultimate ignorance prevails: "The actor does not know with certainty who he is himself." Caution must lead the way here: "man's participatio in being is not blind...there is an experience of participation,...this sense, however, will turn into nonsense if one forgets that subject and predicate in the proposition are terms which explicate tension of existence, and are not concepts denoting objects...there is no thing as a 'man,' as if he were in an enterprise he could as well leave alone; there is, rather, a 'something,' a part of being, capable of experiencing itself as such, and furthermore capable of using language and calling this experiencing consciousness by the name of 'man.'" The lingering doubt about our own identity remains as part of the situation. "Knowledge of the whole is precluded by the identity of the knower with the partner, and ignorance of the whole precludes essential knowledge of the part. This ignorance with regard to the decisive core of existence is more than disconcerting: it is profoundly disturbing, for from the depth of this ultimate ignorance wells up the anxiety of existence." Partial knowledge, however, must not be held in low esteem: "Man can achieve considerable knowledge about the order of being, and not the least part of that knowledge is the distinction between the knowable and the unknowable...even in these early stages there is enough method to allow the distinction of typical features in the process of symbolization."

Voegelin's list of fundamental human experiences is a strategic point of his teaching, and at this point the list is by no means complete. First, "there is the predominance of the experience of participation....The community of being is experienced with such intimacy that the consubstantiality of the partners will override the separateness of substances." Next, he mentions the preoccupation with "the lasting and passing (the durability and transiency) of the partners in the community of being...and the various existences are distinguished by their degrees of durability...under this aspect, being exhibits the lineaments of a hierarchy of existence, from the ephemeral lowliness of man to the everlastingness of the gods....For the more lasting existences, being the more comprehensive ones, provide by their structure the frame into which the lesser existences must fit" (p. 3-4).

At this point, Voegelin introduces "attunement," the attitude required by the fact of participation, and concludes: "In existing we experience mortality; in being we experience what can be symbolized only by the negative metaphor of immortality." Here again, Voegelin warns us of the limits of our knowledge, for "lasting and passing are properties of being as they appear to us in the perspective of our existence; as soon as we try to objectify them we lose even what we have." Attunement differs essentially from certainty. It does affect us positively "when it maintains a tension of awareness for its partial revelations in the order of society and the world, when it listens attentively to the silent voices of conscience and grace in human existence itself. We are thrown into and out of existence without knowing the Why and How, but while in it we know that we are of the being to which we return" (p. 5).

As a third categorial feature, Voegelin lists "the process of symbolization, the attempt at making the essentially unknowable order of being intelligible...through the creation of symbols which interpret the unknown by analogy." Here, for the first time, Voegelin mentions history: "These attempts have a history...compact blocks of the knowable will be differentiated into their component parts and the knowable will gradually come to be distinguished from the essentially unknowable. Thus the history of symbolization is a progression from compact to differentiated experiences and symbols." Two basic forms of symbolization are: one that symbolizes the order of society as an analogue of the cosmos; the other symbolizes the social order as an analogue of human existence; the first a microcosmos, the second, a macroanthropos." When cosmologically symbolized empires break down and in their disaster engulf the cosmic order...symbolization tends to shift toward what is more lasting than the visibly existing world, that is, toward the invisibly existing being beyond all being in tangible existence.... [This] can be experienced only as a movement in the soul of man; hence the soul...becomes the model of order that will furnish symbols for ordering society analogically in its image" (p. 6).

While "the order of being...can be symbolized by using more than one experience of partial order in existence...mutual toleration is accompanied by a vivid consciousness of the sameness of truth at which man aims by means of his various symbols....This tolerance, however will reach its limits when the awareness of the analogical character of symbolization is attracted by the problem of greater or lesser adequacy of symbols to their purpose" (p. 8). Mentioning summodeism, monotheism, and alternative theogonies, he remarks: "The break with earlier tolerance results not from reflection on the inadequacy of pluralistic symbolization, but from the profounder insight that no symbolization through analogues of existential order in the world can even faintly be adequate to the divine partner on whom the community of being and its order depend" (p. 9). Here, Voegelin advances perhaps what is his most profound concept: "And yet, something has changed, not only in the method of symbolization, but in the order of being and existence itself.... Not only will the symbols lose their magic of their transparency for the unseen reader and become opaque, but a pallor will fall over the unseen order of mundane existence...man will turn away from the world and society as the sources of misleading analogy. He will experience a turning around, the Platonic *periagoge*, an inversion or conversion toward the true source of order...[it] results in more than an increase in knowledge;...it is a change in the order itself" (p. 10). This is what Voegelin calls the *leap in being*. Again, he counsels caution: "the leap upward in being is not a leap out of existence. Hence, there is no age of the church that would succeed an age of society on the level of more compact attunement to being. Instead, there develop the tensions, frictions, and balances between the two levels of attunement, a dualistic structure of existence which expresses itself in pairs of symbols, of *theologia civilis* and *theologia supernaturalis*, of temporal and spiritual powers, of secular state and church" (p. 11). Eventually, says Voegelin, "there is an awareness that the new truth about being is not a substitute for, but an addition to the old truth."

One may ask: "How about Voegelin's metaphysics? Has he restored metaphysics to its proper rank? What does his metaphysics say, and do we agree with it?" Voegelin would have rejected these question as *mal posées*. Remember that he insisted on the non-objective character of transcendent reality. Transcendence, he emphasized, is neither a spatial place, nor in any way an external object. In fact, he says, transcendence and immanence are mere "indices," pertaining to the same continuous reality. Hence, metaphysics cannot be rationally conducted as if it were a science describing and analyzing divine or spiritual objects. All the same, metaphysics *is* important. Instead of asking, "what does metaphysics say," however, he asks "how is metaphysics possible?" Knowledge is possible through the inner experience of participation. He whose experience has opened new and more profound insights will feel the urge to communicate. Since there is no language specific to "the whole," the "beginning," the "beyond," or "the meaning of history," everyday language about things must be used analogically—the *analogia entis* of Thomas Aquinas. Since Eric Voegelin's entire philosophy of being is relies on human inner experience as the material source of knowledge, he has, indeed, made metaphysics again possible.

At the end we have to answer the following question: in what way is the recent European development a philosophical problem? It is a problem in the sense that no understanding of this development can be attained by positivist and descriptive methods. Eric Voegelin is the political philosopher who has provided concepts and methods for understanding totalitarianism. What cracked in August, 1991, was not a "novel form of government," as would be described by conventional political science. In Soviet

Russia, as in Nazi Germany, it was not the state that embodied highest authority, but the Party as the guardian of ideology. The party's supersession of the state flowed from the thesis that history's destiny is a re-ordering of Being itself, to be accomplished by the revolutionary action of the Party. Nietzsche's "will to power" was the human disposition on the ground of which this kind of imagery could draw large masses into a disciplined enterprise. Voegelin's formulation here is more precise: Man's lust for power over being. Voegelin defined the structure of this outlook by six points (here paraphrased):

1) A general dissatisfaction with this world and this society.

2) A belief that the unsatisfying condition can be attributed to the fact that the world is intrinsically poorly organized.

3) The belief that salvation from this evil world is possible.

4) It follows that the order of being will have to be changed in an historical process.

5) Changing the order of being lies in the realm of human action.

6) Knowledge—*gnosis*—of the way for men to alter being is the central concern of this age (*Science, Politics, and Gnosticism*, Chicago 1968, p. 87 f). Voegelin comments that this, the (modern) "Gnostic position...is apt to destroy the universe of rational discourse as well as the social function of persuasion" (*The New Science of Politics*, Chicago, 1952, p. 138).

The regime that collapsed recently in Europe is not one of the regular "forms of government," but a by-product of Western Europe's nihilism. The subject populations of this regime who have been totally suppressed, some for three generations, others at least for one, have for a long time been deprived of rational political discourse. In countries without a tradition of philosophy, they may have succeeded in retaining a traditional rational image of reality. In the meantime, the Western nations have not outgrown their nihilism; rather it has come now to the point of epidemic disorder in many day-by-day relations. Thus, both for the West and Eastern nations, the main problem is how to return to ontological premises of rational discourse. The situation favoring alternative experiences and symbolizations of order has been characterized by Voegelin as the breakdown of cosmologically symbolized empires [which] in their disaster engulf the trust in cosmic order" (*Order and History* I, p. 6). We are not in that kind of situation, for Soviet Russia was not a "cosmologically symbolized empire," nor has the collapse of Communism so far been "a disaster." On the other hand, the former rule of the Evil Empire would regularly bring individual lives to the point of "disaster." In some of these cases there indeed happened what Voegelin described as the disaster's result: a "shift toward what is more lasting than the visibly existing world...toward the invisibly existing being beyond all beings in tangible existence." In that such personal gains of experiences of order are tied to the occurrence of personal suffering beyond the limits of endurance, one may say that the peoples of the East, including the Russians, have a hidden treasure of potentiality for order, the like of which the Western nations do not possess.

One concludes that public discussions of order in Central and Eastern Europe should make a deliberate effort to widen the scope of the discussion with the intent of illuminating these hidden metaphysical reserves and thereby demonstrating the possibility of the discussion as such. What is more, the personal experiences that may have generated these higher insights should be philosophically collected and recorded. Finally, the philosophical ordering of both experiences and new symbols of order should become the subject of discussions between people from the East and people from the West. What the West has to give at the present time is money, technology, and administrative or managerial skill. From the East, however, could come the initiation of a renewal of philosophical bases of order. The situation is one that must be called historically open. There is no saying what good will might accomplish at this time.

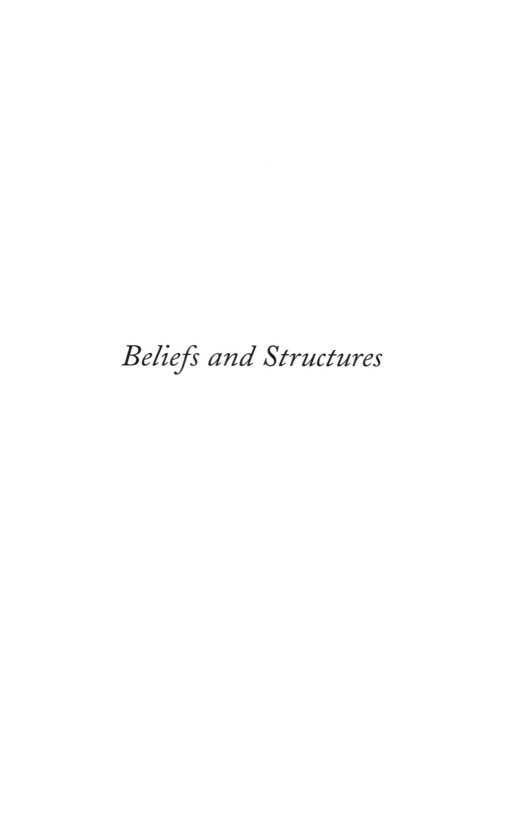

Beliefs and Structures

Forces That Shape the Twentieth Century *

U nderstanding the twentieth century has been a frustrating matter to contemporary minds. Deep puzzlement is found in literary productions and in historical works, and where "shapes" are perceived they appear ambiguous. On the other hand, there is not only an unprecedented loss of shape but the loss does not have the character of replacement. Worse yet, by what name can one call shapelessness? The puzzlement has produced a number of efforts to understand the present by going back to roots either in the Enlightenment, or the late Middle Ages, or even late Antiquity. Prominent among such interpreters are J.L. Talmon (*The Origins of Totalitarian Democracy*, 1960), Norman Cohn (*The Pursuit of the Millennium*, 1957), Hans Jonas (*The Gnostic Revolution*, 2nd ed. 1963), Eric Voegelin (*The New Science of Politics*, 1952), Henri de Lubac (*The Drama of Atheist Humanism*, 1963), and Albert Camus (*The Rebel*, 1956). T.S. Eliot, James Joyce, Ezra Pound, Robert Musil, Heimito von Doderer, and Elias Canetti are ranking literary figures who have wrestled with this problem. Their insights have made possible this brief essay on the topic, which assumes that the historical "present" must be seen, for some purposes, as the last three centuries, for others as

* The remarks made in this essay do not represent scholarly research. They are intended as topical stimulations for a conversation among informed and intelligent people.

the last two, and for still others as at least the nineteenth century. This sketch begins at a point about two thirds through the sixteenth century, for reasons to be explained later.

A prefatory remark on the whole of modernity must be aware of the 180° turn in orientation that marked the end of the Middle Ages. In *The Discarded Image* (1964) C.S. Lewis has shown medieval consciousness looking back to the authorities of the past, Christian, pre-Christian, and extra-Christian ones. The backward orientation does not imply an absence of progressive movement (as the oarsmen rowing a boat moves forward even when looking aft). The Middle Ages saw great innovations in agriculture, the invention of mechanical machineries, new navigational devices, and the beginning of science. Moreover, as Tocqueville remarked, political liberty "had filled all the Middle Ages with its works" (*L'Ancien Regime*, tr. Patterson, Oxford 1952, 20). It is the turning of the inner glance from the past to the future which makes meaningful the designation of an age called "Modernity." This reorientation came as a deliberate rejection of the authority of past knowledge, which rejection was experienced as liberation. Modernity was not merely an observed fact but rather a willed separation.

The turn can be documented in Descartes and Hobbes, possibly prefigured by Machiavelli. Descartes and Hobbes discarded not merely Scholasticism but Aristotle, as they elevated mathematics into philosophy's master method. They signaled a new determination to attain, in philosophy, a certainty like that obtainable in mathematics, even though mathematics does not include man and human existence in its scope. I should like to date modernity, however, not from the time of these philosophers but from a non-philosophical reorientation in politics. It occurred in France, toward the end of those eight frightful civil wars fought between the Catholic League and the Protestant Huguenots. Their hostility seemed interminable. Eventually a kind of party formed between the two enemies; not a religious group, but one whose emphasis was political rather than religious. It supported Henri of Navarre, the Protestant king who had accepted the Catholic faith in order to be accepted by his subjects. The "Politiques," as they were called, made support for the kind their foremost concern. Henri IV ended the religious wars with the Edict of Nantes (1598). The phenomenon of the "Politiques" is the first political shape of Modernity.

Why? If the Politiques foreshadowed the type of political party as one found them a century later in England, and yet another century later in France, still, there were parties all through the Middle Ages, for instance, the Guelfs and Ghibellines in Italy. Medieval rival groups, however, were typically armed and ready to fight each other in the streets. By contrast, the Politiques did not conceive of themselves as one of the armies in civil war. Their self-understanding and their mode of operation were entirely political. That was new. New also was the inclusion, in the Politiques, of both Catholic and Protestant elements who put political unity above religious controversy. For the first time, the state was spontaneously acclaimed as the organization of peace above religious contentions. Furthermore, the Politiques were not an exclusively aristocratic group; they included parts of different social strata so that one might even call them a "grassroots movement." One of their members was a provincial lawyer, Jean Bodin, who in his *Six Books on the Republic* created the new concept of sovereignty, and in his *Heptaplomeres* a powerful document praising universal religious toleration. The outlines of the modern state appear in thought as in action: a strong but tolerant unity of peace above religious as well as feudal factions. In the seventeenth century that kind of thinking generated Richelieu's concept of *"raison d'Etat,"* the first principled separation of statecraft from other normative structures. In our days, Sir Herbert Butterfield, a strong Christian and a philosophical historian, hailed Richelieu's notion for the great good it had brought to mankind. In political practice, then, modernity had already begun before the founding of modern philosophy.

Descartes' *Discourse on Method* was meant as a complete break with past philosophy. Descartes willed, as he described, "to rid myself, at least once in my life, of all the opinions I had hitherto accepted on faith" and "to reject as absolutely false anything which gave rise in my mind to the slightest doubt" (Chapters 2 and 4). One notes that Descartes' systemic doubt was expressed in the language of St. Augustine, who had written, "I am assured both that I am and that I know this," but then goes on to say something that Descartes left out: "and these two I love, and in the same manner I am assured that I love them" (*City of God* XI, 27). Descartes' doubt, then, has a hint of nothingness that is not found in Augustine. Hobbes believed "that scarce anything can be more absurdly said in natural philosophy than that which is now called *Aristotle's Metaphysics*; nor more repugnant to government than much of that he said in his *Politics*, nor more than a great part of his *Ethics*" (*Leviathan*, part III, ch. 46). He goes further: "...there is no *finis ultimum*, utmost aim, nor *summum bonum*, greatest good, as is spoken of in the books of the old moral philosophers.... Felicity is a continual process from the desire of one object to another, the attaining of the former being still but the way to the latter" (*Ibid.* part I ch. 11). Spinoza similarly is conscious of the radical separation from the entire past: "Such a doctrine might well have sufficed to conceal the truth from the human race for all eternity, if mathematics had not furnished another standard of verity in considering the essence and properties of figures without regard to their final causes" (*Ethics*, part I, Appendix).

The enterprise of modern philosophy is thus, in Descartes' words, "a single design to strip oneself of all past beliefs," these beliefs being placed into the category of "prejudices." The elimination of "prejudices" from civilization appears as a process of liberation, as the mind moves toward *les lumieres*, enlightenment.

The mind's confidence flows no more from the sharing of experiences with past great thinkers: from now on one is confident through sharing one's dream of future freedom.

Another founding event of modernity was modern science, a self-perpetuating onward movement in which all answers generate new questions and in which knowledge, unlike that of philosophy, is cumulative. Finally, there is also the enterprise of modern technology, the steady and cumulative increase of human power over nature. Science has been a story of uninterrupted success. Technology, taken merely on its own terms, must also be deemed successful, although it has exacted a steadily rising price in terms of human existence and values. The modern state, continuing through the temporary interruptions of the French and Russian Revolutions, has institutionally spread from Europe over the entire globe.

If, then, we find the twentieth century a time of dissolution, we must first of all look for the causes in modern philosophy. Its founding, as we have seen, was the sounding of a rebellious note. In so far as philosophers rebelled with an apparently good conscience, they based it on the vision of freedom they hoped to gain from purging the mind of residues from the past. This task could only be accomplished step by step, generation by generation. After each step one would discover another unfinished part of the business. Furthermore, as the philosophers moved forward, the horizon receded as the idea of human freedom widened to the point where limits seemed to vanish from sight. But there is also reason to doubt the apparent self-assuredness of the first philosophical rebels, since they took much care to hide their own boldness from public detection. Still, once begun, rebellion proved to have its own dialectic of ever-increasing radicalism. Albert Camus, in *The Rebel* (*L'homme révolté*), has traced in history the dialectic of rebellion turning into destructive revolution, or the will to justice into the will to power.

The suppressive negotiations of rebellion's dialectic may have their ominous coherence, but the history of ideas does not by itself tell us much of our own culture. Descartes, Hobbes, and Spinoza purged philosophy from Aristotle's essence, as well as his perception of ends, in nature. In Descartes, this came as a "fatal bifurcation" of the mind between the two realities of *res extensa*, i.e. bodies and motion, and *res cogitans*, the reality of thought. In Hobbes, as we have seen, the rejection of essences and final causes occurred independently of Descartes. Spinoza denied the existence of particular substances for he defined substance in such a way that only one substance could be conceived. He called that substance *deus sive natura*, God or Nature. Locke rejected, if not the reality of essences, then any possibility of human knowledge of such essences. Modern philosophy, then, postulated a nature which, bereft of ends as well as philosphical intelligibility, is confined to such causes and effects as can be mathematically quantified. This was the "clear and distinct knowledge" Descartes had demanded, which would give man "power over nature," the goal Bacon had postulated.

On the other side of Descartes' divided reality the mind tended increasingly to look on itself as "its own place" (Milton). Erecting mathematics, itself a creation of the human mind, into the sole master method led to philosophy conceived as "reckoning" with one's own definitions as integers. Leo Strauss, commenting on Spinoza, points out: "Now these definitions are in themselves absolutely arbitrary, especially the famous definition of substance: substance is what it is by itself and is conceived of itself. Once you admit that, everything else follows from that; there are no miracles possible then. But since the definitions are arbitrary, the conclusions are arbitrary. The basic definitions are not arbitrary if we view them...as the conditions which must be fulfilled if the whole is to be fully intelligible.... But is Spinoza's account of the whole clear and distinct?" ("The Mutual Influence of Theology and Philosophy," *The Independent Journal of Phi-*

losophy, III, 1979, 111-118). Strauss doubts the truth of the whole as he looks on Spinoza's chapter on the emotions, as we also doubt Hobbes when reading the degree of power he claims for "the great Leviathan"—the "mortal God." Still, the same method of "reckoning" with one's own arbitrary definitions is what holds together Rousseau's *Second Discourse* as well as his *Social Contract*. In most of modern philosophy the mind excuses itself from any objective reality, drawing certainty from its own products. Locke concluded that man could have no certain knowledge other than morality, a notion that forms the core of Kant's mighty system.

First confined to philosophers' books, this idea became commonplace within decades. In his address to the Harvard Divinity School of 1838, Emerson, reducing Jesus to "the true race of prophets," is looking for the new Teacher "who shall see the world to be a mirror of the soul; shall see the identity of the law of gravitation with purity of heart; shall show that the Ought, that Duty, is one thing with science, with Beauty, with Joy" (Quoted in Marion Montgomery, *Why Hawthorne Was Melancholy,* 1984, 66). "Build therefore your own world," said Emerson, "a correspondent revolution in thins will attend the influx of the spirit. So fast will disagreeable appearances, swine, snakes, pests, madhouses, prisons vanish; they are temporary and shall be no more seen...so shall the advancing spirit create its ornaments along its path...until evil is no more seen. The kingdom of man over nature...a dominion such as now is beyond his dream of God" (*Ibid.* 70). The mind, shorn of any experience of transcendence, is construed as man's own power tool, and its proper work is man's kingdom. Thus Comte sketches his vision of a future totalitarian society based on the new science, "sociology," through which morality has become "positive," as quantifiable as physics, and as little to be doubted or contradicted. That plan did not attain reality at Comte's hands, but Comte's Positivism, all the same, has cast its net over all sciences of man, the mind making all of them "its own place," which explains much of the modern narcissism.

The modern state, modern science, modern technology, and modern philosophy, even all combined, do not tell the whole story, unless one also takes into account the liberal world view. A world view is not a philosophy, but it must be called a kind of fuzzy structure especially if it has, like the liberal one, continued for almost three hundred years. During these periods, moreover, neither the world view itself, nor its works, have been the same, so that one hesitates before every generalization about Liberalism. Burke appealed "from the New Whigs to the Old Whigs," and Hayek, furiously attacking the Liberals of the twentieth century, did so not as a Conservative, but as a Liberal of 100 years ago. Now Liberalism, historically astonishing in its tenacity, still does not look to a single intellectual authority for its views, such as the socialists have in Marx. All the same, liberal documents of many kinds abound. Not only are there treatises and speeches like manifestoes, there are also great writers like Charles Dickens, great rulers like Josef II, great initiators like William Wilberforce, and great educators like Pestalozzi. If the French Revolution of 1789 cannot be called liberal, certainly the chief revolutionary movements of the nineteenth century, all over Europe, can. This history, all the same, is ambiguous. One cannot call it good from beginning to end. In our time this ambiguity has been brought to light chiefly by great writers: Dostoevsky, Joseph Conrad, Thomas Mann, Robert Musil, Wyndham Lewis, and Evelyn Waugh. It seems that we cannot come to intellectual grips with our own time unless we manage to understand the roots of ambiguity of the liberal record. The task calls for a generalization capable of explaining both the positive and the negative aspects of this record. It must also range from politics to religion. In a Christian world, one must begin with the Liberals' view of God; in a world first shaped by Greek philosophy, one must also ask about the Liberals' attitude toward nature, then about society, and man—specifically his reason and will.

Liberalism first appears in the form of Socinianism and continues the tendency toward a humanism only loosely tied to Christianity, a tendency that moved from Christianity without Christ to a Christianity without a supernatural dimension, leaving eventually a Christianity limited to a residual Christian morality. The liberal endeavor to pull down restraints left its mark on liberal philosophical assumptions. One can circumscribe Liberalism by means of the following philosophers:

- Locke: In contrast to Aristotle, who pictured the *polis* as that association which in the fullest way corresponded to human nature, Locke pointed to a "state of nature," replete with a "law of nature," and created the concept of natural rights, claims that man supposedly has on organized civil society.
- Rousseau: Prior to civilization, man was both innocent and harmonious; this notion eliminates the Biblical myth of original sin resulting in a fallen human race.
- Descartes and Kant: Man's mind is its own ultimate authority and legislation.
- Condorcet: Believed in the "infinite perfectibility of man," as a basis for a progressivist trust in the future.
- Humboldt, and John S. Mill: The private and creative individual should be left free of any governmental activity protecting certain ideas, beliefs, or truth, since truth will emerge by itself from a completely free competition of all ideas.

Liberalism, however, occurred not merely in an intellectual setting, it occurred also in a Christian society. Liberals were not atheists, at least, for about two hundred years of their development. But Liberals' views on Jesus Christ are not without influence on what happened in the secular affairs of our civilization. Liberals have typically rejected much of Christian dogma and favored pluralism rather than consensus in religious matters. They have found it difficult or even undesirable to make moral judgments and therefore have been permissive in most ways. They have been averse to theology, while welcoming traditional theological language to express nontheological views. They have been less than kind to liturgical forms of worship and given to their own interpretation when using such forms; cultivated what they have called broad-mindedness, which, however, has been an narrower outlook than one that included the transcendent, and they have emphasized the humanity of Jesus while downplaying his divinity. They have gradually moved from a Christianity without Christ to a Christianity without any supernatural dimension, to a Christianity consisting of nothing but residual Christian morality.

In this, as in every respect, the tendency of Liberals has been to pull down restraints—to leave man "to himself." During the nineteenth century, the Liberal mind largely replaced God with Nature, the later conceived as a system of original harmonies and equilibria. This development aimed at the removal of any notion of mystery from belief, philosophy, and religion. It is easy to see that the ensemble of such views amounts to civilizational activities conceived as a kind of salvation, albeit a non-Christian one. The enterprise relies on opposition to the traditions and authorities of the past, which explains the extreme hostility Liberals feel toward conservative views and organizations. The relation of liberal thought and Christian belief is more complex in detail, but this matter belongs to a full history of Liberalism.

Liberalism—benevolent, moderate, optimistic (a word stemming from the end of the eighteenth century), yet restless in its ceaseless push for change-built that house in which the modern West grew up. It was once a cheerful house, filled with self-confidence, adorned with all decency. And yet, we, who have to live in the twentieth century, have come to fear Liberalism as superficial, ignorant of mankind's demonic possibilities, given to mistaken judgments of historical forces, untrustworthy in its complacency. From the outside it has been vulnerable to the lure of radicalism. The word "radical," first mentioned in the last decade of the eighteenth century, was then applied to left-wing Benthamism: no longer a mere "moderate" reform but rather a design to replace the entire social system with another. What the Declaration of the Rights of Man was for French Liberals, the Charter demands and British Reform Acts were for their counterparts across the Channel. In the wake of the French Revolution of 1789 there came Babeuf's Communist conspiracy; the English Reform Acts were followed by Fabian Socialism. What Liberalism and nineteenth-century Radicalism had in common was the anchoring of their highest hopes in the historical future: their kinship in this respect continuously disarmed their criticism of the extreme Left.

How is it that Liberalism, having produced the structure of free government but also the entire culture of the nineteenth century, from which have come the patterns of gentlemanly conduct, the science of economics, the educational ideas of individualism, and international law—how is it that it also has spawned the Raskolnikovs, the Ivan Karamazovs, and the Bazarovs? The Russian writers whose piercing insight created these characters made their parent generation liberal. Liberals always acted from good intentions, but in their furrows there rose a race of men who brutally brushed away the whole Liberal world, benevolence, moderation, and optimism, whose wills were irrational, whose goals knew no limit, who indulged themselves in destructive action. Wrote André Gide: "since Nietzsche, and with Nietzsche, a new question has arisen...and not so much one that is grafted on those other questions but that brushes them aside and takes their place....'What,' it asks, 'is mankind capable of?' That question is coupled with the terrible perception that man could have been something different, could have been more, could yet be more; that he is ignobly relaxing at the end of the first state" (Quoted in Henri de Lubac, *The Drama of Atheist Humanism*, 1963, 176 f). Before Gide, Dostoevsky had this same insight which he embodied in his portraits of "the Underground Man," and *The Possessed*. In his eyes, Liberalism, with its culture-comfort, its self-sufficient rationalism, its secular humanism, its dreamy optimism, and its lack of discernment, could not be acquitted of the catastrophe that is now upon us. Its message has always been ambiguous—an ambiguity others had difficulty in perceiving—given the Liberals' benevolence and moderation.

The Liberals, after all, carried forward a rebellious momentum of modernity, although they advanced it step by hesitant step. Their choice of benevolent change constituted their good conscience which kept them from ever raising the question of where the whole journey might lead to. Their mode of facile self-congratulation blinded them to their spiritual and moral deficiencies. What happened in the twentieth century was, to borrow Marxian jargon, a switch from quantitative to qualitative change, the new "rebellion" battering down not merely traditional "prejudices" but also the Liberal moderate rebellion. The new rebels felt nothing but disgust at the earlier "radicalism" of the Liberals; they managed to conceive a radicalism beyond any known precedent. It attacked all institutions; willing destruction rather than reform; subverting not merely political but all social order; and suppressing no mere political restraints but the alleged "restraints" of God and morality.

Thus Liberalism's time was over after World War I. Its last fling was Wilson's quixotic project of world peace, complete with a Pact "outlawing war." But Liberals, typically optimistic even in their terminal disease, still celebrated an unwarranted later triumph: Britain's Beveridge Plan, Truman's Fair Deal, and the Scandinavian welfare cage occurred simultaneously, and this thirty years after Lenin, twenty after Mussolini, and fifteen after Hitler. These three demonic structures were what Camus had called "revolution": the perversion of rebellion. That pair of concepts may not tell us much, but Dostoevsky's portrait of the "underground man" can help us understand what was going on. If the Western, liberal-trained mind found it beyond comprehension, it was blinded by self-centered confidence and unable to realize different assumptions. As Dostoevsky might say, one was saying "twice-two-makes-four" and the other replied, "but, after all two-two-are-five is rather nice too" (*Notes from the Underground*). One spoke of gentle atheism, the other of Man-God. One saw the bright glow of progress, the other apocalyptic historical destruction. No aspect of reality—God, nature, man, or society—was common to both of these "forces." "In thirty-five years we shall have Europe in convulsions," Nietzsche had correctly predicted.

Socrates had identified tyranny as the political system grown from dreams of lawless passions. Nietzsche had characterized the dark dreams of the nineteenth-century underground as nihilism. Nihilism meant, not the disappearance of structured existence, but a set of self-contradictoral forms. It happened in art before it appeared in politics. Dadism, Futurism, surrealism, and a number of other groups published each a manifesto, complete with their codes for revolutionary attitudes and practices. Russia's Bolsheviks, Hitler's National Socialists, and Mussolini's Fascists borrowed the word "party" from the vocabulary of parliamentary democracy, but the entities to which they applied that term were something unprecedented in politics: they shared some features with churches, but churches they were not. From another angle they looked like states, but states they were not. In still another way they seemed to present themselves as the "true" nuclei of nations, but nations they were not. Nor were they what the word "party" indicated, "parts" of a country's institutions of representation. Wherever they seized and held power, they, both in thought and in practice, burst the limits of politics and entered the region of ultimate beginnings, while acknowledging neither God nor Nature. Since they, all the same, have managed to hold multitudes of embattled people together in a semi-rational, semi-mythical allegiance, one cannot deny their existence as structures, but one should see them as structures *in* politics rather than structures *of* politics, or, better still, metapolitical structures.

Meanwhile, the death struggle of Liberalism throws up certain shapes of its own. The Liberals, in the nadir of their movement, cannot hold on any longer to their diluted Christianity nor to its residual morality. Atheist Liberals already characterized the *fin de siécle* culture. Under the flag of Positivism, a by now utterly secularized liberal world view penetrated the institutes of higher learning, including the seminaries and theological faculties. Eventually there emerged a multitude of ministers, priests, bishops, and theologians who considered themselves liberated from Christian dogma, the definitions of the creeds, the structures of tradition, and the authority of the Bible. The effects of this loosening of sacred bonds were soon to be felt in all nooks and crannies of our culture, and particularly in those of politics.

Churches and politics became entangled in one another in unexpected ways. Between the traditional church, or rather, the remnants of it, and secular government, a no-man's-land opened in which freaks of salvation and specters of politics celebrated unholy matrimony. As for Liberalism, it found itself powerless to preserve even the moral traditions of Christianity. First the *pietas* of formal respect for one another, then the unwritten code of seemliness, then the moral hedge surrounding the family, and eventually all of sexual morality were jettisoned. As Liberalism allowed, or maybe caused, Christian moral principles to slip through its hands, however, it set up new moral structures consisting of Liberal ideas. From the myth of natural rights were drawn many laws of the welfare state, as well as laws restricting police as well as courts in their dealings with persons suspected, accused, or convicted of wrongdoings. An entire branch of law—criminal law—was emptied of the concept of personal responsibility and shifted to a notion resembling medical therapy. Together with the wholesale relaxation of morality in personal relations, the Liberals erected a moral demand, on officeholders individually and on the government as a body, which was derived from an idealized vision of democracy. That same perfectionist standard was allowed to excuse protesting individuals from their national allegiance. Furthermore, an idealizing morality was made the yardstick of international relations, except relations with countries under "progressive" revolutionary regimes. Thus liberal shapes came to resemble, in a structural manner, those created by totalitarian revolutionary movements. In both cases the prevailing morality was born from ideology rather than from the experiences of shared life. In the case of Liberalism, one may say, the ideological element had long been hidden under the surface of surviving remnants of Christian religion and traditional morality. Once these two features, which through the centuries had recommended Liberals to their non-Liberal fellow citizens, were abandoned, the underlying core of semi-rational thinking was laid bare. Possibly it was only then recognizable to Liberals themselves, who had nothing else left on which to base their laws and politics.

So far we have talked only about twentieth century structures generated by dying Liberalism and those rivaling ones typical of revolutionary ideologies. At this point we need to turn to a phenomenon of our century which is neither a shaping force nor is itself shaped, but rather is a widespread incapacity to accept or generate social structure. The word, alienation, brings to mind Marx's concept of a separation between the worker on the one side, and the process of labor as well as its products, on the other. Under those conditions, Marx said, man was alienated from his fellow men, from society as a whole, as well as from his own essence, and the whole of society must be called "alienated." The term, alienation, came to Marx from Hegel, by way of Feuerbach. In Hegel it originally appeared as *Entäusserung*, derived by Hegel from Luther's translation of the *heauton ekenosen* of Philippians 2:7, as "*äusserte sich selbt*," literally meaning "he separated himself from," the word "*entäussern*" also being applicable to "alienating property." Marx and Hegel, however, were not the first ones to have pointed to and conceptualized a condition of self-estranged humanity. That honor belongs to Hölderlin, whose *Hyperion* was published in the last years of the eighteenth century, and who himself may have received an assist from Rousseau, although neither Rousseau nor Hölderlin conceived alienation in economic terms.

Something like alienation was already observed and analyzed in very old documents, the oldest one (ca. 2500 B.C.) probably the "Dispute of Man, Who Contemplates Suicide, With His Soul," for which one should consult the lucid exegesis of Eric Voegelin in his article, "Immortality: Experience and Symbol," (*Harvard Theological Review* 60, 3; July 1967). Another description and analysis of alienation is found in Augustine's *City of God* XIV, 15. In both cases the condition is one which Schelling called "pneumopathology," sickness of the spirit.

Giambattista Vico, in turn, was the first one (1725) to attribute historical causes to such a condition. He called it the "barbarism of reflection," the last degenerative stage of the culture of reflection, which itself is the highest development of social order, after barbarism of sense, the heroic age, and the aristocratic age. "Such peoples," he says, "have fallen into the custom of each man thinking only of his private interests and have reached the extreme of delicacy, or better of pride, in which like wild animals they bristle and lash out at the slightest displeasure. Thus no matter how great the throng and press of their bodies, they live like wild beasts in a deep solitude of spirit and will, scarcely any two being able to agree since each follows his own pleasure or caprice" (*The New Science of Giambattista Vico*, 106). The blame, according to Vico, falls on "the misbegotten subtleties of malicious wits."

A modern writer, Elias Canetti (Nobel Prize, 1981), describes his own problem in writing his *chef d'oeuvre, Die Blendung* (1935): "The world had *crumbled*, and only if one had the courage to show it in its crumbled state could one possibly offer an authentic conception of it. However, this did not mean that one had to tackle a chaotic book, in which nothing was comprehensible anymore; on the contrary, a writer had to invent extreme individuals with the most rigorous consistency.... I made a plan of a human comedy of lunatics...each focusing on a figure on the verge of madness, and each of these figures...different from all others down to his language, down to his most secret thoughts. His experiences were such that no one else could have had the same ones. Nothing could be exchangeable and nothing could mix with anything else" (*The Conscience of Words*, New York, 1973; 210). Flannery O'Connor, writing a few years later, went further in her analysis: "Alienation was once a diagnosis, but in much of the fiction of our time it has become an ideal. The modern hero is the outsider. His experience is rootless. He can go anywhere. He belongs nowhere. Being alien to nothing, he ends up being alienated from any kind of community based on common tastes and interests. The border of his country are the sides of his skull" (*Mystery and Manners*, 1961; 199 f).

Among these various perceptions of what seems to be a besetting, or maybe recurring, condition of men, Marx alone gives it a narrowly economic character which, of course, was his choice before he even set pen to paper. There is nothing to be added to the insights of the other authors. One might attempt a more differentiated hypothesis regarding the possible cause. It may well not be a single one, but two or three casual strands woven together: one of them might be found in the tendency of any highly developed culture to diminish experiences mediated through the senses and to increase experiences coming from words, later words amounting to nothing more than experiences of former words, and derivations from derivations. The experiences themselves take on a more artificial or a prefabricated character. Another strand would be the aforementioned dialectic of rebellion, or of liberation. One abolition of restraint succeeds another, each attainment raising the question whether liberty has now become real, or, as William Wilberforce said on the evening of the decisive vote abolishing the slave trade: "Well, Henry, what do we abolish next?" Two brief examples here, the first from de Sade's *Juliette*, a novel of nihilistic liberation: Juliette, living the life of a wealthy courtesan, is visited by a man who proves that he is her long-lost father, whereupon she first seduces him and then shoots him dead with her pistol. Proud of having reached complete emancipation from morality, she reports to her mentor, who chides her for still being excited about the crime. He says: "Whenever Juliette commits a crime it is enthusiastically. One must proceed calmly, deliberately, lucidly." The second example one hesitates to place directly after de Sade, for it is Hegel. After his death, his disciples remarked that Hegel had, indeed, done away with transcendence by absorbing it into history. But, said Friedrich Richter, Hegel did not go all the way in this endeavor. "I know of no book...of no lecture in which, honestly and openly, precisely and thoroughly, intelligibly and clearly the Beyond is refuted and on its ruins the higher world of immanence be set forth" (Jürgen Gebhardt, *Politik und Eschatologie*, 1962; 72). Whereupon the Left-Hegelians immediately went to work, David Strauss publishing his *Das Leben Jesu* in 1835, and Ludwig Feuerbach his *Essence of Christianity* in 1841, with Marx concluding that, even then, he needed to go further. Finally, in another literary character, Stavrogin in Dostoevsky's *The Possessed*, a similarly endless movement toward nihilism can be observed, from public pranks to political violence to the unspeakable crime that was omitted from the first published version of the book. Thus what "was high yesterday is low today; what was powerful has become impotent. What the parents believed appears to the children as fraud and deception. Reality as a whole more and more loses its reliability as it splinters into confused chaos" (Edgar Piel, *Elias Canetti*, 1984; 18). The resulting experience of nothingness includes social as well as personal existence, the absence of any kind of authority or legitimacy. What needs to be remarked is that alienation, unable to generate a language of its own, needs to avail itself of the Marxist-Leninist jargon to express itself.

Let us see whether we can now say something about "forces that shape the twentieth century." The verb, "shape," points also to the noun, "shape." In general one may assume that shapes of order and structure in human history manifest vectors of under-lying goodness, in the sense that all kinds of being must be seen as linked with goodness. Liberalism, as we know, has been one of the abiding shapes of Western civilization for three hundred years, but as a creative force Liberalism is now in the throes of mortal agony. All of us consider ourselves beneficiaries of the works Liberalism has wrought in its heyday, thus all of us have reason to grieve over its decomposition. Even in its death throes, Liberalism is still a shaping force, but the shapes it produces are no longer wholesome. They meet us as distortions of imagina-tion and judgment, particularly in foreign policy. Morally, they "bind heavy burdens, hard to bear, and lay them on other men's shoulders, but they themselves will to move them with one of their fingers" (Mt 23:4). In other words, they devise codes of ethics conceived in fits of moral perfectionism, and these they lay on the shoulders of individual officeholders, of our national government, and on the governments of other nations, while they, individually, practice an ever broadening moral permissive-ness that leaves judges, teachers, and parents bereft of the concept and discipline of order. In the same way in which Liberalism's influence on Western culture once was all-pervading, the effects of its terminal illness are likewise shared by all of us, including Conservatives. No part of Western civilization is excused from the sufferings of the Liberal's tragedy. Thus, even the political structures that still seem to function with vigor in this Western world do not, in our days, perform with good judgment and sound imagination. In addition there is at least one of the shapes for which Liberals are responsible which continues, if not with vitality, at least with tenacity. I am speaking of Positivism—the blight of the sciences regarding man, still firmly entrenched in the seats of academic power and the dominating foundations, and still preventing a rebirth of genuine philosophy.

If shapes in history have borne witness to the goodness of all being, our century has provided the unprecedented spectacle of negation-shapes, emerging from massively congealing forces of principled hostility. These are, above all, the three totalitarian movements, publicly organized hostility of a postulated future against all of the past and most of the present, or rather, of present forces claiming the perfect future of mankind as their exclusive property. This hostility, ontologically founded in the doctrine of divided being, must conceive itself as irreconcilable. Even though it may be forced into certain compromises with reality that may appear as if they were common sense, the hostility central to this world view must continue as the basic motive force, engendering parties that will not be a part, countries in the service of goals transcending national interests, and governments acknowledging no civil obligation.

A question may arise as to whether a sacred symbol such as the Holocaust might possibly infuse a touch of negativity into the shape that is Israel, which, if indeed present, would induce a certain amount of irreconcilability in the politics both of Israel and its adversaries, by its reference to the suffering of a wrong beyond any conceivable forgiveness. This might be considered a new kind of negation-shape, one rooted not in a claim for total power but rather in a memory of total suffering. If one should think of terrorism as still another type of negation-shape, one neglects the relative shapelessness of this world-wide-yet-nowhere phenomenon. Maybe it cannot be understood except as a marginal effect of the great power existence of historical shapes animated predominantly by negation. Our misfortune is that despairing Liberalism is no longer capable of discerning between historical shapes of goodness, on the one side, and negation-shapes, on the other. Even in this unappeasable situation they continue to dream that all conflicts are solvable by negotiations, that every revolution is nothing but a rational rebellion, and that in any world universal and lasting peace is practically attainable, given determination. Without these Liberal illusions, the peace-movement could not be manipulated as a chosen instrument of Soviet policy, and Liberation Theology would never have reared its ugly head.

As for the alienated flotsam, it is generating its own kind of culture, called now "subculture," now "anti-culture." Its medium is Rock, with its incessant expression of the torment of alienation, and its dissolvent rejection of traditional shapes. It also brings forth a variety of structures, albeit short-lived ones, like that at Jonestown, various Western versions of Eastern cults, pinpointed transvaluations of values, progressively bizarre fashions of dress, hairstyles, skin painting. In the face of individual atomization, there are frenzies of communication, none of them satisfying the endless thirst for unity where there is no unity. The presence of alienated existences in our midst is not without its political consequences. Neither the state, nor government, can count today on being taken for granted in the way they used to be. Nor is any new road to legitimacy available in the present absence of political theory. Vico's term, "aliens in their own countries," meant to apply to the Rome of Augustus, seems curiously fitting to the present West.

Are there no forces in our century capable of giving rise to alternative shapes? One may venture the generalization that, while the shaping of renewal is indeed going on, the shapes have not yet come into existence. Where, then, can one observe the ongoing shaping? Since the degeneration of Liberal theology played such an important role in generating the crisis, it is proper to look first toward religion. Forces of Christian renewal have grown, both in number and in power, in the last third of the century. All branches of Christianity have a share in this movement. It has a popular as well as a liturgical and a theological aspect and thus cannot be shrugged off as a passing fad. Christian publications, not only books but journals and other periodicals as well, must once more be counted as a substantial intellectual presence. Christian education is moving forward toward a new place at the center.

As Liberal culture belonged, first of all, to the educated part of our society, its decline and that of the humanities and the social sciences followed suit. There is renewal also in this field, remarkable in quality, although in its quantity and influence still impeded by Positivism. In a number of scientific disciplines, meta-positivist thinkers have blazed new and important trails: classicists, orientalists, biblical scholars, historians, political scientists, and, *mirabile dictu*, sociologists have blazed new insight. They found support in such metapositivist philosophers as the late Henri Bergson, Michael Polanyi, Bernard Lonergan, Karl Loewith, Wilhelm Kamlah, Hans Jonas, and Alvin Plantinga. Two important political philosophers, Eric Voegelin and Leo Strauss, have gathered many of these disparate strands, the one into a philosophy of History as well as of consciousness, the other into renewed attention to classical philosophers. After the near-destruction of philosophy by Positivism, it now seems possible to recover the lost concept of nature by restoring to nature both purpose and value, without disturbing the eminently successful scientific exploration of causal relations. Above all, the development seems to point in the direction of a restoration of God to philosophical cognizance, not as a mere return to ancient texts, but rather to a new understanding of modern foundations.

These things, however, have been done by scholars and are noticed primarily by scholars. If the shaping were to produce an actual shape, it would need to be molded by someone like Burke who formulated, in a way intelligible to all educated people, principles of discernment between public rationality and irrationality, legitimacy and illegitimacy, philosophy and ideology. Burke's thinking did constitute one of the shapes of Western civilization, in a way that contemporary Conservatism has not been able to attain. A renewal movement *sui generis* is that connected with the name of Aleksandr Solzhenitsyn, to which one may add that of Poland's *Solidarnosc*. Both have the distinction of being born in direct experiences of near annihilation of humanity, from which they have risen to public articulation and world wide authority. Anyone who takes a close look at the breadth and the depth of these developments will be cured from a mood of despair, not only a despair of metaphysical dimensions, but even historical despair concerning the West and its culture. The forces are at work, and the shapes are yet to emerge.

A Christian Sheen on a
Secular World *

The main title of one of Professor Jaroslav Pelikan's most challenging books—*Jesus Through the Centuries*— moves a reader to hold it in one's hand, like a letter from an unknown sender that one turns back and forth before opening, wondering much about the sender and the message the letter might contain. *Jesus Through the Centuries*, by its very subtitle, excludes a treatise on dogma, the development of the faith, or some other theological scholarship.[1] It promises to deal with Jesus "in the history of culture." The setting is familiar, but which "Jesus" would fit into it? The "historical" Jesus, the "son of the carpenter from Nazareth," as his neighbors described him? Or the figure fleetingly mentioned in Josephus and Tacitus? Neither of these Jesus figures deserves any kind of place in history. The other Jesus, however, is the unique person who has so over-whelmingly impressed spiritually sensitive followers that they have felt a need to bestow on him sacred names and titles in Jesus's own lifetime and after his death, for centuries.

From the outset the Jesus who is remembered is wholly what Bultmann called a "faith event," the term slightly hinting at something that is real only to a certain kind of subjective imagination. Still, one need not take the term in this sense, for

---

* This was originally published as a review of Jaroslav Pelikan's *Jesus Through the Centuries* (New Haven, 1985.).

faith at its best has no idiosyncratic character. It is a steady and loving openness to those aspects of reality that lie beyond sense impressions and include the mysteries attending nature, history, and every human life. It is true that people of faith have sensitivities others may be lacking, and that they apperceive meanings where others would not even think of looking, but the same applies, for instance, to those who are in love. Designating Jesus as a "faith event" does not imply any reductionism, but rather a wiser horizon. It was this Jesus whose experience marked, in others, an epoch in human history. Throughout history, epoch-making events have been experiences of timeless meaning in the flow of time. In Jesus's case this would refer not to the experience of Jesus himself, which might have become an object of knowledge had he written a book, but rather the experiences Jesus called forth in people of faith.

By way of comparison, we do have Plato's description of his soul's movements in the process of "discovering the mind" "wondering," "seeking," "being drawn," "questioning," and "loving."[2] It is also significant that behind Plato's own experience and Socrates, which moved him to put most of his work into the mouth of Socrates. Socrates, too, wrote no book, but the Socrates who entered history is the figure of Plato's dialogues, also a kind of "faith event." In Jesus's life it might have seemed that he headed in the same direction as Socrates, for the first title conferred on him by many was "rabbi," or teacher. Soon, however, it turned out that this designation could not sufficiently capture the true dimension of Jesus's person. As Pelikan relates:

> The future belonged to the titles "Christ" and "Lord" as names for Jesus, and to the identification of him as the Son of God and the second person of the Trinity. It was not merely in the name of a great teacher, not even in the name of the greatest teacher who ever lived, that Justinian built Hagia Sophia in Constantinople

and Johann Sebastian Bach composed the *Mass in B-Minor*. There are no cathedrals in honor of Socrates(17).

That is precisely why the title of Pelikan's book makes one wonder how the work could be brought about. For there is no Jesus in universal memory other than the one of Christian experience, and the Jesus of the dogma calls for the bent knee rather than for a treatise on culture. Perhaps this particular approach could not have occurred to anybody, nor have been carried to success by anybody, other than Jaroslav Pelikan. A man of broad and profound erudition, a scholar of recognized authority who has authored three volumes on *The Christian Tradition*, a Lutheran, and Sterling Professor and de Vane Lecturer at Yale, Pelikan is a man who combines professional detachment, lively faith, and poetic sensitivity. Tackling a paradoxical enterprise, the cultural mirroring of high spiritual experiences, he succeeds astonishingly, superbly, convincingly, and memorably. It does not take away from his success that it appears more pronounced in the first half of the book, in chapters of which each is linked to one of the names or titles conferred on Jesus by the faithful. In his later chapters Pelikan himself must hunt, in the literature, for a suitable characterization of Jesus that could represent the culture of a period, *e.g.*, the Renaissance, the Enlightenment, romanticism, modernity. "I think I have always wanted to write this book," he says at the beginning of the Preface. The fulfillment of a life's wish is indeed a joyful event, and Pelikan's joy is contagious.

How does he proceed? We have seen that one must start with the dogmata elicited, by Jesus's appearance, from the faithful, but Pelikan deals with them as data, avoiding any trace of preaching, for he aims not at the dogma but at the image of images of Christ in a succession of cultures. For instance, this remark about Jesus Christ and history:

"The time is fulfilled...in these last days": it is obvious from these and other statements of the early genera-

tions of Christian believers that as they carried out the
task of finding a language that would not collapse
under the weight of what they believed to be the
significance of the coming of Jesus, they found it
necessary to invent a grammar of history...[approach-
ing] the schema of historical meaning that had arisen
in the interpretation of the redemption of Israel accomplished by the exodus from Egypt, and adapted
this schema to the redemption of humanity accomplished by the resurrection of Jesus Christ from the
dead (21f.).

No description of a strange religion could be more neutral than
this, even though a believing Christian wrote it. He knows when
it is imperative for him to preserve the discipline of scholarly
detachment, even in matters close to his heart. That applies also
to the conclusion:

Thus the entire history of Israel had reached its turning point in Jesus as prophet, as priest, and as king.
After the same manner, he was identified as the
turning point in the entire history of all the nations of
the world, as that history was encapsulated in the
history of the "mistress of nations," the Roman empire.

What evidence does he mention? Not, primarily, Augustine's
City of God, although Pelikan does acknowledge the key role of
this work. For the effects on general culture he selects the history
of Eusebius of his own lifetime's events—the fourth century—
and Athanasius's biography of Saint Antony. Eusebius, who
knew Constantine personally and deeply appreciated the significance of that emperor's conversion and victory, nevertheless finds
the decisive event in his narration not in the fourth century but
in the life of Jesus Christ. That, for him, was the event with
universal/historical implications. Similarly, the history of Antony's
personal life centers ultimately on Jesus Christ, rather than the
hermit himself: "Although the purpose of the book is to present

Antony as the embodiment of an ideal, that does not prevent Athanasius from describing his life as an existential struggle, and a struggle that never ends until death. Throughout, it is an effort to describe Antony's life as 'the work of the Savior in Antony.'" The image of Jesus Christ creates perspectives of history both in public life and in the life of a particular person.

Sometimes Pelikan describes the broad cultural effect of Jesus's image more in hints than in full elaboration, particularly in the fourth chapter, "The King of Kings." "King" appeared in Pilate's inscription on the cross of Jesus, as it also did in the Book of Revelation where earthly monarchs are seen acclaiming Christ as "Lord of lords, and King of kings." Pelikan briefly mentions divergent political theories flowing from there: one thing celebrates Constantine's empire as the ultimate fruition of beginnings in Jesus himself and in Augustus, the emperor of universal peace; another manifests itself in Pope Leo I's successful attempt to stop Attila the Hun from capturing Rome, displaying the power which Christ was said to have conferred on the apostles as the first bishops; a third opposes the political kingship of Christ "both in the name of the autonomy of the political order and in the name of the eternal kingship of Christ."

Pelikan gives too little attention to the broadest political development stemming from Jesus Christ: the disappearance of that type of state in which priests were high state officials, and temples and rites were the foremost political institutions. The meaning of Christ's kingship for human life lay above and beyond the political sphere, so that the apparatus of political rule could no longer be seen as the sovereign agent of worship and salvation. Thus, first in Augustine's penetrating analysis and then in the formula coined by Pope Gelasius, two rules and two allegiances came to be distinguished—*sacerdotium* and *imperium*—spiritual and secular rule. Cultural results were found not only in the acknowledged tension between man's legal order and the higher destiny of his soul, but also in the phenomenon of the limited state, and political rule operating within certain permanent confinements. From the sixth century and on, the limited state has been the hallmark of Western civilization. This basic trait alone can account for what Albert Camus has called the "metaphysical rebellion" of the nineteenth and twentieth centuries, for our distinction between political and nonpolitical dimensions of life, and for the Western experience of totalitarian power as an abomination. The Western concept of politics and its limits is certainly one of the broadest cultural effects of Jesus Christ.

Another concept, possibly a broader one, is treated in the fifth chapter, entitled "The Cosmic Christ." This is a curious title, considering what the chapter says, which opens with a quotation from Alfred North Whitehead's *Science and the Modern World* (1925) concerning the contribution of medievalism to the formation of the scientific movement and the belief that

> every detailed occurrence can be correlated with its antecedents in a perfectly definite manner, exemplifying general principles. Without this belief the incredible labours of scientists would be without hope. It is this instinctive conviction, vividly poised before the imagination, which is the motive power of research:— that there is a secret, a secret which can be unveiled. How has this conviction been so vividly implanted on the European mind?... It must come from the medieval insistence on the rationality of God, conceived of as with the personal energy of Jehovah and with the rationality of a Greek philosopher (57).

Whitehead's surmise, at that time not proven, was concretely confirmed by the researches into medieval science by Pierre Duhem and, more recently, the numerous books on the subject by Stanley L. Jaki, theologian, philosopher, and physicist. Several fourteenth-century scholars, among them Buridan and Nicole Oresme, reflecting on Aristotle's cosmology in the light of the Christian faith in the world's creation *ex nihilo* by God, corrected both Aristotle's law of motion and "his insistence on the eternity of the heavens, the endless recurrence of the same ideas and views. 'This is not true,' reads Oresme's terse rebuttal."[3] Through Whitehead, Pelikan points to the entire phenomenon of modern science as essentially linked to faith in Jesus Christ.

Which of his titles is hidden under the chapter heading, "The Cosmic Christ"? It is the title "Logos" as found in the opening of the Gospel according to John: "In the beginning was the Word, and the Word was with God, and the Word was God.... All things were made through Him and without Him nothing was made that was made." Pelikan comments:

> Because the speaking of God (which is one way to translate Logos) made the world possible, it was also the speaking of God that made the world intelligible: Jesus Christ as Logos was the *Word of God* revealing the way and will of God to the world. As the medium of divine revelation, he was also the agent of divine revelation, specifically of revelation about the cosmos and its creation. His "credibility" was fundamental to all human understanding (59).

The Christian fathers drew from this insight far-reaching conclusions: "There was, therefore, an analogy between the Logos of God, which had become incarnate in Jesus, and the logos of humanity, which was incarnate in each person and perceptible to each person from within" (63). After certain starts in false directions (a tendency to glorify the irrational on the one hand and a rash claim that the mind has power to know everything about God on the other), the consensus on which the Fathers settled was, "the cosmos [that] was reliably knowable and at the same time mysterious, both of these because the Logos was the Mind and Reason of God" (65). We have seen how this deep conviction in the fourteenth century led to corrections of Aristotle by Christian scholars that prefigured some of Newton's principles. These new findings were passed on through Leonardo to Galileo, so that the astonishing enterprise of modern science was finally being born in Christian culture after several still births in ancient Egypt, China, and Greece.

It is perhaps bad form for a critic to discuss a particular book chapter by chapter. My departure from this rule is an exception simply because each of Pelikan's first eight chapters deals, powerfully and originally, with aspects of religion and culture that one finds hardly anywhere else. Still, I want to mention one more chapter, that which centers on Jesus's earliest sacred title, "Son of Man"—the title by which Jesus most often referred to himself. Pelikan turns his attention to this title late in his book, and astonishingly so. His topic is the gradual discovery of the mystery of human nature, as Christians were reflecting on the mystery of the incarnate word. Jesus had come into this world to save mankind. Logically speaking one would surmise that men were first conscious of their need for salvation, and this logical order is observed today in all Christian instruction. But it did not happen as such in history where the experience of Jesus came first and the awareness of man's sinfulness later: "Christian thought had to gauge the magnitude of the human crime by first taking the measure of the one on whom the divine punishment of the cross had been imposed and thus (shifting to the original metaphor of salvation as health) making the diagnosis fit the prescription" (72).

The full dimension of man's self-awareness did not come until Augustine's *Confessions*, written almost 400 years after Christ. "First Nicea had to determine what Jesus the Light *was* before Augustine could determine why He *had to be* what He was"(73). History has a parallel in the experience of every Christian who maintains a life of prayer and for whom the gradually deepening knowledge of Jesus Christ becomes the source of an equally deepening discovery of sin in his own life. Augustine himself had traveled this road and experienced this discovery. But if Augustine had left to all of human culture the notion of sin, including original sin, he also had dwelt on the grandeur of humanity in "the face of Jesus Christ," the human image of God. More than a thousand years after Augustine, Blaise Pascal, in his *Thoughts*, found terse words for this knowledge: "The knowledge of God without that of man's misery causes pride. The knowledge of man's misery without that of God causes despair. The knowledge of Jesus Christ constitutes the middle course, because in Him we find both God and our misery" (#426). "That a religion may be true, it must have knowledge of our nature. It ought to know its greatness and littleness, and the reasons of both" (#433).

The maxim "Know thyself" came to us from the Greeks, who claimed it as a divine revelation. In spite of Plato, Aristotle, Zeno, and Epicurus, human self-knowledge had been neither profound nor accurate. Augustine's discovery of the depth of the human soul, in the presence of Jesus Christ, created a psychology which to this day is unsurpassed in scope and accuracy and which, empirically, deals with the universal condition of man. Pelikan demonstrates great sensitivity by placing his chapter on this problem late, among the first eight ones, centering it on Augustine's discoveries, not only in his *Confessions* but also in his *On the Trinity*. He might also have pointed to the very late date when this psychology created a literary form of self-expression in the psychological novel as climaxed by Fyodor Dostoevsky. One is tempted, in fact, to change Hegel's dictum about the owl of Minerva being a bird of the late evening into psychology being a creature of the late night, tardy in making its appearance, more tardy in finding a philosophical expression, and even more tardy in moving the artist's soul. As an example of the latter, Pelikan produces a reproduction of the powerful painting by Siegfried Reinhardt, called *Light*, which shows, in the front, a saxophonist and a person lost in self-centered dreams, and then behind them Christ, his face all appeal, his figure all light. "It is not only that in their self-indulgence they choose to ignore Jesus the light of the world," declares Pelikan. "Rather, it is his very appearing that, for the first time, reveals to them their true condition. Both the misery and the grandeur have become visible through the coming of that light" (72).

The sacred titles of Jesus have provided Pelikan with the themes of his first eight chapters, which compose one half of the book. In the second half the chapters receive their topical unity from various cultural results of the image of Jesus, so that the images of Jesus he describes are not always born from a deep spiritual experience of adoration. Even though Pelikan orders these chapters mostly in chronological sequence of "ages"—the Renaissance, the Reformation, the Enlightenment, Romanticism, the twentieth century—he deals with cultural phenomena more widely spread than the limits of these ages. In his chapter on the Renaissance his central figure is Erasmus, the creator of "Sacred Philology." But Pelikan also includes in this chapter both Dante and El Greco, neither of whom would normally be counted as being within the Renaissance. One expects of a Lutheran professor of church history a strong chapter on the Reformation, and one is not disappointed. Still, the chapter is cultural rather than church history and extends its coverage to the eighteenth century, the time of Johann Sebastian Bach, "the fifth evangelist." A chapter on Christian pacifism appears to deal with the seventeenth century but also ranges considerably further in time. "The Teacher of Common Sense," a title often applied to Jesus in the Enlightenment, illustrates the way in which such titles not only reflect the dogma about Jesus Christ, but also reduce the image of Jesus to the "spirit of the time" (Hegel's *Zeitgeist*), thereby pulling divine transcendence into mundane immanence. In his last chapters, Pelikan gives other examples or varieties of the same endeavor, *e.g.*, Jesus as "the bard of the Holy Ghost" (Emerson), as "the Liberator" of contemporary liberation ideologies, and as a world figure beyond the frontiers of Christendom.

One must wonder whether, in order to write these chapters, Pelikan had to manipulate his portrait of particular ages to fit an image of Jesus that he could find in some of the cultural manifestations. For instance, Pelikan uses the Renaissance term *uomo universale* (universal man) as meant to apply to Jesus Christ. There is no question that Jesus not only is *a* universal man, but in a strict sense *the* universal man, and has thus figured both in dogmatic and generally cultural thinking about him. All the same, the Italian Renaissance coined this symbol to characterize the likes of Leon Battista Alberti, Michelangelo Buonarroti, and Leonardo da Vinci, and when we now speak of "Renaissance Man," we really mean a *uomo universale* in the fifteenth-century sense. If Pelikan ignores this specific meaning of the term in order to concentrate only on the meaning that applies to Jesus, he does justice to Jesus but injustice to the Renaissance. The same kind of distortion is found in Pelikan's report on the Enlightenment with its insistence on Jesus as "the teacher of common sense." There is no denying that the term is used during the Enlightenment, but there also can be no denying that Enlightenment deism emphatically centers on an absentee God without Jesus, and if it centers in turn on Jesus, then it is Jesus without the Cross and the Resurrection. One might even say that in the eighteenth century Zeus and the Olympians were more frequently thought of than Jesus. Examples such as this need to be related in order to avoid the impression that the reality of the eighteenth century is still the same as in the thirteenth, only with a slightly different image of Jesus.

More important is the question of the nineteenth and twentieth centuries. We need to be aware of the Christian component in the message of salvation proclaimed by Marx. But by this time "the human mind left to itself," first postulated by Voltaire, has fully blossomed into a rebellious doctrine. Marx's savior is a Promethean figure, the revolutionary proletariat, and salvation is by way of revolutionary violence rather than a sacrificial death on the cross. On the one hand we can see that ours, a Christian civilization, cannot endure without faith in salvation, that is to say, in some kind of salvation. On the other hand, we find the message of salvation linked to Jesus Christ perverted into its very opposite and claimed by rebellious man as his own work. Again, we are no longer in the same reality in which a mankind composed of sinful persons can count on "the means of grace" and entertain "the hope of glory." Rather, the entire doctrine of reality, and not just the conduct of single persons, has been turned against the divine Savior. The Bible has definitions for this phenomenon. Jesus called it the "unforgivable" sin against the Holy Spirit; and the letters of John speak of "the Antichrist," a political and not a private figure. My remarks here may appear severely critical to some , even impermissibly critical of ideas that are widely held. But in an age that suffers from "spiritual disease" (Schelling's *pneumopathology*) sane persons need this kind of criticism in order to maintain a modicum of order. Pelikan's pages concerning the last two or three centuries are devoid of any trace of critical description of the modern *Zeitgeist*. Does he believe that the continuing image of Jesus, in some radically reduced form, will produce its own critique of the age? Will the fashioning of images of Jesus from the stuff of a rebellious world be sufficient to heal our spiritual disease? Be that as it may, one cannot read the second half of Pelikan's book, particularly the last four chapters, without a sense of drifting, so different from the firm footing provided by the first half.

But such complaints must remain strictly marginal since this is a book that raises broad questions of cultural morphology. Pelikan has demonstrated that the form we call culture issues from great spiritual impulses and experiences. Like Spengler he has shown that a cultural form, once having taken shape, will abide even when a culture seems to have turned its back on the initial impulse. Unlike Spengler he is not committed to looking on cultures as monads or organic unities. The enduring impulse of the spiritual beginning will be able to spread beyond a specific culture by the agency of secondary impulses resulting from it. Pelikan has opened for us ways of looking at ourselves—our form of existence—which may not be entirely new but to which we have by now long been unaccustomed. Many may regard this entire topic as distasteful, but even they, and indeed all of us, will sooner of later acknowledge our gratefulness to Jaroslav Pelikan.

NOTES

1. *Jesus Through the Centuries: His Place in the History of Culture* (New Haven, 1985). All page references are included in the text.

2. *Cf.* Eric Voegelin, *Anamnesis*, translated and edited by Gerhart Niemeyer (Notre Dame, 1978), chapter 6, "Reason—The Classic Experience."

3. Stanley L. Jaki, *Science and Creation* (Scottish Academic Press, 1974), p. 237.

Christianity, in a Time-Bound Perspective

"Be watchful, and strengthen the things which re-main, that are ready to die.... Remember how you have received and heard; hold fast and repent.... Behold, I stand at the door, and knock: If anyone hears my voice, and opens the door, I will come in to him and dine with him, and he with me." — *Revelation 3:2-3, 20*

The title I have chosen for this essay causes me uneasiness. Christianity is a story of the here and now in the presence of the Beyond. "The Beyond" is a term for what is experienced beyond all that is, and can be, seen. Thus Christianity can have no perspective, for a perspective requires a vanishing point on a horizon, and a horizon is the furthest boundary of what is seen. But the Beyond transcends the reality that is seen, so one could not say, "a story of the here and now in the sight of the Beyond." It takes a horizon to establish a perspective, and a horizon is a matter of innercosmic perception. Still, we are at the passing of the second and the coming of the third millennium, and the attention to this particular point in time is that which brought to me the invitation to write this piece. Why? The frequently heard remark, "the third millennium is coming into sight," carries with it the kind of excitement touched off by Halley's Comet, or a spectacular coincidence of stellar eclipses. But Christianity, indeed, was responsible for the first excitement of this type when the year 1000 approached. What may have been foremost in people's minds then might have been the passage in the Book of Revelation which speaks of some future time of 1000 years during which "Satan will be bound, and Christ will reign with his saints." There is no reason, of course, that that period of a thousand years would begin in the year 1000, and in fact nothing remarkable happened at that moment. So, the excitement of passing into the third millennium has ultimate religious roots which makes its recurrence in this areligious time of ours quite astonishing. Indeed, a year of three zeroes has the least relevance for the people of that Lord who said, "watch and pray, for ye know not when the time is. But of that day and hour no one knows, neither the angels in heaven, nor the Son, but only the Father" (Mark 13:22 *f*.).

As we reflect on Christianity at this moment of history, then, let us do it in the context of forces contending with one another for our hearts, souls, and minds. That there are such forces may in itself be a Christian assumption for which non-Christians have little sympathy. Still, this kind of discerning labor is required for an orientation in our time, and such orientation cannot be had at some first glance. Even more could the term "forces" cause raised eyebrows and the desire to end conversation abruptly. Let us say, then, that we focus on "opinion." Not this or that opinion, but opinion in general, in view of the enormously high ranking it enjoys today. Once, at the noonday of philosophy, Parmenides and Plato agreed that to be able to distinguish between opinion and truth was crucial to human life—truth belonging to being, opinion to non-being. Today the imagination of most people cannot even grasp the sense of this distinction. Our children are raised on the dogma that everybody has a right to his opinion, from which as a premise is derived the other dogma that every opinion is as good as every other opinion. Here is an actual letter of a twelve-year-old to his father, a letter I have before me in the original:

> Dad I see what you meant about that opinion stuff. I
> wish it had never gotten taught to the kids at school,
> it's messing up their brains. One kid told me that I was
> an alien and I said does that make it true and he said
> no but IT'S MY OPINION. When I heard this I
> wanted to go over and strangle him. I thought so
> because it was silly and made no sense. Then I tried to
> straighten him out by telling him the rock story. I said
> if you saw a black rock and you said that the rock was
> red would that make the rock red? He said no but IT'S
> MY OPINION THAT THE ROCK IS RED. Some-
> one has got to do something to get this opinion stuff
> out of our school. It's teaching the kids wrong.

The word "truth" has not disappeared from dictionaries but in daily life it functions no longer as the opposite of opinion, nor as something relevant in view of the multitude of opinions. I am turning a glance to the reader, with a silent "Is this not so?"

Behind the indifference to truth is a similar indifference to any concept of "reality." Yet the philosophical distinction between truth and opinion was created in response to a great paradigmatic experience of reality, the ultimate reality in which humans found themselves participating, a reality both constitutive and non-objective (in the sense of non-thingly). Today "reality" may connote pragmatic usefulness, or logical analysis, but there is no appreciation of higher reality. As a result there is both an inability and a refusal to acknowledge authority when one comes face-to-face with it, for there is no authority except in terms of higher reality. Thus, language appearing to invoke authority is barred, and systematic rejection of authority is taught, curiously, as a dogma. One might think that a great enhancement of each particular person would result, but the exact opposite occurs. In the past, a human person could be seen as a "holiness," and in late Romanticism this would transform itself into that other, competing one, "superman." Today, our subjectivist, relativist culture deals with patterns of masses in which no personal reality can be discovered. In politics it becomes increasingly difficult to find a great personality; the same applies to business. In the universities we have the age of the group project. The place of personal greatness has been taken by "celebrity." There is, then, an organized world of appearance which has replaced reality, much as opinion has replaced truth.

Mention has been made of such words as "truth," "reality," "nature," "authority," which have received meaning from exemplary experiences of a hierarchy of being, with higher being as the source of order, and, further, from the mystery of the Beyond, the mystic human awareness of the divine Absolute. By contrast, the equality of all opinions, the rejection of all authority, and the indifference concerning truth seem to derive from the politics of democracy, so that democracy can be said to have superseded the divine absolute. This was already remarked by Plato, in Book VIII of the *Republic*:

> The democratic man will set all his pleasures on a footing of equality, denying to none its equal rights and maintenance, and allowing each in turn, as it presents itself, to succeed, as if by chance of the lot, to the government of his soul until it is satisfied. When he is told that some pleasures should be sought and valued as arising from desires of a higher order, others chastised and enslaved because the desires are base, he will shut the gates of the citadel against the messengers of truth, shaking his head and declaring that one appetite is as good as another and all must have equal rights.... His life is subject to no order or restraint, and he has no wish to change an existence which he calls pleasant, free, and happy (Cornford translation, VIII, 561).

The elevation of one particular political order or mode of existence to the rank of absolute is something that, in this case, democracy shares with the modern ideologies: communism, fascism, nazism, and anarchism. Again, the absence of an ad-equate concept of reality is to blame. Exaltation to the absolute highest rank is rational only with regard to divine reality. Political existence occurs in the stream of history, so it deserves to be seen as passing and relative. The fallacious absolutization of historically relative modes of existence was the source of convulsions, wars, terror, violence, and armed ideological move-ments that filled the first half of this century. These extreme heresies may possibly be over, but the same fallacy continues now as the choice of the erstwhile liberal man. In either case, it is a choice of worship that is hostile to religious truth. The shift from the absolute of divine transcendence to American democracy as the new absolute may eventually be ranked as the salient religious event of the end of this millennium. The Episcopal Church has already furnished us with an heraldic symbol of this shift of absolutes, when it saw fit to set aside the two-thousand-year tradition of Christian ministry by elevating a female, Barbara Harris, to the rank of a bishop, justifying the step as progress in equality, the political equality of American democracy.

A new relation between Christianity and the state seems to be in the making. We already spoke of the armed mass movements which entered the political scene, claiming to represent the absolute of history. Still, their absolute was not political, even though they sought to realize it by political means. It was a new human existence, a new world, a new kind of man. Camus coined a name for this kind of worship: "horizontal transcendence," replacing, since Hegel, the only kind known before, "vertical transcendence." The non-political character of the totalitarian-isms thus established was manifested by the fact that the rule of "the Party" replaced the rule of the state. Conferring rank of absolute on American democracy is a very different matter. Let us remember here the Christian martyrs of old who died not because of general disobedience to the Roman state but because they refused to give to the emperor the honor which belongs to

God alone. The Christian concept of political rule, articulated first by Augustine, moved the state down in rank because it was not, and could not be, an agency of human salvation. Pope Gelasius found the corresponding symbolism by proclaiming two rulers, one spiritual and one temporal. Of the two, the state was limited to the political function of keeping a peace of such kind as was possible in this world, while the Church was likewise limited to a higher ranking function of spiritual order. In one way or another this view has persisted right down to our century; it caused our profound sense of abomination at the sight of what appeared to us as the "total state."

There is no need to review here the history of these two distinct functions of Church and State. Beginning with Henry IV and Richelieu, the distinction emerged into the full light of consciousness, *e.g.*, the new concept, *"raison d'état."* What we are observing is an elevation of this still limited political function to absolute rank higher than that of the Church. The newness of the situation was demonstrated during the 1989 visit of the American hierarchy to Rome, when the Archbishop of St. Louis lectured the Holy father on the right of America's political convictions to supersede the tradition of the Church. This, together with the 1989 elevation of an American woman to the traditional episcopate, seems to point toward a century, probably not before the death of John Paul II, that will see many Christians bow the worshipping knee before a divine majesty, American democracy. One is reminded of the lines in *Burnt Norton* by T.S. Eliot:

> *What might have been and what has been*
> *Point to one end, which is always present.*
> *Footfalls echo in the memory*
> *down the passage which we did not take*
> *Towards the door we never opened*
> *Into the rose garden.*

It does seem as if we were about to "take the passage" which the martyrs gave their lives to avoid. Perhaps we are persuaded that the passage is not sacrilegious because American democracy is committed to human rights and thus can be holy in a way which the Roman Empire could never dream of. But, then again, human rights were not at issue for the martyrs. Rather it was the honor of God, who said, "I am the Lord thy God. Thou shalt have no other gods but me." On the other hand, when, today, we place political principles in a seat of surpassing holiness, do we not ultimately attribute divinity to our collective self?

The canonization of American democracy is the first element of crisis within contemporary Christianity. A second factor is modern Biblical interpretation, a danger increased by the post-Vatican II self-appointment of theologians to the rank of "Second Magisterium." I shall begin with Cardinal Ratzinger's Erasmus Lecture of 1988, "Biblical Interpretation in Crisis," and go on to Eric Voegelin's criticism of Rudolf Bultmann. Ratzinger recalls the high hopes kindled by the new scientific-objective methods of biblical exegesis about one hundred years ago, when one hoped to hear again "the polyphony of history...rising from behind the monotone of traditional interpretations. As the human element in sacred history became more and more visible, the hand of god, too, seemed larger and closer."[1] Too soon, however, it became the case that modern theologians were no longer reading the Bible but dissecting it "into the various parts from which it had to have been composed." Basil the Great spoke of theology as something that issued from prayer and consisted of "words adequate to God." Of modern interpreters, Ratzinger observed: "Faith is not a component, nor is God a factor to be dealt with in historical events," since the method consists in unraveling the various threads of the narrative "so that in the end what one holds in one's hands [is] the 'really historical,' which means the purely human element in events."[2] Modern criticism thus obeys the interpretive precept of Voltaire asserting that

history consists of "what is probable," and the probable is
whatever happens "the way things happen every day," so that
history consists of nothing but the "purely human."

The critical exegete then proceeds to show how it comes about
that the idea of God was interwoven with it all, so that in the end
"one no longer learns what the text *says*, but what it should have
said, and by which component parts this can be traced through
the text." In spite of serious attempts to harmonize historical
analysis and hermeneutical synthesis, Ratzinger says, things have
worsened so that "materialist and feminist exegeses do not even
claim to be an understanding of the text itself...but only whatever
will serve their particular agenda." Ratzinger then offers a "self-
criticism of the historical-critical method," focusing his remarks
on Bultmann and Dibelius whose "basic methodological approaches continue even today to determine the methods and
procedures of modern exegesis." The method pays primary
attention not to the event but rather to what is preached about
it. "Everything in the Bible develops from the proclamation...the
word generates the scene." The result is Bultmann's principle of
"discontinuity": "Not only is there no continuity between the
pre-Easter Jesus and the formative period of the Church; discontinuity applies to all phases of the tradition." As to the criterion
of sequence, it is asserted that "what is simple is original, and
what is complex, must be later," a fallacious application of
Darwin's theory of evolution.

Ratzinger further complains that Bultmann considers everything in the spiritual superstructure as nothing but
"eschatological." "Eschaton" means time's end. It thus differs
from history which occurs within time. Ratzinger's basic characterization of Bultmann's message is a radical separation between
historical events, on the one hand, and the development of otherworldly religious feelings on the other. At this point Ratzinger's
critique, it must be admitted, goes into details that leave the
reader somewhat confused. I thus prefer to continue the argu-

ment on the basis of another critique of Bultmann, by Eric Voegelin.[3]

Voegelin focuses on another example of Bultmann's discontinuity, his assertion that the Old Testament is irrelevant to Christianity. This cannot be proved with conventional historical methods, says Voegelin, since Christianity has emerged from the Israelite antecedents in a continuous stream of history. "And how can historical method justify the exclusion of history itself from theological exploration?" Bultmann, he shows, picks and chooses, but on the basis of a selective principle introduced "from elsewhere." Bultmann's thesis of a "changing conception of history," from the Greek intra-cosmic view, to the intra-mundane view of Israel, to the world historical perspective of Daniel, and finally to the eschatological view of individual lives, asserts that "history is swallowed up by eschatology." This, Voegelin continues, "seems to Bultmann 'the true solution' of the problem: the Now receives eschatological character through the encounter with Christ, because in this encounter the world and history come to their end, and the believer as a new creature is *entweltlicht*." If we translate the elusive German word as "world-alienated," we find in this position of Bultmann the same elements as in ancient Gnosticism: a rejection of both world and history and a choice for radical escape from these realities.

Bultmann's position, says Voegelin, "is not developed through analysis from the sources itself but imposes from the outside," in other words, achieved through a *deus ex machina*, in this case, Heidegger's existentialism. "Since, furthermore, the existentialist conception of man...does not even faintly approach the fullness of the Bible's understanding of man, the definition of 'Christian faith' as the formal object of theology becomes both restrictive and destructive." A "Christian theologian of stature," Voegelin insists, "surrenders the autonomy of his science to one of the intellectual disruptions of a diseased age, which ironically takes its name from the denial of existence to everything but the moment of man's flight from existence toward an eschatoligical future." Some history is still left, but Bultmann dismisses it as mere "profane" history, while the individual experience "of each man by himself" is called "true, or decisive history." Voegelin's precise and penetrating analysis of Bultmann shows that the troubles facing Christian theologians today cannot be solved or even adequately assessed within the purview of theology. They require a critique of philosophy which is able to unravel the ideological element within them, in this case, Bultmann's gnosticism.

We are looking at causes of crisis *within* Christianity itself, for we do not want to fall into the error of modern ideologies, all of which center on blaming others, God included, for the defects of human existence in this world. This is a habit they share with the Gnostics of old. In contrast, Christians have believed that the order of being as created by God is good and that we humans are to blame. The third element I want to mention would seem to lie outside of Christianity, as it is represented by the work of a sociologist, Peter L. Berger, who is a firmly believing, active, and articulate Lutheran, and the title of his book, *A Rumor of Angels*, 1969, clearly invokes biblical language. Berger, moreover, describes himself as a man "whose self-understanding is not exhausted by the fact that [he is] a sociologist but [who] also considers himself a Christian." He deplores the sight of a Christian theologian who asserts that "we must realize [that] the death of God is an historical event, that God has died in our cosmos, in our history, in our existence," quoting from Thomas Altizer's *Radical Theology and the Death of God* (1966). Then, however, he proceeds entirely with sociological method and language, describing "the supernatural and the natural attitude" as two incompatible "cognitive structures" of which the first is "in demise." The sociologist in Peter Berger formulates the conclusion that, "whether one sees the process in terms of the history of ideas [listing factors such as the growth of scientific rationalism or the latent secularity of biblical religion itself], or whether one prefers more sociologically oriented theories [with factors such as industrialization, urbanization, or the pluralism of social milieux], it is difficult to see why any of these elements should suddenly reverse themselves." This seems to be something of a last word, for "the supernatural elements of the religious traditions are more or less liquidated, and the traditional language is transferred from otherworldly to this-worldly referents."

In spite of these hopeless sounding statements, the sociologist claims to have found, within his own science, a future for Christianity. That is astonishing, after Berger has stated that the chief cause of Christianity's demise must be located not in the physical sciences, nor in historians' relativism, but rather in sociology, "the dismal science par excellence of our time, an intrinsically debunking discipline that should be most congenial to nihilists, cynics, and other fit subjects for police surveillance." Human religious experiences and beliefs are referred, ultimately, to "plausibility structures," so that "the magic of faith disappears as the mechanics of plausibility generation and plausibility maintenance become transparent." In other words, "history posits the problem of relativity as a fact, the sociology of knowledge *as a necessity of our condition*." It is precisely this premise of ubiquitous relativism that Berger thinks he can use as a rescue device. He applies this premise to the sociological knowers themselves, insisting that they who issue statements of relativity concerning others are not themselves immune from relativity's annihilation. He sees a way out in "that the entire view of religion as a human product or projection may once again be inverted, and that in such an inversion lies a veritable theological method in response to the challenge of sociology." In this way he hopes to discover that "'in, with, and under' the immense array of human projection, there are indicators of a reality that is truly 'other' and that the religious imagination of man ultimately reflects."

I may unduly abbreviate Berger's effort by saying that he is tracing cases of "inductive faith," looking in them for "signals of transcendence." Now a sociologist cannot even hope to find such signals unless he first knows that there is something called "transcendence," and this he either knows through the traditional language, or else as another sociological "projection." Berger's hope of having found, in the "relativization of the relativizers" a "veritable theological method" has not been fulfilled. The negation of the negation has not delivered us from the octopus of the "dismally debunking science," even though it may have silenced a particular relativizer. Berger, obviously elated at having found "a veritable theological method" within sociology, then feels comfortable in pursuing theological exploration on the basis of "inductive faith," a curious concept particularly if one tries to imagine what might be "deductive faith." For philosophical purposes, he never systematically raises the question of the ap-propriateness of wedding theological concerns to sociological method.

Voegelin, in his earlier reported critique of Bultmann, did object to Bultmann's characteristic use of philological method. "Bultmann's philological method," he says, " while deprecating scriptural proof and allegoresis, uses their very technique of relating successive positions in a continuum on the level of symbols, but since he recognizes only the compact surface of the earlier symbols and disregards the tension of experience pointing to future differentiation, the result is a separation of the history of Israel from that of Christianity."[4] In view of this drastic result, he continues, we should become aware "that the historical process in which experiences and symbols differentiate requires more than philological methods for an adequate exploration.... It is time that prefiguration [Voegelin refers to the prefiguration of Christ in the Old Testament which Bultmann had ignored] emerge from the twilight of benevolent acceptance into the full light of a science of experience and symbolization."[5] Basil the

Great had demanded that theology consist of "words adequate to God." The language of the modern social sciences, with their reductive premises, restrictive methods, and resulting destructive effects on spiritual awareness and sensitivity, is totally "inadequate to God." This fact is relevant far beyond Peter Berger's book; for the chief matter is the deplorable usage of sociological language and jargon in public documents of church leaders aiming at a Christian education of their flocks. The adequacy of method and language to be used in Christian thought and communication is not a subordinate problem in modern culture. In that it involves contention with the positivist tradition in the sciences of man, it is a philosophical question; in that it starts with the Logos as the basis of Christian philology, and the Incarnate Word as the paradigm of human language, it is also a responsibility of theologians.

We have dealt with three problems pertaining to what some term Christianity's sickness unto death. We looked for them not in external factors that might be pressing on Christianity with sheer force but, rather, within Christianity, in the minds of Christians. These modern problems do not resemble those of the early Church, where divergent christologies confronted each other, forcing the Church into a series of authoritative definitions of the faith. What, then, is the nature of these modern problems of Christians? If I may use biblical language, it seems to be a widespread difficulty to "discern spirits," as St. Paul relates it (1 Cor. 12:10), *i.e.*, in spiritual matters to distinguish between what is from God and what is evil. Curiously enough, in our modern culture this "discernment" should have been put in terms of philosophy, in other words, "to discern between sound and unsound philosophy," or "between philosophy and ideology." Earlier, I explained that Cardinal Ratzinger looks on Existentialism as a *bona fide* philosophy, while Voegelin could rightly characterize it as a pseudo-rational *mantel* around an unphilosophical world view. Likewise, ideologies, basically irrational "causes" rather than philosophy born of "the desire to know," have during the last two hundred years appeared in a disguise of apparently scientific thought. One may here call to mind Marxism-Leninism, which its adherents continue to consider "a science." In the presence of a great number of non-philosophical idea structures, and given the destruction of philosophy by positivism, the modern educated man is characteristically gullible when confronted with any idea structure. Even if he had more education, he would probably be unable to distinguish Cartesian from classical philosophy, and Hegelian philosophy from all its predecessors. This inability to discern spirits had a fatal consequence when Neville Chamberlain sought to probe Hitler's mind and, without any power to grasp the nature of ideological thinking, decided that Hitler was basically a passionate German irredentist.

Since then, however, a remarkable burst of philosophical thought has furnished us with penetrating analysis of the ideological passages where irrational fallacies can be clearly grasped. Christian leaders ought to familiarize themselves with the writings of Henri Lubac, Albert Camus, Bruno Snell, Eric Voegelin, Urs von Balthasar, and others, without which they will be defenseless against such powerful ideological thinking as that of C. G. Jung, Martin Heidegger, Jean-Paul Sartre, and Herbert Marcuse, as well as that of those theologians who have inserted ideological elements into their systems.

What about Christianity in a time-bound perspective? Today's fashionable term, "post-Christian age," may suggest to some that Christianity is finished. For instance, it might appear so to intellectual Westerners who have moved from a personally Christian past to modern nihilism or socialism. To them it looks as if they have passed a "point of no return." That impression stands in need of being shorn of its apparent universality. A person's orientation in life may suffer some kind of collapse, but to call this definitive would be to have absolute foresight of the rest of one's life. This applies also to the future of a culture, or of humanity. Today, an African bishop, witnessing the conversions of thousands to Christianity, may likewise speak of a "point of no return," which to him would mean the blessed expansion of Christian truth in his homeland. Although Christianity is still the world's largest religion, in matters of the spirit quantity is surely meaningless. To the rest of the world it may seem as though Christianity's spiritual fountains have dried out in the West. However, religion is ultimately not a matter of printed statements of faith but of experienced contact with God. Every religion traces its origin to a paradigmatic experience of this kind and perdures in time as renewed experiences occur to spiritual giants in its ranks. This is the reason why I considered superfluous an analysis of the difficulties caused by external factors superfluous and turned wholly to internal difficulties of Christian thinking.

Of the three difficulties I analyzed, critical biblical interpretation affects the quality of Christian leadership in our time, so that leaders will give confused statements of the faith. The figure of John Paul II is clearly an exception, but the vigor and clarity of this voice must regretfully be placed in a defensive category. The voice of most other bishops sounds like a trumpet of uncertain sound, and what they have to say can likewise be heard from politicians. That is to say, they may feel that they speak in terms of absolutes, but they may have fallen under the sway of immanentist, political absolutes that are in fashion, be they American democracy, utopian or materialist socialism, or Jung's "collective unconscious." The discussion of a "post-Christian age" certainly must feed chiefly on such examples.

Into this gap have moved the theologians of whom a well-known Catholic author remarks: "They are *a priori* opposed to being told by anyone what the Church teaches. They bristle with pride at the suggestion that their faith has made them captives. They have become a *magisterium* unto themselves.... By and large, they consider themselves to be members of a professional academic group with no loyalties outside it.... And they seem to be in control."[6] Great theologians "have been in control" before, *vide* St. Augustine, St. Bernard of Clairvaux, and, more recently, Karl Barth. They were towers of leadership in that they told a story: the story of Jesus Christ, the God-man, and fellowship between God and man. Today's theologians are not interested in telling a story that has a hero. Instead they work on "problems" the "solution" of which redounds to the glory of their own minds. As for the story, they have split the text into countless bits, so that the object of their research is in each case a fragment and its particular structure. Theirs is a variety of modernity's sickness, the "mind being its own place." One can discover their remote influence as one picks up the countless teaching aids, seminar outlines, discussion work-books, or study projects found on the church shelves of Christian education. It is all there, but reduced to a number of intellectual projects of critical discovery, each leading to a little piece of mastery of the mind. True, they are supposed to add up to Christian faith, but how can that be done when each bears only the stamp of a fragment rather than of a part of the whole?

After looking at two branches of Christian leadership and their respective weaknesses, we may feel that nothing more could be said about the vitality of the Christian faith. That, *mirabile dictu*, is not true. In the second half of the twentieth century an astonishing resurgence of spirituality has begun among the Christian laity and secondary echelon of leaders, with a veritable flood of excellent books and a multitude of personal witnesses. The books are mostly about prayer (particularly contemplative), healing, communion, and individual conversion. Lest I be accused of talking in general terms, here are a few of the many titles, but without author's names for fear of doing an injustice to the many I could not mention here: *Opening to God; When the Well Runs Dry; Soul Friend; The Risk of Love; In the Stillness Dancing;*

Hind's Feet on High Places; *Living Prayer*; *Healing Life's Hurts*; *Spirituality and the Gentle Life*. The character of these books is not traditionalist nostalgia; they report on new experiences of God's presence, new grounds for hope, new ways of living, and new energies. There is not reason to assume that this spiritual resurgence is a short-lived phenomenon. It represents a genuine spiritual outburst articulating new spiritual experiences. True, there is a heretical fringe of this movement, but so did a heretical fringe attend not only the first few centuries of Christianity, but also past periods of strong Christian renewal. On those occasions, Christian authors eventually discovered the nature of the heretical streaks and learned to separate them from the flow of genuine faith, an effort that led toward greater clarity of symbols and concepts.

Finally, even when top leadership appears to be waning, the great story remains. There is Jesus Christ the historical figure, forever pointing beyond history, forever raising the question of the meaning of his life and death. The question abides: "Who do you say that I am?" There is the great Christian liturgy of the Eucharist, "the taking, blessing, breaking, and giving of bread, and the taking, blessing, and giving of a cup of wine and water.... He had told friends to do this henceforward with the new meaning 'for the *anamnesis* of Him'....Was ever a command so obeyed? For century after century, spreading slowly to every continent and country and among every race on earth, this action has been done, in every conceivable human circumstance, for every conceivable human need...."[7] (Dom Gregory Dix, *The Shape of the Liturgy*, 1978, p. 744)

There is still another recent phenomenon in the examples of strong personalities who, having passed through the wasteland of ideologies, nihilism, and totalitarianism, finally discover that the Christian faith has better answers than all its rivals. These conversions seem to embody that ancient promise that the Christian faith will outlast all contrived alternatives. These conversions are not romantic, and as stories they are sober and rational. They give evidence that, between once alienated men and the reality they lost, new contact is possible just when one thought that all had come to a dead end.

The one phenomenon that might seem to contradict this finding is the astonishing growth of Satanic cults, unexpected in a scientifically sophisticated culture. To a mind more deeply aware of the mysteries of goodness and evil, however, the numerous cults of evil may well be seen as a confirmation of all the Christian faith has said about God, man, heaven, and hell.

NOTES

1. *Biblical Interpretation in Crisis: On the Question of the Foundations and Approaches of Exegesis Today* (Rockford, Ill., 1988), p. 3.

2. *Ibid.*, p. 4.

3. "History and Gnosis," *The Old Testament and Christian faith*, ed. Bernhard W. Anderson (New York, 1963).

4. *Ibid.*, p. 87.

5. *Ibid.*, p. 80.

6. Ralph McInerny, "From the Publisher," *Crisis* (May 1989), p. 2.

7. Dom Gregory Dix, *The Shape of the Liturgy* (New York, 1978), p. 744.

The New Need for the Catholic University

B ernard Shaw's still lingering statement, "a Catholic university is a contradiction in terms," is a tautology or a prejudice. A tautology if we read it literally to mean: "A universal university is a contradiction in terms." A prejudice if we supply the historical depth and turn it into a more precise statement, to wit: "A university under such authoritarian strictures by the Church as was the university of the sixteenth and seventeenth centuries contradicts the notion of free inquiry which our century identifies with the university."

We shall see whether the statement is true in this version. Even if true, however, it must be called a prejudice because it judges today's Catholic university in terms of a past situation which no longer applies. If we go further with Shaw and ask what was the objectionable element in the past situation we find that it is not so much the Christian quality of the university as the tendency to identify Christianity with an elaborate set of theological and philosophical propositions which were considered to be comparable to propositions about natural objects, so that there could be competition and collision between the two sets, and one set could be authoritatively superimposed on the other. Furthermore, there had been two centuries of dogmatization not only in theology but also in philosophy, so that formulae and syllogisms came to be taken for reality itself, which explains the tendency to identify Christianity chiefly with propositions. None of these conditions prevails anymore today, so that condemning a Catholic university on the grounds of what a Catholic university was, several hundred years ago, is sheer prejudice.

The first thing to bear in mind, then, when speaking for the need for a Catholic university today, is that we are not indulging ourselves in nostalgia. Today the Catholic university responds to new needs, which must be carefully identified. If we now take a quick look at the medieval universities, all the same, it is not so much to obtain a model but rather to remind ourselves what has been the continuous character of the Western university. Of the five universities extant in the twelfth century (Salerno, Bologna, Paris, Montpellier, and Oxford), Salerno was essentially a medical school. The other four, presenting a wider range of instruction, offered knowledge through which a young man could hope to move into a respectable position in the cities, the episcopal chanceries, or the princely courts. With a grain of salt one may say that they were schools for administrators and counselors in various institutions of authority. But this utilitarian function—and here we come to the distinctive character of the Western university—was from the beginning embedded in a universal pursuit of truth, in knowledge as a universal whole. Of course, a medieval university was a guild, an association of scholars and magisters for purposes of self-protection and self-government. In that way they obtained a certain autonomy from the interference of the surrounding society, represented by prince, church, and city. That autonomy might be seen as nothing more than self-preservation.

But Alexander of Roes speaks of three *principatus*, three eminences: *sacerdotium*, *regnum*, and *studium*, according the university equal rank with the church and the crown. Thus, while the autonomous organization might have been merely self-preservative, the dignity could have come only from the purpose of universal truth to which the autonomous bodies of scholars and magisters had dedicated themselves. In that sense, the

Western university must be distinguished from, let us say, the Japanese university which arose at approximately the same time. In Kyoto, the university also trained administrators, teaching both skills and knowledge, but skills and knowledge wholly immersed in the myth and rituals that constituted the mold of society and the imperial dynasty. In that this university was entirely geared to social and political tradition, the truth it taught had no standing of its own.

Why, then, could it have that standing in the West? Teachers and scholars in the West could conceive of their study as an autonomous enterprise because they had access to two bodies of learning, each subject to its own rules: one was Greek science centering in Greek philosophy, and the other was Roman law. The availability of Roman law seems to have supplied the first impulse toward establishing autonomous institutions of study. If we compare the rise of Bologna with, let us say, Islam, where the law, the *shari'a*, is wholly derived from the Koran, we again notice the difference in the West, of knowledge independent from society and its strictures. The Western university and its ranking of equality with spiritual and secular authorities are thus histori-cally unique. Other cultures have adopted it only within the past hundred years.

The Catholic university, both of the past and the present, must therefore be seen above all as a part of the Western university tradition with its own independent dignity. In today's discus-sions, particularly in the United States, however, some other and narrower concepts of the Catholic university are being used. One of them says that to be a Catholic university, the administration and faculty must be concerned with, and care for, their students in a warm and charitable way. Let me call that, not without malice, "the YMCA concept of the Catholic university." An-other idea specifies that, in order to be a Catholic university, most if not all of a university's faculty and administration must be practicing members of the Catholic Church. That one might call "the fideistic concept of the Catholic university." Thirdly, there is the concept of a Catholic university where the process of learning and teaching is open to the whole of being, including the divine ground of being. We may speak of this as the concept of the "unreduced university." In what follows I should like to address myself to this latter concept which to me appears the one most worthy of consideration.

From its beginning, the Western university, pursuing truth over and above societal contingencies, conducted both inquiry and teaching in the framework of philosophy. In the twelfth century, philosophy meant Aristotle and Plato, and their derivatives. Putting the same idea in different words, one may say that from its beginning the university has understood itself as being engaged in an inquiry into being, as the setting for the concrete analysis of particular beings. It seems to me a valid and necessary assumption that the university has remained committed to this concept all along. Let us fortify this assumption with a brief consideration at a culture that dispenses with the concept of being. I am speaking of Theravada Buddhism, which uses the concept of dependent origination to bar any idea of being from the minds of its adherents. In this culture the place which being holds for us is taken by the idea of nirvana which literally means extinction. Theravada Buddhism has not produced any universities, only communities of monks pursuing their subjective paths to a personal enlightenment.

The Western university, then, not only embodies the concept of being but, is also, a philosophical realism which presupposes that there is an external world independent of the mind, and that it is intelligible. That may not be what modern philosophy departments teach, but it is all the same implied in the manifold of the university's teaching activities, all of which proclaim publicly that something is, that our minds can know it, and that we can transmit reliable knowledge through conceptual constructions of our minds. Let me apply to the university what

Gilson says of every practical person: "The first step...is to recognise that one has always been a realist; the second is to recognise that, however much one tries to think differently, one will never succeed; the third is to note that those who claim that they think differently, think as realists as soon as they forget to act a part....The greatest difference between the realist and the idealist is that the idealist thinks, whereas the realist knows." In this sense, the university is in the business of knowing.

Let us, for a moment, dwell on the concept of *studium* denoting the general business of the university. One may see it as involving three closely related aspects of knowledge. The first is the analysis of concrete objects in this world by the mind's power to take apart, to find components, hidden factors, and forces of motion and cohesion. Let us call this by the Latin word *mens*. This kind of exploration is necessarily set in the wider framework of understanding, comprehending essence, grasping the whole in which objects are parts, arriving at judgments. This would be *intellectus*. But the thinking being who displays both *mens* and *intellectus* is himself a living entity, who before thinking, finds himself existentially tending to what he is inquiring about. That initial commitment has been variously called "wonderment," or "desire to know." One does not wonder unless one is attracted by that which one wonders about. One cannot desire knowledge unless that which is yet unknown can be desired before it is known. The commitment cannot be called either an inference or an axiom. It is an existential endeavor, a given orientation of consciousness, one may even say an affirmative action of the mind toward the ground on which one is walking. In a more general context, G. K. Chesterton relates in this matter: "A man belongs to this world before he begins to ask if it is nice to belong to it. He has fought for the flag, and often won heroic victories for the flag before he ever enlisted. To put shortly what seems the essential matter, he has a loyalty long before he has admiration." In the context of knowledge, this commitment may be called *fides*. In that it has understood knowledge to comprehend *mens* and *intellectus* with *fides*, the Western university has represented the fullness of human knowledge.

At this point, however, the "problem of God" arises. Let us admit that wonderment about being must include the ground of being. Contingency cannot be grasped or satisfactorily explained except in terms of reality. Raising questions about finite things propels the mind toward raising questions about transcendence which intrudes on all knowledge as the dimension of "the beginning," and on all human experience as the realm of "the beyond." In the Greek tradition of philosophy the problem of transcendence was nothing more than a difficulty the noetic consciousness had prepared for itself by explaining the world without resorting to stories about gods and thus keeping apart the cosmos of things and the divine ground. In modern times, however, there is added a subjective difficulty which a man of analytical mind might have with the creed as a set of propositions and which he may come to look on as a personal incapacity for faith. This is so because the Christian revelation has been symbolized not through myths but through concepts and propositions, often cast in philosophical language.

One aspect of faith, then, appears as assent to this body of propositions which in the modern world have come under systematic attack ever since the Enlightenment. Those whose faith has crumbled under this kind of attack may, on account of their personal disbelief, arrive at a general conclusion that all statements about transcendence are incompatible with reasonable discourse. The "death of God" is turned into something playing the part of an allegedly scientific axiom, a "position" which one wears as a kind of badge supposedly capable of certifying the bearer's dignity of rationality. Thus in the West a personal choice to do without God and transcendence has claimed for itself the attribute "enlightened," which, ironically, in Buddhism is the attribute of the person whose soul has opened to the Absolute.

When a number of such men devised systems of what they called "new sciences," the realm of nature was severed from transcendence and man from anything that tended to draw him toward God. Descartes and Hobbes, with assists from Bacon and Ockham, accomplished this feat. On their truncated ontology there arose a body of sciences that were emphatically positive without any metaphysical dimension or setting. These positive sciences, far from accepting for themselves the modest role of a special method valid for special purposes, rather reared themselves to become a universal world view under which rallied all those to whom the refusal of God appeared as the portal to "a brave new world." The positivism of natural sciences came to be hailed as the glory of man's own certainty eventually to extend to all things, the mastery of his mind over the forces of matter and life, the power that enabled him to become a "mortal god," in Hobbes's phrase. Positivism developed into something like a religion of modernity, imperially imposing the methods of natural sciences on the studies of human order and creating the fateful fact-value dichotomy.

These adventures of uprooted minds bore disastrous fruit in everybody's living. Henceforth the nexus between the order of human action and the order of things was disrupted. Insofar as norms of action are acknowledged they lack any ontological support and are drawn from the dreams of subjectivity. Some of these dreams have taken the form of speculations about possible realities of the future, like the new man to be produced by planning, and such futurist dreams present themselves as messages of salvation. The entire movement has the quality of man's self-deification—his assumption of the place of the dethroned God.

By the turn of the nineteenth century, this movement appropriated to itself a mythical symbol: the figure of Prometheus, now revalued and reinterpreted as the revolutionary hero and founder of man's independence from the gods, rather than as a culpable violator of divine majesty. One may therefore speak of Promethean science, the science which finds in its vaunted positivity both a vehicle of human emancipation and the guarantee of eventual full human power over all of nature. In modernity, then

> 1) the knowledge of nature by explicit methodological decision excludes transcendence and metaphysical consideration;
>
> 2) the thus reduced realm of nature is proclaimed as "the whole show";
>
> 3) the order of human existence and the knowledge of human substance have lost any connection with the order of being and lack any authoritative "way";
>
> 4) man, though confidently expecting his future complete mastery over nature, feels alienated from both the cosmos of things and the cosmos of society;
>
> 5) alienated man takes refuge in futurism, progressive or revolutionary, either of them taking the place of religion.

Thus modernity has two faces: on the one hand the positivist natural sciences, focusing on control and manipulation, have given rise to a stupendous technology which, in growing, brought forth ever new impulses for research and new tools for analysis and experiment. There was built up a system of mechanized, chemicalized, electronicized devices and processes originally meant to relive man's burden of work but which now constitute the bulk and the dominant thrust of culture. On the other hand, an ever-deepening erosion has occurred in the areas of spirit, of morality, and political order. Philosophy as well as literature revolves around themes of alienation, absurdity and anxiety. Political revolution is embraced as a permanent way of life. "The center does not hold," unities are crumbling everywhere, and capacity for action in history is waning. In other words, in the substance of culture and order there is progressive devastation, while the technological mastery of nature moves from triumph to triumph.

The two motions are related like two sides of the same coin. The severing of the knowledge of nature from transcendence led eventually to the reductionist ideologies, perverting political order and setting up an idolatrous worship of the historical future. More precisely, the loss of transcendence occurs first in the knowledge pursued and transmitted by the universities, then in everyday life and the marketplace. The loss of transcendence, at times a merely personal deprivation, turned into the prodigious production of public pseudoreligions and pseudomyths. These productions bear witness to the inescapability of transcendence: when man triumphantly celebrates his liberation from the transcendence of reality, he actually introduces a dreamworld transcendence by raising one or the other contingency to the false rank of an absolute. In this cabalist enterprise a reductionist "social science" serves as the magic formula by which economic production, the class struggle, race, and historical progress or the future paradise on earth are invested with salvific character. Political activities are planned to master not only nature but also evil, and the unconditional and unlimited subjection of men to this kind of power is praised as the quintessence of goodness. This is what Peter Drucker has called "the return of the demons." Now many of us are quite ready to blame the political ideologies for the convulsions of our time, but few would admit that the ideologies become possible only in an academic environment which subscribes to the positivistic "taboo on theory." The ideologies and their irrationality are merely a secondary effect of a primary denial of *ratio* that was first established in the philosophy and sciences of nature. This is why the university as a whole, not merely the liberal arts departments, is at the root of the hurricane which is sweeping our culture.

It is time to return to the difference between the function of the Catholic university of the past and that in our time. Then the Catholic university represented the Church which was intertwined in a thousand ways with the structure of secular power, so that Catholic dogma and teaching were considered the chief cement of political unity and stability. This at a time when not only theology but also philosophy had dogmatically hardened so that, the intellectual structure having become brittle, disagreement on any one of its aspects could appear as a danger to the whole of social order. Today the Catholic Church, at least in this country, is disestablished. Politically it is weak to the point of constituting a minority. Both its dogma and teaching have become flexible with due consideration of the ineffabilities of which they are speaking. The conflict of faith and reason is a thing of the past.

On the other hand, Western civilization finds itself in a crisis stemming from the ban of transcendence that originated in natural philosophy and natural science. In this situation, a university in which the pursuit of truth and the transmission of knowledge are systematically kept open to the presupposition of a divine creation and the reliance on divine salvation has something to give that is now lacking at secular universities. Hence it is most important not to confine the contribution of the Catholic university to the field of personal relations and personal ethics. One could go so far as to say that, unless the Catholic faith makes a difference in its approach to knowledge, no other features of personnel or atmosphere could constitute a Catholic university. Today the Catholic university stands out among other universities not as an institution where learning is kept on a leash, but, on the contrary, as one with the capacity and equipment to liberate science from the positivist "taboo on theory," as it reopens the flow among *mens*, *intellectus*, and *fides*.

Restoring this mission of the Catholic university should not be looked upon as something like bringing back Latin. The restoration of the *ratio* of science has been under way for about half a century now, even without the help of a university. In quite a few disciplines imaginative scholars have broken out of the positivist sterility, rediscovering the full extent of reality by reintroducing the dimension of divine transcendence. Most spectacular advances of this kind have been made in oriental studies, classical studies, biblical studies, comparative religion, and political science. A similar movement can be observed in literary history, literary criticism, psychology, and sociology.

Natural science, ever since leaving behind the relatively narrow confines of Newtonian physics, has self-consciously come face to face with transcendence. Niels Bohr observed that his starting point, in moving towards his theory of the structure of atoms, was "not at all the idea that an atom is a small-scale planetary system and as such governed by the laws of astronomy. My starting point was rather the stability of matter, a pure miracle when considered from the standpoint of classical physics." Werner Heisenberg has described his own advances in the following way: "If, as we must always do as a first step in theoretical physics, we combine the results of experiments and formulae and arrive at a phenomenological description of the processes involved, we gain the impression that we have invented the formulae ourselves. If, however, we chance upon one of those very simple, wide relationships that must later be incorporated into the axiom system, then things look quite different. Then we are suddenly brought face to face with a relationship that always existed, and that was quite obviously not made by men." Later on he adds that "the genuine solution of a difficult problem is neither more nor less than a glimpse of the simple, large relationships, a glimpse that helps us to clear away other difficulties whose existence we had not even suspected at first." Similarly in astronomy, it has been found necessary to entertain some notion of the whole in which all the partial objects of knowledge are encountered, and it has turned out that the whole remains always the essentially unknowable in which knowledge is necessarily embedded. Thus in cosmology, the problem of the infinite is bracketed and maintained at the distance of a mystery, a fact which presumably must have induced Sir Bernard Lovell of England's Jodrell Bank Laboratory to remark that in the foreseeable future astronomy will merge into theology. The problem of the whole plays a role in a number of disciplines, above all in the philosophy of history where, again, the mystery of the whole has been rediscovered against the ideological assertion of the essential knowability of the whole of history. In all of these instances, transcendence has opened up as an inescapable dimension of knowledge brought into view by the methods of inquiry intrinsic to the various sciences.

The restoration of the *ratio* in science thus is not a nostalgic hope but an ongoing process. What has been missing so far is the official recognition of this process by the universities which for the most part are deeply caught in the prejudices of the Enlightenment and nineteenth-century scientism. To some extent I find that the way in which the problem of the Catholic university is put by its defenders partakes of the same prejudices as it adopts a defensive stance vis-a-vis the triumphalist positivism particularly of the American academic establishment. I would like to suggest that the questions most frequently asked in this context be turned around. Instead of asking the question: "Is science an adequate or possible basis for a belief in the existence of God?" (in other words, can the existence of God be academically secured by the cosmological argument?) I would propose: "Is a science centered in a denial of God and of transcendence deserving the name of science?" Instead of asking: "Is the Catholic character of a university sufficiently guaranteed by the requirement that all its faculty members be practicing Catholics?" I would ask: "Would a university consisting entirely of practicing Catholics in its faculty be necessarily a Catholic university?" Instead of asking: "Must a Catholic university necessarily hamstring the academic pursuit of truth by its dogma?" I would ask: "Does the commitment of a body of scholars to exclude the transcendence from its inquiries admit of a genuine university?" Instead of asking: "Is mention of transcendence compatible with analytical knowledge?" I would ask: "How can the various parts of analytical knowledge ever amount to more than unrelated fragments, compartmentalized pieces of information without an overarching metaphysical unity?"

The men and women I earlier alluded to who have encountered personal difficulties in accepting the Creed, or praying to a personal and transcendent God, permitted these difficulties to dictate to them an axiomatic "position" as scholars. If one thinks of a Catholic university as an institution committed to an "unreduced science," one would think of its faculty as men and women who either have no personal difficulty in that respect or who do not allow such difficulties to spill over into their scholarship. In their scholarship at least, the basic commitment of *fides* must provide the orientation for the *intellectus* and the agenda for the *mens*.

Today's Catholic university has the potential to be a trailblazer, ahead in its encouragement of the boldest and most penetrating scholarship of our time. What about toleration? The superimposition of dogma on inquiry is no longer conceivable, but a Catholic university would have every right to insist on the absence of an antitheistic or antimetaphysical prejudice. It could legitimately refuse to hire those whose minds are artificially closed against man's religious experience, against the transcendent dimension of reality, and are given to dogmatic shortcircuiting of knowledge by reductionism. Many of its faculty members, of course, would believe in the Christian God. Since Christians do not turn up apart from denominational differences, one has to make a denominational decision in running such a university. This type of a decision would not necessarily bar the employment of faculty from other denominations, nor even of faculty without a particular Church affiliation, provided that their religion does not commit them to the "taboo on theory," the exclusion of transcendence from science.

This university, then, is emphatically "unreduced," in that the religious and metaphysical dimension of knowledge is acknowledged and embraced, without being minimized to personal ethics or put in a fideistic Sunday corner. An openness of mind and spirit pervades this university, an atmosphere immediately understood when experienced but impossible to define. I do not see how it could be forced into a hard-and-fast code of hiring practices. Those who themselves have this openness of mind and spirit would have to find others by empathy and intuition. The implied vagueness may remain unacceptable to positivists and quantifiers. It is, however, the only way in which great institutions in this world have arisen and perpetuated themselves. Without trying to presume, one might say: "The wind bloweth where it listeth, but thou canst not tell whence it cometh and whither it goeth: so is everyone that is born of the spirit."

In Praise of Tradition

Without apology I shall begin with unstinted praise of tradition, a reality of political existence and cultural creativity. Tradition implies awareness of being, along with awareness of history. Tradition is not merely a remembrance of ancestors, but an openness to God as well. Tradition results in appropriate humility of individual persons, while it denies not freedom of choice: indeed, freedom of choice presupposes awareness of tradition. Tradition is the basis for both authority and continuity; it makes possible the "bringing up" of children as well as the conception of projects. Tradition provides a framework for decisions, particularly those that have to be made without delay; it also provides the material for deliberation when time is available. Tradition attends all relations between particular persons—with the possible exception of fashion. Tradition is public memory—the stuff that Aristotle describes as "civic friendship."

In Cicero's *On the Nature of the Gods*, three persons, with Cicero as observer, debate problems about the existence and manifestation of gods. One of them is supposed to be Gaius Aurelius Cotta, a distinguished orator and politician, consul for the year 75 B.C., and Pontifex, who in the discussion represents the Academy, Plato's school. He is content and able to use rational arguments against the Epicurean and Stoic philosophies of Velleius and Balbus, and in favor of the Academy. However, in the end he moves beyond the entire discussion itself. "You were doubtful," he says to the others, "whether the proposition was as obvious as you would have wished, and so you were anxious to bolster the existence of the gods by many arguments. For me one was enough, that this was the traditional belief of our ancestors. But you despise authority and appeal to reason. So let me meet you on your own ground. You deploy all these arguments to prove that divine beings exist. But by these very arguments you cast doubt on something which to my mind is not doubtful at all" (*The Nature of the Gods* III, 9, Penguin Classics edition). The man of action is willing to join in a game of the mind, but for reality he looks to tradition. His partners in the discussion could have returned his bluntness by explaining that tradition is something "handed down," not assured by any proof, and not even with a reason for its acceptance, to which Cotta did reply: "Now all this I have said about the nature of the gods was not said in denial of their existence, but to make you realize how difficult a question this is and how dubious is every theory which has been evolved to answer it" (III, 93). The passage may well be a *locus classicus* for "tradition," an attitude for which the ancient Romans coined the grave word *pietas*.

This being so, how can we explain the manifest dissolution of tradition in our time, how the almost hysterical negation at the slightest *soupçon* of authority? One should not expect a quotation comparable to the one from Cicero stemming from the centuries of high Christian culture. Christians were preoccupied, above all, with the will of God. There was no problem with the Ten Commandments, nay, even with "The imitation of Christ." But along with Christianity a new problem had entered human consciousness: history. It could not be avoided, if only as a result of God's Incarnation in a human being, at a certain time and place. In addition, though, the problem of Christianity and Israel had been made explicit by the ninth chapter of Paul's Letter to the Romans. The last book of the Bible, moreover, contained the vision of an angel laying hold of "the dragon, that serpent of old, who is the Devil and Satan, and bound him for a thousand years ...And I saw the souls of those who had been beheaded for their witness to Jesus...And they lived and reigned with Christ for a thousand years" (Rev. 20:2,4,7). Regarding this passage, St. Augustine had admonished Christians not to try to apply it to the future, for "the devil was thus not bound only when the Church began to be more and more widely extended among the nations beyond Judea, but is now and shall be bound till the end of the world...the Church could not now be called His kingdom or the kingdom of heaven unless his saints were even now reigning with Him" (*The City of God*, XX, 8-9).

Augustine's prohibition of speculations about the historical future was strictly obeyed until the beginning of the thirteenth century, when Joachim of Flora presented his scheme of three ages of history, of which the last one, the one of perfection, was yet to come within historical time. In addition, however, there was the question of the direction in which Christians would normally be looking, whether with their face to the past or to the future. Augustine's *City of God* had made clear that that fulfill-ment which alone could give meaning to history, belonged not to time. That placed it in what the Greeks called the*eschaton*: "the furthest, uttermost, extreme"; or, in other words, "beyond time." Those who were looking for this fulfillment in historical time were called, according to Augustine, *Chiliasts*, or, in Latin, *Millennarians*, and had to be refuted (*op.cit.* XX, 7). Thus, St. Cyprian, although preceding Augustine, was not theologically mistaken when he proclaimed that "the world is now old, nor has it that vigor and force which it formerly possessed," and thus had to expect the apocalyptic woes which the Gospels as well as the book of Revelation had predicted.

It was the Reformation of the sixteenth century, however, which touched off widespread speculations about the particulars of this last age. It was no accident that such speculations came from the Protestants, for they had then recently identified the

Pope with "the Antichrist," a figure briefly mentioned in the first Letter of John (2:18,22; 4:3), thus providing some historical concreteness to their inquiry into the probable events of tribulation. All those involved in describing the "last age" in historical detail used the Book of Revelation for their yardstick, but actual historical data for their material.

It was not long before at least some writers discovered that a history of sheer doom and gloom ill-fitted a God of love and redemption. Thus they began to add to their dark pictures of coming tribulation a final chapter of improvement and order; still in the context of the book of Revelation. The argument for this eventual improvement, however, was largely based on the new achievements of the physical sciences. The corresponding myth implied a silent or open rejection of religious authority. In the words of Mark Schorer: "The new myth finds its modern beginnings as far back as Bacon's denial of authority ('Bacon has broke that scarecrow Deitie') and the beginning of scientific investigation.... And this protest was summarized once and for all in that era by the metaphysical speculations of Locke and the argument of the tabula rasa. The myth is of man's native goodness, a vision of the liberated individual progressing into dignity when released from the most crushing forms of authority, whether economic, political, or theological. It is the concept of regeneration not in the next world, but in this—the regeneration of the social man. This is the chiliastic hope of seventeenth-century Protestantism given specifically political form, the millennium conceived anew in terms not of graves burst open but of institutions broken down. It is perfectibility" (Mark Schorer, *William Blake. The Politics of Vision*, Vintage Book 1946, p. 37).

The resulting belief in inevitable progress was not slow in taking the place of religion. The "religion of modernity" involved a complete turnaround in outlook. Man had, until that time, seen himself in the position of the oarsman in a rowboat: moving forward while looking backward. Beginning approximately in the middle of the eighteenth century, the inner eye was looking out on the expected progress and the resulting future perfection in the social and political setting of human existence. The forward-turned face, however, beheld dreams rather than given reality.

Not until this century was this outlook appropriated by Christian theology, with the implied or explicit derision of the past, and thus of authority. That revision of the faith was not necessarily dangerous, however, until a way was found to locate authority in history's future—and that by leading Christian theologians. Let us examine one of these theologians, Johann Baptist Metz. God's promises, Metz says, concern that which is to come or to be realized. Using a formula coined by Ernst Bloch, Metz calls the present the "not yet." One cannot speak of "not yet" unless the future "exists" as a more or less clear vision, sometimes (since Thomas More) called "utopia," which literally means "no place." As More makes clear, his "perfect" city could exist were it no for man's "superbia" (pride). In Metz's thinking, that future is not to be conceived as a perfection of nature, as it is not based on present knowledge of what is given. If any present knowledge plays a part in the shape to be expected, it is the knowledge of human suffering, the *memoria passionis*. Thus Metz plays a number of illicit games with key concepts. On the one hand, *eschaton* no longer means "beyond time," but, on the contrary, a coming political order in time and space. On the other hand, the concept of nature is changed, from a *cosmos*, to that of a raw material for human enterprise, so that nature turns from something to be obeyed into something to be exploited. Finally, salvation, a concept stemming from man's wonderment at God's mighty and saving acts, now appears as a purely human political project, precisely the "coming being" that is the meaning of Metz's "not yet." It is all based on scripture but one misses the Savior in that salvation project.

This reference to one of today's leading theologians does not imply that those who today think and act without any awareness of tradition and authority have studied contemporary theological works. Both tradition and authority belong largely to the pattern of habit, on which alone institutions can be erected and maintained. Tradition, as Cotta said, is belief with implicit rather than explicit reason, but the contemporary denial of authority to the point of committing murder is devoid even of implicit reason. While young people are frequently the perpetrators of such destruction, it is their parents who have failed to honor tradition in speech and gesture.

Seeing as how our century's public reality has been dominated, since the end of World War I, by ideologies advancing fallacious reason as their conviction, the ultimate blame must fall on those who could and should have taught parents reasons for not tolerating the disorder of such nihilistic movements. Parents cannot be expected to have undergone philosophical instruction. Still, where there is order, at least a vaguely perceived concept of being prevails even in uneducated minds. That includes the being of nature as well as human being, in terms of human nature. Moral and legal reasoning flows from such foundations. Most of this presents itself to non-intellectual citizens as, indeed, reality without explicit reason, the reality that Cotta placed above speculating philosophy. Today too many people cannot find images of any kind of reality within themselves, or their upbringing. Thus, when children, even before their teens, behave disorderly, destructively, meanly, or even hatefully, parents are bereft of any words of order to oppose to their children's chaos. They may even ask themselves what their children are "trying to say to them."

We are not yet at the point of inevitable dissolution. That will come when even those who direct and move public institutions cannot find in themselves any reason for their institutions except power. Then mankind will have returned to the condition of

Hobbes' "war of all against all." Even before we come to that point, however, there will be a period in which any number of nations will have acquired nuclear weapons, because there also will no longer be any reason for the limitation of armaments. Power has its own rules, indeed, but these rules which apply as well to animals and even vegetation. So, dissolution will not necessarily bring with it the remedy of social and political anarchy. History alone will not "compel" humans into an ordered existence. There is no substitute for the will to acknowledge the higher reality that permits concepts of meaningful order.

After Communism—What?

S trictly speaking, Communist expansion differs from any
national desires to acquire possession of, or dominant influence within, certain territories, the kind of drives which created
the international problems typical of the eighteenth and nineteenth centuries.

Communist expansion comes not so much from a desire to see
boundaries change, but rather from an interest in fundamental
changes of political loyalties, moral principles, and traditional
values of people. It seeks to impose, by force and manipulation,
exclusive allegiance to the Communist Party, thereby excluding
all other allegiances. Thus a Communist drive for a certain
political territory, say South Korea or South Vietnam, concerns
itself only secondarily with territory as an increment of the
conquering nation's wealth and power.

Primarily it aims at control over the governmental machinery
of coercion that would enable Communists to make more
Communists, and to impose Communist ideology on an entire
population. To the rest of the world falls the responsibility, vis-
a-vis this kind of drive, to defend unwilling people from thus
having their lives and beliefs turned upside down, and this is
accomplished, among other methods, by defending the integrity
of territorial boundaries. Hence politico-military contention
over territories will continue to trouble the world as long as the
Communist conviction continues to motivate the small and

tight-knit groups that now control such great countries as Russia and China.

Communism, a historical phenomenon, is bound eventually to run its course. We may assume confidently that one day there will be rulers in Moscow and Peking (provided that Peking will still be the capital of China) who would look on themselves as stewards of their respective nations and servants of their respective peoples, rather than as leaders of a militant band marching toward a Utopian future.

What might be the pattern of international relations after the passing of the Communist threat?

One could plausibly assume that no other political irrationality would succeed Communism. Of all the political ideologies of the past century and a half, only three have produced armed organizations for revolutionary political action *viz.* Anarchism, Communism, and Fascism, and only the latter two have succeeded in subjugating entire nations and obtaining control of vast power resources.

The new ideologies marking the mid-century have developed neither organizational structure nor strategic discipline. They are therefore unlikely ever to attain or hold ruling power in a country. If this should actually turn out to be the case, the passing of Communism would mark the end of the era in which ideological drives overshadowed world politics and practically obliterated the line that separates internal and external affairs. It would also bring to an end a pattern of world politics which, in spite of the global range of conflicts, still bore the stamp of a Western intra-family quarrel. For Communism is an outgrowth, albeit a perverted one, of Western political, philosophical, and religious thought. It arrived in both Russia and China as a foreign import, and the strenuous efforts of Lenin and Mao to adapt it to their native cultures have not succeeded in converting Marxism-Leninism into an autochthonous product.

In parentheses, one may here remark on the irony of the indifference displayed by some non-Western leaders toward the Communist threat. While the leaders of Western countries have perceived, even though in very uneven degrees, the character of Communism as a total negation of Western political rationality, non-Western leaders often feel that Communism need not amount to a radical denial of *their* non-Western political order. Abiding, possibly with secret pride, in their inviolate culture which they believe immune from Communist destruction, they actually promote by their attitudes the chances of a Communist triumph which, should it happen to their country, would bring about nothing less than a forcible though horribly perverted Westernization, a dictatorial imposition of Western thought at its lowest and most demonic level. That, however, is a question other than the one to which we wish here to address ourselves: the possible pattern of post-Communist international relations.

As long as great powers are managed by units of the Communist movement, that fact and its inherent dynamic surely must rank as the most significant in world politics. After the demise of Communist power, the most salient fact would probably be the clustering of great industrial productivity in three of four great areas of the world: Western Europe, Russia, North America, and East Asia. Industrial capacities in other parts of the world would probably tend to fall further back by comparison.

What induces one to speak of these industrial areas as "centers" is not so much their clustering in space—because that cannot always be predicated of such widely dispersed industrial capacities as are found in the Soviet Union or the United States—as rather the cluttering of industrial capacity in political units pervaded by a common culture, and the perception of profound politico-cultural differences between various of these "centers."

Further reflection might lead one to remark that such differences are relatively slight between Western Europe and North

America which might justify the anticipation of a single large Atlantic "center." Similar considerations might regard Russia as a country that has been effectively Westernized by a long period of Communist rule. We could not know, of course, in what manner Russia would bounce back from Communist domination, particularly whether she would emphatically return to her Christian-Orthodox tradition with its marked differences from Western culture, in which case the Atlantic center might remain just that and not extend to the Urals.

Could one further assume that these various centers after a period of growth would reach a plateau of technology on which there would be little motive or even occasion for invidious rivalry? One has learned to be very cautious with predictions regarding technology, but the plateau concept seems to have been corroborated repeatedly as one corresponding to reality. Not that invention or improvement would cease, but they would probably not push any one of these centers so far ahead of the others as all of them are ahead of the rest of the world. Thus they would move, but presumably on the same relative level.

What, then, might be the characteristic problems of international relations that one could expect in this situation? One notes, of course, that some of these centers, particularly East Asia and Western Europe, are not abundantly endowed with natural resources. They depend on imported raw materials, which fact alone puts the highest priority on their foreign trade. The intricacies of trade between nations and their effect on domestic welfare, are bound to loom very large in government councils.

We have recently had a telling example of the dilemmas besetting this field of decisions. When similar dilemmas confronted governments forty years ago they resulted in a series of foreign policies by great powers aiming at autarky, i.e., boundaries that would comprise a maximum of required economic factors within one political jurisdiction. In other words, the breakdown of trade and international payments led to a widespread quest for new territorial possessions. Since then, however, some of the nations which at that time entered on the path of conquest have demonstrated to the world that a high level of industrialization and great accumulation of wealth can be realized without political dominion over the sources of raw materials and market areas. In that respect, the lessons of Japan, Korea, and Taiwan are particularly impressive.

Will it be possible to maintain the steady flow of international trade on which such nations must depend? Economists agree that the problems of economic order are not insuperable provided one allows the market forces to exact the price of periodical adjustments in the movements of capital and labor. This, however, is precisely the point at which economic problems tend to acquire a political surcharge. Any state or political community exists primarily for the sake of the good life of its citizens. While the necessity of making great sacrifices for the sake of the community is generally accepted in the case of external military conflicts, no such general acceptance covers the need for sacrifices for the sake of foreign trade or, even more, for the sake of the general flow of international trade.

Economic adjustments elicited by foreign trade pressures are therefore not made as willingly as adjustments brought about by shifting factors within the national economic system. In fact, economic pressures from abroad are rarely even seen as purely economic phenomena. They tend rather easily to appear as something like a threat directed at the life—or the livelihood—of groups of one's fellow citizens. The history of economically growing nations is replete with examples of economic competition that caused general attitudes of political suspicion and even hostility toward another nation.

The world, it is true, has passed through a period of bitter experience in the '30s which has led to determined efforts not to let similar things happen again, efforts that have taken a good many tangible shapes in the last twenty years. Thus in the present climate it seems almost inconceivable that political emotions aroused by international trade factors would be allowed to grow into something like causes of war. That fortunate fact, however, should not obscure the disturbing political surcharge which always attaches to trade conflicts between national economic systems.

Within such conflicts, two dangerous tendencies inhere: first the tendency to move toward attitudes of conflict, and develop means and procedures of conflict, in other words, to convert international trade into a battleground. The other tendency would induce particular nations to turn their back on the order of the market on which, after all, international trade must rely, and convert to a planned economy. In any planned economy, however, all trade is perpetually subject to political considerations, so that the solution of trade problems on economic grounds with a simultaneous minimization of political factors becomes impossible.

In the present time, this fact is recognized in the existence of two trade systems, one between nations with planned economies subject to the primacy of political purposes, and the other between nations adhering, at least partially, to market economies with their relative autonomy from political dictation. It is this separation of mutually incompatible trade systems that has made possible the achievements in international trade on which Japan, Korea, and Taiwan, among others, have flourished.

From these developments one may reasonably derive hope that in a post-Communist world problems of territorial possession are not likely to become causes of conflict involving the threat of war. That hope is fortified by a look at Europe whence nearly all international conflicts originated for more than 200 years. Today, the nations of Europe proceed on the confident assumption that no boundary question is important enough ever again to plunge them into war. In the twenties, this statement would have been taken for a description of Utopia, and in the mold of thinking which then prevailed, it probably was.

The present basic assurance of international peace within Western Europe stems from no patent solution like the League of Nations Covenant but simply from the development of conditions and attitudes that have pushed boundary problems to a very low level of political priority. This same outlook has recently embraced even a territorial problem induced by Communism, in the Soviet-German Treaty on the Reunification of Force. One may be entitled to doubts whether this kind of problem, which centers in basic loyalties and human values rather than boundaries, could or should have been included in the NATO dispensation of peace. That aside, however, there is every reason to look on the general unconcern of NATO members for boundary questions as one of the real promises for a post-Communist international order.

We conclude, then, that it would not be frivolous to assume a post-Communist world with two or three centers of highly industrialized nations among whom neither technological rivalry nor international trade nor boundary questions would be allowed to mount to the level of international hostility. How stable could one expect this world to be? Among the lessons which this astonishing quarter of a century has taught us, the most recent one seems to cast grave doubt on the stability of an industrial society as such. After World War II it looked for a while as if the discipline of labor and management, the prospect of rising incomes and improved job opportunities would furnish nations with a novel substance of political order.

It was on this premise that the Marshall Plan and subsequent foreign aid programs of the United States countered the Soviet political offensive by defenses of economic prosperity, and so persuasive was the underlying argument that it even caught on in Moscow and induced Khrushchev to make his ill-advised boasts about "catching up with, and overtaking" the United States. Germany, a defeated and truncated country which had in effect lost its history because it could no longer confidently embrace its own public past, resorted to the *Wirtschaftswunder* as the content of its renewed political existence. More recently, however, that kind of faith in economic discipline and hope as a substitute for a missing political order seems to have been profoundly shaken. In the United States great disappointment has been reaped from the twenty-year record of foreign aid. Soviet leadership no longer seems to pin its prospects of eventual triumph on demonstrations of rapidly rising production.

More important evidence, however, has come from the widespread attitudes of alienation in industrial societies. The so-called "New Left" owes its existence largely to fresh ideologies; that is, it should be explained in terms of perverted political ideas of the kind that look for a wholly transformed new life. Around the New Left, however, cluster groups of men and women who recognize each other in a common sense of disillusionment with industrial civilization. For them, neither economic discipline nor technical prospects hold any meaning. Their sense of unfulfillment in the industrial world frequently takes the form of dropping back into an emphatically simple and pre-civilized way of life. Most of these people do not know what they want. They demonstrate their sense of emptiness by casting around in weird ways for some substance by which to orient their lives.

The industrial society of our time has adopted the mentality of quantification, which is often mistaken for the spirit of science. Nations measure well-being in figures of gross national product. Economics and political science have endeavored to ban any qualitative considerations from the research they will permit. Managerial and many other jobs have come to resemble each other except in the salary figures attached to them, and salary figures at the same time determine a person's position in society.

Recently, there has been much evidence of revolt against the cult of the idol of quantity.

In France, the student rebellion of April, 1968, began at Nanterre University with demonstrations against the sociology department and its positivistic approaches. A small number of leading economists and political scientists have resolutely turned to problems of quality and substance which they seek to illuminate through disciplined inquiry. Most of the discontent, however, still remains formless and undirected, even though it is aware of what causes its *malaise*.

One may assume, then, that industrialization and economic discipline cannot ultimately substitute genuine political order, i.e. order rooting in a qualitative meaning of life, based on commonly held insights into the ground of reality. Business organization, soberly quantitative calculations, principles of public relations, and personnel management, and other norms of production and trade may superficially keep a nation going for a while. But people living mainly for job opportunities and advancements, for higher incomes and purchases of durable goods, for automobiles and television, for gross national products and rates of productivity become aware fairly soon that all this says nothing to man's profound concern with the quality of life.

The awareness of a qualitative void will generate not merely unhappiness but deep and vocal dissatisfaction with one's nation. At present, these dissatisfactions in the major industrial countries are clustering around the ideological symbols of the "New Left." Those symbols will pass, but the underlying dissatisfaction seems to attach not so much to a particular ideology as to a quantified and procedure-directed existence in a system of industrial performance. That dissatisfaction is likely to remain. It may appropriate other ideologies, produce new ones, or possibly even not dress itself in any ideological mantle at all. Instead, it might express itself through concepts of political rationality that would in effect maneuver the "establishment" into a position where it would seem to defend irrationality.

If one can not implausibly assume a post-Communist world to be relatively free from disturbances originating in international relations, one would plausibly also expect that industrial nations would be threatened by internal instability stemming from a void of qualitative order. Such instability, obviously, would also affect the nations' external affairs, even though indirectly. National productivity might suffer. The costs of maintaining public order might rise steeply. Mercantile ethics and confidence might suffer a severe decline. Democratic politics might turn out to be unworkable and might give way to despotisms, with an attendant increase in deadweight bureaucracy. Even thinking of such possibilities serves only to corroborate the plausibility of the basic assumption: the troubles of leading nations in a post-Communist world are more likely to come from the political or qualitative insufficiency of their internal order than from their external relations as such.

If that assumption be not altogether unreasonable, one must infer that the major problem confronting modern industrial nations during the post-Communist century will be the search for a concept of order to fill the void of industrial instrumentalism. We postulated as the starting point of this essay the assumption that Communism as a world power would decline. That implies that Communism would be unable to persuade the non-Communist parts of the world to believe in the future classless society à la Marx. It would not be inconceivable that the urgent quest for meaning of political order might result in new ideologies to which meaning-starved masses could adhere. More probably, however, one could anticipate that Nazism, Communism, and Anarchism might have left a distaste of ideology in general, so that new ideological movements would tend to remain relatively small and marginal.

Where, then, will people look for criteria of political order? The situation is not altogether unprecedented: after the long period of turbulence and violence, the quest for order at the beginning of the Han Dynasty took the form of an enrichment of ancient religious foundations with Confucianism and Taoism, a combination of ancient rituals with theogonic speculations and precepts of moral wisdom. Similarly, when the Roman Empire emerged from prolonged civil wars, revolutions, and dictatorships, it experimented with a number of higher religions among which finally Christianity was victorious. Religion and philosophy, on the one hand, and ideology, on the other, are antithetical: the first two have man looking for the sources of order in the direction of what Paul Tillich called "the ground of being," the cosmic reality of which men know themselves to be a part, and its divine origin.

Ideologies, by contrast, are attempts of men to look upon themselves as the creators of their own being and the source of order; they end up in invidious distinction between the few who claim to be the true source of order (Nazis, Communists, revolutionaries, "progressives") and all others who are at best objects to be formed, at worst obstacles to be removed. We have seen that ideologies had resulted in convulsive amounts of disorder. A return to order after the era of ideologies could be hoped for only if men once again were to look for the sources of order in the larger reality that we perceive around us, in nature, as well as in our own souls.

The great industrial nations of the future will have to delve into their own patrimony of religious and moral insights unless they want to emulate the ancient Romans and import a higher religion from abroad. The present historical situation does not seem to be propitious to such a process. Rather, one might expect to see some kind of mutual stimulation and fertilization among the various nations of common culture that make up each of the industrial centers. If this should occur, the industrial centers would come into stark relief as *centers*, a common field of culture embracing various nations, the field constituted by ancient religious, metaphysical, and moral foundations. It would also become manifest to what extent there is a link between these foundations, on the one hand, and both economic and political order, on the other. Natural science has developed in many parts of the world, but its rapid and full development in the past 300 years occurred on the soil of the *doctrina christiana*, the amalgam of Christian theology and Greek philosophy that founded the countries of the West. Nor can it be a coincidence that the great economic success stories of contemporary Asia were all written by countries or peoples who belonged to the Confucian culture, peoples, incidentally, who had demonstrated through many centuries a supreme ability to erect and maintain political structures with a high degree of stability.

It would seem likely, then, that in a post-Communist world great industrial centers of the Christian tradition would rival with great industrial centers of the Confucian tradition, each endeavoring to achieve a qualitative order of human existence under conditions of large-scale industrial production and voluminous trade. In other words, the cultural differences of these centers would seem to play a more significant role in their mutual relations and conditions than the relatively similar economic and technical structures. One foresees here not so much conflict as noble rivalry, but competitive efforts on behalf of the good human life. In so far as this kind of rivalry might be reflected in international relations, however, the shape of international relations for the first time would not depend on intra-Western difficulties but on a confrontation—albeit a peaceful one— between West and East.

At present, it must be admitted, Western peoples are just beginning to be aware of Asia. Centuries of parochial thinking within one's own cultural confines have yet to be overcome. During the century following the demise of Communist power, however, the main problem for the peoples of the West will be

Asia, and for the peoples of Asia it will be the recovery of a genuinely autochthonous political order reconcilable with an imported industrial system. For both sides the great tasks will be those of comparative social sciences and those of a profound and accurate interpretation of meaning in each other's culture, tasks to which positivist approaches are simply not equal. For both sides, the regaining of qualitative order would largely depend on whether they find it possible, in the presence of large-scale industrial production and high-rapidity trade, to find possibilities of men being men without having to talk or do, just by being, in each other's presence. In both cultures there are seminal terms to designate this state: "contemplation" in the West; "meditation" in the East.

An industrial civilization can recover some kind of qualitative order only as it acknowledges that either contemplation or meditation do not negate industry, technology, and trade, but are presupposed as the open soul's stillness from which right words and actions flow.

Social Forces and
Concepts of Order

A Reappraisal of the Doctrine of Free Speech

A s this paper purports to deal with some of the difficulties that a consistent application of the traditional doctrine of free speech has caused to arise in modern society, a working definition of the subject of inquiry is a necessary first step. Without attempting to establish a formula for all purposes, I shall use the term "freedom of speech" as denoting a principle which precludes any classification or judgment of public utterances on public matters aiming at selection of some of these utterances for favorable and others for unfavorable treatment by the authorities. Under freedom of speech, all ideas bearing on common affairs are considered to be equally entitled to expression, regardless of their content and intrinsic value. The principle calls for an official attitude of neutrality on the part of the authorities, denying them the right to establish and practice any public preference for one class of ideas over another. In this sense, freedom of speech may be called a nonpreferential treatment of the contents of public utterances by the community as a whole. Thus defined, the doctrine of free speech would not seem incompatible with an occasional curtailment of utterances based on the fear that certain prevailing circumstances might lend a damaging effect to otherwise permissible ideas. The characteristic feature of the doctrine of free speech must be found, not in the complete absence of any restrictions at any time, but in the refusal to allow value distinctions between various types of ideas to have influence on the public treatment of utterances.

This principle of nonpreference in matters of public expression is based on certain of characteristic beliefs which it is useful to recall at this point. They may be conveniently classified under three headings: belief in the free quest for truth, belief in the free determination of the will of the people, and belief in the rational method of discussion as a "common good" of the social order. Each of these values is conceived to be desirable from the point of view of individual interests as well as from the point of view of the common interest. Truth is approached in a continuous process of intellectual advance, progressing from one insight to another by way of criticism and correction. The stimulus for this movement is found in the critical faculties of each individual mind, so that a guarantee of free expression must be considered the best condition for a rapid and general advance to higher levels of rational insight. Similarly, the freely formed popular will is posited as that form of social organization which is of the highest value both to the individual interests of men and to the community as such. The people's will is held to be free when every individual member is assured of an active contributing function in it. The outvoted minority of today must be allowed a chance to win members of the majority to its views, and an unhindered circulation of ideas is the obvious means by which to secure that end. Again, discussion as a method of social change and of settlement of conflicts is considered to be of equal value for each individual and for society. It is seen, above all, as the method of peace. Only rational clarification of the issues of conflict can pave the way for a true settlement, while irrational methods must lead to violence. Freedom of expression is held to be the prerequisite of any rational discussion. When all parties involved in a dispute have an unhindered chance to express themselves and to air their grievances, error will be publicly revealed and solutions will suggest themselves. Moreover, freedom of speech is considered the best antidote to hatred, because the relief felt by the hater for having spoken his mind and the patience of the victim in being willing to listen eliminates hard feelings more effectively than all repression and restriction could.

If it is true that the doctrine of free speech is inspired by these axiomatic beliefs, we must allow it to stand and fall with the soundness of these assumptions. This paper is an attempt to criticize the traditional doctrine of freedom of expression at the point of its underlying assumptions. The attack is directed not against these assumptions in themselves but against the effect which the doctrine has on them when consistently applied. For the purposes of this paper, we shall therefore accept the basic beliefs while attempting to prove that the principle of free speech tends to discredit and invalidate every one of them in course of time. In other words, this doctrine deserves to be criticized because it is so ill conceived that it deprives itself of its own justification by destroying the value foundations on which it rests. Like much of political liberalism, it turns out to be a self-defeating proposition.

Considering first the idea of truth, it is obvious that freedom of speech is meant to express the deepest possible respect for the preeminent value of truth. Freedom of speech constitutes a guarantee against any interference on the part of those in power with the ceaseless pursuit of truth, regardless of whether the motives for such interference may stem from selfish or from legitimate social interests. Thus even where the cause of truth might result in damage or injury to the functions of social power, the doctrine of free speech gives it precedence over the interests of sovereignty. Henceforth, it is clear that the demand for free speech has sprung from profound reverence for the royal majesty of truth and a disposition to place it above all kinds of human self-love. But it seems that freedom of speech operates like some of the measuring devices described by physicists, devices which when applied change the very reality which it is supposed to measure.

For the principle of free speech, although born of reverence for truth, proceeds to dethrone any truth already gained by guaranteeing that the further quest will not be affected by respect for what insight has been won. It establishes the official assumption that all new ideas have an equal chance to be true, but it likewise establishes the assumption that all accepted ideas have an equal chance to be false. Once found, truth is supposed to stand up under the impact of criticism and to prove itself in the crucible of discussion. While this assumption itself may be questioned on the ground that truth is often disagreeable and unpopular, it means in practice that accepted truth is not conceded any kind of official preference over new ideas. Although believed to be true, it is entered on equal terms with untried propositions in the general race of ideas. Thus an official stamp reading "Very likely untrue. Shake well before using and apply with extreme caution!" is placed on every kind of truth known to men. Hence, the very expectation on which the entire doctrine of free speech is based is destroyed. That doctrine cannot have any meaning unless the exchange of ideas is believed to yield some result. Nevertheless, the official skepticism implied in the principle of free speech eliminates that goal, for when the result has been attained, the competition is encouraged to continue without pause. In this sense it can be said that realized truth is not treated as involving any obligation: it is not held to demand any deference, nor to impose any restraint on will or thought. Victor today, it is once more contestant tomorrow; its reign, in the light of freedom of speech, is that of a fleeting moment and implies no commitment.

Now the dialectic movement of the mind from step to step and from lower to higher insight is certainly the only practical method of gaining human knowledge. However, there is an important difference between a Socratic open mind and the nonpreferential attitude implied in the doctrine of free speech. A gradual ascent on the dialectic ladder requires that insights once gained should be treated with the profound respect which is due to the hallowed ground of truth: they are the rungs on which we stand, be it for further advance or for the wide view they enable us to have. In a regime of free speech, nothing is considered worthy of such respect; every truth is treated as a potential untruth, and every untruth as a potential truth. Thus the very concept of truth recedes into a nebulous background: a goal never to be attained; while at the same time the quest for truth begins to assume a value of its own. In the place of deepening knowledge we find an ideal of constant change. To the extent which the "pursuit of truth" is identified with discussion, the latter takes the place of the preeminent value, thus usurping the quality of an end which ought to be attributed only to truth as such. It seems good and desirable to keep talking, while the result of the talk becomes something of secondary importance—a by-product which is destined to be discarded as soon as it has been obtained. In this way, the quest for truth is turned into an exciting game rather than a serious and exacting endeavor, a game in which, like the Caucus Race in "Alice," all are winners and receive the prize of official recognition.

It is important to remember that what we expect to emerge from free public discussion is, above all, truth regarding standards of conduct, i.e., moral truth. Scientific knowledge is certainly an eminent value and as such has inspired the demand for free speech, but moral truth is what we have in mind when considering most of the problems of free speech. "Free trade in ideas," as Justice Holmes stated this belief in the Abrams case, is the best way to reach the "ultimate good." What follows if we treat all kinds of ideas concerning the ultimate good in the same way, granting to every one of them the same claim to the title of potential truth? Firstly, such practice implies an admission that no moral truth is known to us as deserving preference or protection. At least this would be so if freedom of speech were rigorously applied without any restrictions. Since in reality the principle is not extended to utterances which constitute slander, libel, fraud or other attempts to do harm to some private individual, a distinction must be made between moral truth regarding interindividual relations and moral truth regarding political affairs. It is only with respect to the latter that freedom of speech maintains an attitude of moral agnosticism. We have no doubt about moral obligations in private affairs, and we expect the authorities to defend recognized truth concerning such matters with all the means at their disposal. If, on the other hand, we demand a neutral attitude on the part of the authorities in all moral questions of political concern, we thereby acknowledge that the moral insights of our private relations have no bearing on these issues, and that standards of political morality are a matter of discussion rather than of careful cultivation.

Secondly, a nonpreferential treatment of all ideas concerning the "ultimate good" means that disinterested ideas are not publicly conceded to deserve preference over self-interested ideas. We find therein an implied suggestion that moral truth might be expected to emerge from the clash of highly powered interests just as well as from the exchange of detached insights by scholars and saints. The protagonists of free speech seem to believe that only when all individuals have a chance to make known their particular desires can an "ultimate good" emerge. The "ultimate good" thus begins to appear as a constantly changing and shifting resultant of interests, rather than as a product of common thought.

In a society in which truth is officially treated as but a passing rest in an endless movement of discussion, and goodness is considered a matter of popular agreement, a general indifference regarding absolutes begins to spread. Under the influence of relativism, ideas as such lose that intended relations to truth which originally caused them to be guaranteed the fullest measure of free expression. Where absolutes are no longer taken seriously, political ideas are sought not for the sake of knowledge, but for mere effectiveness. The more such relativization progresses, the more the guarantee of free speech serves to bring about something quite opposite from what was originally intended. In a general relativistic atmosphere, ideas become above all formidable weapons. There is an emotional vacuum in such a society, and ideas which are capable of filling it are apt to engender great political power. While in an age of rationalism liberty of speech served the individual as a defense against tyrannical monarchs and majorities, in an age of relativism it turns into aggressive power in the hands of demagogues and dictators. In such an environment, the rigorous adherence to the free speech doctrine is tantamount to an official encouragement for tyrants, their success being made possible by words and ideas which have been conceived, not from a desire for truth but from lust for power, and which are meant not to dispel ignorance but to exploit it. No amount of free discussion can conduce to truth when such ideas dominate the marketplace. The masses from whose mental world the awareness of common standards of truth and goodness has receded are prone to accept not that which is true but that which is emotionally best fitted to their prevalent mood. Hitler's racial doctrine was thus received, in spite of many effective refutations by scholars and philosophers. In the absence of real respect for truth, not the best insight but the most powerful weapon of propaganda prevailed. A regime of free speech in a period of relativism means that all those who are anxious to join in a general race for power by means of ideas find the whole arsenal of mental weapons officially reserved for any misuse they care to make of them.

The second underlying belief of the doctrine of free speech is that in the supreme authority of a freely formed popular will. The notion of the "people's will," conceived as the collective willing of all individual members of the community, implies respect for the opinion of each and seems to demand a guarantee for every member to express his ideas freely and thereby to make his contribution to the collective will. Unhindered circulation of ideas is thus considered a requisite for the conversion of minorities into majorities, and as the only conceivable remedy for errors. In order to visualize how free speech is linked to the concept of the people's will, it will be well to recall the model of the assembly of free men in which every member was respectfully listened to and a consensus was reached after all possible points of view had been stated—a model which certainly has inspired the doctrine of freedom of speech.

It is here that we can find the hidden clues to the meaning of the concept of the "people" and to the effects which freedom of speech has on that notion. The democratic assembly implies a selective conception of membership. It consists of very definite classes of people. Not only is its membership restricted according to age (and sometimes sex), but it also excludes the foreigner, the traitor, and the rebel. It also implies a certain selectiveness regarding the contributions of members to the common will. Ideas that have a right to be heard in the assembly are characterized by a certain quality, the quality of public faith which the individual members owe to each other. Against the background of a fundamental will to stay together and to keep faith with one another, differences of opinion are held as valuable contributions to common wisdom. When differences develop to the point where they disrupt the bond of mutual loyalty, they constitute either treason or rebellion and involve forfeiture of the right to be heard peacefully. Thus the concept of "the people" seen in the light of the right of speech is a concept of exclusion and inclusion. It implies an element of moral obligation and moral qualification which is the basis for the authority attributed to it. Only within the limits of these qualifications do public utterances have a right to public hearing. Our thesis is that the doctrine of free speech tends to obliterate this criterion of moral qualification and thus to deprive the concept of "the people" of its distinctiveness and authority. In doing so, it destroys the very foundation on which its claim to validity rests.

The problem with which we are dealing here is not that of defining treason and sedition—a very difficult question which does not come within the purview of this paper. At this point the question which concerns us is whether the doctrine of free speech admits of any criterion by which utterances may be recognized as either belonging to the circle of mutual loyalty or denying the basic community. Such a criterion would not be invalidated by the circumstance that it might be very difficult to apply in practice. Even if its application were a matter of great delicacy and numerous doubts, the very acknowledgment of a difference between qualified and unqualified utterances would be of the utmost importance. Actually, the doctrine of free speech knows of no such distinction. The guarantee of free expression means that any kind of idea, any public statement, any political intention is officially treated as if it were born of a spirit of public faith between the members of the community. A general presumption of loyalty is thereby established for any political will which cares to express itself. No kind of political idea is denied the potential quality of being "the people's will." Sedition and treason are confined to overt action. The notion that there are ideas which maintain and nourish the community and others which disrupt and dissolve it is explicitly rejected. No statement as such, whatever its content and implication may be, is held to indicate disloyalty or lack of public faith.

Under the influence of this all-inclusive sanction of every possible utterance, the concept of "the people" tends to lose its selective and exclusive character. The element of qualification for the right of a public hearing gradually disappears, and "the people" is conceived more and more simply as a physical multitude of persons rather than as entity held together by mutual obligation. Since there is no criterion of exclusion, there is none of inclusion either. Anything may claim to belong to the "will of the people," hence everybody may claim to be "of the people." If anything publicly said must be accorded full respect because it could conceivably develop into the communal will, the concept of the community loses any limitation and shape which it may have had. At the same time, it also loses the underlying justification of the authority of "the people," insofar as that authority is grounded in moral qualities. "The people" seen as a mere physical multitude, as but a statistical concept, can command respect for nothing but its physical power. It no longer obligates, it merely compels.

Under the influence of the nonselective doctrine of free speech, "the people" gradually loses the appearance of an ordered, structured entity and begins to figure in men's minds as something shapeless, formless, bottomless and entirely incomprehensible. Who or what are "the people"? What does it take to be one of them? The less clear our principles become by which such questions must be answered, the more speculative and demagogical are the answers offered to the public in practical politics. Communists maintain that only they and their adherents constitute "the people," because they claim to stand for the alleged will of the masses. Fascists assert that their movement alone embodies the true character of "the people," because it breathes a spirit of national resistance and heroism. Both movements deny all their opponents the capacity to be part of the "real people," excluding them thereby from participation in political life. Such tendencies are living evidence of the uncertainties arising from the dissipation of genuine criteria of exclusion and inclusion regarding the community of "the people," the latter understood as the supreme authority of political will. If a church that had defined itself at first as the community of all who believe in certain religious truths, later discarded that criterion and in a spirit of broad-mindedness included in its membership all who had expressed an interest by sometimes attending services, and later still all who had discussed or come to know its beliefs, the concept of the church would simply evaporate. Thus the concept of "the people" as the supreme political authority has tended to evaporate in our age, and the nonpreferential doctrine of free speech has been one of the main contributing factors in this development. At the same time, this evanescence of "the people" as a criterion of moral authority has also deprived the doctrine of free speech of its own justification. Like Midas, this doctrine seems to be unable to use whatever it touches.

"But," some will object, "this is a complete misunderstanding of the doctrine of free speech. Far from being neutral in respect to morality, it insists on the rational process as the only moral way of conducting social affairs. It is definitely committed to reason as the supreme "common good" and promotes this highest social value by compelling everyone to listen to others, to answer argument by argument rather than by force. The reasoning process is the only practical alternative to violence in human relations. Men will not be prepared to reason unless they are taught that others may have arguments as good or better than their own. It is the official insistence on open-mindedness which gives rise to that attitude of practical reasonableness which is our only hope for peace. Hence readiness to allow any argument which people may want to advance is far from moral neutrality. On the contrary, it constitutes essentially a moral commitment." In this or a similar way one would expect the proponents of free speech to formulate the idea of the "common good" on which the doctrine is based. Again, leaving aside any argument about the correctness of this assumption, one may ask what becomes of it when freedom of speech is applied to this concept.

The moral value which is here invoked is that of reasonableness. The principle of free speech, however, compels its adherents to refrain from any official preference of words which are uttered in a spirit of reasonableness over words which spring from a rejection of both reasonableness and reason. As a matter of fact, the rational motive is implicitly presupposed. In the words of Professor Cooper:

> Indeed, no opinion or doctrine, of whatever nature it be or whatever be its tendency, ought to be suppressed. For it is either manifestly true or it is manifestly false, or its truth or falsehood is dubious. Its tendency is manifestly good, or it is manifestly bad, or it is dubious and concealed. There are no other assignable conditions, no other functions of the problem. In the case of its being manifestly true of good tendency *there can be no dispute. Nor in the case of its being manifestly otherwise;* for by the terms it can mislead nobody. If its truth or its tendency be dubious, it is clear that nothing can bring the good to light, or expose the evil, but full and free discussion. Until this takes place, a plausible fallacy may do harm; but discussion is sure to elicit the truth and fix public opinion on a proper basis, and nothing else can do it.[1]

Both rationality and reasonableness are here taken for granted as the sole or dominant motives of public expression. There values are not seen as a "common good" which must be eagerly sought and carefully guarded, but as a natural disposition of man upon which one can count as on the rising of the sun. Free speech is considered as but the proper method to derive the maximum benefit from that trait of human nature.

Obviously there is a difference between discussion carried on with an open-minded attitude and a fight for power in which words are used merely as the main tools. Speech is not the chosen and reserved instrument of sweet reasonableness, nor force the only method by which the irrational will can avail itself. Words and force are both tools, and either tool can be used for varying ends. As the doctrine of free speech sanctions all public utterances regardless of their ends, it tends to blur this distinction. Under its influence, people no longer aim at rationality or reasonableness as the supreme "common good," but cling to the external forms of discussion as such. The doctrine of free speech may have been meant to insure rationality, but when actually applied to political life it simply insists that everything in politics be done in the form of speech. Thus it tends to convert the underlying notion of a moral good into a concept of method rather than spirit. Its protection is granted to the process of talking rather than to the attitude of reasonableness, thereby according to the means of discussion and persuasion the dignity of an ultimate end. In the words of Professor Sidney Hook: "The strategic freedoms are those of method; *they* must be maintained above all." When official policy emphasizes the interlocutory forms of politics, people tend to believe that the externals of this process are a guarantee of an underlying moral will, and that abidance by these forms constitutes the supreme "common good." Observance of rules rather than cultivation of a certain spirit becomes the mark of obligation and the governing principle of social relations.

Once the idea of the "common good" has been formalized and emptied of its content, freedom of speech actually amounts to an official encouragement for every person or group that knows how to use the methods of democracy for the end of destroying its substance. The technique of talking, in and out of parliamentary bodies, is assured of official protection regardless of the underlying motives or intentions. Consequently, he who can master that technique can always count on a certain amount of support and approval, by both the authorities and the public. As the "common good" appears to be identical with procedural forms, any literal observance of the methods substitutes moral legitimation. To the extent which the methods are misused for ends that conflict with the ideal of rationality and reasonableness, this legitimation breaks down in practice. To the same degree the notion of the "common good" in itself becomes obscure, hazy, and more inapplicable to realities. A people which experiences this kind of progressive dissipation of the moral core of public life will one day become conscious of its lack of direction, and will in mortal fright embrace any ideological substitute that happens to present itself in a plausible disguise.

We arrive at the conclusion that the traditional doctrine of free speech, when consistently applied, has the tendency to destroy its own premises, such as the concept of truth, the notion of the authoritative "will of the people," and the ideal of rationality and reasonableness as the supreme "common good." While this erosion of the foundations may occur beneath the surface and not come to light until it has made considerable progress, a number of practical consequences can be observed immediately. We shall touch here briefly on (1) the question of criminal subversiveness, (2) recognition of foreign governments, and (3) the problem of the defense of a free society against its ideological enemies. In every case, we shall endeavor to show how the principle of free speech prevents these questions from being answered satisfactorily.

(1) There is general agreement that subversion is a crime. Criminal activities are not protected by the doctrine of free speech, as is evidenced by the fact that no utterance is allowed which is made with the intention of injuring the life, limb, or property of others. Such an utterance can be recognized as a direct attack on the person of a human being, classified as a clear evil, and thereby placed outside of the scope of freedom of speech. Now one can use this analogy and define subversion as an attack on the existence of the entire community. But what is injury to the "life, limb or property" of the community, if these terms can be applied figuratively? Can we recognize an intention to do harm to the people as a whole unless we have a clear notion of what it takes to keep the people in a state of healthy and vigorous being? Under the influence of freedom of speech, any awareness of such conditions of communal existence is gradually dissipated. When "the people" is conceived as a mere physical

multitude, a statistical group with no shape, order, or meaning, it is difficult to see how it can be injured or attacked except from the outside. If it is not clear what harm subversion causes and what good it attacks, it is impossible to distinguish subversive from other political activities. Still, no society, not even the most relativistic one, can do without protection against subversion.

A relativistic society finds itself thus caught in a dilemma, between the necessity of defending itself against its own internal enemies and the impossibility of finding a clear moral criterion of subversiveness. It escapes this dilemma by confining subversion to attempts to overthrow the government. The curious paradox results that a "free" society classifies injury to its government as a crime while looking with indifference on activities which undermine the spirit of community that is the only basis of freedom and mutual acceptance. The arbitrary and tyrannical possibilities contained in this "solution" do not come to light in normal times in which freedom of speech offers a wide leeway to all kinds of political tendencies. But in times of danger, when the problem of subversiveness becomes pressing, the application of the government protecting concept of subversion leads to gross injustices. The government, in possession of this keen weapon, then feels justified in constructing a protective wall not only for its own safety, but also to protect any chance policy on which it may have decided. Thus the shocking decisions of the repression years 1918-1921 may be said to result from a doctrine which is incapable of conceiving an injury to the community in any other way than as an attack on the government. When the notion of "the people" as a moral community disappears, "public order" remains the only point of reference for defining subversion, and governmental infallibility its ultimate ratio.

2) Similar consequences result from the traditional doctrine of free speech in the field of international relations. While the absence of a satisfactory concept of "the people" spoils the definition of "subversion," the policy of recognition is handi-

capped when the notion of the "common good" turns hazy. In ordinary times, when the recognition of governments is not a vital matter in international relations, any *de facto* criterion will serve as a formula by which one can decide which government should be recognized and which should not. But in an age in which international wars are closely related to domestic tensions and different types of government represent strongly conflicting ideologies, recognition becomes more than a mere formality. It is then of vital importance to know which government should be supported by recognition and which weakened by a policy of nonrecognition.

It appears however, that nations which have become used to identify the value of the "common good" with the external methods of democracy have the greatest difficulties in distinguishing between good and bad governments. For instance, the only definition of dictatorship of which such a nation can conceive is in terms of violent methods as distinct from nonviolent methods. If a dictator is shrewd enough to use parliamentary practices on his way to power and to maintain a parliamentary front when in power, he may live and die as a fascist ruler with the approval of the democratic governments. What he does to the community of the people over whom he rules, how he influences their daily lives, their trust in each other, their values, their inner balance—these are matters which do not enter into consideration. Nations that are accustomed to slight such questions in their own domestic policies are not inclined to let them influence a policy of recognition of foreign regimes. The same agnosticism regarding the moral basis of communities induces many people in democratic countries not to distinguish between conflicting national causes in terms of moral worth. The habit of shrugging one's shoulders about the ideal of the "common good" regarding one's own country results in a general skepticism concerning all national causes. One arrives at the conclusion that the others are probably fighting for objects which are just as good or as bad as those of one's own country, or even that no causes of moral concern are involved in war at all. People who fail to see a distinction between contending causes must ultimately come to feel that really nothing is at stake but survival.

3) The greatest difficulty produced by the traditional doctrine of free speech is that encountered by a "free" society which is compelled to define its attitude toward those who desire to end its freedom. Is it not the nature of liberty to provide a comfortable berth even for those who oppose the existing order of things, and would that principle not demand toleration for the very enemies of freedom? Could not the foes of a "free" society claim that they desire to destroy the existing order of freedom merely in the name of a higher freedom, and would not that claim have to be allowed, in view of our basic lack of certain knowledge of what freedom is? In other words, is a "free" society entitled to defend itself at all? The problem is not identical with that of criminal subversiveness. Nor does is arise from the appearance, in our time, of totalitarian movements as such. Some totalitarian movements have been recognized as obvious enemies against which a "free" society has decided to defend itself and its institutions. But others are still in an ambiguous relation to "free" societies, a relation in which their character of either friend or foe is not clear.

Fascism, once its characteristics were fully known, could be classified as an enemy because it lacked a clear and consistent political philosophy, perverted ideas for political effect, and substituted romantic slogans for rational objectiveness. These traits were so opposed to liberal principles that it was not difficult to perceive an irreconcilable hostility between the two. Fascism became, in liberal minds, identified with the violent methods of the concentration camps and storm troops. Those are just the kind of methods against which a liberal society would feel justified in defending itself with all the means at its disposal.

But what about communism? This movement, unlike fascism, has sprung from a fully grown philosophy. True, it later developed its methods of violence, but it declared them justified by the repression which its ideas provoked. Communism claims to have a rational cause to which a liberal society must not deny a hearing. It opposes the entire order of a "free" society, including the methods of free speech and democratic government, but it presents this opposition first in the form of a logical argument. Communists demand the right to destroy liberal society by means of the very liberties which that society grants them. Hence it is not fascism but communism which has significantly posed the relation between a "free" society and its enemies as an insoluble problem. To deny those enemies the use of liberty of expression is equivalent to making freedom of speech dependent on certain moral qualifications. Hence the need to take a stand on this question forces us to open once more the drawer in which we thought the metaphysics of politics had been put away forever.

The metaphysical issue cannot be evaded by a willingness to be inconsistent and to take action without regard to the subtleties of the doctrine of free speech. The question is not what one can or cannot prohibit, but how to defend a "free" society and to strengthen its powers of resistance. Any policy adopted by a "free" society which contradicts its own basic beliefs is likely to act as a boomerang. A downright prohibition of communist agitation would be opposed not only by the "progressive" part of the people but would also cause many other fair-minded persons to feel grave doubts about the nature of such a "freedom." Legally and politically, a limitation of free speech in order to exclude the foes of freedom might be feasible, but it would tend to weaken rather than to strengthen the community, as it would create moral confusion and uneasiness within its own ranks and cause many people to detach themselves mentally and emotionally from their fellow citizens. The difficulty of a "free" society is not one of determining what it actually can or cannot do against communists, but how to make any kind of meaningful decision about what must be rejected and what can be tolerated by the community. For a long time, the people of "free" societies have been accustomed to disregard the moral laws of community life, because the traditional doctrine of free speech with its official neutrality led them to believe that such criteria could not be known and need not be cultivated. If then we were now to impose strict limitations on the communists, many among us would be led to the conclusion that "vested interests" and "imperialistic policies" rather than genuine moral distinctions had been the underlying motive. As long as that is the case, we cannot excuse the communists from political life without doing ourselves harm. Even a superficial observation of the public temper must confirm this view, for the hysterical shouting by which some people cover their own inner uncertainty weakens the social fiber no less than the gnawing doubts of the "progressives." Blindness to the basic values of community life cannot be cured by a sudden resolution of the problem raised by the presence of communists in a society practicing freedom of speech. Such a society, when facing this enemy, seems to be caught in the dilemma of publicly disavowing its own fundamental principles or resigning itself to the idea that suicide is also a "legitimate" use of freedom.

What then is the alternative? If the traditional doctrine of free speech leads to such insoluble difficulties, must we resort to repression? Would anybody want to see the Goldman, Schenck, and Abrams cases multiplied and elevated to the dignity of a publicly recognized principle? The answer must clearly be negative. Inquisitorial control of public expression cannot be the remedy for the failure of free speech. But is the reverse equally true? Must we argue that since repression is utterly unacceptable, freedom of speech, in spite of its shortcomings, is the only possible method? This is a popular but fallacious conclusion which is uncritical and superficial because it simply turns from one position to the other without a close examination of why repression must be rejected.

If we may again refer to the notorious decisions of the first postwar period as our star exhibit of a repressive policy, we should ask ourselves what it is that causes us to consider them unsatisfactory. It cannot be the mere fact that public expression had been limited, because most of us accept some limits of speech as a matter of course, as a discipline of behavior practiced normally within the family, the club, the school, and the dictates of tact. Those postwar decisions were shocking not because public utterance was limited, but because this limitation was based on farfetched, artificial, and unconvincing criteria. We cannot accept an interference with the right of speech which is made without really good reasons. What were the reasons advanced by the courts in those cases? All of them were in the nature of an argument from circumstances. Under certain circumstances, the intent of the indicted person is constructed; under certain circumstances, otherwise harmless utterances are assumed to be highly dangerous; under certain circumstances the community is held justified to do what it normally would reject. This might be an acceptable principle if the circumstances were clearly recognizable by everybody, so that an adjustment could be made. But if we look again at the repressive decisions we find that the definition of the circumstances and their implication is in the discretion of the courts, so that sentences which are based so entirely on an appraisal of the situation often bear the marks of the judges' subjective fears. Even the "clear and present danger" test of Justice Holmes is nothing but a circumstantial criterion, allowing the court to judge an action on the basis of the court's own estimate of a situation.

In all of these repression cases, it was not the content of the speeches which was held to reflect loyalty or disloyalty to the community. The intent of disloyalty was constructed from the effect which the speech was considered to have under the prevailing circumstances, measured in terms of alleged detriment to established government policies. Since only the judge held the key to what could be considered detrimental to which aim of whose policy, nobody else could possibly be expected to know or recognize the limits between permissible and nonpermissible statements. The result was arbitrariness of judicial decisions, and the introduction of most inconsistent ideas into the doctrine of free speech.

In the light of those decisions based on an estimate of circumstances, the doctrine carried the implication that utterances of all kinds would be permissible in peace, while in times of war nobody could in any way predict what would be tolerated and what would be condemned. Even the Declaration of Independence drew a sentence for sedition when published in the Philippines. It is this completely arbitrary latitude of repressive power in a crisis, compared with completely uncritical toleration in "normal" times, which revolts our conscience when we examine those infamous decisions. They remind us, for instance, of the man who might undertake to justify adultery by saying: "Normally I would not dream of doing such a thing, but with the nervous strain under which I have been laboring, and business going so bad, I felt that I had a right to sow some wild oats." It is the basic immorality of such reasoning which makes us reject the repression cases.

If the arbitrary curtailment of public expression on the ground of pressing circumstances must be rejected as immoral, so must freedom of speech, on the same count. We have seen how awareness of the moral quality of political ideas is gradually undermined when society as a whole, through its official representatives, declares itself neutral in regard to political judgments. Such a laissez-faire principle in the field of political ideas implies that community is essentially not an entity of mutual loyalty, public faith, and devotion to a "common good," but a vast and loose network of little significance as a whole. Freedom of speech implies that the community as such really has no moral demands to make on its members beyond the requirement that nobody should interfere with his neighbor's desire to express his ideas. If anything may be thus advocated and everything must be tolerated, and if one opinion is potentially just as good as another, the test of ideas must be found in their historical success. From this point of view, World History becomes the supreme tribunal. "Whatever is and can maintain itself must be right—whatever can conquer must be good—whatever finds acceptance must be true." Any successful government must be considered just, simply because it has found acceptance with its people. Thus justice is emptied of its meaning, truth identified with popularity, and goodness confused with preference. Such a "directionless freedom," to use Professor Heimann's words, can only result in a "ruinous confusion of opinion and values."

Could this doctrine of free speech be defended on the ground that a regime of official impartiality is the best contribution to the triumph of the good? It seems that such a defense could be valid only if one assumes either that the state has no positive function in the struggle between good and evil, or else that truth in these matters is so uncertain that no government can do anything but repeat Pilate's query, "What is truth?", thereby washing its hands of the problem. On neither of these two grounds can the defense of free speech be successful. A defense on the first assumption would question the entire institution of the state and thereby undermine the protective functions through which the state undertakes to guarantee free speech. Nor can a defense of freedom of speech be advanced on the second ground, for if we cannot know what truth is, there is no point in carrying on an endless discussion about it. Thus, left without defense, the traditional doctrine of freedom of speech stands indicted for destruction of the moral basis of society, a destruction not undertaken in the name of a higher morality, but in a spirit of neutrality, agnosticism, and complacency.

Is a third way conceivable? If the indictment of freedom of

speech stands, the only justifiable alternative is a limitation of public utterances by a general awareness of the obligation which community life entails and the public faith which it demands from us. There ought to be no public neutrality in questions concerning the moral basis of society, whether one approaches them from the point of view of moral obligation or from that of vital political interest. The members of a family are aware of certain boundaries of speech, without needing to have these boundaries imposed on them by arbitrary dictate. Such awareness must be carefully nourished and cultivated by exhortation, rebuke, and selection of things preferable over those that are nonpreferable. In a society which has been accustomed to take the cohesion of community for granted, people must attune their minds to the moral needs of common life through a long process of practicing moral distinctions. They must be helped by a cautious official attitude of *parti pris* in matters concerning the moral requirements of community life.[2] Such an attitude should not attempt to shield the government and its policies from criticism, but rather promote the development of a broad and firm ground of common convictions, principles and standards which would serve as a generally understood criterion for drawing meaningful boundaries of public expression. When people enjoy a common awareness of what allows them to live together, and what demands common life makes, not only on actions but on dispositions, no arbitrary repression of public speech will be held necessary or indeed possible.

In the meantime, a firm, official stand for what is known as right, true, and good is required if an awareness of the moral nature of political community is to return. Moral judgments of political issues should not only not be avoided, but also faced with resolution and made with clarity and determination. Above all we must once more become confident that such judgments are possible. In our private affairs, our actions are guided every day by judgments made in the light of moral standards. As there are sources of knowledge which enable us to make these daily decisions, we can securely count on bases for similar judgments in political matters, provided we begin to consider ourselves bound to make them.

But who is to decide on the standards which are to enjoy official favor? Whoever it may be, is he not always exposed to the danger of mixing his own interests with the standards of morality? Is not our limited knowledge, our egotism, our shortsightedness, our lack of understanding, a continuous handicap in the exercise of human power, and should we not therefore be hesitant in the extreme to take such power into our hands? Indeed we should. The inadequacies of the human race in the its present stage of development are too obvious not to command the utmost caution. Thus the entire question of what moral standards deserve public approval and official support can be approached only in a spirit of deep humility. But humility is something very different from neutrality. Neutrality springs from a profession of ignorance, humility from a confession of imperfection. Neutrality displays an attitude of indifference toward standards, humility implies their definite acknowledgment. Humility is not possible without a sense of the objective reality of oughtness, an awareness of what is demanded of us, accentuated by the realization that we are falling short of the mark. Hence humility, unlike neutrality, is compatible with clear decisions and judgments according to moral standards, although such decisions should always be overshadowed by the knowledge of their provisional character. The spirit of humility inspires that courage in the midst of hesitation which enables us to go forward, at once boldly and with "fear and trembling," a spirit which Abraham Lincoln put in the words, "With firmness in the right,—as God gives us to see the right."

NOTES

1. Quoted in Theodore Schroeder, *Free Speech for Radicals* (New York, 1916), p. 43 (italics mine).

2. Some misunderstanding might arise at this point regarding the role of the government in the matter of public expression. This paper, it must be emphasized, does not address itself to the problem of what methods are best suited to achieve desirable ends with regard to public speech. It studies the question whether distinctions between right and wrong uses of speech in public life exist and whether they are relevant to the preservation of freedom in a political community. This problem must be clearly distinguished from another one, viz., the identification of the categories of right and wrong regarding divers situations, and a third one, viz., how to set up a procedure for making and applying such distinctions in practice. The need for an official attitude of *parti pris* has been mentioned here not as a device of procedure, but merely as a way of stressing the necessity of making significant distinctions between public utterances vis-a-vis the traditional doctrine of free speech. This doctrine denies that distinctions between public utterances are relevant to the health of the community and clothes its theory in the demand that the authorities observe a strictly noncommittal attitude. Rejection of the theory thus involves rejection of the official policy by means of which it presents itself. That is all that is implied in my insistence on an official attitude of *parti pris*, which does not prejudice any further investigations regarding the important problems of where leadership in the making of these distinctions should be located, and how agreement about them could be secured.

Myth and Order in Our Time

Myth narrates a sacred history; it relates an event that took place in primordial time.... Myth tells how, through the deeds of Supernatural Beings, a reality came into existence, be it the whole of reality, the cosmos, or only a fragment of reality—an island, a species of plant, a particular kind of human behavior, an institution. Myth, then, is always an account of a 'creation,...' (concerning) not only the origin of the World but also the primordial events in consequence of which man became what he is today—mortal, sexed, organized in a society, obliged to work in order to live, and working in accordance with certain rules (M. Eliade, *Myth and Reality*, pp. 5, 6, 11).

Myth, as Eliade describes it, has everywhere been the foundation of human societies, as a public truth concerning the ground and meaning of all reality, while at the same time furnishing concrete guidance for human actions. Through myth men have been instructed what to do or not to do in a variety of situations, so as to participate in that great and mysterious reality pulsating around and within us with ever renewed powers of life, growth, form, and order. The myth regulates actions not so much through a separate ethic, but rather through sacrifices, purification rites, initiation, marriage, birth and burial ceremonies, incantations, and taboos. This kind of order, then, concrete and detailed, always pertained to a particular society which it fitted like the skin fits the body.

Obviously, we no longer live in a ritually ordered society. The precise and concrete guidance of myths was superseded by universal concepts of philosophy, ontological as well as ethical, and ritual prescriptions of detailed conduct were replaced by the more general duty to attain those permanent dispositions called virtues. Even so, fragments of myths continued in the constitution of order. Recently, positivistic radicalism has set out systematically to "de-mythologize" one aspect of life after another, finally reaching even religion. The impression is widespread that "modern man" is self-sufficient through the power of his autonomous reason and no longer has need of any myths.

The impression is profoundly mistaken. First, men and women do not make their daily choices and assessment of situations on the basis of either critical analytical concepts or pure reason but rather through what one might call "see-abilities," images relating appearances to more ultimate realities. In our days, such imagery no longer comes in the form of ancient myths, i.e. stories about gods and their manifestation in intracosmic things and processes, although men still invariably entertain some indistinct pictures of time and space, their own origins and the origins of everything, the destiny of their lives, death and immortality. One might call the vague and nonanalytical "views" in which these dimensions of life appear, analogies. In all probability they are diluted residues of former myths. At any rate, most people orient themselves in this life, even today, through such crypto-mythical premises. Second, the modern process of de-mythologization has resulted in the surreptitious introduction of a new kind of myth, a myth claiming the attributes of divinity for some intra-historical entity, be it a master race, a class, a unique party, an economic system, a revolution, or a government program. These are not myths like those about which Eliade reports, "accounts of creation," narratives of "Supernatural Beings;" and their introduction into public life has historically produced not social order but divisive ideological movements engaged in perpetual civil war. The appearance of such movements has confronted us with the urgent need to distinguish between the perverted theologizing from which they spring and mythical "see-abilities" capable of promoting order, and to find the criteria by which one may separate myths true from pseudo myths, or perverted myths, just as Plato found the criteria by which to distinguish government from tyranny.

Myths' true, concrete, and poetic imagery about the origin and relatedness of all things, constitutes a vast range from crude animism to such highly developed religious networks of symbols as Hinduism—necessary outgrowths of human consciousness which even on the simplest level finds itself both encompassing and transcending the realities given to immediate experience. It was not in a void but rather in a world wholly ordered by such myths that philosophy emerged as what one writer has called "the discovery of the mind" (Bruno Snell, *The Discovery of the Mind*, English ed. 1960), or, more properly speaking, the discovery of the soul as "the sensorium of transcendence" (Voegelin) and of the *nous*, or reason, as that element of the soul that is "itself also divine or only the most divine element in us" (Aristotle, *Nicomachean Ethics* 1177a15), the luminosity of which is the specific human way of participating in the divine ground of all being.

Philosophy undertook to develop a way of life illumined by knowledge cast into insights without the help of stories about gods, but the great originators of *philosophia* also resorted to the form of the myth in order to preserve the link between the new consciousness and the mythical past from which the "discovery of the mind" had mysteriously proceeded. In the words of Eric Voegelin, "the philosopher must of necessity establish this link if he wants to articulate his experience of reality integrally, because there is no reality of noetic consciousness independent from the mystery of its emergence. If the mystery is forgotten, consciousness loses a fundamental dimension...." Plato created myths of his own when his thought touched the points at which man looks beyond death or speculates about his beginnings and the beginnings of all things, or the possibility of truth. He thus distinguished analytical thought concerning phenomena given to observation from the mysteries of transcending absolute reality about which the mind indefatigably inquires, even while acknowledging basic mysteries. Thomas Aquinas insisted that one can speak of such "non-objective" realities, which do not have the character of "things," only by way of a rough analogy with things (*analogia entis*), so that one must take such analogies not as descriptions of analyses but rather as evocative renderings of human experiences of the Ineffable.

When the United States were founded, the Fathers seemed to use the critical and antimythical language of the Enlightenment. The apodictical statement "We hold these truths...," however, is not an end-product of a preceding analysis or syllogism, and the terms "nature" and "nature's God" obviously are crypto-mythical. More explicitly mythical, though of doubtful quality, is the slogan of the Great Seal, *Novus Ordo Seclorum*, which reflects America's self-interpretation as the creator of a new existence exemplary for all mankind, the doubtful character of which pops up in the later version: Manifest Destiny.

With regard to everyday actions, the waning of the myth left a gap that for many centuries was closed by custom. Custom, the traditional way of doing things, to this day faintly reflects ancient myths as well as Christian teachings. It was through their knowledge of custom and tradition that men could confidently move through the varied situations in which they had to make choices. Medieval countries would look on their custom, and on the web of their vested rights, as their inviolable substance which kings ought to respect and protect. Thomas Aquinas, mindful of this, required of human law that it be "just, possible to nature, according to the customs of the country, adapted to time and place" (*Summa Theol.* 1a 2ae, qu. 95, 3), which is the very opposite of what rationalists of the eighteenth century expected of law. One may say, then, that the ordering function of the ancient myth came to be discharged by three sources of obligation: religion teaching about god, creation, death, and destiny; rational natural law and ethics teaching about virtue; traditional customs and vested rights guiding concrete decisions; with human law drawing on all three of them. As long as no direct clash was experienced between the three, one could speak of a Christian society even though the Church might not officially be established.

The present crisis can be explained as the cumulation of attacks on the following three sources of obligation.

1) Christianity has been attacked from many sides: first by the Enlightenment atheists and Deists, then by the superman-devotees Marx and Nietzsche, then by Evolutionists, Vitalists and Naturalists, then by psychoanalysis, then by the Existentialist prophets of the Absurd.

2) Reason, the principle underlying natural law and virtue, has been shoved aside by the enthusiasts of the Unconscious and Subconscious, and by the emancipators of the passions.

3) Custom and tradition have been the prime targets of the futurists who expect to find goodness nowhere but in the phantasmal new society they assume will emerge from the total destruction of what now exists. Eighteenth-century rationalists, however, have also vigorously denigrated any body of order that grew historically.

The extant sources of order and obligation have been rejected and assailed by teachings that set up man as his own creator, savior, and inspirer, tolerate no divinity or higher norm above man's will, replace custom and common sense with subjective "lifestyles" of persons who vaunt their having "dropped out" of the social continuity. These denials and rejections, in turn, have been allowed to attain public standing by the keepers of the social order, whose positivism made them dismiss religion, philosophy, ethics, and myth, as irrational "personal preferences" and who thus remove from society all spiritual and rational substance, with the result that now they are unable to comprehend any differences and to withhold any permission.

This is the situation in which we ask ourselves what myths and crypto-myths can do for us in secondary and primary education, to the end that our children may be spared the agonies of utter disorientation and be protected from the perversity of irrational ideologies.

Instead of probing for a direct answer to this question, I shall at this point try to sketch certain guidelines for the work of restoration in an educational process set in the midst of both antinomian dissolution and ideological irrationalism. The following points are conceived as a kind of agenda, each of them entailing a host of subordinate problems that should be investigated cautiously and with severe discipline. One might think of this agenda as five *foci* of attention, to wit:

1. Education must be very alert to avoid communicating any of the pseudo-myths that center on god-ridded man, natural strength shorn of divine grace, man posturing as the self-creator, self-redeemer, and sole master of his destiny. That way lie the monstrosities of Nazism, Communism, and Anarchism, "politics become religion," with the ensuing elevation of murder to official legal standing. In this context one might begin to wonder to what extent America's political self-understanding might not also be affected by a certain amount of the-world-saved-by-political-action mythology, manifesting itself in Wilson's "Make the world safe for democracy," in Lyndon Johnson's save-the-

world pretension, in Richard Nixon's "peace for a generation," in our general propensity to declare "war," sacred war, on cancer, pollution, poverty, and any number of other evils, all of which we are confident of conquering by good civic intention plus the organized might of the dollar and the bureaucracy.

2. Along the same line, one should be distrustful of any tendency to produce myths at will, myths as political instruments, myths that are called into existence because someone desires a certain political effect, and not by the love of truth. This disposition tends to treat not only the world but the entire creation and its divine ground as something that should be considered above all as useful to human purposes. As long as one invents no such myths as the thousand year *Reich* or the Communist *Realm of Freedom* no disastrous harm might be done, because the myth-inventing people who want to manipulate others into supporting their designs also operate under all kinds of traditional limitations and inhibitions that cause them at least to bow to sanity. All the same, once the ends of policies are elevated to the rank of the highest good, outranking principles and eternal verities, then the gates to irrationality in politics are open, and of the inbreaking waves the Nazi and Communist ones are merely the ones that top the ground swell.

3. Myth in education serves above all to reinforce prime awareness of that ultimate reality the desire for which is the chief motive of knowledge. Aristotle's *Metaphysics* opens with the sentence: "All men by nature desire to know," meaning that knowledge is preceded by desire which, of course, is desire for *something*. Anselm of Canterbury expresses the same truth in his formula *fides quaerens intellectum*, meaning that underlying all efforts at knowledge is the will's primary embrace of reality, a commitment and an awareness on the part of a rational being, which commitment includes the quest to be clear in one's mind what the will's "tending to God" implies. What Anselm means is that knowledge concerns the reality which we first note and

also affirm with our will. Human consciousness, then, operates in no void, whence its structure as consciousness of something. This "perspectivity" of consciousness can be called its *ratio* (Cf. Eric Voegelin, *Anamnesis*, p. 289). Bergson hints at the same truth when he links knowledge with the "open soul" (*The Two Sources of Morality and Religion*, Anchor Books, p. 38). Speaking of the "open soul" implies also the possibility of a "closed soul" in which the perspective of consciousness is willfully ignored and cut off. Consciousness then suffers the loss of reality, which means that instead of illumining the "serious play of life" and thus guiding human actions it gyrates wildly around itself, disseminating confusion. Now it is the ancient myth, the true myth, that serves to recall us again and again to the awareness of reality, to the commitment to the whole in which we participate. Thornton Wilder gave expression to this in a pithy sentence: "Joy is praise of the whole and *cannot exist where there are ulterior aims*" (*The Eighth Day*, p. 186; emphasis supplied).

4. The idea of "human nature" stems not from the myth but from Greek philosophy, chiefly from Plato and Aristotle. In the course of time, however, it became a figure of speech conjuring up images rather than a strictly defined concept, images often containing a set of immutable attributes. Recently, that notion has been passionately assailed on the grounds that man is a) malleable and ultimately perfectible, and b) changes himself continuously by his own historical decisions and thus never remains the same. Among those who operate with the notion of human nature, on the other hand, there is a tendency to equate that in nature with the observation of sick or depraved men and to infer that the sordid side of man reveals all there is to human nature. This reduction of the idea of human nature began with Thomas Hobbes who, in the face of the full view of human beings as being motivated by both *amor sui* (self-love) and *amor Dei* (love of God), chose to eliminate the latter, thus identifying man wholly with the former. We find this truncated notion of

human nature widely reflected in the modern, so-called "realistic," literature.

Restoring the notion of human nature to its adequate fullness is one of the most important educative tasks. We are presently witnessing such a restoration in the work of the great Russian writer Aleksandr Solzhenitsyn, who himself was raised to accept the reductionist Communist idea of man as the mere adjunct to historical economic forces, but who, in his novels, regained a full and comprehensive view of what man really is. Logically, Solzhenitsyn became a full communicant of the Russian Church in 1971. Perhaps the idea of a permanent set of attributes deserves not to be restored, as there is hardly any evidence to support it. If, however, we go back to the sources from which the notion of "human nature" stems, we find in Plato the awareness that man is "midway between ignorance and wisdom," "halfway between mortal and immortal," the "spirit" in him plying "between heaven and earth" (*Symposium* 203e, 202e). In other words, he is a being existing characteristically "in between." This "in between" must indeed be called a constant of human nature, which alone enables man to have a history, namely, the history of his various and successive attempts to illumine his insights into this "in between."

5. Sometimes, in modern contexts, we hear the phrase "the human condition" used as a synonym or substitute for "human nature," the latter concept applied chiefly to the structure of individual persons, the former to the setting in which persons find themselves. That setting can be circumscribed by a number of features:

a) Each human being lives in the society of other human beings; that society was there when he was born and will continue after he dies; he comes into it and goes out of it, and, while in it, must acknowledge the company of others like himself as a given and a norm. Thus it will not do to think of the human condition as one in which a person can have full satisfaction of all his desires. Plato made that clear in the *Republic* (259d-360b), when he had Glaucon tell the story of the ancestor of Gyges the Lydian, who, first a shepherd, went to town, possessed the queen, murdered her husband as well as other people who stood in his way, pursuing every wish of his as if he were in the world all alone. What gave him that illusion, said Plato, was a ring which could make him invisible. Since such a ring does not in fact exist, Plato here tells us that all live under the watchful and critical eyes of our fellow beings to whom we have to account for our actions.

b) Beyond society, which outlasts our little span of life, there is the everlasting God. Our experience of obligation issues ultimately from the experience of acting as stewards of being in the sight of God, to whom we return just as we have come from him. Christianity, behind the truth of which there is no going back, even for those who do not accept the Christian faith, teaches that fellowship of man with God has become possible and constitutes man's ultimate destiny. In view of this, man cannot consider himself ultimately at home in any political society, as he strives for a goal to be attained only beyond time, through grace in death. A permanent tension between man's ultimate destiny and his mundane existence in society results, and this tension is a basic characteristic of our civilization, reflected in the side by side of state and Church, and the limitation of the state within certain boundaries of its authority.

c) Society, the setting of man's mundane experience, is nonetheless neither wholly profane, nor devoid of grace, nor negligible. The naive conclusion that man ought to live in a society identical and coextensive with the Church is a fallacy; no wholly spiritual or theocratic order is possible, and a society representing our natural common good is both necessary and natural. Its order embraces all types of men living together and thus cannot be realized at the highest level that is possible of attainment only to a few. Soviets, with all their necessary shortcomings, form little "worlds," universes of meaning, custom, norms, and institutions, apart from which man is never found to exist: Robinson Crusoe as a paradigmatic figure has nothing to teach us. Societies resemble families: man would not be born or raised without them, and is existentially so tied up with them that he can only say: "May it always be right, but right or wrong,—my country (or: my family)", meaning that partnership in existence in some way transcends moral approval and disapproval. A particular person may turn his back on a particular society, but he cannot evade human society in some form or other, since wherever he goes men live in families and societies, with their authorities and norms.

d) Human existence is set in societies, each organized for action in history. Humanity, by contrast, has no such existence; it is a mere fiction and most certainly not the subject of history. The term, "humanity," when it means "humankind," expresses the kinship of all who bear a human face, but that experience comes rarely and only to rare persons. The average man lives in a "closed society," i.e., a society which in its pattern of custom, norms, religion, authorities is introverted, excluding men who live beyond its boundaries. Yet even the closed societies of higher civilization acknowledge, in some of their features, the universal brotherhood of all human beings (e.g., asylum). These features stem from the impact of those rare persons whose souls are open and can transcend the limits of their own social order. Their teaching, of universal applicability, eventually will be incorporated into the closed society's order.

e) Societies are the primary units of human order, even though the truths by which they live may stem from higher-ranking authorities than their own instituted leaders. Whatever is thus incorporated trickles down to form a kind of rudimentary rationality, of which the Scotch philosopher Thomas Reid said: "There is a certain degree of it which is necessary to our being subjects of law and government, capable of managing our own affairs, and answerable for our own conduct toward others: This is called common sense, because it is common to all men with whom we can transact business, or call to account for their conduct" (*Essays on the Intellectual Powers of Man*, 1785). This is what Burke termed "prejudices," i.e., unreflected judgments abiding as vulgarized residue of the best knowledge attained by mankind's highest-ranking authorities. Ordinary men are not capable of more than this residue of rationality which, however, suffices them for a tolerably decent life. Common sense, therefore, must not be despised or deliberately destroyed, and in times of crisis may even be the last resort of hope.

f) Man's existence is necessarily the outcome of past actions, and memories of those actions. Standing on his past as if on a platform, he looks into a future that is a series of open possibilities among which he must choose. The choices are limited both by the past and by natural givens, and political action can never attain to more than rational choice among available possibilities. "The art of the possible" is what Bismarck called politics. Some modern pseudo-myths speak of man's ability to create a new world, a new man, a new culture, and usually those "new worlds" are envisaged as totally different from anything that has occurred before. These pseudo-myths then deny that politics is the "art of the possible," as they aim at the impossible (the title both a popular TV show, and an equally popular hit song), thus arrogating to man a godlike role. This way lies the quest for total power, the only kind of power that would be deemed adequate to the task of creating worlds, cultures, men. The adepts of the "new world" concept also invariably despise and combat the past. In our restoration program, then, the past must never be despised or rejected, lest history be destroyed and man deny his own condition. That does not mean that this or that act should not be condemned, only that a rejection of the past as a whole is tantamount to a presumption beyond the limits of man's condition. The way we came must be recalled and accepted, as the landmark of our identity in history.

g) Man's existence is embedded in a process of history of which he is simultaneously the protagonist, victim, and observer. The mind observing this process has discovered—late in time—lines of meaning *in* history (Cf. Karl Loewith, *Meaning in History*, 1949) and this discovery, held in modest bounds by Augustine, was later abused to support an ideological assertion of a meaning *of* history, encompassing past, present, as well as future. In view of the prodigious career of this pseudomyth in the last two centuries, we should remain ever-mindful of the characteristic of human historical existence, formulated by Herodotus, Polybius, Ibn Khaldun, Bodin and Vico, that there is an unavoidable up and down in human affairs, that the imperfections of human nature doom every historical attainment before its highest fruition, that in the end *hubris* or pettiness bring down the proudest city or the mightiest empire.

6. Education, to convey these insights, no longer depends on the myth. Even the sagas of heroes and tales of exemplary feats in history are received only with great difficulty, an observation

that one might have to rethink in the light of the success of Tolkien's *The Lord of the Rings*. In general, though, any suspicion of a moralizing intent attached to a story stands in the way of its effectiveness as a teaching device, the reason being that the ontology underlying the ethics has been lost and must first be restored. Author William Golding has realized that and has undertaken, in one book after another, to rebuild in his readers the consciousness of being which alone can receive any talk of morality. Thus preference should be given to literature and traditions that establish the basic assumptions of an ontological character from which the rest follows. Solzhenitsyn's *Cancer Ward*, Thornton Wilder's *The Eighth Day*, C.S. Lewis's trilogy *Out of the Silent Planet, Perelandra, That Hideous Strength*, are examples of such literature. On a more advanced level, Dostoyevsky's *The Brothers Karamazov* is one of the world-restoring books, as is his *Crime and Punishment*, and Mauriac's *Viper's Tangle*. Much greater difficulty is encountered in such disciplines as history, although there are possibilities of concentrating attention on other times of crisis (the Athens of the Sophists, the Rome of the Manicheans, the Middle Ages of the Brethren of the Free Spirit, the Hussites, and the Anabaptists). At no point can one rely simply on presenting results; everywhere the foundations must be resecured by stimulating their rethinking.

The problems of various means, however, can be thought through only by a group of men and women who have become clear in their minds about he ends. Fortunately, the crisis itself causes more and more thinking people to grasp for those ends.

Nations, Myths, & Mores

A political community abides in time; it endures with the sameness of truth in the flux of temporal vicissitudes and thus, in an important sense, "imitates eternity." Yeats speaks of "man's two eternities, that of race and that of soul." What is the relation between these "two eternities?" Do they confront man with a necessary conflict of loyalties? If they diverge, which would be the more authoritative?

Time-bound man lives in tension toward the eternal, so the tension toward the "eternity of race" should be seen in the context of other pertinent tensions. As Yeats saw "two eternities," so Aristotle saw two parts of man's soul, the rational and the irrational. In the latter there is both a vegetative and a concupiscent element, the concupiscent element standing in tension toward the rational part which corresponds to Yeats' "eternity of soul." Is there, perhaps, an irrational element "of race" that persists in similar tension toward the "eternity of race," and can tensions be discerned between either complex and the other?

Aristotle did not use the words "rational" and "mind" (*nous* and *noetic*) to connote what we, the heirs of the Enlightenment, associate with "rational"—namely a disposition to consider nothing but a logical approach based on abstract concepts. "Rational" in Aristotle meant noetic openness toward the divine ground of being in which the transparency of being becomes the *ratio* of human existence and action. The term *nous* retains in Aristotle a deliberate ambiguity, connoting "what is most divine in man," the divine itself, as well as man's participation in the divine; then again, on the strength of this triple meaning, it indicates what is "best" and "highest" in man, for the sake of which man is to be loved with the kind of love which, being selfless, endures in time.

Similarly, Aristotle's "concupiscent" element of the soul must be understood as connoting not merely appetites but all the opaque motives, promptings, and impulses which go under the names of habits, prejudices, reaction, passions, desires—in other words, the muddy stream of "forces" and "patterns" so familiar to the discourse of contemporary psychology and sociology. They are not capable of transparency as is the *nous*, but Aristotle reminds us that they can heed the *nous* or refuse to heed it. If they do, a man is at peace with himself; if not, he lives in a kind of intra-soul civil war and self-hatred. Thus Aristotle distinguishes a tension of the soul's rational part toward the divine ground of being, for which the proper term is participation, and another tension of man's opaque psychic force toward the *nous* in him, the name for which is ethics.

What about the corresponding tensions in the political community? Yeats' "eternity of race" obviously refers not to the human race as a whole which has no entity in existence, but rather to the political communities abiding in time whose participation in the divine ground is symbolized in what Yeats calls "artifices of eternity," and "monuments of unageing intellect." In the case of Israel, one can discover the genesis of a political community in the theophany of the Exodus, an illumination of being. Israel's "monument of unageing intellect," then, was the story of Yahweh's deliverance of "Jacob and his sons," countlessly retold. The story of the Exodus and Israel's corresponding relation to the Lord of History must be seen as the *nous* of the community, the opening of transparency for the participating men. Thus the people as a whole, its rulers, and its institutions, represented the truth of being, as illuminated by the Exodus story. Yet this relationship implied the neverending temptation to confuse or even merge the community's existence with the divine truth, to assume identity rather than participation, and thus to let go of the tension toward the divine on which the community had been founded. Against such tendencies there stood the warning of sensitive men, men of "vision" and authority, who in the course of succeeding generations repeatedly called Israel to that tension toward the divine which represented, in this case, the "eternity of race."

A community also has its "irrational" dimension—its opaque "forces" and "patterns" which, although incapable of transparency in themselves, still abide in time and are passed from generation to generation. They are the habits, customs, conventional standards of approval and disapproval, prejudices, superstitions, property relations, gradations of respectability, and other "ways of doing things." Such norms, as Bergson has pointed out, operate through unorganized pressures to which people respond unreflectively, each obedient response itself adding to the pressures on others. As a result, psychic and customary patterns are the most tenacious and ubiquitous manifestations by which a political community distinguishes itself.

While customs are distinctly evident to the point of being "picturesque," they are incapable of that transparency that gives meaning to existence and action. The transparency of being can reside only in what Yeats has called the "eternity of race," the commonly acknowledged truth regarding God, nature, man and society. The psychic and social patterns can resist or defy the "eternity of race," or conform themselves to it, so that a community's habits stand in unceasing tension toward the "eternity of race," the name of this tension being justice. Where habits and customs drift away and develop in terms of their own impulsive causality, the community will eventually lose its reason for being and, as Vico has reminded us, eventually lose its language and arms, too.

Note that there is also a tension between the "eternity of race" and the "eternity of soul," as Aristotle indicated by his distinction between the "good citizen" and the good man. Under normal circumstances the "eternity of race" seems to be accorded higher rank, in all probability because it is examined much more carefully than anything that a single individual can work out in his lifetime. This hierarchy also obtains because a community cannot be maintained on everyday notice by critical individuals. On occasion, however, an outstandingly sensitive person experiences what Bergson has called an opening of the soul and attains insights into reality and the moral order beyond those underlying the existing community. His life then manifests a quality that attracts people for whom the previously accepted truths suddenly become opaque; a new transparency appears, and the "eternity of soul" confronts the "eternity of race" with an authoritative: "You have heard it said...but I say to you!" These are the words of Jesus, but they also characterize Xenophanes' confrontation with Homer and Hesiod, Socrates' with Athens, and Gautama's with Brahmanism; they produce a tension which Bergson has explored in his *Two Sources of Morality and Religion*. This is not the tension of man's irrationality toward the "eternity" of his consciousness, but rather the confrontation of one rationality with a higher rationality, in a mode of gentle persuasion—resulting not in obedient subordination but in supersession of the lower by the higher authority and a "leap" in the level of existence.

We may now turn to the question at hand—and for these purposes we will need some suitable terminology. We are accustomed to speaking of a "community" or a "political entity" or a "people" or "society." These terms are inadequate. "People" is a quantitative concept suggesting a living multitude which at the margin could be counted. Actually one cannot fix on a multitude as constituting the "people," since the membership of a political entity constantly fluctuates with each birth and death. Numbers, moreover, do not convey the quality of *gestalt* or enduring identity—nor that of authority—both of which we really have in mind when we speak of "a people." Cicero, to be sure, identified a people with an association acknowledging principles of true justice; but while this definition accounted for the authoritative aspect, it was subject to Augustine's criticism that it corresponded to no empirical phenomenon. Augustine proposed as an alternative the concept of "an assemblage of reasonable beings bound together by a common agreement as to the objects of their love." This concept avoided Cicero's idealization; but it also set up the unascertainable requirement of agreement, and postulated more homogeneity than Augustine himself might have been willing to concede to any existing "people." Earlier, Aristotle, in trying to identify a political community through constitutional forms impressed on the "people" as "matter," had found this definition impracticable; and Polybius emphasized this point by explaining that a people may pass through a whole cycle of constitutional forms without losing its identity. As for Augustine's criterion of a "common love," the weakness of the test can be seen in subsequent applications: Ibn Khaldun thought that political entities transferred their "common love" from "bedouin life" to "sedentary life"; and Vico's idea of the *mente eroica*, wandering from patricians to people to monarch, suggested a similar mutation, from savage barbarism to the "barbarism of reflection."

If neither the total quantity of component members, nor common principles or loves, nor political forms can adequately define that which politically exists, we must assume something to "exist" which is more fundamental than all of these, more fundamental than even the "people," and of which the "people" would be an attribute. We propose the term *realm* for this time abiding existential entity, noting that realm implies a unity of consciousness as well a certain geographical limits.

A realm is, first of all, a phenomenon of history. Realms are not properly attributable to logical, psychological, or material necessities, nor are they to be explained in terms of "agreement," "form," "principle," or "factor." Vico has said that the world of history is the one part of reality of which the "principles are to be found within the modifications of our own mind." But neither he nor anybody else has succeeded in reducing realms—concrete historical realms—to an act of "position" by men. Recognizing the existence of realms does not therefore require taking a position with regard to them; we should approach them, rather, as what are commonly called "facts of life." On the other hand, realms are entities of political order in an atmosphere of moral neutrality.

There are, then, two approaches to realms. One seeks to understand what order is, illuminating from within, the experiences on which order is based; this approach cannot escape judgments, since the experience of right and wrong is basic to any political order. The other approach recognizes that order occurs among men in the form of a multiplicity of realms, many of which can be perceived at any given time. Each realm can be understood from within—an order claiming to represent mankind as such; but precisely because of that, the multiplicity of realms must be confronted as a phenomenon. This means that realms are, in fact, available to people as vehicles of order; it makes little sense to argue with this fact, or to postulate something different which does not exist.

Every realm is multilayered. At the top we find a "We hold these truths...," the *keinon* of Aristotle's *koinonia*, the insights through which being has transparency, which spell out the terms of participation in the divine ground. This common perspective of consciousness renders possible a broad and deep area in which actions and language symbols are commonly understood: a rich soil of taken for granted assumptions, associations, and references enabling persons to communicate by gestures, hints, signs, or even silently, and to act toward and with each other with a great economy of decision energy. From this soil common aspirations grow—the "agreed-upon objects of love" which Augustine pointed out. It also produces unwritten but highly effective structures, the patterns of custom, conventional judgments, the do's and don't's usually more strictly obeyed than written statutes. Here, above all, confidence flowers—the assurance with which a person moves among his fellow beings, knowing what to expect and on what grounds to engage in cooperative efforts.

All of this, however, is confined to a *limes*, a spatial boundary. The definition of this boundary may not be possible to draw with precision, but there are recognizable areas in which a particular order does *not* obtain. With the *limes*, however, there is a world of familiarity to which every one of its members "belongs"; there is something like a "whole" of which he as a single person feels to be a "part," moving among other "parts" like him. The whole structure of meaning and familiarity makes for the possibility of friendship, the public friendship of which Aristotle treats in the *Nichomachean Ethics*. It is a basic openness and benevolence toward all other "parts" even though they are not of one's personal acquaintance.

Note, however, that this entire world of familiarity and conventionality stands in existential tension toward the highest ranking truth which elicits the conscious public effort at justice. For the confinement of this order to a certain area circumscribed by a *limes*, and to certain persons who are its bearers within this geographical line, attaches the order of consciousness to a corporeal and material matrix. Thus there is always the possibility of destroying the entire order by destroying the matrix. For this reason, it makes perfect sense to say that a realm *exists*.

The commonly held truths at the top of the realm's structure may be called *myth*. The word, in this context, does not mean a historical variant of order—i.e., a "cosmological myth," an order that prevailed "before philosophy," as Frankfort put it. Rather, myth in this context applies to any set of symbols through which a multitude of people living together symbolically secure the transparency of life and awareness of participation in the divine ground.

In this sense one must say that no realm, ancient or modern, is without its myth. Philosophy, or noetic consciousness of participation, has made a difference in the quality of life, but no realm has ever been founded by a philosopher or been held together merely by syllogistic propositions. In countries that have degenerated to "barbarism of reflection," the underlying myths are certainly no longer symbolized by express celebration, and thus they are hardly recognizable. Such countries resort, on their festival occasions, to phrases and slogans derived from analytical thought rather than to restatements of their myth. All the same, the myth effectively determines in these cases what most persons take for granted, the tacit assumptions they make about reality, about the meaning of life, about God, man and nature.

If it were not for the myth, even in these cases, the mutual comprehensibility of actions and language symbols among the "parts" would atrophy after a while, and in place of familiarity and confident communication a universal assumption of hostility would arise—the kind that prevails in desert life. In the course of time a myth that is not supported by appropriate cultic celebrations may suffer a decline and recede far into the subconscious. But there is a decisive difference between that kind of weakening and the total collapse of the myth, which causes an opaqueness of life and befalls men as a major disaster.

The lower layer of non-transparent motivations—customs, habits, prejudices—may be called the *mores* of the realm. The realm as a whole is made up of myth and *mores*, justice and conventions, the whole and the parts, with multiple tensions prevailing between these aspects, and between the realm as a whole and the divine ground. The individual soul acknowledges, as authoritative, the myth of the realm, but it also knows of the tension of the person toward God, and of the soul as the "sensorium of transcendence" (Eric Voegelin). On occasion, the illumination of truth in the individual soul turns out to have authority vis-a-vis the public myth, particularly when the myth has been weakened and the *mores* are drifting guideless by the force of impulses. Then, as we have seen, the authority of this or that individual soul may address itself above all to the *mores* as measured by the truth of transcendence, particularly in a tradition in which righteousness constitutes the chief terms of participation in the divine ground. The individual whose personal sensitivity moves him to a high degree of righteousness then moves into the position of a judge vis-a-vis the decadent *mores*.

In all of this we find no answer to the question of why certain realms appear and exist at a given time and place, and why realms are as they are, and, above all, why there is a multiplicity of different realism by virtue of which men exist in a variety of communal orders, rather than one single realm which encompasses all humanity. Nobody has come close to answers for such questions; and since it seems unlikely that anybody will, it is wise to leave the diversity and multiplicity of realms in the class of *phainomena*, to be accepted and understood for what they are, without yielding to the temptation of positing potentially different *phainomena* and speculating on what life might be if they existed.

One more word is required about the problem of change. It was obvious to Aristotle even before he finished the *Politics* that it would not do to identify a *koinonia* with a particular constitutional form in the sense that every change of form would bring into existence a new *koinonia*. Realms survive constitutional changes, they also survive dynasties and various ruling classes; they may even survive a period without rulers. A realm, to be sure, presupposes and is subject to, a myth; but on occasion a realm may even survive a change of the myth, as did the Frankish realm when Clovis converted to Christianity. Similarly, Augustine's "commonly agreed upon objects of love" may change within a continuing realm, as exemplified by Ibn Khaldun's mutation from "bedouin life" to "sedentary life."

This brings us to the role of "the people" in the realm. We commonly accord authority to the people, but we have seen that authority derives from the myth which spells out the terms of participation in the divine ground of being. The people, then, are the bearers of the myth at any given time, and as such serve as the organ of representation of the public truth; this is what gives authority to the *vox populi*. No authority, however, derives from sheer numbers alienated from the myth, when the thoughts they commonly accept and resort to are representative of abstract analysis and arbitrary positions apart from the myth, when the *mores* are regarded as a law unto themselves, then the people cease to represent. In this case, the bearers of the myth may be concentrated in a "remnant" or even in a single person, like Jeremiah in sixth-century Judah or Socrates in fifth-century Athens.[1]

In such situations neither king nor people can speak with authority, and things move either toward dissolution or a renewal of the myth. Kind, people, government, laws and arms, peace and justice, are attributes of a realm rather than its substance. The substance, a public truth in which life becomes transparent and meaningful, is genetically elusive, mysterious, and in a sense "given," particularly since it appears in history as an existent subject to laws of biological nature, nor to mere morality, but pertains to the area of complex tensions between consciousness and the divine ground, psyche and *nous*, and to the general relation of things mutable to eternity.

NOTES

1. Eric Voegelin, *Israel and Revelation*, p. 467.

The Social Whole and
the Solitary Thinker

We know that a mature human being is a work of art produced partly by education, partly by habits of his own choosing. The best education is that which produces vision and virtues. By vision we mean the knowledge of a reality higher and wider, as it were, than both the individual and the social whole. For most of humanity, in most of its historical past, knowledge communicating vision was imparted to single persons by the social whole, consisting of beliefs in mythical form. Some of these beliefs were appropriated by the individual through observation of daily habits and occasional festivities. The rest consisted of knowledge which, even before philosophy, was conveyed by the spoken word that constituted initiation. This education opened the mind to the relation between the sacred and the profane, the validation and limitation of the profane by the sacred. The sacred, in distinction from the profane, was seen as eminent reality, enduring reality. Possession of such knowledge enabled the individual to order his attitudes and habits for participation in both the social whole and the cosmic whole. The order he experienced did not depend on any particular person but precisely on the existing "whole" and its enduring tradition. How, then, was it possible for there to arise solitary persons to whom there accrued authority strong enough to rival the tradition?

The myth, wherever we encounter it, consists of images and symbols regarding the relation between the sacred and the profane. One aspect of the myth is a focus on the names of divinities, spirits, or semidivinities, together with stories about their acts. Most of these acts explain the origin of the cosmos and the "10,000 things," as the Chinese say. This is the narrative component. The other component is ritual, consisting in sacred days or periods, the order of sacrifices, and hymns. Thus, the *Veda,* for example, is essentially a collection of hymns. And so the basic social unity of existence is the unity of cultic and political order, whether in terms of tribe, city-state, kingdom, or empire.

Some data may illustrate this relation. In Japan, the word *uji* ("clan") means "those who worship together" the *uji-gami* ("clan god") and thus are led by the *uji-no-kami.* Now *gami* and *kami* are virtually the same word, *gami* meaning "god" or "power", *kami* meaning "lord." We realize the political significance of this myth when we learn that even slaves who worship the *uji-gami* were accepted as members of the clan.

In ancient Egypt, the kind, an incarnate god, has *ka* ("vital power") originally stemming from *Re,* the sun god. Each commoner's *ka* is derived from the Pharaoh's *ka. Ka* is what holds life together, both in the world of the living and in that of the dead. The entire complex might be compared to Marx's "unity of theory and practice."

Sacrifices and hymns are verbal actions, having a permanent, sacred form. Each and every word is vital to the effectiveness of the ritual; therefore, even the pronunciation may not be altered. Hieratic language thus does not have the instrumental character that modern language has; it is invocative language. Sacrifices and hymns establish man in reality, secure his existence within the limits of mortality, purify him from contamination, and sustain the sociopolitical unity.

Today we talk of order in terms of consciousness; believers of myth, however, made no distinction between consciousness and ritual. The acts that constituted the rite established meaning in profane reality, set down limits (taboos) for humans, and confirmed authority. This kind of knowledge requires no written, discursive language as the carrier of education. Sacrifices, hymns, rituals were passed on by memorization and protected against erosion of time by rules of grammar and pronunciation, as well as by a hereditary elite charged with the task of passing on correct ritual forms, including the words. This was the structure of "tradition." Education consisted in being initiated and skilled in the tradition, the "form" of both the collective body and each personal life. In China, Heaven and Earth were acknowledged as the chief cosmic realities, with Man in the middle; and so only the Emperor could perform the horse sacrifice. The principle was the same in India, where other sacrifices were performed by brahmans. Regardless of their personal wealth and power, brahmans still rank highest in Indian society; in the order of ritual they rank even above the king.

In the context of these cultural differences, Bergson's distinction between "open" and "closed" societies is relevant. So also is his point that "our civilized communities, however different they may be from the society to which we were primarily destined by nature, exhibit indeed, with respect to that society, a fundamental resemblance. For they too are closed societies. They may be very extensive compared to the small agglomerations [of earlier ages, but] their essential characteristic is none the less to include at any moment a certain number of individuals, and exclude others."[1]

It is against this background that we must understand the phenomenon of solitary thinkers who appear from time to time with the claim of an authority different from, yet higher than, the order of the myth. The middle of the sixth century B.C. seemed propitious for this appearance of solitary thinkers. At roughly the same time we find Confucius and Lao Tzu in China, Siddhartha Gautama (the Buddha) and Vardhamana (the Mahavira) in

India, Deutero-Isaiah and Jeremiah in Israel, Parmenides and Heraclitus in Hellas. Only slightly before this time in Israel, we find Amos, Hosea, and Isaiah as initiators of a succession of prophets who left a message cast in discursive language; and slightly later in Greece, we find Socrates and Plato, the founders of philosophy. None of these figures held a public office; none of them was a person in instituted authority. The fact that they did stand out, not merely with considerable authority but with an authority higher than that established by the myth, is a phenomenon that calls for critical explanation.

The two Indian figures of the Buddha and the Mahavira do not quite fit our category. Inasmuch as each of these men surrounded himself with a group of monks and proclaimed a version of salvation different from that of the mythic tradition, it is easier to compare them with Luther and Calvin than with Confucius and Plato. It makes sense, then, to drop India from this discussion and confine ourselves to Israel, China, and Hellas, where the solitary thinker is soon elevated to a cosmic rank of his own. Thus in China, to Heaven and Earth is now added the "Sage." This word also appears in the Greek tradition, albeit reserved for great lawgiving figures of political rule. In Israel, there were prophets before Amos, Hosea, and Isaiah, but "The Prophets" as an authority alongside that of "the Law" is something that appears only after the eighth century. What is common to all of these solitary men of authority is that they constitute a newness: a newness that is not a departure from the community, but rather an addition to order of a further dimension, that of the representative inner experience of the solitary thinker. It may be due to this experience of the new within the enduring that Israel, China, and Hellas are the only places in humanity where history is experienced as a dimension of ontological order, and where great historiographic works are produced.

Let us return to the history of China. A kind of religion consisting of five concepts (Heaven, Earth, and Man, plus *yin* and *yang*) existed side by side with a mythical past, the three emperors of the beginning (Yao, Shun, Yun [now transliterated as Yu]), and the elements of an earlier religion (spirits and ancestors). Unlike India, Hellas, Italy, and the Germanic North, China never had a pantheon. Rulers came by way of dynasties, each lasting many hundreds of years, individual rulers measuring themselves by the yardstick of the mythical emperors. At the time of Confucius (551-479 B.C.), the *Chou* (*Zhou*) dynasty was nominally still in existence, having lasted for more than half a millennium. Its order, however, was badly deteriorated, and its rulers were no longer virtuous but degenerate and vicious. Treacherous vassals proclaimed themselves kings, without right to this title; legitimate rulers proved corrupt; there was widespread disregard for piety; struggle for power characterized nearly every human relation; and truth was no longer discerned. This kind of description, however, came from none of the men entrusted with guarding the tradition; rather, it came from a private citizen, a man who held no office. When asked later what he would do if he had public power, he reportedly said, "Rectify names." In other words, the universal struggle for power had eroded the names of offices and public institutions to such an extent that they no longer represented truth.

Confucius did not come forward with any revolutionary message, not even one that could restore the traditional order of offices. Classifying human relations according to five types, he taught that an improvement of the world must begin with a man's own person, his decision to obey the discipline of these five relations. A similar reform would then move to the family, and then to the city, and only lastly to the kingdom. Unlike Siddharta Gautama, Confucius proclaimed no religious discovery or faith; indeed, he explicitly refrained from this. What he recommended to his countrymen was a program that did not depend on any premise of power, faith, or high intelligence; it was limited to that area of life which every single person could see, understand, and influence. Thus Confucianism had no need to compete with, or argue against, the existing religion(s). Instead, it added to them a liturgy of manners.

Confucius did stress, however, a set of concepts, somewhat in the same way in which Aristotle spoke of the *spoudaios*. Confucius distinguished between the *chun-tzu* (*junzi*, "gentleman"), who can be taught virtue, and the *hsiao-jen* (*xiao-ren*, "common man"), who cannot be thus taught. Confucius himself was placed, by Mencius, in the new category of the *sheng-jen* (*sheng-ren*, "sage"), who simply possesses wisdom and virtue, without having to be taught; it was Mencius who accorded the sage the authority of eminent reality (Heaven, Earth, the Sage). As a program for praxis, Confucianism contains two further concepts: *jen* (*ren*), meaning "humanity," "benevolence," "right disposition"; and *li*, meaning "correct ritual and music," "correct conduct," and the practical charge, "each man to rectify himself."

About two and a half centuries passed between the death of Confucius and the end of Chinese feudalism, with its attendant corruption of order. The kind of change for which Confucius had yearned was not realized, but a number of philosophic schools appeared, and through them the notion of order as emanating from discursive speech and the appeal of argument gained acceptance. Mencius, who acclaimed Confucius as the "secret ruler" of China, ascribed importance to the fact that Confucius had come 500 years after the Chou Dynasty. He concluded the existence of 500-year cycles in Chinese history, a theory which in turn inspired the great historiographic works of Ssu-ma Ch'ien and of his father, who had celebrated the victory of the Han Dynasty over the antiphilosophic Ch'in (Qin) dynasty. The Han Dynasty (207 B.C. to A.D. 220) adopted Confucianism as its public orthodoxy, thus making it a part of China's tradition. From then on, the traditional order was communicated not only in the form of stories, rituals, hymns, and music, but also by rational thought in discursive speech.

The case of Greece goes both farther and deeper. At the time of Socrates, the Athenian tradition was the lore of the pantheon headed by Zeus; knowledge of this tradition was communicated above all by the *Iliad* and *Odyssey* and by Hesiod's *Theogony*. For a century, Athenians had been able to boast of a unique educational device that spelled out the moral implications of the tradition: the publicly performed tragedy. Had their religious-ethical world view continued, neither Socrates nor Platonism might have arisen. It was the terrible corruption of life resulting from their success in the Persian wars that degenerated the Athenians' religious tradition and moral integrity. Socrates single-handedly resisted this process, confronting the teachers of moral perversion, the Sophists, in their own teaching places. Socrates was not, however, the first solitary thinker in Athens; he came after nearly two hundred years of philosophizing by private persons, the pattern beginning in Ionia and Southern Italy and centering first on something like metaphysics. If we think today of Socrates as the exemplary solitary thinker, we do so because in the late fifth century Socrates was indeed alone, a solitary in the midst of a city that was rapidly losing its tradition and its essence. Socrates' resistance made his life a heroic event, culminating in his memorable death. As a philosopher rather than a religious preacher, Socrates taught "conversion," a "new life." Two key concepts were *anamnesis*, knowledge emerging from the depth of the soul (from recollection, as it were), and *dialectic*, the mind's capacity to move in adversarial conversation, from cognitive step to cognitive step, towards well-founded truth. His central message was life as an ongoing task of self-examination. Unlike Confucius, Socrates philosophized in a way that was explicitly critical of his people's tradition, but—like Jesus' "You have heard it said...but I say unto you" formula—with the accent on fulfillment rather than negation.

It was Plato who established a school, in the form of a small circle of followers who continued the practice of looking for the order of existence in the depth of the human soul, and in the soul's mystic experiences. This development from the solitary thinker to an institutionalized school had already occurred in China. Plato, however, envisaged, at least in the middle of his life, a radically new political order centering on the "philosopher-king." Only after his one concrete attempt to bring this about had failed, did he confine his expectations to the enduring companionship of a few followers (*Letters VI*). Yet his enormous impact on the entire gamut of the Middle Ages, his enduring authority among philosophers, and his ongoing influence on political institutions make Plato the prime example of a successful solitary thinker. Eric Voegelin, whose five-volume *Order and History* has given us the most profound analysis of this phenomenon, points to three historical events which he calls "leaps in being": Israel and Revelation, Greece and the discovery of philosophy, and Christianity and salvation. If I may quote my review of his first volume, it mentions

> the reader's bafflement at discovering that Voegelin, in one stage of history, sees Israel's political order reduced to the vision of one solitary person, the rejected Prophet (Jeremiah). Here obviously is order potential, but is it also order actual? Can it be called political existence if rejected by the people and retained only in the breast of the lone seer?...The difficulty is compounded as Voegelin tells us that the creation of new symbols on a higher level of insight brings about a qualitative change in man's existence, a "leap in being." Does this change occur only in the life of the symbol's creator? Or does it extend to the entire community? Does it come about as a direct result of knowledge gained, or does it require an act of authoritative will to convert ontological symbols into political structure?[2]

Such questions must be disquieting, above all, to the solitary thinker himself. Precisely as a man of unusual and deep insight into the order of being, he cannot look upon himself and his isolation from the body politic without having doubts about seeing "authority" attributed to his mind, the mind of a citizen. Now Plato reports Socrates' declarations that he alone "practiced statesmanship" in Athens (*Gorgias*, 521d), that the oracle at Delphi had called him the wisest of all men, and that God had appointed him to the duty of leading a philosophical life (*Apology*). Thus the solitary thinker knows himself at once called by God and rejected by the authoritative community; all the same, he has no rebellious soul, is no alienated critic of the order in which he himself has been brought up (*Crito*, 50b-51c). He knows himself as one who comes "not to destroy but to fulfill" (Mt. 5:17). All the same, Plato confronts the Athenians with a critique of myth and legend. In other words, philosophical truth about being, the good life, virtue, and wisdom cannot just slip in comfortably alongside the tradition, as they can for Confucius. The point is made without apology as Plato excludes "the poets" (meaning Homer and Hesiod) from the political order Socrates composes in speech (*Republic* 377d). The critique is severe, but neither hostile nor total. Socrates and Plato are not alienated from Athens in general. They are engaged in resistance to the corrupters of the wisdom, virtue, and vision that used to be the glory of the city. Theirs is a critique that never abandons the common ground of faith, loyalty, and love bonding the community.

This much conceded, problems nevertheless remain as to how the solitary thinker can authoritatively represent the whole. One problem is the predictably violent reaction of the organized society. Socrates was executed. In China, the reaction came only when all of erstwhile feudal China was united under the "First Emperor," of the Ch'in Dynasty: he banned all philosophy and burned the philosophers' books. As for the prophets of Israel, we know from Jesus' word that the pharisees and lawyers "built the tombs of the prophets" and that their fathers were the ones who had killed them (Lk 11:47).

A more profound and difficult problem is the one which Saints Paul and John refer to as "the discernment of spirits." John tells us, "Do not believe every spirit, but test the spirits, whether they are from God; because many false prophets have gone out into the world" (1 John 4:1). Paul says the ability to discern spirits is a "gift" (1 Co 12:10). It is also of interest that Ignatius of Loyola devotes an entire chapter of his *Spiritual Exercises* to discernment.

In any case, the social whole as the source of forms and acts of order needs no proof. It is the solitary figure in a place of authority that cries for explanation and justification. Let us try to furnish these with regard to four different types: (a) the shaman, (b) the "false Christs," (c) the public articulator of alienation, and (d) the solitary philosopher.

Almost by definition, the shaman is a solitary figure. Unlike the priest, he is not the holder of a given office, but just the same "the magico-religious life of society centers on [him]."[3] Shamanism is sometimes a hereditary quality (and thus a profession), at other times a "spontaneous vocation." At all times, however, the shaman is a solitary specialist:

> Usually sickness, dreams, and ecstasies in themselves constitute an initiation; that is, they transfer the pro-fane, pre-"choice" individual into a technician of the sacred....The content of these first ecstatic experiences...almost always includes one or more of the following themes: dismemberment of the body, followed by a renewal of the internal organs and viscera; ascent to the sky and dialogue with the gods or spirits; descent to the underworld and conversation with spirits and the souls of dead shamans.[4]

The shaman has secret knowledge of "dreams and trances, the tradition of shamanic techniques, e.g. names and functions of the spirits, mythology and genealogy of the clan, secret language, etc.[5] Besides shamanism, the clan usually has its own body of myths and sacred activities, as well as some version of political representation. The shaman does not act in their name, nor in opposition to them. In fact, his activities are concerned exclusively with the afflictions, needs, or desires of particular persons. His help and remedies are in the realm of magic; his is an authority of special situations rather than an authority the order of the whole. While there is no tension or conflict between him and the instituted authorities of the whole, his authority of is different from that of priests, chiefs, judges, and even medicine men.

The next type, that of the "false Christ," is not a problem confined to the Christian faith. It was indeed Jesus who said, "If anyone says to you, 'Look, here is the Christ!' or, 'Look, He is there!' do not believe it. For false christs and false prophets will rise and show signs and wonders to deceive, if possible, even the elect" (Mk 13:21, 22). The type, however, is universal. A "false Christ" is one who fraudulently exploit a faith in ultimate reality to which a people adheres. Norman Cohn's book, *The Pursuit of the Millennium* (2nd ed., 1961), contains numerous examples of such individuals, each of whom was able to gather around himself large crowds and even armies. The wholesale fraudulence of these leaders was evidenced by their love of these leaders for splendid clothes, money, and power. While they pretended to come in the name and authority of Christ, they practiced violence and had swords carried ahead of them. It was not unusual for one of these men to have with him a wife whom he addressed as "the Virgin Mary." Cohn's work is particularly valuable in that it shows that the so-called Reformation was only in part attributable to Luther, Zwingli, and Calvin—that there was another component consisting in the surfacing of various false Christ movements that had been suppressed. Passing themselves off as God's representatives, Tanchelm, Eudes de l'Etoile, Jan van Leyden, the Bohemian Taborites, and the Brethren of the Free Spirit claimed absolute authority and had worldwide aspirations. In fact, however, theirs was the authority of Herman Melville's *Confidence-Man*. The false Christs, incidentally, have their counterparts in the "false prophets" of whom Jeremiah and Ezekiel spoke and in Socrates' "false philosophers," the Sophists.

Modernity produced a different kind of false Christs: people who wrote books promulgating an entire theory of total revolution. What qualifies such people as Comte, Marx, Bakunin, and Lenin as con men is a complex double fraud. They were false Christs inasmuch as they purported to offer salvation to the whole of mankind. As eschatological as the Gospels and St. Paul, as salvation-promising as the Sermon on the Mount, they were as total in their claim to people's commitment as any religion has ever been. This fraud is compounded by the fact that their underlying analyses of history and human nature made sense only in terms of severe reductions of reality. They should have done what Thomas More did: they should have put at the end of their books an acknowledgment that their goal could be realized only if the sin of "*superbia*," (pride) could be done away with. More thus protected himself against the charge of lying; neither Comte nor Marx, Bakunin nor Lenin, however, was sane (or perhaps honest) enough to append such a cautionary remark. And so distortion of reality remains forever their last word—no correction or even deviation permitted.

But there is a second fraud involved here as well: the promise of a total change of human nature and political existence. A "new man," a "new life," a "new age" as the eschatological end of history was foretold as something the human race would certainly be able to achieve. The term "salvation," which had always been symbolic of God's redeeming power, was now drawn into the politics of revolution. In this way revolutionary leaders aroused an enthusiasm that was ostensibly religious but in fact atheist—again, without a word of apology or explanation.

One might even add a third dimension to this fraud: the appearance these revolutionaries created of being "rational" and "scientific," when in reality their books were written primarily for the purpose of swaying through emotion masses of people explicitly forbidden to use their critical reason. These con men came, as it were, in the vestments of priests of scientific truth, while their real aim was to found, along with Flannery O'Connor's Hazel Motes, "the Church Without Christ."

Curiously enough, though, there is yet another group of solitary thinkers. These people, unlike Comte, Marx, Bakunin, and Lenin are not in the business of forming mass movements to change nature and man; they are, however, living in the age of nihilism created by these high-powered con men. Nietzsche predicted a period of thirty-five years before Europe would be "in convulsions." He was right, even to the year, about these "convulsions"; but he was mistaken when he said, in the last quarter of the nineteenth century, that nihilism was at hand. It took twice thirty-five years more for nihilism to be felt or even seen as a kind of daily environment. But come it did. It came as a suffering that could coexist with an orgy of "fun," a dizzying sudden increase of technological power, a flood of "definitive" triumphs of medicine, a near total subjection of nature by man—an environment one did not feel inclined to lament. Thus nihilism entailed a suffering that had no voice. Then there came solitary thinkers who could supply a voice for the suffering: Kafka, Becket, Joyce, and Canetti; Alban Berg and Schönberg; playwrights for the theater of the absurd; artists painting without object or line; and rock stars. Their function in society is to put into words, music, pictures, and action the agony of the Nothing, so that the millions of its mute sufferers can feel understood. It fits with the character of these works that one feels no urge to give a name to the solitary men who produce expression where there is nothing to express. But let us try to imagine Jeremiah's *Lamentations* without the element of lament.

Finally, let us turn to the type of solitary man whose thinking and teaching amounts to that "qualitative increase" in human existence which Voegelin calls a "leap in being." There is a need to remember such men, restudy them, rediscover them, if only to reproduce the language, images, and concepts which made possible their amazing "foundations." Thus fortified, let us then attempt to sketch a similar figure potentially to appear now. This would have to be an independent thinker, for the intellectual establishment of today's society seems to be solidly positivist and psychologistic, while its general culture lives on the remnants of Enlightenment. To imagine our new solitary thinker ("not a Thomist but a new St. Thomas," as Voegelin stipulates) and the tasks that that person would have to carry out, let us begin by counting our losses. First, let us listen to the words of Hans Urs von Balthasar:

> The globe, inhabited everywhere, resembles as a whole a one-room flat in which the whole family lives, eats, and sleeps, begets children, is sick and dies, in a community that admits of no escape. Socialized man suffers from spiritual asthma and fits of suffocation. The more he number his interior void with the drugs of civilization, the more incapable he becomes of loving his neighbor who has come too close to him. In his enforced solitude which he is unable to master he can only become a neurotic.... The solitary man of today differs from the hermits in that he is the man of the anthropological age. He has been lifted out of nature and can no longer understand himself in the mirror of the macrocosm, hence he is alone with himself as with a stranger. All he knows with certainty of this unknown person is that he is alone, that it

belongs to his essence to be alone.[6]

Let us now listen to a similar lament by Hans Jonas:

> That which has no nature has no norm. Only that which belongs to an order of natures—be it an order of creation, or of intelligible forms—can have a nature.... That makes modern nihilism infinitely more radical and more desperate than gnostic nihilism ever could be for all its panic terror of the world and its defiant contempt of its laws. That nature does not care, one way or the other, is the true abyss. That only man cares, in his finitude facing nothing but death, alone with his contingency and the objective meaninglessness of his projecting meanings, is a truly unprecedented situation.[7]

Thus, both the experience of and the linguistic symbols for "the one and the whole" must be regained. The potential solitary thinker of today, faced with the mammoth structure of natural science, is confined to cause-and-effect exploration and is sworn to use nothing but the mathematical method. It is precisely in the physical sciences of today, however, that scientists find themselves compelled to resort to a modicum of speculation. In the epochal quarrel between Einstein and the Copenhagen School, it was faith that had Einstein insist on the rational order of the universe (all the more problematic since "the universe" is a concept far removed in meaning from "the cosmos"). At any rate, the context of theoretical physics might provide a foothold for the rare solitary climber.

Another loss is that of "the present." As Jonas says,

> Theoria had a dignity [in antiquity] because of its Platonic implications—because it beheld eternal objects in the form of things, a transcendence of immutable being, shining through the transparency of becoming. Immutable being is everlasting present, in which contemplation can share in the brief durations

of the temporal present. Thus it is eternity, not time, that grants a present and gives it a status of its own in the flux of time; and it is the loss of eternity which accounts for the loss of a genuine present.... In the words of Nietzsche: "Who once has lost what thou hast lost stands never still."[8]

Our solitary thinker will not need for us to tell him what to do. But we will need to know by what traits or marks he can be recognized. How will we know him? How can we avoid confusing him with a madman?

The following words of Whitehead should be considered:

At last [a new planet] is discovered by human reason, penetrating into the nature of things and laying bare the necessities of their interconnection. The speculative extensions of laws, baseless on the positivist theory, are the obvious issue of speculative metaphysical trust in the material permanences, such as telescopes, observatories, mountains, planets, which are behaving towards each other according to the necessities of the universe, including theories of their own natures. The point is that speculative extension beyond direct observation spells some trust in metaphysics, however vaguely these metaphysical notions may be entertained in explicit thought. Our metaphysical knowledge is slight, superficial, incomplete. Thus errors creep in. But, such as it is, metaphysical understanding guides imagination and justifies purpose. Apart from metaphysical presuppositions there can be no civilization.[9]

Such words as "nature" and "being" came from profound experiences in the open souls of the founding minds. Different words may be used, but the underlying mystic/philosophical experience remains always the same, and that is the real source of authority. Unless our solitary person speaks from love of wisdom and of the good, he is not the one we need. To be the one we need, he will have to embrace all of man—his mundane interests, his abilities, his fears and hatreds, the soul with its capacity for infinity, the mind with its power to see the unseen, the spirit able to soar and to convert, the heart that ultimtely moves us. He can bear witness to reality only if he takes all of this into account. He will be new—his ideas, his words, his symbols and concepts will not be those of yesteryear. But he will be in the company of all the great open souls of every age and continent. And in the end there will be no question, no hesitation, as to who he is.

NOTES

1. Henri Bergson, *The Two Sources of Morality and Religion* (Doubleday Anchor Books, 1954), p. 30.

2. *Review of Politics*, vol. 19, no. 3, p. 407.

3. Mircea Eliade, *Shamanism*, revised and enlarged English edition, 1972), p. 4.

4. *Ibid.*, p. 34.

5. *Ibid.*, p. 13.

6. Hans Urs von Balthazar, *The God Question and Modern Man*, English tr., 1967, p. 105f.

7. Hans Jonas, *The Gnostic Religion*, 2nd ed., revised 1963, pp. 334 and 339.

8. *Ibid.*, p. 388.

9. Alfred North Whitehead, *Adventures of Ideas* (Mentor Books, 1955), p. 132.

A Query about Assumptions on International Organization

In seeking a rational solution to policy problems, we select and approach the relevant facts in the light of underlying assumptions. Both knowledge of the object[1] and rational certainty about the course to be taken can be attained only by proceeding from assumptions concerning values as well as causal relations. Our thinking is scientific (or, if one prefers another term, rationally disciplined rather than merely emotional) insofar as these indispensable assumptions are made deliberately, methodically, and critically. In applying thought to the problem of international organization, we have not done as well in this respect as we ought. It may be worthwhile, therefore, to call attention to the task of critically examining the assumptions on which the study of problems of international organization actually proceeds.

Some illustrations may indicate the range of possible assumptions and their relevance to the way in which research is done in the field.

Fundamental approval of international organization (i.e., the assumption, "International organization is good") has inspired a kind of research in which disapproval of national policies supposedly unresponsive to international organization guides the inquiry. In a study of international organization, this would probably produce an analysis of world politics in terms of the behavior expected of members of a world society; in a study of national policy, it would probably result in exclusive emphasis on the part that interest in the United Nations plays in United States motivations. (One may, e.g., assume that the United Nations is good because "united policies" are preferable to other kinds of policies; research would then presumably concentrate on obstacles to the shaping of "united policies" by international organizations. Similarly, one's effort can be guided by such notions as, e.g., "The United Nations is good because it brings about a world governed by law'" "The United Nations is good because, even though it may not bring about world peace now, it at least affects beneficially the general atmosphere of international relations"; "The United Nations is not a final, but a primitive, stage and should be approved because it is designed to create conditions for further growth," etc.)

One need not go to the other extreme (i.e., the assumptions, "The United Nations is bad because it is un-American"; "The United Nations is bad because it includes Soviet Russia," etc.) to realize that there may be alternative assumptions, all of which are not necessarily unreasonable. If alternatives are simply disregarded or brushed aside, our chosen assumptions are allowed to rest on purely emotional grounds or to play the role of dogma. In that case, we would do research in the light of concepts that are not themselves subject to questioning. The result of such studies could hardly be credited to rational knowledge of what is true and untrue. Particularly in a field in which the human race cannot look back on centuries of experience, the assumptions themselves must be continuously subjected to the process of dialectic reasoning. "United policies" may well be better than disunited ones, but should we not deliberate this premise by stating why policies are to be held more valuable if united to other policies than if disunited? This would enable us to consider the point of view, for instance, that policies protecting recognized values do not necessarily become more valuable when they are united with other policies detrimental to those values. International organization may indeed deserve support because it stands for a world governed by law, but should we not test this assumption against, for instance, the view that a world governed by law would be a nightmare if that law were Soviet law or likely to develop into something like it? Again, approving of the United Nations because it makes possible "further growth" is reasonable, provided that "further growth" is a good thing. Maybe it is, but should not this question be discussed? What are the values underlying this judgment?

Value assumptions create the perspectives in which we see political reality and the object of research. If one assumes that international organization is good, one asks particular questions and marshals facts in a certain way. (On this assumption, it makes sense to ask, e.g., how it would be possible for people to transfer their loyalties from the state to the "larger group," and, in the course of research, to report favorably on any successful examples of such a transfer. Most likely, however, a research motivated by this assumption would not inquire sympathetically into the possible damage to other values that the transfer of loyalties may have caused.) Still, value assumptions are necessary for research, inasmuch as research should help men to decide rationally upon the kind of political system they prefer. The problem, therefore, is how to proceed from an underlying value assumption toward a rational grasp for truth.

Pretending that we do not make any assumptions has turned out to be an illusion. It is also unsatisfactory merely to mention one's preference in a footnote and let the reader make allowance for it, for assumptions do more than inject a little subjective note into reasoning; they guide the asking of questions, the method of inquiry, and the anticipation of solutions. It is therefore important to keep not only the reader but also the researcher himself and his colleagues continuously aware of the values that govern the researcher's procedure. This means that we should decline to take our chosen assumptions for granted, and remain ready to reexamine them in the light of maturing thought. One might then, besides those studies that assume the value of international organization, have other inquiries which would begin by saying, in effect: "We are here confronted with a phenomenon that is new in international relations. It has an ideal purpose which we need to known, but, since it is an experiment, we also need to know whether this type of institution actually promotes that purpose, and furthermore what other effects it may have on international politics." If this approach were chosen, a different type of research problem would arise, different facts would be focused upon and related to each other in a different way.[2]

For another illustration, we might look at the range of assumptions regarding the role of the United Nations with respect to the East-West conflict. We may assume that the East-West conflict is taking place within the framework of an existing world society of nations that may be tangibly expressed by the United Nations; or, alternatively, that the central fact of the contemporary world is the conflict between two superpowers representing hostile ideologies and the United Nations is a political instrument which both sides are seeking to use in the struggle. One assumption considers the United Nations more basic than the struggle, the other takes the conflict to be a weightier reality than the United Nations. Either assumption would result in its own set of research questions, its own characteristic perspective on the facts, and its own methods of seeking answers. A third assumption might picture the United Nations as neither a community nor a pawn in the great power conflict, but as an island of neutral ground between hostile forces—a facility the political significance of which would depend on changing circumstances rather than on fixed principle. Unlike the value assumptions previously mentioned, these are assumptions about the contemporary scene and the forces at work in it. No less than the first type, they tend to give color and direction to research and should therefore be made an explicit part of the discussion.

A third type of assumption can be found in research questions that aim at "strengthening" the United Nations, the overcoming of "frustrations" in the organization, further development of this or that function (economic development, promotion of human rights, peaceful settlement, etc.). Such questions not only take certain values for granted, but, in addition, assume certain theses about the nature of international politics, peace, and war. It is fairly obvious that one who seeks ways and means to strengthen the United Nations must have in mind not only some notion of what a "strong" rather than a "weak" international organization would look like, but also an idea of how any international organization—strong or weak—is likely to affect international politics. Likewise, someone who is deeply concerned with "economic development" as an international task might not be untouched by the concept that wars in the last analysis spring from economic causes, just as another, who urges the greatest energy in the international promotion of human rights, is probably convinced that wars begin when certain human rights are flouted, and that international organization is a proper and effective agency for the promotion of a given set of rights.

There can be no reasonable objection to making such assumptions as these, or any others. Without them, we could not even begin to ask questions, much less increase our knowledge. But should we not in our studies avoid treating them as self-evident truths or as articles of faith, if knowledge is what we are seeking? Should we not consider them hypotheses which may serve to raise questions and direct studies, but which should in turn be subjected to criticism as we move ahead in knowledge and understanding? The profession is inviting blame not as it makes assumptions that others may object to, but insofar as it fails to make clear the assumptions and to examine and reexamine them in the growing light of maturing rational thought.

Without real knowledge of the object, we cannot let reason make a judgment. Particularly in matters concerning policy, the objects we seek to know cannot be conceived except in terms of values.[3] One might say that in matters political we attain knowledge as we achieve an understanding of how institutions, rules, actions, and events relate to given values, especially what value choices they posit and what value prospects they set up.[4] If this is valid, the big question facing the scholar in this field is where to find the value standards to which he may relate to phenomena. If it were a question of studying government, the answer could be considered relatively easy: the values constituting the enduring consensus of the political community would furnish his standard. These would be his starting point, even if he pressed beyond their current formulation and postulated higher norms. In international relations, the matter is different, and when we come to international organization, with its quasi-governmental functions, we are necessarily perplexed. The very nature of the institution seems to demand that it be related to value standards transcending those of any particular nation. Where do we find them? From what manifestations of human life do we draw our knowledge of their substance? Whom do we acknowledge to have authority to decide upon them? Is there, with respect to international organization, anything that plays the role the people play with respect to government? Can we derive the standards of value from a pattern of living, a recognized tradition, a set of symbols, a body of representative thought that could furnish evidence of decisions which may possibly have crystallized in an unspoken plebiscite over the centuries?

If we as scholars cannot identify an objective standard of good relevant to the object of our studies, a standard that we are aware we did not make up subjectively, but recognize as in reality standing over against us, we have only two possibilities left. Either we can attribute value standards to an ideal community that is postulated, or we can introduce valuations that are frankly unrelated to any community decision. In the last analysis, these two solutions may amount to the same thing. At any rate, we find that this is what has occurred in the field of international organization. The world society, the family of nations, the international community—these are formulas through which we have contrived to conceive value systems relevant to international organization. And what is the substance behind the formula? Is there evidence of a consensus, of substantive agreement on which political structures could rest and to which they should be beholden? Artificial as those formulas may seem, they need not necessarily be devoid of real meaning. At certain times in history, one could actually perceive something like a community transcending nations; there was cumulative evidence of loyalty to common values binding together men and women of different nations without negating their loyalty to their own community. With a certain amount of justification, one could name this a family of nations, a wider community, or something similar. Whether such a wider consensus exists at any given time is, however, a question of historical fact. Under present circumstances, it would appear most unlikely that, with the political world deeply divided on ideological lines, terms like "world society" or "international community" denote anything that has reality at all. If this is so, whence *do* we draw the value standards to which we relate international organization? From the consensus of the "free world"? From the golden age of nineteenth-century peace? From an alleged residuum of common humanity allegedly still linking the Soviet regime to the non-Communist world? From cultural traits common to all humanity?

One can hardly avoid the conclusion that the profession has not succeeded in making up its mind on this problem. It can know, and given rational advice based on knowledge, only as it relates the institutions and policies of international organization to acknowledged values of human life. In the present world, there is no discernible community of values other than that of the nation and, from the perspective of our own nation, possibly the so-called "free world." Both of these are smaller-than-global communities. In what way can we relate global institutions to a plurality of smaller-than-global value communities? Will it do to postulate values that have no support in actual community consensus? Would this not expose the profession to all the dangers of subjectivism and deprive its findings in this field of the dignity of rational objectivity? Whatever the answer, we can no longer avoid facing the question with courage and circumspection.

It is clear that the assumptions we are making in the study of international organization are not confined to value premises. In addition to them, we also make assumptions about cause and effect, including estimates of the interaction of various political forces. Again, the main problem here is: In the field of international organization, are the assumptions we have been using fruitful, in the sense that they have enabled us to increase our hold on truth by rational thought? The present writer, having grave doubts on this score, would like to press on to a deliberate examination of this problem: If the economists, for instance, methodologically assume an ideally free interplay of supply and demand (and, incidentally, get quite impressive results by this device), what causal assumptions could be equally productive of good method in the field of international organization?

It would be well here to recall first the assumptions that we have been in the habit of making in this field, although it is difficult to identify them clearly, since so few researchers have taken the trouble to make them explicit. International organization being primarily a device to achieve peace, the most important causal assumptions naturally would concern the causes of war and the forces making for peace. The League of Nations Covenant furnishes some clues regarding these assumptions.

They might be roughly outlined as follows: Among the primary causes of war are competitive armaments, lack of international judicial procedures, inadequate information on the part of nations about each other's objectives, passionate feelings, and nationalistic prejudices. The Covenant seems to assume that, if these defects were eliminated, nothing would prevent governments from settling their disputes peacefully and uniting their forces for the common repression of an occasional lawbreaker. The United Nations Charter seems to embrace the additional assumptions that among the indirect causes of war are the unequal economic development of nations, certain types of domestic injustice, and colonial rule.

If it is not unfair so to summarize basic assumptions, one may venture similarly to sketch some of the subsidiary assumptions on which research in our field has proceeded for two generations. They concern: (1) the kind of support international organization is likely to receive in the contemporary world (e.g., "Today the entire world is united in an overwhelming desire for peace"; "The common danger threatening all nations today is war itself"; "Technological development has made the world one"; "Nations realize that without common action to meet common problems we are all lost"; "The United Nations is as far as present world opinion will go in the direction of world federation," etc.); (2) the role an international organization would play in the contemporary setting of world politics (as exemplified by such notions characterizing international organization as "the town meeting of the world," "the moral power of world opinion," "our best hope for success," "the majority of right," "the community forming moral judgments," "the Constitution of the community of states," "the combined force of the community of nations," "organizing the determination of the world against aggression," "a useful forum for negotiation," etc.); and (3) a gradual transformation of world politics expected as a result of the influence of international organization over a period of time (represented by such concepts as "the passing of power politics," "a primitive stage which will make possible a more highly developed organization," "It changes all who participate in good faith into better members of world society," "It can influence the growth of world law," "By discouraging one aggressor, it discourages all future aggressors," "It induces governments to form the habit of resorting to peaceful methods of settling conflicts rather than to war," "It will convince nations that aggression does not pay," "It will teach nations to pursue common instead of selfish interests," "Every success of collective security is bound to increase the likelihood of future successes," etc.).

It may be unfair to ask whether these assumptions have served us well, in the sense that thinking based on them has reliably guided us in the actual political situations involving international organization. Those who are opposed to collective security, for example, would claim that the failure is obvious and that the underlying thinking must have been inadequate; but those believing in collective security could simply reply that the time to judge has not yet come and that the flower may yet be plucked from the nettle. We may therefore have to pass up the pragmatic test. But it may be useful to ask how plausible these assumptions look at first sight. In doing so, let us recall that, for all the precedents in literature and even in the practice of some other civilization, the League of Nations and the United Nations are novel experiments creating, rather than building upon, precedent in international politics. So far as scientific knowledge is concerned, they have opened up new territory, one that we mistakenly assume to be familiar. It is submitted that we do so because it reminds us of familiar terrain: the problems of government. On the whole, we are well acquainted with the way people act when confronted with institutions of government (authority, laws, judges, police, etc.). In this respect, the experience of the race is extremely old and we feel on firm ground even though we may grope uncertainly for a better grasp of details. On the other hand, we have little or no experience of states acting under the influence of similar institutions. Since, therefore, no concepts derived from international relations are available for this situation, we imply, *faute de mieux*, the analogy of government-citizens organizing themselves in a world society ("We the peoples of the United Nations..."). This is understandable, but it must be recognized that use of this kind of assumption may lead researchers badly astray, unless they remain ever-mindful of having borrowed the concept from an entirely different context. It may, therefore, be preferable to abandon this analogy and to try for assumptions that are more representative of the international scene.

A critical review of those assumptions would incidentally raise doubt about the applicability of certain concepts which we have been prone to transfer, together with our convictions attached thereto, from the field of government to that of international organization. How much sense does it make, for example, to speak of "democratic procedure" when it is not the mind of free individuals but the instruction of government delegations that has a bearing on the "communal" deliberations and decisions? How useful is it to speak of the "majority principle" when governments of many nations, large, small, and minuscule, are assembled, and each of them counts for one in the total number? Is it meaningful to employ the term "public opinion" to denote the result of the voting of UN delegations? Where and how can the "common interest" of nations be authoritatively determined? How closely do we move to reality when we speak of aggression as a "crime"?

A deliberate and systematic critique of our own assumptions is necessary if we are to advance the contribution of the profession regarding the problems of international organization. To this end, it would be desirable not only to aim at fuller awareness of the assumptions made in the asking of question and the devising of methods, but also to have some research projects focus directly on the methodology and the adequacy of a variety of assumptions. The objective here would be to raise the quality of scholarly inquiry and discussion through the most vigorous rational discipline. But beyond this, we should always be mindful of the needs of policy makers. If we have to state and discuss our assumptions in order to advance knowledge, policy makers have to decide among various possible assumptions in order to operate with energy and consistency. It seems that scholars could help in this respect by presenting, in the clearest possible fashion, the available choices and their implications. This would probably involve explaining a number of different assumptions not only as adequately (or inadequately) reflecting the facts of life, but also as logically (or psychologically) leading to certain types of policies. If this were done well, the profession would contribute not only to more intelligent and realistic United States attitudes toward the problems of international organization, but also to a more rational correlation between these attitudes and other national interests in the total picture of United States policies.

NOTES

1. "That of which the mind by any of its activities takes cognizance" (Webster).

2. This is not a plea for one assumption in favor of another. Assumptions are means for understanding reality. Precisely for that reason, however, we should be aware of all the available means and the problem of using them judiciously and rationally.

3. *Cf.* David Easton, *The Political System*, New York, 1953, pp. 228ff.

4. This is, of course, not equivalent to saying that the study of these matters should be value-bound, in the sense of refusing to see reality unless it happens to confirm one's own preferences. The scholar's probing mind can and should be detached and objective even as he seeks to grasp the value significance of the affairs that he studies.

Enlightenment to Ideology

More than any other historical period the eighteenth-century Enlightenment tempts one to make generalizations. A close reading of the historical record gives most of these generalizations the lie; for any one thinker of this period who strikes us as "typical" there are others who oppose him. "Ambiguity" does prevail, indeed. What tempts us to generalizations, however, is the flow of ideas and emotions from this century to the next, experienced as a unified legacy. I do not conceive it my task to enter, once again, into the fray about the "character" of this century. For what I should like to say, the Enlightenment is a *terminus a quo*. I do need a *point d'appui* for a characterization of that terminus, and I have chosen Ernst Cassirer's *The Philosophy of the Enlightenment*, fully aware that thus I must stand or fall with what this mentor has to say to me.[1] Since Cassirer has asked the kind of questions that I would ask, and dealt with them in the manner I prefer, that situation suits me well.

Cassirer regards the eighteenth-century concept of reason as the key factor in the picture. If it was radically "new," so was that of the preceding century, with Descartes' "bifurcation" of reality into a *res extensa* and a *res cogitans*. But to some extent Descartes still had one foot in scholasticism, and, anyhow, the eighteenth century depended on Newton and Locke rather than on Descartes, great seventeenth-century philosophical systems gave an impression of stability, sameness, endurance, quite the opposite mood prevailed in the eighteenth-century ones. Said D'Alembert, in his *Elements de Philosophie* (1759): "It is difficult not to see...a very remarkable change in our ideas...a change whose rapidity seems to promise an even greater transformation to come," and called this "a revolution." This change centered in the eighteenth century's radically different conception of reason and what effects this had on the strivings and beliefs of the entire civilization. "Reason" is seen as "an original spontaneity of thought," an agency, a force, an "imminent activity" not so much engaged in an imitative function but in "the power and task of shaping life itself" (vii, viii).

Descartes had emphasized mathematics and had discovered analytical geometry. From then on, analysis was the only conceivable method to arrive at knowledge consisting of "clear and distinct ideas," ideas focused on the composing parts of any whole. But mathematics applied to a system derived from a few dogmatic axioms was one thing; Newton and Locke were empiricists, and that was quite another thing. Newton "does not begin by setting up certain principles, certain general concepts and axioms, when he is investigating 'the factual.'" Rather, "his phenomena are the data of experience, his principles are the goal of investigation. If the latter are first according to nature, then the former must always be first to us."(7) Hence the true method of physics can never consist in proceeding

> from a hypothesis...for such hypotheses can be invented and modified as desired; logically any one of them is valid as any other.... A scientific abstraction or "definition" cannot serve as a really unambiguous starting-point, for such a starting point can only be obtained by experience and observation. [This] means that facts as such are not mere matter, facts exhibit an all-pervasive form. This form appears in mathematical

determinations and in arrangements according to measure and number. But such arrangements cannot be foreseen in the mere concept; they must rather be shown to exist in the facts themselves. The procedure is thus not from concepts and axioms to phenomena, but vice versa.(8)

The Enlightenment, then, models philosophy on the pattern of contemporary natural science, particularly physics. It demands that the mind "abandon itself to the abundance of phenomena and gauge itself constantly by them. For it may be sure that it will not get lose, but that instead it will find here its own real truth and standard." This is how Cassirer describes the *fides* on which the Enlightenment travels to "understanding." Cassirer perceives in this spirit two principles: the first is the identity of "the positive" with the "rational," not a mere postulate but a "goal attainable and an ideal fully realizable." (9) In this perspective reason appears as a dynamic force that, beginning with disciplined and systematic observation, will from there move, greatly expanding the horizon of knowledge, from the finite to the infinite, from the concrete to the universal. The other principle holds reason to have become the lever of a new age, characterized by the combination of the "positive" and the "rational," in which combination "reason" becomes "the unifying and central point of this century, expressing all that it longs and strives for, and all that it achieves." (5)

D'Alembert greeted this philosophical method as a "revolution" because it replaced faith with certainty, dogma with process; and Lessing proclaimed that the real power of reason is found not in the possession but in the acquisitive pursuit of truth. The eighteenth century itself provides an illustration of this spirit, as it frees itself from the authority of mathematics at the very moment of relying on it, by extending the analytical process beyond quantity and number. Thus the "positive" which combines with the "rational" is no longer confined to a particular field of knowledge; it applies also to the psychological and sociological fields.

It was Condillac, in his *Treatise on Sensation* (1754) and *The Language of Calculus* (1798), who showed the way to this further expansiveness of "reason." This is remarkable in that Condillac agreed with Descartes on the immateriality and spirituality of the soul, and on the obvious conclusion that what is immaterial and spiritual does not consist of parts in the way "extended things" do. All the same, he found a way to subject psychological phenomena to mathematical analysis, relying on Locke's sense perceptions. Particular psychological phenomena, he argued, are continuous developments from a common source of all psychological phenomena. A continuous series of "impressions" and the temporal order in which they are produced "are sufficient to build up the totality of psychological experience and to produce it in all its wealth and subtle shadings. If we succeed in producing psychological experience in this manner, we have at the same time reduced it to the quantitative concepts." (25) The "higher powers of the mind," Condillac concluded, are "in reality only a transformation of the basic element of sense perception....The mind neither creates nor invents; it repeats and constructs. But in this repetition it can exhibit almost inexhaustible powers. It extends the visible universe beyond all bounds; it traverses the infinity of time and space; and yet it is unceasingly engaged in the production of ever new shapes within itself." This passage from Condillac can well serve as an explanation of the central orientation that united thinking people in the eighteenth century. It is attention to "the mind...concerned only with itself." The immensely popular Helvetius was the chief herald (*On the Mind*) of this good news. One step further, and the same conception will be applied to theoretical distinctions.

Judgment is said to consist only in "grasping similarities and differences between individual ideas." But at the beginning of this process the Enlightenment thinkers presuppose "an original act of awareness which is analogous to, and indeed identical with, the perception of a sense quality." (27) Here Cassirer adds, "both the edifice of ethical values and the logically graded structure of knowledge are demolished." The *analogia sensationis* has replaced the *analogia entis*, but while the latter applies to the desire to know higher reality, the former is the mind's desire to know itself and the newly discovered uses of this instrument.

If the revolutionary concept of reason may serve to represent the character of the Enlightenment, a brief look at the concepts of nature and history will round out the impression. Cassirer points out that the patterning of all reason on natural science must not be mistaken for just an addition of some different features to the scope of knowledge: "The knowledge of nature does not simply lead us into the world of objects; it serves rather as a medium in which the mind develops its own self-knowledge" (37). The new discoveries point toward the illimitable, "one world and one Being are replaced by an infinity of worlds.... But the important aspect of this transformation does not lie in the boundless expansion, but that the mind now becomes aware of a new force within itself...proving its unity equal to the infinity of being....The power of reason is our only access to the infinite...." (38) The autonomy of intellect "corresponds to the autonomy of nature....The philosophy of the Enlightenment attempts to show the self-sufficiency of both nature and intellect" (45). In the century of Newton, the idea of natural science

> is no longer shaped after the pattern of geometry, but rather after that of arithmetic.... On the question of the certainty or uncertainty of knowledge the roles have been switched about strangely as a result of this transition from the constructive to the analytical ideal of natural science....We can escape deception only by penetrating beyond mere appearance, by relating the empirically given to concepts and expressing it in concepts which carry their proof in themselves...truth

and certainty must be found in the body of knowledge which the principle validates (54).

Thus, with regard to the important assumption that past experience points the way to future ones, a Dutch philosopher argued that the validity of this axiom stemmed not from necessity of the object of thought but from the necessity of action. Cassirer comments: "Mathematical empiricism here stands on the threshold of skeptical empiricism" (62). Hume, of course, takes the further step when he divests belief of all its transcendental elements and reduces it to purely psychological grounds, to an immanent necessity of human nature. In a similar way the Enlightenment eliminates the notion of substance by insisting that "the idea of a thing is simply the idea of a mere sum or aggregate of qualities." Says Cassirer: "The attempt to eliminate all metaphysical elements from empirical philosophy finally gains so much ground that it casts doubt upon the logical foundations of this philosophy as well" (64).

Nature, then, no longer justifying an inference from deduction, now justifies inference from the part to the whole.

> But if the experimental method is to be completely effective, we must grant it full autonomy and free it from all tutelage. It is therefore necessary in the field of natural science to combat the systematizing spirit in mathematics as well as in metaphysics. As soon as the mathematician develops not merely his own conceptual world, but is convinced that he can catch reality in the meshes of his concepts, he has himself become a metaphysician.... [This amounts to] a demand for a purely descriptive science of nature (74f).

In this sense, materialism—which did form only a small part of the Enlightenment—presents itself not so much as a dogma but a an imperative (69). And Buffon, himself not a materialist, insists that in nature "there are only individuals, there are no species and genera" (79). Cassirer asserts:

But as the center of gravity of thought shifts from definition to description, from the species to the individual, mechanism can no longer be considered as the sole and sufficient basis of explanation; there is in the making a transition to a conception of nature which no longer seeks to derive and explain becoming from being, but being from becoming (80).

This may be the right point at which to turn from an historical account of the Enlightenment to the problem of the links between this century and the ideologies of the nineteenth and twentieth centuries.

I shall approach this problem not with the rationalist methods of the past but rather with the greatly enriched political science of our time, which has room for the awareness that reason is born from experiences of the soul, the *open* soul participating in transcendent reality.[2] The characteristic trait of the Enlightenment is its universal cult of "reason," a cult quite evident even before November 10, 1793, the day when Robespierre turned Notre Dame into the Temple of Reason.

The entire century, particularly in France, seems bent not so much on knowing reality but on knowing and admiring the human mind. It was Locke who put the Enlightenment on this track, with his analysis of knowledge composed of sense perception and reflection. Beginning with Condillac, French thinkers rang the changes on this simple sequence, all the while obeying a canon of certain exclusions. "System," in the sense of seventeenth-century philosophy, was declared taboo, as was metaphysics, and as was any reference to transcendence. There may have been no unified concept of reason in the Enlightenment, but there emerged a unified attitude toward reason, the attitude of regarding it as an instrument, an agency, a force. Of what was it to be an agency, toward what force? The answer is, "power," even though this end had already been put on its pedestal by

Francis Bacon and Descartes. "For this age, knowledge of its own activity, intellectual self-examination, and foresight are the proper function and essential task of thought" (4).

Reason is no longer experienced as a partnership between the human soul and the divine inspiration—man's exclusive possession and favorite and powerful tool. "The lust for knowledge, the *libido sciendi*, which theological dogmatism had outlawed and branded as intellectual pride, is now called a necessary quality of the soul" (14). The Enlightenment does not ignore that man is born into this world, but it rejects any obligation to deference as flowing from this fact. "As soon as the power of thought awakens in man, it advances irresistibly against this form of reality, summoning it before the tribunal of thought and challenging its legal titles to truth and validity" (18). Not even facts are allowed to form a kind of metaphysical upper story: "The mere togetherness of the facts must be transformed into a conjuncture; the mere coexistence of the data must upon closer inspection reveal an interdependence" (21). Thus rational order demands "strict unification," which means that "the manifold of experience [must be] placed into such a relationship [of its parts] that, starting from any given point, we can run through them according to a constant and general rule" (23). "Reason," hence, means ultimate control not only of nature but also of what philosophers used to call the mysterious soul, as well as power over the equally mysterious reality of social order. The Enlightenment, throughout its course, was celebrating the final attainment of reason's "almost limitless power," before which every reality had to prostrate itself in abject servitude.

At this point I must argue with Cassirer, my mentor, and with his statement that "the autonomy of intellect corresponds to the autonomy of nature." It was not the autonomy of nature that the Enlightenment had discovered; that discovery had already been made by Aristotle and his Milesian antecedents. The Enlightenment forced its concept of nature into obedience to its newly acquired power tool of reason. Only that was nature which could be fully possessed and dominated by that power tool. Thus the Enlightenment eliminated, from the autonomous nature that Aristotle knew, the ends and purposes, the final causality, which went perfectly well with an autonomous nature but not with the demand of an all-powerful empirical reason.

The new attitude toward reason, and nature, carried with it a new moral attitude which may well not have been part of the design. Just as the actual adoration of reason in its own Temple came late in the century, so the moral attitude of the Enlightenment did not become fully articulate until the next century, when its postulate, the superman, was openly and formally proclaimed. The idea that life is, above all, man's power began to stir in the last two decades of the eighteenth century as Europe's young poets revived the ancient myth of Prometheus, turning it upside down, so that now Prometheus is no longer the victim of divine punishment for his metaphysical rebellion, but the heroic leader of mankind against that "pack of gods." Man, in pursuit of "Promethean" power, needed to "transvaluate all values," which was initiated at that time by the Marquis de Sade and Lord Byron.

As a general principle of life, however, this vision of power was enthroned only by Romanticism. Thus Ralph Waldo Emerson spurred on "the American Scholar":

> It is a mischievous notion that we are come late into nature; that the world was finished a long time ago. As the world was plastic and fluid in the hands of God, so it is to so much of his attributes as we bring to it...in proportion as a man has anything in him divine, the firmament flows before him, and takes his signet and form. They are the kings of the world who give the color of their present thought to all nature and all art, and persuade men by the cheerful serenity of their carrying the matter, that this thing which they do, is

the apple which the ages have desired to pluck, now at
last ripe, and inviting nations to the harvest. The great
man makes the great thing.[3]
In Germany, the young Marx saw himself as a modern Prometheus
and superman.[4]

The postulate of reason's limitless power entailed certain
manipulations of reality. Two types of manipulation are widespread: the reduction of non-corporeal reality to assumed artificial parts into which it appeared divisible; and the reduction of
one kind of reality to another kind that appeared quantifiable.
The latter appeared first: "[The Enlightenment] seeks another
concept of truth and philosophy whose function it is to extend
the boundaries and make them more elastic, concrete, and vital.
The Enlightenment does not take the ideal of this model of
thinking from the philosophical doctrines of the past; on the
contrary, it constructs its ideal according to the model and
pattern of contemporary natural science" (7). Mathematics,
particularly after the discovery of calculus by Leibniz, became the
dominant technical discipline. Where analytical division seemed
impossible, as in the science of man's soul, of the social whole,
of the moral order, a reduction to composing parts is achieved
artificially, as previously noted. Reducing human society to its
economic component made it suitable for both analysis and
quantification. Thus any thought of mystery was disallowed;
there were only things already known and things that eventually
would be known.

Even more did an impression of enormous power flow from
the postulate of unity, a postulate that grew more urgent as more
emphasis was placed on the particularity of facts as the sole reality
given. "Knowledge" could not stop at particularities, it had to
pull them together into a unified whole. The postulate soon
came to play a very practical role, as Robespierre and St. Just
sought by all means of power to achieve, out of the multiplicity
of citizens, the seamless unity of The People. The new concept

of reason also gave eighteenth-century man an utter confidence in his ability to shape human life according to whatever design he had in mind. In the past, as long as thinking men reflected not on the power of their mind but on the cosmos, the order of things which they knew not to have brought about, ignorance was the essential starting point of all philosophy. "All men by nature *desire* to know" is the opening line of Aristotle's *Metaphysics*, attributing the urge to move from ignorance to knowledge to "all men," as a "natural" velleity.

The Enlightenment, by contrast, focused on the mind's power as its chief object. It identified that power with a particular method of inquiry and, if the reality was unsuited for this method, so much the worse for the reality. Reason appeared no longer as a process of partnership between the human and the divine, but as a self-sufficient faculty possessed by man, a force that could be turned even against nature, tradition, and God, so that the kingdom of God could be replaced by the kingdom of human reason. The business of this kingdom was rebellion, for from rebellion against authority, superior norms, and the divine being, reason's new self-sufficiency had originated. As Albert Camus states: "From this moment, every question, every word, is an act of rebellion. The rebel is a man who is on the point of accepting or rejecting the sacred and determined on laying claim to a human situation in which all answers are human—in other words, formulated in reasonable terms."[5] Camus continues: "It would be possible to demonstrate in this manner that only two possible worlds can exist for the human mind: the sacred (or, to speak in Christian terms, the world of grace), and the world of rebellion."

Before exploring the link between Enlightenment and the nineteenth-century ideologies, we should recall that the eighteenth century was not unique. Enlightenment is a type of human form; other civilizations have known periods of enlightenment, too. In Athens the Sophists' dominance continued for about a century. Of their books, however, only one is still known, and that only through a summary. Gorgias of Leontini wrote *On Being*, where he said, among other things: nothing exists; if anything exists, it is incomprehensible; if it is comprehensible, it is incommunicable. Regarding being he argued thus: "It cannot be everlasting; if it were, it would have no beginning and therefore it would be boundless; if it is boundless, then it has no position, for if it had position, it would be contained in something, and so it would no longer be boundless.... Hence, if Being is everlasting, it is boundless; if boundless, it has no position; if without position, it does not exist."[6]

Similarly there was a period of enlightenment in China, a reaction to the rise of philosophy from Confucius and Mencius. Its protagonist was Han Fei Tzu, in the early third century B.C. As Confucius aimed chiefly at the restoration of public order in China, so Han Fei Tzu wrote about the same subject. Confucius' way was that of moral regeneration, beginning with each person and each family. Here, by contrast, are samples of Han Fei Tzu's advice:

> In the state of an enlightened ruler there are no books written on bamboo slips; law supplies the only instruction. There are no sermons of the former kings; the officials serve as the only teachers.... Therefore, the way of the enlightened ruler is to unify the laws instead of longing for men of good faith.... Benevolence may make one shed tears and be reluctant to apply penalties; but law makes it clear that such penalties must be applied.... Men of antiquity strove for moral virtue; men of middle times sought out wise schemes; men of today vie to be known for strength and spirit.[7]

In China, the period of Enlightenment culminated in the Ch'in Dynasty, which to this day is proverbial for harsh rule and the burnings of philosophers' books. But the Ch'in Dynasty lasted barely two decades and was followed by the Han Dynasty, which elevated Confucius' thought to the rank of public philosophy. The Sophists in Athens had their way for not quite one hundred years. Then Socrates and, after him, Plato, rose to philosophical prominence, with the result that their insights are still taught to this day.

Now to return to "our" Enlightenment. The concentration of the mind on itself involved a new concept of history, that of necessary progress. About that something will be said later. Here we should remember the ancient distinction between *intellectus* and *ratio*, the latter connoting discursive thinking that produced concepts of perception; the former, the higher understanding of contemplation. The Enlightenment recognized only *ratio*, and when Kant, on top of this, reversed the meaning of the two terms, there resulted an entire civilization that oriented itself exclusively by *ratio*, the power of *concapere*, perception as grasping. In Milton's words: "The mind is its own place, and in it self can make a Heav'n of Hell, a Hell of Heaven."[8]

At this point a child of our age who has been listening with mounting impatience might burst in with: "What is wrong with that? Is thinking *not* power, and nothing but power? Look at the results: Haven't we freed agriculture from weeds and pests? Haven't we put a man on the moon? Aren't we on the point of generating life itself?" This is, indeed, a "powerful" argument. The phenomenon of modern science, and the resulting technology, is and remains utterly astounding. As for Enlightenment's concept of reason, has it not created human liberty and prosperity? It was indeed a great and significant movement that began early in the seventeenth century and culminated in the nineteenth. But an even greater and more profound movement began a little more than two thousand years before that time. Bruno Snell has aptly called it "The Discovery of the Mind."[9] The small people populating Attica's city-states brought it forth, and men of great authority in human history were its stars. And if we are ready to praise the Enlightenment for the prodigious achievement of natural science, should not the Greek discovery of the mind be justified for focusing on the human soul and its public order? It was the combination of Greek philosophy and Christian faith that accounts for the opening moves of Western science. Neither Copernicus, nor Kepler, nor Leibniz, nor Newton had felt a need to forget the knowledge of things human embodied in the earlier tradition. The Enlightenment's "prohibition of remembrance" cannot be explained as an intellectual necessity.

Plato was no follower of Parmenides, but he has Socrates speak of Parmenides as "a revered and awful figure. There was a sort of depth in him that was altogether noble."[10] Parmenides was the one from whom came the concept of Being, in close connection with the *nous* (reason). Parmenides reports a vision of a deity and her words to him: "One should both say and think what Being Is; for to Be is noble, and Nothingness is not possible. This I command you to consider; for from the latter way of search first of all I debar you. But next I debar you from that way...of blind, uncritical hordes, by whom To Be and Not To Be are regarded as the same and not the same...."[11] And Socrates says of himself: "I have gained [my] kind of reputation, gentlemen, from nothing more or less than a kind of wisdom. What kind of wisdom do I mean? Human wisdom, I suppose. It seems that I really am wise in this limited sense. Presumably the geniuses whom I mentioned are wise in a wisdom that is more than human.... But the truth of the matter is pretty certainly this, that real wisdom is the property of God."[12]

The astonishing Greek achievement of originating philosophy came both from the consciousness of ignorance and the realization that true wisdom is divine and that men, as men, are wise when they love divine wisdom. Plato establishes that "soul is prior to body, body secondary and derivative, soul governing in the real order of things, and body being subject to governance."[13] Of the *nous* he spoke of not only as an aspect of the human soul but also as a divinity. Similarly Aristotle, Plato's student, said of the *nous*: "Whether it be reason or something else that is this element in us which is thought to be our natural ruler and guide and to take thought of things noble and divine, whether it be itself also divine or only the most divine element in us, the activity of this in accordance with proper virtue will be perfect happiness."[14]

Thus the human creators of philosophy never spoke of reason in the way the Enlightenment thinkers did. Parmenides experienced the Is in a vision; Socrates, Plato, and others experienced being "drawn," "pulled," even "dragged" to the true reality beyond the cosmos. They respond to these experiences with something they call "the quest," "the arduous way," "the search," clearly conveying that the authority of truth is not found in themselves, nor in their method, but in their participation in a higher reality. Their attitude was one of love of the cosmos and of divine wisdom. Where in the Enlightenment do we find mention of "love" to characterize the attitude towards the cosmos or divinity? Enlightenment focuses on the objects of knowledge which mind can convert from multiplicity to unity, or from unity to composing parts, all for the sake of human control and mastery over nature.

Enlightenment's "reason" is a myth of human power, a myth eventually generating another myth, that of human "self-salvation." It was not until a century later that Nietzsche gave a name to this attitude: the will to power. How much this had become a feature of culture in general is made clear by a letter from Beethoven to Nikolaus Ameskall von Domanovecz: "I refuse to hear anything about your whole moral outlook. *Power* is the moral principle of those who excel others, and it is also mine."[15] A few pages later we read what Beethoven wrote about the addressee, his friend: "I regard him [von Domanovecz] and S. merely as instruments on which to play when I feel inclined."[16]

A few words may be said about the Enlightenment's idea of

nature. Classical Greek philosophy experienced nature as an autonomous order whose structure and laws could be independently explored. Even Descartes, insisting that the human mind had "innate ideas," embraced a conviction that there was something as knowledge "by nature." Locke banned this concept. He, along with Voltaire and D'Alembert, agreed that knowledge of essences was impossible. Still, a tiny remnant of metaphysics was left in the Enlightenment, the "uniformity of nature," by virtue of which they trusted in conclusions drawn from today's experiment to future experiments. But the idea of substance was discarded in favor of that of a mere sum or aggregate of qualities. Cassirer declares: "The attempt to eliminate all metaphysical elements from empirical philosophy finally gained so much ground that it cast doubt upon the logical foundations of this philosophy as well" (64).

On the other hand, the concept of nature serves the Enlightenment as a barrier against theology, and also against a rational order of ends. The exploration of nature was restricted to causes and effects. It was not supposed to include any teleology of nature, because it might become a science of ends in human life. A contemporary philosopher, Hans Jonas, has recently begun to argue that there was no need for this exclusion. "For natural science," he says, "it is enough that in the measurable regions the qualitative-mechanistic accounting always tallies; that is, that its equations each time stand the test of event and its method is rebuffed by none. And that is quite compatible with an underlying teleology."[17]

The eighteenth-century elevation of the human mind to something like divine rank was attended by a turbulent development of metaphysical concepts, notably nature and God. God was somewhat demoted from Almighty Power and Source of Life to "architect," or demiurge. The energy of motion was seen as energy. In this company nature figured as "the force which partakes of matter by its origin and of the Supreme Intelligence by is laws."[18] It was a kind of metaphysics made to measure for a human mind that eventually would leave nothing unknown. The sense of awe which originally produced the idea of nature gave way to a spirit of conquest fortified by the certainty that the mind's power to penetrate and possess had no limits. The admiration for nature in the eighteenth century had a trace of impurity about it which probably lowered men's capacity of drawing from nature's image standards of human conduct. The place of Aristotle's *Right by Nature* was vacated. Into the gap moved, slowly at first, but rapidly gaining speed, a new concept of history. Not that history as a symbolic form of consciousness had been absent.

From St. Augustine's *De civitate dei* the symbolism of history had been present in Western civilization. New was the idea that history could be known as well as nature. We remember that conceiving a way to divide psychic processed into parts led to the application of natural science methods to these processes. The same thing occurred in the case of history. History, both past and future, was divided into parts (or stages, or phases), each of which could be rendered intelligible by attributing to it a specific character. Turgot was the first to do this, as he suggested that mankind had a childhood, from which followed the conclusion that there would be an adolescence and a maturity. His friend and biographer, Condorcet, suggested ten different parts of history; Saint-Simon distinguished between three successive parts; Fourier assumed thirty-two successive ages; Marx distinguished now five, now six stages of history; and Comte returned to the ritual number three. At any rate, without postulating stages, or parts of history, no knowledge could be even dreamed about. One should add that it is one thing to distinguish different phases of the past and another to extend that postulate into the future.

Once this fad had begun speculations about histories appeared at the rate of about one every ten years. In this wave of production, Marx was the latest, and his sociological method of perceiving different characters of the states was able to impress people as "scientific." There resulted a well-nigh dizzy wave of lining up history's total number of stages, and momentum from one to the other, all of them spelling out mankind's "destiny" as something knowable in details and totally predictable. All this was worlds apart from living with an "inner sense of history," an awareness of the "flowing presence of God" in the passage of generations and kingdoms. It was Augustine, of course, who correctly had placed the goal of history in the eschatological beyond, while denying to the stream of political and military events any meaning.[19] For a brilliant analysis of a people's finding the meaning of their collective existence in history, one should consult Eric Voegelin, *Israel and Revelation*, particularly chapter 4.[20] Unlike nature, history is not a "given." To the Christian civilizations, as well as to the Jews and to Islam, history has become the symbolic form of their consciousness, so that if they reject one philosophy of history they will immediately crave and obtain another, even though the other can be an irrational ideology.

History as an inner sense of human existence, then, was necessarily linked to the experience of God in "flowing presence." The antitheistic modernity could not accept this outlook. Yet there was no way in which the eighteenth century could have embraced the utterly ahistorical view of life that characterizes, for instance, Hindu civilization. Admitting that something must be said about history, Turgot, in the middle of the century, lecturing on "the advantages of Christian faith" in human history, asked a completely new question: "Does mankind, then, have a childhood?" It is a question that might have occurred to any philosopher at some time, but it is a question pertaining to the context of and growth in nature. When Turgot raises the question in the context of history, he implies that history as a whole can be known by analogy with the phases of a human life.[21] By means of this question Turgot set aside all philosophy of history since Augustine, as well as what the Bible had said about history. Israel knew God chiefly through his "mighty acts," and itself as the specific target of these divine acts, and thus it could understand its own existence as a drama in time punctuated by the time-bound presence of the eternal God. By contrast Turgot removes the character of history as a story. His seeing history as an organic process eliminates history from our civilizational consciousness. This becomes clear as his questioning stops at mankind's "maturity," so that he avoids the category of death, which alone could have brought up history's character as a drama. Turgot's follower, Condorcet, is even clearer about this feature when he identifies history with "the infinite perfectibility of mankind," suggesting process but no end. There can be no philosophy of history without meaning in terms of history's end. In this sense history no longer figures in the Enlightenment's consciousness.

Still, paradoxically, Voltaire creates a new outlook on history, saying that it deals with "*histoire en philosophe*," thus launching the concept "philosophy of history."[22] So did Schiller and Herder write on history, as did Kant. What is more, Turgot was followed by any number of minor thinkers, e.g., Dom Deschamps, Paul Rebaut, Chastellux, Abbe de St. Pierre. Among them, two stand out in this period—Saint-Simon and Fourier. All of them seem to have been excited by the prospect, which Turgot had created, that one could now calculate history on the basis of empirical evidence, emphatically "doing without God." From then on history was in everybody's mind as a newly discovered field for "positive thinking." Turgot constructed it as an effect of impersonal forces, working catastrophes and destruction, but in the process favoring the flowering of geniuses through whom great things would be accomplished. Saint-Simon speculated that "military societies" had come to an end and that the future would belong to "industrial societies."

The most widely accepted view assumed a self-generating process of inexorable progress, an inevitable upward movement of mankind, and the absolute elimination of every kind of evil in the course of things. All of these concepts precluded what used to be the center of existence-in-history: the memory of crucial events and features of the past, and their meaningful relation with both present and future. The book of Deuteronomy still preserves, in the form of a prayer, this constitutive memory of Israel:

> My father was a wandering Aramaean, who went down to Egypt with a small group of men, and stayed there, until he there became a great, powerful and numerous nation. The Egyptians ill-treated us, they oppressed us, and inflicted harsh slavery on us. But we called on Yahweh, God of our ancestors. Yahweh heard our voice and saw our misery, our toil and our oppression; and Yahweh brought us out of Egypt with mighty hand and outstretched arm, with great terror, and with signs and wonders. He brought us here and has given us this country flowing with milk and honey. Hence, I now bring the first-fruits of the soil that you, Yahweh, have given us.[23]

Without memory of this kind, there can be no history as the symbolic form of a people's consciousness, or even as a consciousness of history shared by an entire civilization.

What used to be the drama of mankind's relation with God turned into a secular dogma of mankind's steady and autonomous ascent, but now toward God. Instead of history we find an optimistic metaphysics of time in worldly terms. This kind of thinking has a vulnerable point, the question of "the end." Kant was the first one to note this problem. From the assumption of a steadily maturing human reason he infers "Nature's" secret purpose: "a cosmopolitan condition to secure the external safety of each state." Nature's "Idea" (as he calls it) will help man to bring the millennium to pass in the not too distant future. But Kant was aware of an undeniable bit of irrationality in the scheme: "It remains strange [*befremdend bleibt es allerdings*] that the earlier generations carry through their toilsome labor only for the sake of the later, to prepare for them a foundation on which the later generations could erect the higher edifice which was Nature's goal, and yet that only the latest of the generations should have the good fortune to inhabit the building...."[24] It would seem that history as the symbolic form of Western consciousness might have come to an end, its place taken entirely by some progressive processes of nature, including evolution, and that an "end" could be envisaged only in terms of maturing human reasons. In fact the opposite took place. As Enlightenment changed to Romanticism, history asserted itself and became the quasi-religious core of the next century's ideological movements.

What in historical retrospect looks like a radical break with the past, to the point of intended oblivion, is hardly noticeable in the continuity of daily life. Looking at the concrete multitude of figures in the eighteenth century, one found hardly anyone to whom one could attribute responsibility for a break, yet one did occur between the Cartesian philosophy and that of Newton. Descartes, in turn, still had contact with scholasticism, and then Leibniz, a philosopher in the Cartesian mode, did gain entrée into the middle of the Enlightenment through the *Essays on Human Understanding*, not published until 1765. Similarly, Romanticism slowly emerged while the Enlightenment was still flourishing, even though Romanticism constituted a break with Enlightenment. Both break and gradualism can be observed in Rousseau. His language is that of the Enlightenment: short, sharp, apparently clear sentences giving the impression of being strictly obedient to facts and governed by sheer logic—in reality a shallow rationalism that kept its eyes closed to anything that might be mystery, transcendence, spiritual experience, or metaphysics.

Yet in Rousseau one finds many deliberately ambiguous words through which mystery, spirit, and metaphysics enter through the back door. One of them is the word "alienation," the substance of the social contract. It is by no means clear whether the particular persons, each of whom has to consent to the contract, survive the "total alienation to the community" or merge into the new entity of the whole. When a citizen, having dissented, is "forced to be free," is it his own better self that "forces" the resisting lower part of his soul or the mass of the majority that crushes a powerless individual? Concerning the *volonté generale*, which is said to replace the multitude of individuals by a collective moral body, with "its collective self its life, and its will," is it an *ens*, an object, a thing in the way of other things in the cosmos, or does it remain a composite structure, a function of the characters, virtues, and vices of its many members? It is said to have "absolute power over its members," but does that deprive its unity of its moral character, or is it something like the power of a natural body over its natural parts?

"The Sovereign [the general will] needs only to exist in order to be what it ought to be...." Does this mean that fact amounts to norm? The general will "is always right [*droite*]," but it can be mistaken. When it is mistaken, is it still the core of morality, and is it still an existential truth, in the sense in which Jesus said, "I am the way, the truth, and the life"? In addition to the general will there is also a legislator who, while having no public office, is there to "design the laws." Is he something comparable to a British Royal Commission, or is he like the Athenian Stranger in Plato's *Laws*? Is it his task "to change human nature...to strip each man of the resources that are his and his alone, in order to give him new resources that are foreign to his nature," which would be like the task that Lenin took upon himself? And what about the "unquestionable miracle of his own great spirit"? All this ambiguity moves Rousseau into the realm of Romanticism.

The same can be said of Hegel. Coming half a century after Rousseau, he grew up in the decade of emerging Romanticism. Still, there is the famous sentence that commits philosophy to come "nearer to the form of science—that goal where it can lay aside the name of *love* of knowledge and be actual *knowledge* [*wirkliches Wissen*]."[25] This ideal comes straight from the eighteenth century, and so does the entire tendency to move the transcendent God into the realm of things subject to actual *knowledge*. But then come the multitude of ambiguous words and ideas designed to leave the reader in a state of uncertain profundity. When Hegel asserts the identity of "subject and substance," is substance used in the manner of Spinoza (*deus sive natura*), and is subject the Absolute Mind, the human mind, or both? The word "*aufheben*" that characterizes what happens between thesis and antithesis—does it mean "to do away with," or "to preserve," or to "sublimate," or to "lift up"? Any of these meanings can apply to the term. There can be no question that Hegel used the word precisely for its ambiguity. When speaking of "absolute knowledge" that would prevail at the end of history, is this to be God's knowledge of Himself, or man's, or both God's and man's? Is history, passing from one state of consciousness to another, the drama of mankind, or of an evolving deity? The Romantic longing for depth and height and wonder, which the Enlightenment had discarded, is common to Rousseau and Hegel, but there is also their common determination to grasp that "certainty" which was the Enlightenment's most alluring promise. Both men are concerned with absolutes, perfection of being, salvation, and transcendent reality; both, however, look on the human mind as a powerful tool that enables men to shape this world according to the image of man. The way is pointing toward ideology.

Ideology, the fallacious immanentization of divine salvation, eventually generated armed mass movements that threw the entire globe into convulsions. There are other strands of fallacious thinking which did not jell into organized political forces. The former encountered founders, in the nineteenth century, whose writings came to be looked upon as if they were sacred books. The latter can be said to have continued straight from the Enlightenment to our time. Positivism and psychoanalysis occupy a middle position. Positivist thinking was one of the central imperatives of the Enlightenment. It came upon a "founder" figure in Auguste Comte, who would have produced a political mass movement if he could. He did proclaim a new religion, the worship of humanity as the *grand être*, complete with a hierarchy and a liturgy, and he sent out his apostles to win not only religious converts but also political allies. With the exception of Brazil he produced no direct political effects.

Similarly, psychoanalysis is a concept generated in the middle of the Enlightenment which also found its "founder" figure in Sigmund Freud, who saw himself as a kind of cult person and also as the fountainhead of a new social order, but who likewise did not produce an organized movement. All the same, both positivism and psychoanalysis have become dominant forces, chiefly in the institutions of higher learning, but indirectly also through the attitudes they engendered in the mass of half-educated people. The myth of inexorable progress never had a nineteenth-century founding person and process, but Charles Darwin's biological elaboration provided it with a late *imprimatur* and converted it into a secular substitute for a *credo*. All three must be considered continuing the effects of the eighteenth-century Enlightenment in contemporary Western civilization.

At the beginning of the nineteenth century in Europe it seemed that the Enlightenment had been stopped in its tracks, as the Sophists had been by Socrates and Plato. Hegel saw himself as philosophy's restorer and redeemer. An antitheistic animus had characterized the Enlightenment; Hegel came from Pietist Swabia, he had studied at a religious seminary, and he, Hölderlin, and Schelling, still young men, had sworn to each other not to rest until they had realized God's kingdom on earth. Hegel rejected not only atheism and Deism but also the Enlightenment's dry and shallow rationalism. He was determined to return the experiences of the soul to the center of philosophy. He might very well have become the German Plato of the nineteenth century, dooming the Enlightenment to oblivion. Plato, however, was taught by Socrates whose starting point was the awareness of ignorance, ignorance of that wisdom which is divine.

Hegel was deeply impressed with the prodigious career of the modern mind, "left to itself." He also was convinced that the human mind had reached the level of power where it could attain full certainty even in regard to ultimate matters. Hegel's God was the Absolute Mind, the "identity of subject and substance," whose history was the evolution of human consciousness, through various stages, to the terminal point of Absolute Knowledge, where all separation of subject and object had been vanquished and the Mind (or mind) would know only itself (or Himself). The mind as "its own place" had turned out to be God Himself, something Hegel could "open like a book" (one remembers that this is what Irenaeus had remarked of the Gnostics). He did reintroduce the soul's experiences, but as the soul's mighty actions. In other words, Hegel's great mind merged the secularizing tendencies of the Enlightenment with the religious imagination of Pietist Swabia, and as a result his work became a starting point for a number of philosophical and political movements of self-salvation.

Thus Hegel's disciple, Feuerbach, would make an anthropomorphic explanation of deity into a fully immanentist philosophy. One of his books, *The essence of Christianity* (1841),[26] became a catalyst for the young Marx who then moved in the company of Left-Hegelians, all of whom were bent on removing from philosophy the last vestiges of transcendence that Hegel had left in place. Feuerbach, in the eyes of Marx, had successfully completed "the critique of religion." But since he had left intact the concepts of man and nature, even Feuerbach had spared some residual transcendence. Moreover, he had ignored history, which Hegel had so impressively restored. Marx now resorted to one of the reductions of reality that we have already encountered in the Enlightenment in that he reduced man's social order to economic production. Aristotle once said, "More than anything else, reason is man." Marx retorted, in effect, "More than anything else, labor is man." That reduction enabled him to transform Hegel's romantic view of history, as God's and/or man's salvation, into a materialistic construction of salvific history. Marx replaced Hegel's succession of states of conscious-ness with a succession of "modes or production," and added revolution as a Promethean act that would bring about the final and perfect stage of history. Marx had used the eighteenth-century materialism of LaMettrie, d'Holbach, and Helvetius—a completely static condition—and equipped it with revolution as an impetus of historical movement from one type of society to the next. The proletarian revolution was conceived to bring the movement of history to an end by abolishing private ownership of the means of production and thus the class struggle.

Marx's teaching was a mixture of eighteenth-century positiv-ism with romantic Promethean chiliasm. That mixture turned out to become the incendiary force capable of engendering fanatic and armed mass movements. Through its scientific wrapping it offered certainty in lieu of faith. Instead of imprecise philosophy it relied on economics. Instead of hope for a utopia it insisted on its claim to know mankind's future. Instead of pale thought it called to action. Socialism has had other, earlier heralds, most of them in the eighteenth century. Marx, the latest advocate of socialism, appeared with the power of a prophet of history, claiming his power in the name of science. On the basis of a "scientifically" established necessary succession of modes of production, he pointed to the last of these modes as a future fact rather than a hope or a desire. Nineteenth-century economists were quick to spot the vulnerable points of Marx's economics, but then his chief work, *Das Kapital*, used economic concepts not to demonstrate economic effects, but to indict capitalists of the sin of exploitation. Marx wrote in the language of science, but his message spoke of unjust systems and their end by revolution.

Curiously enough it was another Enlightenment legacy that added to Marxism the eventual result of totalitarianism. A brief moment of totalitarianism had occurred in the French Revolution, when Robespierre and Saint-Just ruled over unlimited governmental terror. They had come to power as advocates of Rousseau's general will, apparently a plea for democracy. As mentioned above, Rousseau appeared to most of his contemporaries as a prophet of human self-salvation, by means of a perfectly rational and perfectly good social order. When France's National Convention, structured as the image of democracy itself, failed to produce unity, the Enlightenment's faith in the mind's power to unify came to be applied by Robespierre, the dictatorial ruler who believed that he was acting in perfect obedience to Rousseau's principles. If the Assembly did not produce unity it must be because of vice prevailing in it. To eradicate vice Robespierre used the guillotine with a calm conscience.

Another legacy of the Enlightenment, August Comte's Positivism, had likewise arrived at the conclusion of a totalitarian society, in this case on the assumption that a sociology having become "positive" could be doubted as little as physics, so that neither disagreement nor disobedience could be permitted. In Marx's *Communist Manifesto* it might appear that the proletarian "dictatorship: would be merely a temporary necessary evil. If it continued beyond the few months following the Revolution, it was because of the claim that Marxism-Leninism was "a science" and as such an unquestionable truth; that mankind's eventual destiny was proven to be socialism; that anyone not lending his hand and complete obedience to this cause must have a criminally distorted mind. The assertion of certainty regarding social and political order had come from the Enlightenment as "socialism." Both Mussolini's and Hitler's totalitarianism had sprung from this root. Mussolini was a socialist before becoming a fascist, and Hitler called his party the National Socialist Worker's Party.

Here special attention should be given to the problem of history, both during and after the Enlightenment. The Enlightenment talked quite a bit about history, but in effect ignored history in favor of nature. On occasion, it was not even nature that took its place. Voltaire, in the 1850s, and Schiller, in the 1880s, said in no uncertain terms that history was an aesthetic product of the onlooker, who selected, from what was otherwise a "chaos" (Voltaire), elements which together made an interesting and pleasing scenery. Schiller expressed his greatest joy at the wide gaps of historical knowledge which enabled him, the poet, to fill them up with products of his own imagination. Otherwise, however, when speaking of history, Enlightenment thinkers meant aspects of nature, either something like organic growth of nature's entities, or evolution of the ensemble, or an aspect of it. Until then history had been experienced in terms of events of great importance in that they contained elements by which human political order could orient itself, or, to express it in Socrates' terms, events that served the virtue of measurement.

Such events, however, were immune to oblivion. They constituted an abiding past, and an eternal present. With the Enlightenment's emphasis on either organic growth, or else on evolution, both within the order of nature, the past came to be not only disregarded but also despised, and willfully forgotten.

The inner eye was riveted on nature's promises regarding the future. That is even true of Kant, who calls his piece an essay on "history" but actually speaks of the unfolding of "nature's secret purpose." There results a curious situation in which history is a word used frequently by thinkers, while history as the symbolic form of consciousness is rapidly waning.

A great event did take place at the end of the Enlightenment: the French Revolution. On this occasion the traditional inner sense of history awakened suddenly. Leading thinkers everywhere greeted the event as the beginning of a new age—not just any age, but an age that would finally overcome shortcomings of human order that had appeared to remain in a besetting state of imperfection. Wordsworth, Kant, Goethe, Hegel, not to speak of public figures of second rank, responded to the event with "Hail!" and "Glory!"

The only one who responded with a serious effort of thought that constituted his life's work was Hegel. There can be no doubt that Hegel singlehandedly reawakened the dormant sense of history as the form of human existence. In this capacity he may be compared to St. Augustine. All the more important is to ask the question, Why did Hegel generate not an historically symbolized order of existence but almost universal disorder? There emerged not only the various ideological movements, each centering on a writer's body of practical ideas about history, but also the unbalanced and fanatical version of nationalism and the shortlived fever of imperialism. All this was accompanied not only by propaganda, but also by supporting versions of scholarly works, so that the disorder was not limited to practice but extended into the very core of reason, which in turn was reflected in art.

Mention has been made of Hegel's God, the Absolute Mind (*Geist*, another ambiguous German word combining the meanings of mind, spirit, and ghost; unfortunately there is no English word that could render this ambiguity). Hegel's crucial remark appears in Baillie's translation as follows:

> That the truth is only realized in the form of system, that substance is essentially subject, is expressed in the idea which represents the Absolute as Spirit [*Geist*] — the grandest conception of all, and one which is due to modern times and its religion. Spirit [*Geist*] is alone Reality. It is the inner being of the world, that which essentially is; it assumes objective, determinate form and enters into relations with itself...."27

This passage illustrates the ambiguous character of reality, as Hegel uses this concept, which is transcendent and immanent, divine and human, being and becoming. Hegel may have seen himself as a modern Plato; he refers to Plato's cave in the introduction, and he certainly is determined to philosophize on the basis of spiritual experience in the way Plato did. He also wanted to reintroduce God into philosophy in the sense in which philosophy, from Plato to Kant, always has the divine, and also theology, by its side, and as its point of origin.

We remember, from the *Gorgias*, that Socrates felt only one virtue could be taught: that of measuring. Today we might say, "distances" in the sense in which Flannery O'Connor called herself a "realist of distances." Plato was most certainly a "realist of distances." In Hegel, however, distances disappear, or rather, now they appear and then they seem to be nonexistent. History is construed as man's relation with the *Geist*, which can be called the distance that matters above all. But then the *Geist* is also the human consciousness and the discursive mind. Hegel constructs the forward movement of history, in time, by analogy with the forward movement of the mind, in dialectics, as it moves from insight to higher insight when it negates the one that has turned out to be inadequate to the matter. This has been called "the movement of the concept," and, as Hegel strongly emphasizes, it is the "enormous power of negative thinking." The distance between man and society disappears, as does the distance between society and God, and ultimately the distance between man and God.

As all other virtues, so Socrates taught, depended on that one virtue of "measuring" distances, so now, as a result of Hegel's blurring of distances and differences, virtues tend to disappear, or to mutate into their opposite. History appears as an enormously important undertaking of mankind, as outranking all other importances because it is not only the movement of the concept but also the movement of the Absolute *Geist*. Primarily the *Geist* moves from one to the other states of consciousness, each one true to some extent though not fully, and thus moving on to its opposite, and from there to another, higher state, and so on always driving forward by negations. The negations are the equivalent of Camus' "rebellions."

For a moment one might look with the inner eye at this astounding spectacle of the whole of mankind climbing the stairs of truth from step to step, always in company with the *Geist*. But, then, history is not consciousness alone. It is a succession of political order, societies, nations, and civilizations. And the results of power conflicts, great hostilities, conquests, battles, growth and decline are all parts of the movement. This aspect cannot be grasped with such intuitive immediacy as the "movement of the concept," but it is the same movement. If the pragmatic and political aspect eludes our understanding, it is all "reasonable." Hegel returns to Parmenides' equation of being and thinking. "All that is rational is real, and all that is real is rational." If that is not immediately apparent, the "cunning of reason" is to blame which uses even the destructive ad evil aspects of reality to further the ends of reason. In the same manner, Hegel introduces the "historical figures," men with the genius for power, who bestride history like "a colossus," who are themselves not conscious of the way in which they serve the *Geist*, but who are nevertheless its most important instrument.

All distances have disappeared in the thick fog. All differences appear as sameness. What alone remains is the one process of the universe—history—and it is not clear whether men or God are its prime movers. What is clear is that history, not philosophy, must be the chief activity of the self-respecting man, that here alone he can become the equal of God, or even—who knows?—the savior of God. The Establishment's "Will to Power" has here found its religious expression, even though the Enlightenment had no real taste for religion. From then on action is the one virtue remaining. It is, essentially, action in the dark, but with the positive certainty that full light, "absolute knowledge," will be its attainment at the end. What end? Augustine's eschatological end of time and history, at which alone one may look for the "beatific vision"? No, this one is an end *in* time, history's end and fulfillment. Well, then, when history ends, what will come thereafter? That is one of the great unanswered, and unanswerable, questions of our time. We have lived through the movement of the "Third Reich," through that of the "classless society," through the "end of the illusion," an entire century of organized, celebrated, soul-lifting enterprises of self-salvation. We have reaped nothing that looked like salvation, only destruction, convulsions, annihilations, alienations, oblivions, separations, and loss of common bonds of all kinds.

Hegel's ideas inflamed the imagination of successive generations. They saw dream castles which they mistook for history. Hegel did indeed generate something like a new sense of history; it was not, however, issuing from a past revered because it was experienced as the active presence of God. Nor was it the "flowing presence" that one finds in Israel's historiographers. On the contrary, Hegel's "historical consciousness" focused on the remote future that was beyond any human experience. The futuristic orientation served to excuse the present from both natural limits and moral discipline. Hegel's history had this in common with Auguste Comte's: that both saw history as a process of the mind's perfection, with absolute knowledge at the end. but souls who were "supernaturally" excited by Hegel's speculation showed little interest in the mind and its progress. One must say, then, that Hegel did save the West's awareness of history as its symbolic form of consciousness, but in the act lost the rational substance of this consciousness. We who are living a century and a half after Hegel's death are the first ones to see a faint beginning of a return to imaginative sobriety with regard to historical "destiny."

Of the important thinkers after Hegel, two managed to escape his spell: Nietzsche and Kierkegaard. But when you delete Hegel from the thought of the nineteenth century, to what or to whom can you return? In the Enlightenment there was only the mind, as "its own place," "left to itself." There was also a myth of nature. Nietzsche, who had no more respect for the Enlightenment than for Hegel, did embrace a myth of "eternal return," precisely reflecting nature without history. Kierkegaard's existentialism, however, eventually bore Hegelian offspring. It was Heidegger, praiseworthy for his renewed attention to Being, who could conceive being only as something that would come to be, in the remote future. Heidegger's attachment, for a time, to Hitler reminds us of the Hegel who, on the day after the battle of Jena, saw Napolean riding by in the city's streets, and could think of nothing else but his thrill at beholding a "world historical individual." Genuine history is rooted in genuine adoration of the living God; dream history causes great minds to become idolaters.

NOTES

1. Boston, 1965. Page references from *The Philosophy of the Enlightenment* are included in the text.

2. For the concept of the open soul, cf. Henri Bergson, *The Two Sources of Morality and Religion* (New York, 1935), ch. 1.

3. Quoted in Marion Montgomery, *Why Hawthorne Was Melancholy*, vol. III of *The Prophetic Poet and the Spirit of the Age* (La Salle, Ill., 1984), 31 ff.

4. *Cf.* Leonard P. Wessell, Jr., *Prometheus Bound: The Mythic Structure of Karl Marx's Scientific Thinking* (Baton Rouge, 1984).

5. *The Rebel* (New York, 1956), 21.

6. K. Freeman, *Ancilla to the Presocratic Philosophers* (Boston, 1966), 128.

7. Han Fei Tzu, *Basic Writings* (New York, 1964).

8. *Paradise Lost*, Book I, 245/5.

9. *The Discovery of the Mind* (New York, 1960).

10. *Theaetetus*, 183e.

11. Diels-Kranz, B6.

12. *Apology*, 20 d-e, 23a.

13. *The Laws*, 896c.

14. *Nicomachean Ethics*, 1176 a, 13f.

15. Emily Anderson, *The Letters of Beethoven*, vol. I (1961), 32.

16. *Ibid.* at 63.

17. *The Imperative of Responsibility* (Chicago, 1984), 72.

18. A. Le Flamanc, *Les utopies prerevolutionnaires et la philosophie du 18eme siecle*, (Brest, 1934), 42.

19. *The City of God*, Book XX.

20. *Order and History*, vol.I: *Israel and Revelation* (Baton Rouge, 1956).

21. *Cf.* This author's Between Nothingness and Paradise, 1971, ch.2.

22. *Essai sur les moeurs at l'esprit des nations*, 1759.

23. *Deuteronomy* 26:5b-11.

24. *Idea for a Universal History from a Cosmolpolitan Point of View*, 1784.

25. *Phenomonology of Mind*, J.B. Baillie, ed. (Rev. ed., 1931), 70.

26. New York, 1957.

27. *Op. cit.*, 86.

On Authority and Alienation: A Meditation

In a mental experiment that divested man of all institutions of order, Thomas Hobbes called the resulting imaginary situation "the state of nature," and described it as "war of all against all." In other words, he established an assumption that aggression is the original quality of human nature, an assumption he supported with correct observations. I submit that, if such a mental experiment made sense, it would be more to the point to call this imaginary nonsocial man "confused," and I am ready to support this assumption with correct observation: I have found myself in a country whose language I could not speak, whose writing I could not read, and whose habits I did not know. The native person accompanying me as an interpreter was separated from me by crowds. Here I was, all alone. I did not know the name of my street, the look of my house, or even the direction of the compass, since the day was clouded. The confusion that befell me was general, all-encompassing, basic, and utterly frightening. While I was completely free to go in any direction I wanted, all these possibilities were the same to me, like to Buridan's ass, so that I could not move for simple lack of discernment. I can easily conceive an imaginary nonsocial man being in the same mental condition, much more easily than a warrior engaged in a big enterprise such as a "war against all." This is the assumption underlying the following investigations on authority and alienation.

Hobbes's eventual conclusion that all men, "in the state of nature," are equal is not based on his denial of observable inequalities between men. He mentions such inequalities, either of brain or of brawn, but declares them irrelevant, since, as he says, ultimately they cancel each other out. I submit that the observable inequalities are relevant, since they result in a variety of different authorities, each of which has its ordering function in human life. Let us make a provisional list of some such authorities.

"It is in the impartial practice of life, if anywhere, that the perfection for (the writer's art) can be found." (Joseph Conrad, quoted in Robert Penn Warren's introduction to *Nostromo*.) In the "impartial practice of life" are found a few whose speech is heeded and revered above that of others, because it strikes others as reflection of truth pertaining to that which is, or wisdom pertaining to what to do. To such few people belongs what one may call *gnostic authority*. Then there are, still fewer, those persons who lead a life of exemplary quality so outstanding that many others flock to this person, powerfully attracted. Here we have *charismatic authority*. Yet different are persons excelling in initiative, competence, and energy in various kinds of enterprise, so that others willingly and even enthusiastically obey. Of them one may predicate *functional authority*. Yet another type of person may conduct himself *comme il faut*, speak *comme il faut*, dress *comme il faut*, so that others fear his disapproval and seek to earn his approval. Theirs would be *traditional authority*.

What takes place in these instances? Obviously, there is an experience of something special and impressive, even something to be imitated. The experience seems to have the character of an "invasion," one might say. If we would look again for a nonconventional word, this time we might go, not to Latin but to bankers' English, using the term "friendly takeover." This tells us that, first, authority is not something fixed but an event; secondly that it is a relation; thirdly, that there occurs not only a recognition but also an expansion of order. The resulting kind of authority is an abstraction from the particular incidents of conduct, a general image of some exemplary behavior which from then on functions as a model for others. Consequently there emerges a distinction between what may be called "upper" and "lower." One might regret this kind of division as a reduction of freedom. If we compare the situation with the above mentioned imaginary condition of basic confusion, where freedom is paralyzed through indecision, it will be clear that the experience of various types of authority nor merely creates order, but serves freedom, in that the conscious perception, the *mirare* of some kind of conduct as an object of *admiratio* makes possible distinctions between varieties of potential action, and thus provides the mental capacity of choice. One can again support this thesis with the correct observation of many persons of quality who, with a sense of great freedom, consent to a life of personal service, from *Upstairs—Downstairs*, to Kent, in Shakespeare's *King Lear*. I myself have encountered a number of such persons in my life. Let us say there is an experience and inner acceptance of a *subjection*, remembering that one meaning of the verb *subiicere* is "throwing up from below. It is an *ontic subjection*, resulting from a distinction of qualitatively different aspects of being.

One may point out that this kind of distinction is what Mircea Eliade means when speaking of "the sacred" and "the profane," when Parmenides pointed to the difference between being and becoming, when Heraclitus pointed to the *logos* in contrast to the flows of things, or Augustine said that living-according-to-God is "truth" but living-according-to-man is "a lie." Instead of subjection, one may also speak of this as a condition of being *bound*, meaning a normative binding of the person's will, or rather, striving. It is this kind of binding to which Plato referred when he called Love a product of the union between "Need" and "Fullness," the Fullness binding, through the emptiness of Need. A similar figure of symbolic speech is Aristotle's universal "desire to know," or Anselm's "will tending to God." Being, fullness, the sacred, truth, God—all stand for higher ontic levels against which one experiences an awareness of one's own lower ontic level, and, at the same time, the desire to "be" higher. Let us call this desire *ligatio*. A Latin term is chosen to avoid the need for continuous explanation of some much used English word capable of receiving many oscillating shades of meaning. It has the further advantage of its closeness to such words as obligation, and religion.

As *ligatio* is a social phenomenon, emerging in Conrad's "impartial practice of life," it has consequences of social order. It results in a particular and continuing pattern which Henri Frankfort has called a *Form*. Of "form" one may predicate both time and place. This enables us to define what a people is: a people is a multitude of human beings sharing "the impartial practice of life" and linked to each other by a common *ingenium ligationis*, a disposition that is also a kinetic structure of generally shared and communicated awe, respect, deference, striving, a multitude bound by an awareness of higher being as represented by authoritative persons. Hence: *ubi populus ibi auctoritas*, a formula capable of being reversed. In the presence of this kind of "form," authority as such is abstracted from the various types above mentioned, and a possibility results of experiencing a new type of authority representing not this or that specific excellence, but the goodness of human life as a whole. Let us call this authority, belonging to the incumbents of certain public offices, *sovereignty*. It, too, has a binding effect, by virtue of which these incumbents have "power" to elicit general public compliance.

Sovereignty differs from the variety of authorities mentioned at the beginning in that it claims rank superior not just to those who are linked to each other by a common *admiratio*, but to all men within a given territorial boundary. The Chinese even say: "to all men, to the entire cosmos." Sovereignty also is an authority that claims active powers over persons and property, powers covering the full range of life and death. Aristotle remarked: this power has to do with the whole of human life. Hence this authority has been called by the medieval Latin term *superanus*, "above all other earthly authorities."

Sovereignty, as it relates "to all men" leaves the original face-to-face relation of authority behind. The personal experiences are still there, but no longer referred to, in the work of sovereignty. Even in that personal field, an abstraction occurs, very soon. Authority then appears as a set of types. Before there can be sovereign authority, even the type must be further abstracted, into a norm. What is essentially a living relationship appears in the norm as concepts, definitions, verbal generalizations, and, above all, applications to the form of command. On the other hand, it is the norm that expands concrete experiences and relations of authority to the universality of human nature. The norm is the way in which sovereignty appropriates the living wisdom found in "the impartial practice of life," so as to make it serviceable to the business of ruling indefinite multitudes. That original recognition and acceptance of living truth becomes an image, maybe even an *imago abscondita*, the problem of which resembles that of the *deus absconditus*, the hidden God. It means that the ultimate source of order has moved out of the orbit of attention. In its place, we must be content with representation, which, of course, abides in perpetual need of renewal. Sovereignty is further complicated by its character a an institution of command and enforcement, in addition to which there is the power of blinding interpretation. These power aspects have their own problems, which usually are mistaken for the whole. Here, however, we are focusing on the element of authority, which surely is not absent from any version of sovereignty. It is the quality of authority in sovereignty that enables us to speak of the "representation of truth," recognized by Eric Voegelin as the central problem of all politics.

Much misunderstanding, and many false problems, have

resulted from confusing sovereignty as such with its attribution either to kind (rather than to people), or to people (rather than to king). Calling a king sovereign is a metaphor like, for example, calling Charles the Bold "Burgundy," or Francis I "France." We have spoken of a people as a multitude linked one to another by *ligatio*, a common awareness of higher reality in contrast to an also experienced lower reality, of being. This mind of multitude is capable of producing government, through what one may call *conatus imperii*, an endeavor for unity of command. The resulting authority then differs from the first mentioned types of special authority in that the authority of rulers belongs to the office rather than to the person. *Rex est a populi voluntate* (John of Paris).

The multitude united by common *admiratio*, and *ligatio*, does not exist as a unit capable of action in history until it has "thrown up" (from *subiicere*) a rulership. We have thus used the term "people" for a multitude capable of producing government and one that already has produced government, which explains the fact that Poland, for example, was spoken of as a people even during the more than 100 years in which it had no government of its own. On the other hand, it is possible that a people living under sovereign authority will lose the *conatus imperii* and thus pass out of historical existence (an example, the Herules, is mentioned in Paulus Diaconus's History of the Lombards, quoted by Eric Voegelin, *The New Science of Politics*, 1952, p. 46 f.).

As a problem, the question of legitimacy was first formulated in 1814, by Talleyrand. Why then? Political authority then began to be seen as a psychological problem: "written in the hearts of men."

The mythical symbols that represented *ligatio* were chiefly two: (a) the king, (b) "by the grace of God." As for political theory, there had been clusters of ideas and concepts regarding both king and people, as related to each other in the whole of the body politic. The execution of the King of France, in 1793, had produced widespread uncertainty about both *ligatio*, and its representative. Albert Camus has said: "The condemnation of the King is at the crux of contemporary history" (*The Rebel*). The deliberate murder of the person under the *ligatio* of the French people amounted to a rebellious rejection of the *ligatio*. A mere switch from monarchy to Republic would not have been catastrophical, except that a corresponding political theory would have had to supply the legitimation of he people as ruler, as it had supplied the legitimation of the king.

Since 1650, however, political theorists had produced works that were alien from both "the constitution that is written in the hearts of the people" and from the constitution of being. Thus, in the field of political theory there were available only two alternatives to the traditional *ligatio*, both bad theory in terms of philosophical quality: utility and collectivity.

Utility (Hobbes, Locke, Bentham) is the straight opposite of *ligatio*, in that it attributes obligatory power to man's lower motives instead of his higher striving. These authors appealed to human self-centeredness and therefore were not community-creating. The social bond now had no longer the character of *ligatio* but became *pressura*, (the first of Henri Bergson's *Two Sources of Morality and Religion*). As for the much advertised *social contract*, it is admitted by Hobbes to be a fable. Even when others do not present it in this manner it is still an undefined legal transaction that does not carry on its face the power of binding people's wills, or striving.

As for collectivism (Rousseau, nationalism), it too rejects *ligatio*. In Rousseau's words, the people is sovereign because "they are always everything that they should be," which amounts to a denial of the tension between higher and lower reality experienced in human life. Rousseau's "General Will" represents an identity between existence and perfection, an identity predicated of an historical phenomenon rather than of God. It follows that virtue is construed as "becoming one" with this historical phenomenon.

We have spoken of a people as a multitude possessing a *conatus imperii*. In a parliamentary system of government, parties develop and are eventually considered indispensable for daily political life. A party might be called a multitude of citizens possessing a *conatus dominandi*, the endeavor to wield power over the whole. There is a question whether such a party is still a part, or has itself become "the whole." As long as the *ligatio communis* still continues in force, political parties may well differ from each other prudentially rather than ontologically. In other words, though differing on courses of political action, they still feel bound by something ontologically higher, to which belongs the *conatus imperii*. In this sense, they function as true parts of the whole, and deserve the name "party."

There comes a time when the ontic bonds of society crumble. Fragmentation and alienation may result. Persons withdraw into shells as if they were their own worlds. Meaning, direction, and choice are lost or nebulous. Sex and violence, both rock bottom experiences, may begin to appear as absolutes. In such a situation, parties take on a different character. They pretend to represent an ontological alternative, rather than a prudential one. They pretend to be able to offer the creation and establishment of a world, new or old. If new, they claim authority as representatives of the future seen as a gigantic project. If old, they pretend to be the sole representatives of tradition, all other representatives having fallen away. Thus the *conatus dominandi* flows not from *ligatio communis*, but from a Promethean *libido creandi*—the passion to be as the divine Creator.

Such a party is no longer part of a whole but itself claims to be the whole. If it does not offer itself as a world, it points to itself as the sole way to a world. Hence it does not itself receive authority but pretends to bestow authority on its supporters.

There are three types of such parties:

(1) Totalitarian parties, beginning with a *total critique* of all that is, and endeavoring to make everything new, particularly consciousness;

(2) Centripetal parties, mostly armed forces, in countries having lost *ligatio*, where, consequently, there is no more "people;"

(3) Centrificent parties, in countries that have never had a tradition and, thus, where no people has ever existed (as, *e.g.*, in Africa).

Such parties have no relation between themselves and their subjects with the character of *ligatio*. Sheer compulsive, or even terroristic power takes its place, so that the government has the gaining of support as its chief, or only goal. This condition may continue for a long while, if rival groups are systematically and effectively squashed. There is power without a people, order without legitimacy, and rule without spirit.

Before we turn to the phenomenon of alienation, we should briefly look at the family. What wish do we hear more often, from a grown-up person, than "I want to go home"? One must assume that there are other periods of time, and other localities and persons in one's past, to which one would ardently desire to return. Still, the longing for "home" seems to be more widely shared, more deeply felt, more frequently mentioned, than any other. One can only guess the reason. Modern analysts mention, typically, the nurture, care, and attention one then received. Psychoanalysis even stoops to hidden sexual motivations: forbidden sexual desire for the mother or the father, and sexual play with siblings. Of necessity, the following tentative analytical remarks must be personal, for which I plead for the reader's indulgence.

The more I myself try to penetrate into my own deep attraction for my home, the more the image of home looks like a place where all the major aspects of life occurred, together, in one relatively small place, within a small circle of persons, so that "the whole" was both visible and fully there. The presence of two persons appears dominating, or rather, the dominating person of the father appears unthinkable without the less dominating but utterly indispensable person of the mother. Nor can the siblings be mentally eliminated, nor childhood friends. But still, more important than anything or anyone else is the experience of being guided, in the circle of the same persons and the same locality, into the order of life. In retrospect, it is remembered as an altogether astonishing series of discoveries, one after another, a little like being introduced by a narrator into a fairyland (could Chesterton have had some influence on my memory there?). The image is replete with the moments of deepest unhappiness when the four, or five-year-old, was first aware of his own lack of understanding, was baffled, and defeated by what appeared frighteningly strange. The image grows brighter, and altogether radiant, when, about ten years old, the child attained some confidence that he could look around him with some recognition of what he saw, heard , or experienced. This period lasted about three years, after which time the powers of the mind seemed to suffice for the task of thinking up one's own portrait of the world, of reality. That is the point at which the remembrance of erstwhile happiness stops, for then began the fights with the parents, particularly the father, then the rebellion, even revolution, and wave after wave of unhappiness.

So it must be the experience of being opened to the order of life, under parental guidance, which is so unique, so enormously attractive, that to it we wish to return. And Thomas Wolfe is right when he says, "You can't go home again," if for nothing else but for the reason that you cannot return to being an ignorant child, helpless for lack of understanding. And the image of home is essentially not so much a place where one was fed, where one had a room, meals at certain hours, toys and friends, but where the hierarchical figure of the father represented the mysteries of the world's order. If, in my case, it was the father, I would imagine that it would be the same if, in other cases, it was the mother who opened that important door. But my strongest recollection was my utterly consuming, ardent love for my father who for me embodied what I later came to call, "wisdom." In the general social field of authority, that of the parents must rank very low in original substance, but extremely high in social effectiveness. All the same, one should call it "borrowed authority."

As for alienation, the last two centuries have provided us with direct experiences of its variegated and well-known phenomena: Persons having "dropped out" from the community of truth, values, strivings, manners, into which they were born, but also aware of this condition and celebrating it by means of appearance, speech, conduct, and artifacts. Primarily they appear intent on shocking those not as atomized. On principle, they deny any authority. They disclaim any loyalty once accepted, to the point of joining their country's enemy. These, however, are symptoms. What is behind them? For an early analysis, we might recall the words of Jan Ruusbroec, the great fourteenth-century Flemish mystic, in his *Spiritual Espousals*:

> When, therefore, a person possesses natural rest in a state of empty idleness, intends himself in all his works, and remains obstinately turned away from God...he lives without charity in a state of unlikeness to God....[Such people] are contemplatives. They think they are the holiest people alive.... Because of the natural rest which they feel and possess within themselves in a state of emptiness, they believe that they are above all practices of the holy Church, above God's commandments, above the law, and above all virtuous works which might be practiced in any manner, for they consider this state of emptiness to be so great a thing that it must not be disturbed by any works, however good they may be, since the emptiness is

nobler than all virtue.... Consequently they hold that they may freely do whatever their corporal nature desires, for they have arrived at a state of innocence and are bound by no law. If their nature is drawn toward something which it desires and if this proves a hindrance to their spirit's state of emptiness, then they satisfy the desire of their nature so that the emptiness of their spirit might remain undisturbed.... In many respects and in many of their works they behave in the same way as good persons, but in some respects they are different, for they believe that everything to which they feel interiorly driven—whether it is something lawful or unlawful—comes from the Holy Spirit....They are also so self-willed and hold so fast to their own ideas that they would rather die than abandon a single point to which they are attached.

One may disregard the elements of Christian doctrine in this text and still find the analysis fitting the observations we make today. Ruusbroec continually points to the "emptiness" as the crucial mental factor. As a mystic, he is familiar with the kind of emptiness that is the proper preparation for the soul's potential union with God, an "emptiness" characterized by the "naked intent to God," as *The Cloud of Unknowing* puts it. The emptiness Ruusbroec found in the alienated people of his day (the Brethren of the Free Spirit) is characterized by its confinement to this "natural" world, to one's self, and to inactivity. His other emphasis is on the resulting lawlessness. He concludes that, as human beings, "they are different," in that they acknowledge no norm of order above their self-will.

Manifestly, it is very difficult to find out the place of alienation in being and history, which is why sovereign authorities had no answers to the phenomena of alienation. But another fourteenth century mystic, this time Henry Suso of Cologne, provides us with adequate language. Norman Cohn quotes him:

sitting in meditation [when] an incorporeal image appeared to his spirit. Suso addresses the image: "Whence have you come?" The image answers: "I come from nowhere."—"Tell me, what are you?"—"I am not."—"What do you wish?"—"I do not wish."— "This is a miracle! Tell me, what is your name?"—"I am called Nameless Wildness."—"Where does your insight lead to?"—"Into untrammeled freedom."— "Tell me, what do you call untrammeled freedom?"— "When a man lives according to all his caprices without distinguishing between God and himself, and without looking before of after" (*The Pursuit of the Millennium*, p. 186).

How does this compare with the structure of authority? Authority resulted as another person's conduct, or skill, or speech, or taste were recognized as being ranking "higher" than one's own. Briefly, one may say, there is, in this situation, "apperception" of being. There is no apperception in the case of alienated persons; indeed, Heimito von Doderer coined the formula "refusal of apperception." In addition there is something like sweeping denial, or rejection, of all that was apperceived before, and is still apperceived by others. When the person recognizing authority says Yes, the alienated person says No. When being is met by denial, refusal, or rejection, how can the resulting Nothing be described? One is limited to the symptomatic phenomena, for example, to the anarchic pseudo-mysticism of the "Free Brethren." To match this with a case of our times: The son of Hannelore Schmidt, a "child of rock," escaped from East to West Germany, was asked to which city he preferred to go, answered: "It is all the same," was sent to Hamburg, after some time there again she escaped back to East Germany. The escapes, going and coming, provided moments of excitement. Other than that, nothing was real to him, nothing better or worse. The only thing he lived for was the release of the next cassette of rock music.

Authority results from the apperception and affirmation of being. This is an ontological event occurring in historical society, which is what makes history possible. In the case of alienation, there is neither apperception nor affirmation. Being is denied, rejected, and, to that extent, destroyed. In other words, there is no process one can report, because nothing is created or maintained. "Nothing" is indescribable. The genius of Suso has captured this problem in language that could only be attributed to an incorporeal apparition. Since nothing occurs that pertains to being, both meaning and history are destroyed.

They cannot generate order, at least not the order of being. On their own terms, they need to feel excited by movement and newness. They do not have leaders, but leaders only to stir up in them the sense of fast movement. Hence they need exciters, and instigators, and they incline to give superstitious veneration to persons who appear to them to possess "the magic of the extreme," for example, Hitler, and Charles Manson. "The magic of the extreme" is original in Nietzsche's *Will to Power* (749), and appears in Eric Voegelin's Meditation, "Wisdom and the Magic of the Extreme" (*Collected Works*, 112: 315-75). The most this state of mind can produce is an order of battle, rather than an order of peace (cf. my *Between Nothingness and Paradise*, 1971, pp. 120-25).

This brief list of observed phenomena must remain both incomplete and inadequately analyzed. An attempt to penetrate to anything like a structure of alienation would necessarily have to make use of the literary products of the alienated multitude; the works of Kafka, Robert Musil, Elias Canetti, Samuel Beckett, and similar writers. Such remarks as Marx's, on alienation, are of less value as they are not empirically founded. It is still noteworthy that this literature is not confined to the twentieth century but has such forerunners as Büchner, in Germany, and Blake, in England.

It is possible, however, to analyze the progressive structure of critical thinking, which first began with the "discovery of the mind," with philosophy. Philosophy established a pattern of criticism, with the intention of moving man from lower to higher forms of existence. This philosophical intent criticized opinion, in the name of truth; existence, in the name of essence; imperfection, in the name of perfection; human ways, in the name of divine ways; vice, in the name of virtue; injustice, in the name of justice; becoming, in the name of being. Even though it produced such embracing criticism as that of the Sophists, by Socrates, the critical attack always relied on experiences of the good, the true, and the beautiful that were shared between the critic and those whose views, or habits, or loyalties were criticized.

A new pattern resulted from the proclamation, by Descartes, of absolute doubt as a desirable starting point. The resulting pattern of critical thinking denounced religion, in the name of reason; morality, in the name of nature; society, in the name of progress; the past, in the name of the present. In other words, whole chunks of civilized existence were put on trial in the court of critical thought. In the eighteenth century, the criticism went further to the point where the critical mind challenged the entire reality of reason, and succeeded in substituting a completely new meaning of that term. Critical thinking thus became the preeminent work of an entire civilization, so that having brought to fall this or that institution, or structure, was seen as an occasion for celebration. Excessive emphasis on analysis replaced concepts symbolizing the whole of reality, such concepts as being, nature, man, soul, with concepts belonging to parts of the whole, and to process. Among the followers of Hegel, *critique* was cultivated as the foremost task of philosophical minds. There was a succession, from the critique of religion (as such), to the critique of the state (as such), to the critique of nonpolitical society (the civil society). Each of these critiques was launched with a sense of obligation to remove a still remaining bit of transcendence that Hegel might have left intact, each critique discovering some remaining inattention in the previous one. This led to Marx's rejection of "political revolution" as insufficiently radical, and to his demand for a type of revolution that would not leave "the pillars of the house standing." Even Marx, however, began to look tame, first to Nietzsche, but then to such people as André Breton, the founder of surrealism. *All* values must be revalued, *all* traditions abolished, reason itself emphatically included. If that appears as a message attributing positive value to destruction as such, the impression is not incorrect, as demonstrated by Bakunin's teaching.

Critical thinking, particularly in the second half of the nineteenth and the entire twentieth century, may be said to culminate in what I have called *total critique*, a new type of critical thinking not found previously. It is characterized by an attitude opposite to that of Socrates. An illustration is Socrates' criticism of his death sentence as wholly unjust, and, by contrast, his refusal to flee Athens, because flight from Athens to a foreign city would amount to a *total critique* of Socrates' native city, including his own life as benefited by Athens' laws. I remember being asked, in Madrid, in February of 1936, by a worker: "Are you an anarchist?" When I answered negatively, he said, with a gesture of absolute separation: "Then there can be no dialogue." What is denied is Conrad's "impartial practice of life." The denial includes necessarily such images as "the cosmos," and "the transcendence." But with all these destructions there results also the inability of orienting oneself in life.

Modern alienation, then, is utter disorientation. Some kind of measure, some kind of limit, some kind of distinction are still needed, as everyone experiences. Since they cannot be found either in one's mind or in one's soul, they must be made, by an act of will. Thus we have the flood of "codes of ethics," of this or that profession, or institution; the multitude of laws covering the smallest details which, in a sound society, would be left to the common sense of the citizens; also the enormous flood of litigations, and the disappearance of any kind of balance in the financial awards made by juries for all kinds of damage, physical or psychological. The totalitarian movements arising in such a situation are in the business of creating a "new world" where none exists, but a totalitarian regime not only presupposes an atomized multitude; it leaves an even more atomized wasteland in its wake. Jane Kramer, in a remarkable piece of research on what was then East Germany ("Letter From Germany," *The New Yorker*, 18 June 1990), reports Hannelore Schmidt, the mother of one family, saying that she knows only three kinds of people: "Children of the War, Children of the State (by which she meant the Communist regime), and Children of Rock," all three crippled for any real human life. Her own son, belonging to the last group, eventually committed suicide.

Such phenomena are not limited to countries ruled by totalitarian movements. Eliot's *Wasteland* after all, reflects American reality. Since this poem was written, the century has moved towards its end, and the disorientation has become more widespread. Still, life goes on, the government functions in its own way, and as for disoriented citizens, they think of new reasons for association.

The state, as we have seen, is an association centered on the idea of being. That concept is gone. In the second half of the twentieth century, the state, together with *being*, is de-emphasized. In its place, the recent emphasis is on dissatisfactions. Dissatisfaction as a motive for political association produces a type different from the state. Richard Hooker has introduced the concept, *cause*, for association erected on the ground of nihilistic dissatisfaction (for a discussion of Richard Hooker's concept of *cause*, see Eric Voegelin's *New Science of Politics*, pp. 135-140). Where there is no recognition of authority, no awareness of a tension between higher and lower being and thus no *ligatio*, dissatisfactions alone provide motives for association. Each one is real, or irrational, dissatisfactions lends itself for the creation of a corresponding *cause* a public organization with a *libido dominandi*. The chief characteristic of *causes* is their need to divide the world into two hostile parts: the purity of one's own partisans, and the guilt of "the others," not to say "the enemy." Every *cause* speaks, feels, and operates as if it were engaged in an apocalyptic war. There is a basic difference between the state (*sovereignty*) and a *cause*. One recalls Thornton Wilder's poignant sentence, in his novel, *The Eighth Day*: "Joy is praise of the whole, and it cannot exist where there are ulterior motives." Every state, no matter how limited in terms of territory and citizenship is, to use Eric Voegelin's concept, a*cosmion*, a genuine whole. Any *cause*, no matter how far-flung its membership throughout the world, is an *ulterior motive*, and remains that even if it succeeds in gaining control of the state's government. We know only of states limited in territory and citizenship, in other words, of *closed societies*, in the sense of Bergson's *The Two Sources of Morality and Religion*. But, being a *cosmion*, even a limited state is compatible with a love that embraces all humanity, even though such openness of the soul to universal mankind can be attained only by way of worshipping a universal God. In other words, a philosophical or religious universalism always envisages the whole, which no *cause* can ever do.

Meanwhile, the "free" societies try to cope with the wasteland situation by means of the principle of pluralism. There is something to be said for that principle, but not when it becomes a kind of fanatical fixation for laws, preachers, and educators. Particularly, the commitment of a public school system to indoctrinate the children with*pluralism* can lead to nothing but the systematic raising of generations of nihilists. Thus, the public school system effectively blocks the *Wasteland* from any potentially healing influence. It is difficult to see how a widespread spiritual disease (*pneumopathology*, in Schelling's language) could heal itself, since such ordering factors as authority, hierarchy of being, and recognition of communal *ligatio* are on principle excluded from consideration. Pluralism cannot accept the fact that all spiritual outbursts, all breakthroughs to higher insights, have always occurred within the limits of a particular people or country, and more often than not, a small one. Theologians, speaking with reference to Jesus Christ, have a name for this. They call it "The Scandal of Particularity" ("scandal" in the sense of: "a scandal to the Jews, and a foolishness to the Greeks"). Thus, *pluralism* itself is a kind of great dissatisfaction that such breakthroughs and revelations did not happen to all of mankind simultaneously (See Marion Montgomery, *Virtue and Modern Shadows of Turning,* 1990). The self-destruction of highly developed civilizations was not unknown to philosophers of previous times, as fitting the concept Vico coined for this phenomenon: "The barbarism of reflection," meaning by "reflection" that intellectualism which the Enlightenment launched and which still continues.

Certain evidence from the other *Wasteland,* that left behind by the totalitarian regimes, hints at potential modes of recovery. I should like to mention two events. The first happened to Alexander Solzhenitsyn, the Soviet Bolshevik sentenced to eight years of labor camp for having included, in a private letter, a joke about the "man with the mustache" (Stalin). Solzhenitsyn was spared no suffering during his years of interrogations and systematic cruelties of forced labor. But, in his case, there was a difference: *He had accepted his sentence.* After seven years, Solzhenitsyn was struck by cancer. There was an operation in the camp hospital, but it was inadequate. After this operation, Solzhenitsyn had a long conversation with a doctor Kornfeld, a Jew recently converted to Christianity by a cellmate. For hours, this doctor tells the patient about his own spiritual discoveries. During these hours, Solzhenitsyn himself was converted, not yet to Christianity but to a belief in God. As was his habit, he put his reflections into the form of a poem which he easily memorized.

These are the last three verses:

> *But passing here between being and nothingness,*
> *Stumbling and clutching at the edge,*
> *I look behind me with a grateful tremor*
> *Upon the life that I have lived.*
>
> *Not with good judgment nor with desire*
> *Are its twists and turns illumined.*
> *But with the even glow of the Higher Meaning*
> *Which became apparent to me only later on.*
>
> *And now, with measuring cup returned to me,*
> *Scooping up living water,*
> *God of the universe! I believe again!*
> *Though I renounced you, You were with me!*

In *Gulag Archipelago*, this poem is accompanied by the following words: "I had come to understand why everything had happened to me: both prison and, as an additional piece of ballast, my malignant tumor. And I would not have murmered even if all that punishment had been considered inadequate. Punishment? But...whose? Well, think about that—whose? (part 4, chap. 1). All the details of this experience are less important than Solzhenitsyn's attitude as he describes it. In spite of his excruciating sufferings, his attitude was not one of rebellion, and emphatically not that which Camus has called *metaphysical rebellion*. In the midst of suffering, he remained obedient. His is by no means the only case; it may not even by the only case described by a writer. It seems that this kind of obedience, through seemingly endless years of suffering without hope, has worked in certain persons a thorough purgation, in the sense of deliverance from self-centeredness and "ulterior motives." Whether or not they believe in God seems not to be the most important question to ask. They are once again capable of being aware of reality, of order, capable of recognizing authority when they see it, and to realize its connection with the "Higher Meaning" of Solzhenitsyn's poem.

The other event occurred in Czechoslovakia, in the breathtaking days of November 1989. The people have rallied in the streets, though no summons from any political office called them there. They are just assembled, with each other. And then, spontaneously, they decide on two men as leaders of their country, one an anti-Communist, the other a Communist: Vaclav Havel and Alexander Dubcek. One has spent most of his adult life in political prison, the other has been in Coventry, for twenty-one years. Neither of the two has announced his desire for office. The people, though, are unanimous on the choice of these two. Why? Because of their political views? But their views oppose each other. No, it is because of their character. What was it that attracted the masses of people to these two characters? On what principle did they seem united? One can only conclude: on the principle of the good. The good of which Plato said the following: "You will agree that the Sun not only makes the things we see visible, but also brings them into existence and gives them growth and nourishment.... And so with the objects of knowledge: These derive from the Good not only their power of being known, but their very being and reality; and Goodness is not the same thing as being, but even beyond being, surpassing it in dignity and power" (*Republic* VI, 509b).

One should see these events not in their concreteness, but as an indication that, after many decades of *Wasteland*, something like a return to rational awareness of being, authority, virtue, order, is not excluded. Both of these events, in themselves, are paradigmatic as well as constitutive, and constitutive because paradigmatic. Could it be that the suffering of those peoples under Communist Despotism has put them, or some of them, into a position that now, coming out "from under the rubble," it is they from whose candle we may take light, rather than we, who can give them anything beyond material goods? And between material goods, no matter how urgently needed, and goods of the mind and the soul, it is the latter that "surpass in dignity and power."